From the Jaws of Victory

The publisher gratefully acknowledges the generous support of the Humanities Endowment Fund of the University of California Press Foundation.

From the Jaws of Victory

THE TRIUMPH AND TRAGEDY OF CESAR CHAVEZ
AND THE FARM WORKER MOVEMENT

Matt Garcia

UNIVERSITY OF CALIFORNIA PRESS

BERKELEY LOS ANGELES LONDON

University of California Press, one of the most distinguished university presses in the United States, enriches lives around the world by advancing scholarship in the humanities, social sciences, and natural sciences. Its activities are supported by the UC Press Foundation and by philanthropic contributions from individuals and institutions. For more information, visit www.ucpress.edu.

University of California Press
Berkeley and Los Angeles, California

University of California Press, Ltd.
London, England

Library of Congress Cataloging-in-Publication Data

Garcia, Matt.
    From the jaws of victory : the triumph and tragedy of Cesar Chavez and the farm worker movement / Matt Garcia.
      p. cm.
    Includes bibliographical references and index.
ISBN 978-0-520-25930-0 (hbk. : alk. paper)
1. Chavez, Cesar, 1927–1993.   2. United Farm Workers—History.
3. Labor leaders—United States—Biography.   4. Migrant agricultural laborers—Labor unions—United States—History.   I. Title.
    HD6509.C48G37 2012
    331.88′13092—dc23   2012011880

Manufactured in the United States of America

21 20 19 18 17 16 15 14 13 12
10 9 8 7 6 5 4 3 2 1

In keeping with a commitment to support environmentally responsible and sustainable printing practices, UC Press has printed this book on Rolland Enviro100, a 100% post-consumer fiber paper that is FSC certified, deinked, processed chlorine-free, and manufactured with renewable biogas energy. It is acid-free and EcoLogo certified.

In Memoriam
Tam Ngoc Tran and Peggy Pascoe

For
Timotea

CONTENTS

NW STATE COMMUNITY COLLEGE

ILLUSTRATIONS

Northwest State Community College

MAP

FIGURES

ACKNOWLEDGMENTS

To write a book, an author must draw on the support of his friends, family, and colleagues. Fortunately, I have plenty of all three. First, I thank all the veterans of the farm worker movement that made time to be interviewed. Without them, I would not have tried to write this book. Special thanks go to the incredible staff at the Walter P. Reuther Archive of Labor and Urban Affairs at Wayne State University, especially former director Mike Smith, acting director Kathy Schmeling, research archivist William LeFevre, and audiovisual archivists Elizabeth Clemens and Mary Wallace. In spite of budget cuts and various other challenges, they have maintained the UFW Collections and distinguished theirs as the best labor archive in the country. Paul Henggeler, a professor of history at the University of Texas, Pan-American, who passed away before completing his biography of Cesar Chavez, unearthed important audio recordings at Wayne State and laid the foundations for an online archive that has helped many scholars. Miriam Pawel shared documents and ideas while pursuing parallel interests. I also wish to thank Bill Seacrest at the Fresno County Public Library, Polly Armstrong at Special Collections in the Stanford University Library, Gabriella Gray and the staff in UCLA's Special Collections, Neena Sachdeva at the National Archives, and Peter Blodgett at the Huntington Library. Thank you also to the staff at Fresno State University's Madden Library, Special Collections; the Beinecke Library, Yale University; Amherst College; the Mandeville Special Collections, University of California, San Diego; and the U.S. Department of Agriculture Library in College Park, Maryland. The independent writer and antiwar activist David Harris donated his personal archive on the United Farm Workers. Michael Sesling and Patrick Emond mobilized the team at Audio Transcription Center to accurately and efficiently transcribe all of my oral histories.

My old friend Karl Jacoby played a crucial role in helping me hone ideas, edit down a long first *and* second draft, and maneuver through the uncharted waters of publishing a second monograph. My newer friend Don Critchlow played an equally important role in helping me make difficult cuts to the final draft. Madeleine Adams brought her editorial expertise to bear on the final draft, for which I am grateful. Kay Mansfield, the manager of the Program in Agrarian Studies at Yale University, also helped whittle down the first draft. I was fortunate to be a fellow in the nineteenth cohort of agrarian studies in 2009–10 with Ponciano del Pino Huaman, Yuka Suzuki, and Annu Jalais, all of whom gave me critical feedback. The directors of the program, K. Sivara-makrishnan ("Shivi") and Jim Scott, have created an intellectual treasure, and I am grateful for their generosity and guidance. I also benefited from a fellowship at the Cogut Center for the Humanities and a Solomon Grant at Brown University, and a research fellowship at the Huntington Library. Several Brown University students contributed to my research, including two former graduate students and now assistant professors, Mario Sifuentez and Mireya Loza; Alma Carrillo, a public humanities master's graduate; and two summer undergraduate research groups that included Monica Martínez, Sophie Harris, Armando Garcia, Aracely Pérez, Stella Klemperer, and Liliana Ornelas (2005) and Jackie Martínez, Adriana Sandoval, Rochelle Garza, Annette Shreibati, Grisel Murillo, and Veronica Cortez (2006). My research assistant and graduate advisee at Arizona State University, Cali Pitchel Mc-Cullough, helped track down incomplete endnotes. Thank you too to my new colleagues at Arizona State University who saw the relevance of my work to their goal of building a more inclusive American university.

I appreciate Nelson Lichtenstein and Ralph Armbuster-Sandoval at UC Santa Barbara, Dave Gutiérrez and Luis Alvarez at UC San Diego, Alessandro Monsutti at the Graduate Institute in Geneva, Switzerland, Bruce Schulman at Boston University, and Daniel HoSang at the University of Oregon, who hosted me at their campuses while I was still formulating my arguments. I also received helpful feedback from attendees at a colloquium for immigration studies at the Massachusetts Historical Society. Vicki Ruiz has taught me everything I know about this profession and continues to be a source of inspiration and strength. The following friends, family, and colleagues contributed something positive to this project: Peggy Pascoe, Tam Tran, Susan Ferber, Lolly Tran, Mark Padoognpatt, Marilyn Halter, Elpidio Rocha, José Alamillo, Anne Martínez, Mike Willard, Matt Delmont, Kariann Akemi Yokota, Bill Deverell, Robert "Roy" Ritchie, Ed Escobar, Gayle Gullett, Carlos

Vélez-Ibañez, Elizabeth Cantú, Victor Becerra, Eileen Boris, Dana Frank, Todd Holmes, Melanie DuPuis, Laura Pulido, Howard Winant, Stephanie Birdsall, Giovianna Roz, Steve Velasquez, Magdalena Mieri, Peter Liebhold, Kristine Navarro-McElhaney, Elizabeth Francis, Sarah Heller Steinberg, Marv and Linda Karsten, Mellissa Martínez, my beloved children, Mauricio and Timotea, and my parents, David and Janet Garcia. Two anonymous readers, later made known to me—Cindy Hahamovitch and David Montejano—made insightful contributions and helped make my arguments much sharper. A final anonymous reader serving on the University of California Press editorial board made helpful, last-minute suggestions. I am eternally grateful to them. Neils Hooper at the University of California Press saw the potential of this book early on, and encouraged me to be more ambitious in the end.

Finally, I offer my love and appreciation to Desirée Garcia, who helped me through the most difficult moments of this project and the most challenging years of my life. I am grateful for her insights and affection, and I look forward to helping her achieve her goals as she has helped me achieve mine.

ABBREVIATIONS

AFL-CIO	American Federation of Labor and Congress of Industrial Organizations
ALRA	Agricultural Labor Relations Act
ALRB	Agricultural Labor Relations Board
AWFWA	Agricultural Workers Freedom to Work Association
AWOC	Agricultural Workers Organizing Committee
CRLA	California Rural Legal Assistance
CSO	Community Service Organization
IFPAAW	International Federation of Plantation, Agricultural, and Allied Workers
ILWU	International Longshoremen Workers Union
ITWF	International Transport Workers Federation
MLK	Martin Luther King, Jr.
NAWU	National Agricultural Workers Union
NEB	National Executive Board of the United Farm Workers
NEP	New Economic Policy, Richard M. Nixon administration
NFLU	National Farm Labor Union
NFWA	National Farm Workers Association
NLRA	National Labor Relations Act
NLRB	National Labor Relations Board

SCFC	South Central Farmers Committee
SDS	Students for a Democratic Society
SNCC	Student Nonviolent Coordinating Committee
TGWU	Transport and General Workers Union, Great Britain
TUC	Trade Union Congress, Great Britain
UAW	United Auto Workers union
UFW	United Farm Workers union
UFWOC	United Farm Workers Organizing Committee
USDA	U.S. Department of Agriculture

Introduction

[The role of the] organizer [is to] work with the people where they are, not where you are, or where you think they ought to be.

FRED ROSS
"Book Outline (Bell Town and Casa Blanca)," from his unpublished
autobiography, Fred Ross Papers, Stanford University Library

An organizer is an outsider in many cases—there's nothing wrong in that. But then he assumes a sort of special position in that program. If you organize a good group, pretty soon you find yourself hoping, "I wish I had a vote in this outfit."

CESAR CHAVEZ
"What Is an Organizer?," in *Cesar Chavez, An Organizer's Tale*

I aimed at the public's heart, and by accident I hit it in the stomach.

UPTON SINCLAIR
The Jungle

BEFORE PUBLISHING HIS PROVOCATIVE NOVEL, *The Jungle*, on the meatpacking industry in 1906, Upton Sinclair embedded himself in the Chicago stockyards as a worker and an investigative reporter. Dedicated to the plight of immigrant workers, he sought to produce sympathy for the less fortunate producers of meat products from those who consumed the fruits of their labor. Like so many issues involving food, his was a cultural problem as much as a political one. How do you communicate the experience of working-class, Lithuanian immigrant laborers in a way that *moves* middle-class, English-speaking consumers to care? More important, how do you get those consumers to pursue reforms that serve the interest of people other than themselves?

To his chagrin, Sinclair succeeded in meeting only the first challenge. *The Jungle* prompted progressive-era activism and reform—the Meat Inspection Act and the Pure Food and Drug Act of 1906—motivated primarily by the public's horror over what went *into* the food and consequently *into* their bodies. The question of workers' rights, as Sinclair and others discovered, required further activism up through the 1930s. During the Depression, Congress passed the National Labor Relations Act (NLRA) of 1935, but an executive order later excluded agricultural workers from the collective bargaining rights that went to industrial laborers. The task of extending these rights to farm workers would fall to a new generation of activists, most famously Cesar Chavez and the many people responsible for building the United Farm Workers Union in the 1960s and early 1970s.

Cesar Chavez created the most successful farm worker movement in United States history. Born into a farm worker family, Chavez fought his way out from under the tyranny of the fields to become a community organizer whose mission it was to convince poor people that they could achieve justice through collective action. Like Sinclair before him, Chavez entered a world not completely his own. Chavez too had to find a vehicle for explaining the need for justice to the public in a convincing manner that would move them to action. Although he used many strategies to achieve this goal—long marches, fasts, and the age-old tool of the strike—it was the boycott that had the greatest impact in reaching across the divide between farm workers and consumers.

This book examines the strategy and leadership that sustained the farm worker movement for nearly two decades, from the beginning of the 1960s until the end of the 1970s. During that period, the United States experienced unprecedented economic change. The country moved from being the dominant producer of goods on the world market to a country that imported more than it exported. Rather than relinquish their attachment to military spending or stake all of their hopes on a struggling automobile industry, U.S. lawmakers worked to expand the reach and profitability of U.S. growers by reducing restrictions against the trade of U.S. agricultural products. This shift in economic priorities brought new prestige to California agriculture; it also renewed the public's attention to rural poverty. Chavez offered his solution to the problem by working toward an end to the exploitative guest worker program (known as the bracero program) and creating a union. By using community organizing efforts begun in the wake of World War II, he and his early allies forged a broad, new coalition of workers, students, social justice activists, and religious affiliates. Throughout the 1960s and the first half of the 1970s, the United Farm Workers won most of their battles by leveraging this diversity. Farm owners, on the other hand, remained committed to ethnic cliques and business models that made it difficult for them to communicate a common message.

Chavez achieved his early success through a combination of political savvy and attentiveness to workers' concerns. As a former director of the Community Service Organization (CSO), a group of working-class citizens committed to electoral empowerment, he understood the capacity of organized citizens to accomplish tangible goals. Although he became frustrated by the nonpartisan and urban orientation of the CSO, the organization served as an important training ground that provided opportunities to cultivate support for a new farm workers union. This outreach, as his mentor Fred Ross had taught him, required a tremendous amount of patience and listening. Rather than push a solution upon communities in need, Ross encouraged members to meet, argue, and eventually come to collective decisions. Strategically deployed, such democratic methods gave participants a sense of ownership over the goals of the movement and inspired deeper investments among its adherents. Chavez urged organizers to be creative in their tactics, which enabled many volunteers to discover new methods for achieving their goals. The nimbleness and independence that Chavez encouraged among his organizers led to a union with deeper roots and more effective strategies than any of its predecessors had achieved.

The challenge of building an effective organization also requires decisive leadership. Chavez exhibited this attribute early on, offering a clear path for those who joined the cause. This began in his years as an organizer for the CSO, when he determined that the organization lacked the capacity and appropriate membership to address the particular needs of farm workers. His departure from the CSO in 1962 to start the National Farm Workers Association (NFWA) was just one moment among many over two decades in which Chavez asserted his leadership in a way that propelled the dream of building a farm workers union forward. In making these decisions, Chavez not only assumed great risk for himself and his family but also jeopardized the security of his allies. When the NFWA evolved into the United Farm Workers union in 1966,[1] his decisions—and the decisions of a small national executive board—threatened to compromise the jobs of thousands of workers and volunteers who sacrificed their time and their bodies in the pursuit of Chavez's vision of justice. This awesome responsibility weighed heavily on him, but his propensity—in the beginning—to seek counsel from trusted advisors helped distribute this burden.

This book shows that the task of striking a balance between cultivating creativity among organizers and providing strong, timely leadership ultimately was a challenge too great for Chavez to sustain. After achieving the first collective bargaining agreements for farm workers in California in 1970, Chavez made a series of missteps that compromised the health of the union. Initially, his encouragement of debate among organizers produced inventive solutions to new problems that arose throughout the first half of the 1970s. Yet the failure to channel this ad hoc democracy into a permanent structure of governance eventually led to personal and systematic failure. As some of his closest advisors and friends testify, Chavez became increasingly invested in his power to dictate the strategies and priorities of the union as the decade wore on. His isolation in a communal living arrangement at the union's head-quarters, La Paz, augmented his infatuation with control over the organization and the individuals who composed it. According to advisors and staff members who worked alongside Chavez during this period, the living arrangements separated him from farm workers and union staff in the field at a time when he needed to incorporate more perspectives into solving an increasingly complex situation.[2] Chavez's physical and emotional distance contributed to an alarming lack of accountability to union members and allowed him to abandon the principles of democracy preached by his mentor and friend, Fred Ross. Ironically, Chavez abused power and manipulated the powerless like the employers and the state he had become so critical of. Sadly, by the end of the 1970s, he had alienated most of his early allies and compromised most of the gains made during the late 1960s and early 1970s.

Unlike the overwhelming majority of authors who have written about the United Farm Workers, I explain how and why the union achieved most of its goals through 1970, *and* how and why it failed to live up to its tremendous potential after that. Most historians writing about the union have celebrated its triumphs only and, in the process, canonized Chavez as a leader who could do no wrong. Mario T. García, for example, recently declared Chavez "one of the great figures in the history of the United States" for "accomplish[ing] what no other U.S. labor leader had been able to do: successfully organize farm workers."[3] While Chavez accomplished much, I believe his legacy is far more complicated. To begin with, his success is debatable if we consider that by the end of the decade the union lost most of the contracts it had gained in 1970. Some authors have depicted Chavez and the UFW as helpless victims of the Teamsters union or hostile Republican administrations in Washington and Sacramento to explain these shortcomings. Although these wealthier and more powerful foes created barriers to UFW growth, their influence alone cannot explain the union's rapid decline during the late 1970s.

What is missing is a consideration of how Chavez employed strategies and management techniques that compromised the union. Such self-inflicted wounds were particularly damaging in the late 1970s, when Chavez benefited from the support of a sympathetic California governor, Edmund "Jerry" Brown, and enjoyed the fruits of the Agricultural Labor Relations Act, a state law that gave California farm workers collective bargaining rights starting in 1975. From the mid-1970s through the end of the decade, Chavez squandered political advantages and the esprit de corps he and other leaders had cultivated. In interviews with organizers and volunteers, I found that many veterans of the movement hold Chavez accountable for these failures. My oral histories are corroborated by findings from the Farm Worker Documentation Project, including a valuable archive of listserv discussions in 2004–5 among people who lived through these tumultuous years. I also consulted previously uncatalogued archival material in the United Farm Workers Collections at the Walter Reuther Library of Labor and Urban Affairs at Wayne State University that include rarely heard recordings of the union's national executive board meetings during the mid- and late 1970s. Taken together, these sources reveal that Chavez had much more to do with the union's decline than previously acknowledged.

Chavez's mishandling of the boycott and his failure to replace it with an equally effective strategy was among his most important strategic blunders. From 1965 until January 31, 1978, union volunteers extended the reach and power of the UFW through a successful boycott of grapes and, to a lesser extent, lettuce and wine. Described by Chavez as "capitalism in reverse," the boycott emerged as the sine qua non of the movement, expanding the struggle beyond the fields in rural California to urban storefronts across the United States and Canada and docks and union halls all over Europe. Such consumer activism falls within an American political tradition dating as far back as the Boston Tea Party, although, as most consumer historians note, the vast majority of boycotts have been "putative failures."[4] In some cases, U.S. companies, in a fit of economic nationalism, encouraged the boycott of foreign products that served corporate rather than worker interests.[5] The United Farm Workers, on the other hand, maintained firm control of their grape boycott campaign, driving growers to the bargaining table in 1970 and keeping their adversaries in check throughout the first half of the decade. In doing so, they bucked the trend of unions before them who had mostly treated the boycott as a supplement to strikes and picket lines at the workplace.[6]

The United Farm Workers distinguished their use of the boycott in three primary ways. First, Chavez expanded the use of the boycott by appealing to consumers to participate in the pursuit of social justice.[7] Prior to the farm worker movement, most unions had used the boycott to create class solidarity by asking fellow laborers not to purchase a particular product linked to the unfair treatment of workers.[8] Chavez, however, transformed his campaign into a social movement akin to that of the abolitionists who appealed to northern consumers not to buy southern-made textiles as a protest against slavery, or that of the Montgomery bus boycotters who asked blacks and white allies not to use public transportation until the segregation of buses ended. The UFW's insistence on presenting the campaign in a social justice framework irritated national union sponsors, although Chavez and other UFW leaders understood the potential of the civil rights moment and its influence on the farm workers' struggle. In hopes of capitalizing on a heightened civil rights consciousness in the nation, Chavez used the boycott to draw attention to the injustices of a farm labor system that employed mostly Mexican and Filipino laborers. By matching long marches in rural California with picket lines at urban markets, he drew a connection between the conditions of farm laborers and the buying habits of urban consumers. To the surprise of traditional union leaders, his tactic mostly succeeded. In doing so, the United Farm Workers articulated the possibilities of uniting protest for social justice with labor organizing in a new social movement that renewed faith in labor unions across America.[9]

Second, although initially Chavez and a handful of union leaders started the boycott to occupy volunteers' time between harvests, he and union leaders eventually came to regard the boycott with at least as much respect as they did strikes and marches. Here, however, Chavez had to be convinced. Throughout most of the boycott's first year, he remained focused on building membership in the fields. Nevertheless, many young, mostly white (and several Jewish) volunteers believed in the power of the boycott and campaigned to make it a stronger component of *la causa*. At a time when Chavez listened to advice, his acceptance of their opinions paid tremendous dividends. From 1966 to 1968, young college students joined with veteran organizers and aggrieved farm workers to build an effective boycott network that stretched across North America. Key to this network were the many boycott houses where people from all walks of life took up residence and formulated the best strategy for appealing to local consumers. In these cities, far from the front lines of the rural struggle, volunteers often cut their teeth as organizers, learning how to build a farm worker justice movement where none had previously existed. Many applied tactics borrowed from a variety of sources, including the counterculture group the Youth International Party, or Yippies; fellow civil rights organizations such as the Student Nonviolent Coordinating Committee (SNCC) and Congress of Racial Equality (CORE); and local unions who supported the UFW. In short, boycott house volunteers adopted a "by any means necessary" approach with great success.

Third, the United Farm Workers pursued a strategy not available to most labor unions: the secondary boycott. In 1947 the Taft-Hartley Labor Act amended the National Labor Relations Act to restrict labor unions from running campaigns against companies that were not abusing workers but were selling products of companies that were. In 1959, the Labor Management Reporting and Disclosure Act strengthened the restriction against this practice, which was known as a secondary boycott.[10] For farm workers who had been excluded from the NLRA, however, the secondary boycott remained a viable tool. The United Farm Workers availed themselves of it thoroughly, setting up picket lines in front of markets that had nothing to do with the production of grapes but had become targets because they carried the produce. Grapes proved to be a particularly good product to boycott since most consumers regarded them as a nonessential luxury item that they could easily eliminate from their diet.[11] Initially, UFW volunteers persuaded many consumers to forgo shopping at markets that carried nonunion grapes. When growers with UFW contracts began sharing their labels with peers in an act of corporate solidarity, the union called a boycott against all California and Arizona grapes, and consequently all markets that carried the fruit. Rather than sacrifice their entire sales, many market owners dropped grapes altogether.

The secondary boycott initiated a game of global cat and mouse between the union and growers that played out over a decade. When the grape boycott began in earnest in 1965, incredulous grape growers dismissed the action as a weak publicity stunt. The union proved, however, that it could affect the top North American markets. Growers shifted their sales to other cities, believing that they could outrun the boycott and outlast the poorly funded United Farm Workers in a war of attrition.

The union applied an organizer's logic to the construction of the boycott by aggressively recruiting volunteers and consumers as if they were potential members of the union itself. The more growers expanded into new markets, the wider and stronger the boycott became. Ultimately, the UFW showed the powerful growers that grapes were not the moveable feast that they thought they were.[12]

If the success of the boycott taught the growers the limits of their strategy, it also imbued Chavez with false confidence. The story of the UFW *after* the historic signing of the first grape contracts in 1970 is mostly one of tactical errors caused in part by Chavez's refusal to take counsel from his advisors. Chavez assumed he was infallible, which led to self-destructive behavior that short-circuited the movement. Disappointing the many people who dedicated their lives to the farm workers struggle, Chavez ultimately managed to snatch defeat from the jaws of victory. Nonetheless, the boycott's veterans and supporters continued to hold him accountable to the workers he purported to serve, even after the boycott network had been dismantled. This spirit of resistance extended to some members within Chavez's inner circle, preventing a complete dissolution of the union.

An exploration of the successes *and* failures of Cesar Chavez and the United Farm Workers is valuable now, at a time when a new food justice movement is on the rise. On college campuses, a new generation of students have created gardens, demanded new courses, and challenged their universities to serve "real food" in dining halls. Their ideas have also had significant influence beyond the ivory tower, compelling consumers to spurn fast food, shop at local farmers' markets, and invest in community-supported agriculture (CSAs).

In many ways this new consciousness about food and its contents builds upon the longer American tradition that starts with Sinclair and runs through Chavez and the United Farm Workers. Most similar are the large number of young people drawn into the movements then and now. In the 1960s and 1970s, many young people dedicated a summer, a semester, or even years to working for the United Farm Workers, participating in strikes or traveling to far-off cities to picket stores carrying nonunion grapes. Such volunteers were most effective in the boycott, where their cultural affinity with consumers and their urban upbringing made them effective advocates for the movement. At the height of their power, hundreds of boycott volunteers killed the grape market in nine of the ten most important North American cities and blocked (or "blacked," as they called it in England) grapes from reaching European markets, contributing to the final push for contracts. In the process, volunteers gained valuable experience that propelled them into a life of activism and so-cial justice.

Today advocates for food justice have a similar passion for their cause. I fear, however, that the motivation of many participants stems from concern for themselves rather than for the lives of workers. Like Sinclair's audience who worried about what went into the hot dogs more than the conditions under which laborers produced them, many of today's activists are inclined to think of their own diet or their impact on livestock animals before they think of the workers. Such positions are a product of popular food writers who often privilege *consumer*-oriented food justice over the equally impor-tant challenge of achieving better working conditions in the fields.[13]

The history of the United Farm Workers grape boycott offers a reminder that this has not always been the case. Safe and humane working conditions and fair wages for farm workers served as the primary motivations for boycott volunteers throughout the 1960s and 1970s, compelling some to sacrifice their own lives for the cause. This is not to say that moments of tension did not seep into the movement; however, the overwhelming majority of those who volunteered saw themselves as servants to an idea that went well beyond concerns for their own health. And although boycott campaigns often in-volved familiar warnings about pesticides, the message focused on workers who endured exposure to potentially harmful chemicals in the fields. At root, the boycott was a consumer strategy for achieving *producer*-oriented goals.[14] That most of the intended beneficiaries of this movement were Mexican and Filipino is a testament to the power of the intercultural understanding that thrived in the union throughout the better part of two decades.

The United Farm Workers, therefore, symbolized the potential of peace-ful protest by a multiracial, intergenerational coalition of men and women at a time when social movements had begun to grow weary of such approaches. Students for a Democratic Society splintered into the Weather Underground, a group that carried out bombing campaigns on unoccupied government buildings in the early 1970s.[15] Similarly, the Student Nonviolent Coordi-nating Committee turned toward a politics of "black power" that privileged black (male) voices, excluded white ones, and questioned the viability of peaceful protest.[16] During this same period, the United Farm Workers in-creasingly became the last, best hope for those still committed to a world without violence and racial division. As groups like the Black Panthers, the Brown Berets, and the Young Lords chose a paramilitary character that earned them increased surveillance from federal and local authorities, the union projected an image of inclusivity and cooperation that attracted new recruits and won the support of the media and urban consumers.[17] Although this approach moved the nexus of power farther from Chavez's hands and into the public, it also gave him more bargaining power than his contemporaries in other movements.

Some readers may wonder why I focus on organizers rather than farm workers. In some instances, the distinction between the two is blurred since many organizers had experience in the fields, including Chavez himself; however, by the mid-1960s, most had left this line of work. The union relied heavily on volunteers who lived in cities and suburbs rather than the California countryside, a fact that initially did not trouble Chavez. As he noted, the organizer is often an outsider to the people he represents. A lack of strike funds and the constant migration of agricultural laborers created what Chavez called "a movement without members" that was kept alive by the volunteers who had little or no experience in the fields.[18] It was not until the mid-1970s that some members of the UFW executive board became concerned about the authenticity of a union run by people other than farm workers, although they failed to produce a viable alternative.

The experiences of organizers have also been better recorded than those of workers. In addition to my oral histories, the Farm Worker Documentation Project and the United Farm Worker Collections at the Walter Reuther Library provide more insight into the lives of organizers, reflecting the origins of these archives. As a web-based, English-language project, the Farm Worker Documentation Project attracted computer-savvy veterans to upload memoirs, documents, and photos and to engage in discussion online. Regarding the collections at Wayne State, most documents and recordings focus on organizers who ran the union and, to a lesser extent, the farm workers who benefited from their activities. This is not to say that farm workers' voices are absent or that worker opinions are not available. Nevertheless, a systematic collection of oral histories and documents from farm workers during the heyday of the UFW remains to be done.[19]

These limitations notwithstanding, *From the Jaws of Victory* conveys a tale of hope, triumph, and disappointment that will be useful to anyone who has harbored the goal of bringing justice to this world.

The book is organized into a balanced focus on the United Farm Workers before and after the historic grape contracts in 1970. Chapter 1 explores the many activists who revived an effort to end rural poverty in California and explains how Cesar Chavez and the United Farm Workers emerged as the leader of this new movement. Chapter 2 examines the evolution of the boycott as the primary tool for the union and the many tactics employed by boycott volunteers to make it effective. In chapter 3, the conditions that contributed to the signing of the first UFW contracts for grape workers, including the efforts of boycott volunteers on both sides of the Atlantic Ocean, are explored. Chapter 4 considers the changes in the U.S. economy and the policies President Richard Nixon employed to expand the "free trade" of California's agricultural bounty. This policy included encouraging the Teamsters to organize farm workers in an attempt to divide (and conquer) the farm labor movement. Chapter 5 examines the UFW's decision to enlist the support of California's state government in regulating labor relations through the revolutionary Agricultural Labor Relations Act (ALRA). Chapter 6 explores Chavez's failed attempt to shift consumer activism generated by the boycott to support for Proposition 14, a California initiative that aimed to resolve funding and legal ambiguities in ALRA. Chapter 7 examines the fallout from the failure of Proposition 14, including Chavez's attempt to root out disloyal staff who dared to criticize him. Chapter 8 explores the struggle between Chavez and the boycott volunteers, staff, and members of the national executive board who challenged his increasingly autocratic management of the union and resisted his plans to focus the union's energy on the creation of an intentional community at La Paz. Although these brave volunteers and organizers failed to bring democracy to the UFW, they succeeded in preventing Chavez from taking the union down the path of notorious cults of that age. Taken together, these chapters tell a new history of the United Farm Workers, one that honors the service of volunteers who have been overshadowed by a previous generations' search for heroes rather than usable knowledge.

ONE

Birth of a Movement

FARM WORKER ADVOCATES have often contrasted visions of rural California as the land of milk and honey with the gritty reality of farm workers' lives. This, in part, was the approach that novelist John Steinbeck, photographer Dorothea Lange, and other agrarian partisans used in the 1930s to arouse the nation's appetite for reform. Their ability to undermine growers' idyllic impressions of the California countryside led to the creation of programs that brought temporary relief to field hands. Although the New Deal ultimately fell short, artists and union organizers proved that they could counter advertisements celebrating the bounty of nature and, for a time, shift the balance of power in favor of workers in the long struggle to end rural poverty in the Golden State.

Such a tactic was at the heart of a 1948 film, *Poverty in the Valley of Plenty*. A coproduction of the National Farm Labor Union and Hollywood filmmakers, the film drew attention to the anti-union practices of the DiGiorgio Fruit Company located in the lower San Joaquin Valley. An Italian immigrant, Giuseppe "Joseph" DiGiorgio, began modestly, growing fruit on 5,845 acres in 1919. By 1946 he had expanded production on thirty-three square miles worth $18.2 million, becoming the largest grape, plum, and pear grower in the world.[1] According to NFLU organizers, much of this wealth had been built on the backs of laborers who lived in substandard housing. With the film and their activism, they sought to make the DiGiorgio Fruit Company more accountable to its employees.

In 1947 union organizers at DiGiorgio petitioned for a 10 cents per hour raise, seniority rights, and a grievance procedure. The company promptly responded by expelling striking workers and replacing them with several hundred Filipinos, undocumented workers, Tejano recruits, and 130 Mexican guest workers, known as braceros. The employment of the last group violated the agreement between Mexico and the United States that stipulated no foreign workers would be used during labor disputes. Members of the Hollywood film unions regarded DiGiorgio's reaction as so hostile that they waived all wage and pay contracts to get the film made.[2]

The collaboration between the NFLU and filmmakers marked a new phase in the evolution of farm worker activism. Besides evoking the contrast between growers' wealth and farm workers' poverty in the title, they portrayed the stark differences between the natural beauty of the fields and the ramshackle homes of employees. The first thirty-seven of fifty-seven scenes accentuate this contrast, offering viewers a visual context for the last portion of the film, which is focused on the DiGiorgio strike. In terms of activism, the union paired *Poverty in the Valley of Plenty* with highly public appeals to consumers across the nation not to buy DiGiorgio's products. The first large-scale consumer boycott of its kind, the strategy worked, cutting deeply into the company's profits and provoking angry clashes between loyal employees and strikers on the farm.[3]

If the NFLU's film and boycott signaled a new level of sophistication among farm worker activists, it also demonstrated the resolve of DiGiorgio to maintain the status quo. In addition to hiring a photographer and filmmaker to produce a visual counter to *Poverty in the Valley of Plenty*, the company unleashed a legal torrent on the NFLU, suing them for libel and fighting to suppress any further screenings of the film. Although an independent investigation by CBS News and Congresswoman Helen Gahagan Douglas revealed the company's version to be false and the repression of workers to be real, DiGiorgio simply overwhelmed its opposition with images and lawsuits. Unable to match the wealth and power of the company in the courts, the NFLU agreed to destroy all copies of *Poverty in the Valley of Plenty* and end the strike and boycott in exchange for DiGiorgio's dropping charges against the union leaders. The settlement brought an end to the NFLU, which ceased to exist by the summer of 1950.[4]

DiGiorgio achieved its intended goal of destroying the NFLU and ending the circulation of the film, but the episode signaled a core truth about agriculture: consumer opinion matters. The union's ability to engineer a boycott demonstrated to both sides that the conflict extended well beyond the fields, and that simply replacing workers at the point of production could not solve the conflict. Indeed, DiGiorgio's suppression of *Poverty in the Valley of Plenty*, even at the expense of free speech, demonstrated how seriously the company took this challenge. Although DiGiorgio won this battle, growers remained susceptible to such campaigns as long as they refused to take responsibility for solving the problem of rural poverty.

It took time for activists to recover from the collapse of the NFLU. Although Ernesto Galarza, a labor intellectual and the former director of education and research for the union, reconstituted the NFLU as the National Agricultural Workers Union (NAWU), the new union struggled as a consequence of the bracero program. Throughout the 1950s, the single goal of ending the program consumed farm worker advocates, delaying the use of tactics briefly employed by the NFLU. By the beginning of the 1960s, however, new voices emerged that revived some of the hope in the fields, where conditions remained as difficult, if not worse than they had been in the 1940s. Armed with new research and imbued with a sense of purpose, these grassroots activists hit the countryside intent on making a difference.

RURAL CALIFORNIA AND ITS DISCONTENTS

Those wishing to tackle the thorny issue of rural poverty have often begun their fight in the Imperial Valley. Its location in the most southern portion of the state made it the first destination for desperate Mexican immigrants crossing the border to apply their substantial knowledge to the state's massive agricultural economy. The tumult of the Mexican Revolution and the recruitment of Mexican workers by labor contractors during the first three decades of the twentieth century made Mexicans the preferred group in a racial-caste system that remained in flux until World War II.[5] The flood of Mexican workers generated a surplus of labor that facilitated competition among a diverse population segmented by race and enabled growers to pay their employees below subsistence wages. As the first to employ farm workers for the season, Imperial growers often established the going rate for many crops in the state. The desert climate aided this process. An inversion of the typical North American growing season from a spring-to-summer to a winter-to-spring trajectory meant that Imperial growers could deliver warm-weather, drought-tolerant crops such as cotton, peas, melons, and lettuce to the market at a time of the year when such products were rare. When cultivation moved northward, so did wage levels and workers.

A researcher studying social stratification across agricultural sections of the United States in 1959 found that the Imperial Valley had a two-class system: a few farm managers in the middle class and a mass of laborers, mostly Mexican, in the lower class. These conditions strongly resembled those in the Deep South, where white landholding elites and farm managers profited from the labor of African Americans. In Tunica County, Mississippi, and West Baton Rouge County, Louisiana, for example, "lower class farm personnel," defined as "all those who perform only the labor function on the farms, plantations, and ranches in the United States," constituted approximately 80 percent of the workforce. By comparison, Imperial Valley farms employed 87 percent of their laborers at this level. Moreover, while all three counties employed a small middle- and lower-middle-managerial class, in the Imperial Valley these managers constituted a much smaller portion of the total population than in Mississippi or Louisiana. Such numbers suggest that the rural Southwest was a world as deeply southern as the South itself.[6]

After World War II, many farm worker advocates accused the federal government of exacerbating the problem with the importation of Mexican guest workers. Begun in 1942, the bilateral agreement between Mexico and the United States known as the bracero program delivered Mexican nationals to rural California to harvest crops and maintain railroads. Although initially meant to be temporary, the program continued well beyond World War II. In 1951, agricultural lobbyists convinced Congress to pass Public Law 78, formalizing the bracero program, by making spurious claims that the Korean War had compromised the agricultural labor force and threatened domestic production.[7]

Many scholars have documented the detrimental effect the bracero program had on farm wages and the employment of local workers. During the initial years of the program, between 1943 and 1947, California employed 54 percent of the Mexican nationals who came to the United States; however, by the late 1950s, most worked in Texas. Growers invested heavily in the program to take advantage of the discrepancies between the wages Mexican nationals would accept and what local workers needed to survive. Although the bilateral agreement required employers to pay braceros at or above the standard wage in a given region, in reality they earned far less than what their contracts promised and between 10 and 15 percent less than their local coworkers. The difference in the standard of living and wages between Mexico and the United States compelled Mexican nationals to come north despite receiving ill treatment and false promises from contractors and employers. Many braceros maintained families in Mexico with wages that far surpassed what they could have made by staying at home. Locals who had to raise families at the higher U.S. cost of living felt the pinch of the program's downward force on agricultural wages. By one account, the willingness of braceros to work at starvation levels widened the gap between farm and industrial wages by 60 percent.[8]

California growers' dependence on the bracero program varied from south to north and from crop to crop. Throughout the twenty-two-year history of the program, reliance on Mexican nationals skewed southward toward the desert regions and the south coast of the state. By the last year of the program, 1964, 42 percent of the seasonal employees in the desert came from the bracero labor pool, compared to just 9 percent in the San Joaquin Valley. On the south and central coasts, where orange and lemon production dominated, braceros constituted 38 and 31 percent, respectively, reflecting the citrus industry's historic dependence on the program. In fact, California lemon producers, who accounted for 90 percent of the lemons grown in the United States, drew 74 percent of their labor from the program. In the desert, where a significant number of braceros worked, melon producers in the Palo Verde and Imperial Valleys drew 44 percent of their labor from Mexican nationals, while date growers located in Coachella Valley depended on braceros for 91 percent of their labor. In the San Joaquin Valley, melon producers were the biggest users of braceros, drawing 41 percent of their labor force from the program. Among grape growers, only those in the south coast region relied on Mexican nationals for more than half their labor needs, and in the San Joaquin Valley, they constituted a mere 2 percent of workers. Grape growers in the desert region had a slightly higher dependence on Mexican nationals, at 11 percent of the total number of employees, although California grape growers in general used the program much less than their peers in other crops.[9]

In the San Joaquin Valley, farm worker advocates worried about the impact of the bracero program on wages, but other factors shaped poverty there. In a study of rural labor conditions in Fresno County over a six-month period, from January to July 1959, a team of researchers based at Fresno State College (which later became Fresno State University) found that braceros rarely totaled more than 1 percent of the labor force in the area and recently had been eliminated from the fruit harvest altogether. Instead, growers had become dependent on what researchers referred to as "day-haul" laborers: settled workers who brought in local harvests and returned to their homes each day. In some instances, workers traveled as far as Salinas, near the coast. Most San Joaquin Valley farm workers found ample employment in the crops immediately around Fresno, which enjoyed a harvest cycle that started in April and lasted

MAP I. California growing areas and locations of UFW activity.

until October, the longest in the country. According to the researchers, only a small minority of Anglo melon pickers based in the county followed a year-round cycle that took them first to the harvests in Arizona and the southern California deserts, up through Kern County, and back into Fresno. Known as "aristocrats," these workers often earned between $8,000 and $10,000 per year, making them the highest paid farm laborers in the county.

Most workers earned far less due to a system that facilitated constant labor surpluses and disrupted potential worker solidarity. Researchers found evidence of growers who had invested in labor camps for Mexican nationals and Mexican Americans but had recently abandoned these projects in favor of hiring through local labor contractors. Camps promised a more stable labor pool, though growers grew to resent the cost of maintaining such settlements. Most growers found it more convenient to outsource the hiring process to a third party that bore the responsibility of finding workers and making sure they got to the farms. The county Farm Labor Bureau, financed through tax dollars and grower contributions, served as one source, though researchers found that most growers preferred the completely independent labor brokers who operated without restrictions from the government. According to the authors of the report, "The farm labor contractors expressed the feeling that the Farm Labor Office [i.e., the Fresno County Farm Labor Bureau] does not play a role of significant importance in the present agricultural pattern."

The disparities in the cost of day-haul laborers compared to camp laborers encouraged this transition to labor contractors. Fresno State researchers found that growers paid labor contractors a going rate of between $1.10 and $1.15 per worker per hour. Contractors were expected to hire workers at an average of $.75 per hour, although frequently they increased their shares by driving down wages at the point of contract. In one instance, a contractor working to fill jobs at a nearby sugar beet farm arrived at the corner of Tulare and F Streets in Fresno to recruit among a large pool of unemployed men. The contractor offered to pay workers by the row rather than by the hour. One worker told the researcher, "The pay is $1.90 a row but the row may stretch from here to Sacramento." His friend had taken the same job the day before and "netted one dollar (for about ten hours' work)," while another, more efficient worker finished two rows, earning a total of $3.80.[10] Although many balked at the wages, the informant told the researcher, "Guys will get hungry enough," and the contractor will eventually have his crew. The authors of the report alleged that workers could do better with contracts with the Farm Labor Bureau, earning as much as $6 to $7 per hour, though such opportunities were few and far between. In fact, the terms of contracts varied so widely that researchers were unable to offer an average in their report.

By comparison, workers found much better pay and living conditions on the few ranches where growers still maintained camps. At the Weeth Ranch west of Fresno, for example, thirty-five permanent employees lived in clean one- and two-bedroom units made of concrete block with functioning kitchens and bathrooms. Weeth attempted to pay his workers $1.10 per hour but found that they slowed their pace and did not complete the task in a day. When he increased their pay to $2.50 per hour, his work crews finished their tasks in five hours, earning approximately $15 per day. Although Weeth expressed satisfaction with his workers, he was doubtful that he could maintain this system, given the cost and competition from local growers who used contractors. He preferred machine labor, although researchers concluded that the cheapness of labor under the current system forestalled such developments.[11]

The trend toward hiring through labor contractors had a detrimental effect on the living conditions of most workers. Under this new system, growers no longer took responsibility for their employees' well-being, including where or how they lived. These concerns fell to the county, which now experienced many incidents of lawlessness, dependency, and unsanitary conditions in the numerous "fringe" settlements that completely encircled Fresno in 1959. Labor contractors drew the vast majority of their recruits from these "blighted areas" that existed in various stages of decay. The authors of the report gave the following description of Three Rocks, a typical fringe settlement: "Housing consists of tar-papered, very small shacks (condemned housing from labor camps) with outdoor privies, no water is available in the area where the housing is, must be carried from the grocery store which is on the road that borders the property."[12] Six hundred people occupied this particular settlement, a majority of them Mexican American. Most settlements, however, consisted of black or ethnic Mexican residents, while poor whites made up as much as 10 percent of the total fringe area populations. Only 33 percent of the inhabitants owned their own home, although 75 percent owned a car, reflecting the importance of mobility in getting to and from job sites and recruitment centers.[13] In areas where single men predominated, high levels of alcoholism, prostitution, and violence occurred, creating constant challenges for law enforcement officials. In settlements where families resided, county restrictions against public assistance for free and able-bodied men drove many unemployed fathers to "habitually seek to be jailed" so that their wives and children could secure food subsidies from the county. "In many cases," researchers found, "the noon meal at school [was] the only full meal many of the children received."[14]

In the end, the authors depicted a view of rural poverty that differed in form if not severity from the one found in the southern deserts. The heavy employment of temporary Mexican guest workers and undocumented immigrants in the South undermined local wages, precipitating the migration of workers northward. In the San Joaquin Valley, local residents struggled against declining wages caused by a changing employment system in which growers increasingly externalized the cost of labor and placed a heavier burden on contractors and the county government. Fringe areas that served as the major source of labor swelled in the postwar era with the migration of

FIGURE 1. A child stands in front of a derelict house in an undisclosed farm labor camp. ALUA, UFW Collection, 7118.

undocumented Mexican immigrants and former braceros who had "skipped" their contracts. For the authors of the study, however, migration constituted a less important factor in the creation of rural poverty than the maintenance of a large pool of desperate workers living on the margins of society, whose conditions led them to accept whatever wages contractors offered. "Steps need to be taken immediately," they concluded, "to bring about more equitable rates of pay, better housing, better educational opportunity, better police and fire protection, increased access to medical care, and all the other advantages which might be expected to accrue to citizens in our wealthy, productive economy."[15]

Such studies confirmed what most on the ground understood: life for farm workers had gotten worse since World War II, despite massive government investments in irrigation projects and during a time when growers expanded their production. U.S. Secretary of Labor James F. Mitchell, speaking to a gathering of farm labor specialists in 1959, confirmed these losses, testifying, "There is very little evidence that the underemployed and unemployed farm worker is passing out of society." The relative rootedness of workers in the San Joaquin Valley notwithstanding, Mitchell reported that the number of migratory farm workers in the United States had not decreased in a decade. Wages had declined over a seven-year period, leading Mitchell to remark, "We must remember that these workers not only do not have the protection of most of the social legislation which places a floor under the economic wellbeing of most Americans; but they are also deprived even of the 'automatic' action of a free labor market, in which a labor shortage tends to bring its own correction."[16] In spite of his observations, Mitchell possessed little power to alter the conditions undergirding this system. In the 1960s, local activists, community organizations, and workers themselves would be quicker to address these problems than government.

Rural labor advocates did not sit idly by as growers' profits increased and workers' conditions worsened. In some cases, local activism rose organically from the righteous indignation of people who applied their own analysis to the injustices that they witnessed around them. In other cases, workers circulating in and out of rural areas carried with them knowledge of how to leverage the power of unions and initiate reform through labor organizing. Still others attempted to adapt an urban model of reform to rural areas. Whatever the approach, in the 1960s advocates increasingly took matters into their own hands.

In the southern deserts, advocates for reform prioritized the goal of ending the bracero program, given the dramatic impact it had on the lives of farm workers in the area. The presence of Mexican nationals upset social relations in these rural communities, often pitting the guests against residents who felt entitled to local jobs. As I have described elsewhere, conflict occurred over employment as well as courtship, leading to violence and sometimes murder.[17]

In 1960, a coalition of workers in the Imperial Valley tried to increase their wages by striking the lettuce fields. Two AFL-CIO representatives, Al Green and Clyde Knowles, had begun to organize local workers with an eye toward starting a new union, the Agricultural Workers Organizing Committee (AWOC). Green and Knowles believed a new, statewide union movement could be built among migratory Mexican and Filipino workers who began their seasons in the southern deserts with the lettuce harvest. Growers' importation of braceros, however, complicated this dream and led some organizers to take out their frustrations on Mexican nationals in the fields. Fights in bars between braceros and striking workers also erupted in vice districts on the outskirts of many rural towns, leading to a chaotic situation.[18]

Two local activists, Miguel and Alfredo Figueroa, participated in these early attempts at unionization as a consequence of their upbringing. When the Figueroas were children, the family moved from Blythe, California, to nearby Oatman, Arizona, where their father took a job in the gold mines and joined the local mineworkers' union. Although mineworkers and farm workers occasionally overlapped within working-class communities, their rights and expectations differed considerably. The success of the United Mine Workers union provided miners with the leverage to insist on fair pay and better social services. In contrast, the lack of collective bargaining rights for farm workers meant that they often suffered discrimination on and off the job and had relatively little faith in their ability to change their condition. Occasionally, however, families like the Figueroas worked in both mining and agriculture, leading to a cross-fertilization of cultures that benefited farm worker communities. As young men, the Figueroas assisted their father in the mines and the melon harvest in and around Blythe.

During the early 1960s, Miguel and Alfredo threw themselves into farm worker activism across the desert region of southern California. Their trips to the Imperial Valley caught the attention of local law enforcement officials who maintained communication with their peers in Blythe. According to Miguel, the surveillance of Mexican Americans depended on a network of police officers, bankers, and deputized growers who kept tabs on anyone who tried to improve the lives of farm workers living in the Tri-Valley region. When Miguel and Alfredo returned home from working with AWOC in the Imperial Valley, town leaders called them to a meeting at the local bank and threatened them with violence. Miguel recalled their line of questioning: "What the hell [are] you guys doing down there? Do you know that those people have guns? Do you know that you Figueroa boys might get hurt?'" The town leaders eventually let them go, but other incidents of harassment followed. In 1963, for example, Blythe police officers dragged Alfredo from a local bar and publicly beat him, provoking a confrontation between his brother Gilbert and the police. Alfredo Figueroa won a case against the department, although a jury in Coachella awarded him a less than satisfactory settlement of $3,500. Investigators with the U.S. Commission on Civil Rights later wrote that the incident epitomized the kind of intimidation and abuse Mexican Americans encountered in the rural Southwest.[19]

Such threats and acts of violence did not deter everyone, least of all the Figueroas. The election of John F. Kennedy inspired hope that the federal government might intervene to improve conditions for farm workers in California. The newly formed Mexican American Political Association, led by the labor intellectual Bert Corona, organized "Viva Kennedy!" campaigns in the West, which sought to rally Mexican American voters and offset the considerable advantage the Republican candidate, Richard Nixon, held in California in 1960. The Figueroas participated in these electoral efforts in the Tri-Valley area, although they became disillusioned with Kennedy after he was elected, when he appealed to AFL-CIO leaders to call off the AWOC lettuce strike in El Centro.[20]

Many local activists were also angered by Kennedy's refusal to heed the calls of the labor intellectual Ernesto Galarza to end the bracero program. Galarza, a former policy advisor for the Pan American Union, became involved with farm worker unions, although his main contribution came by way of his scholarship. Utilizing political connections and social science methods, he studied the effects of the bracero program on the wages and work conditions of all farm workers in California. In 1956, he published a short book, *Strangers in Our Fields*, and spoke critically about the program in public. His interventions initiated a quiet reassessment of the policy by the Department of Labor, and by 1960 the program began to fall out of favor with lawmakers.[21] In 1961, Congress passed a two-year extension of Public Law 78 after tremendous debate, and the following year the Kennedy administration finally took a public position against the program. In 1963, Galarza published a longer, more critical book on the bracero program, *Merchants of Labor: The Mexican Bracero Story*, which helped push the contract-labor agreement to the brink of extinction. Although Congress and the president would honor requests from Mexico to gently wind down the program rather than cut it off immediately, lawmakers, growers, and activists acknowledged that the Mexican contract-labor program would soon come to a close.[22]

Studies such as those by Galarza and Fresno State College provided momentum for changes in the farm labor system as activists pressed the issue on the ground. Many reform advocates combined criticism of the bilateral agreement with a commitment to creating an institutional presence in rural California. The slow death of the bracero program allowed advocates to think about conditions after its demise, specifically how to reform a rural labor system dominated by disempowered migratory workers and day-haul laborers. In the early 1960s, both unions and community organizations vied with one another to assume leadership as the fight to end rural poverty moved into a new phase.

No one disputed the need to end the bracero program, although little consensus existed on what to do beyond this goal. In addition to assisting AWOC in the Imperial Valley, Miguel Figueroa worked with Ben Yellen, one of two physicians in the valley who had served braceros and saw first-hand the abuses of the program. Yellen distributed a self-published pamphlet known as the "yellow sheet" that criticized the bracero program and exposed local growers for their circumvention of the National Reclamation Act. Like Galarza, he campaigned for an end to the Mexican contract-labor agreement, but he saw it as a by-product of a larger problem related to the unequal distribution of public wealth in the form of irrigated land. Yellen believed that the problem of rural poverty could be eliminated by the enforcement of 160-acre limitation and residency requirements on megafarm owners who received federally funded water. He argued for the dismantling of these lands and their redistribution to farm workers, thereby achieving the novel solution of turning farm workers into farmers. Although Yellen counted among his supporters the University of California economist Paul Taylor, his was mostly a one-man crusade that had little support from labor unions and community organizations.[23]

Organizing workers was a far more common approach among activists, although not all agreed on the method. Union organizers like Al Green and Clyde Knowles believed that a union should be the ultimate objective, but their plans became mired in the conflicts between local workers and Mexican nationals. Consequently, prior to 1964, AWOC organizers and affiliates found themselves spending as much time campaigning against the bracero program as they did organizing workers for collective action. By the time the Mexican contract-labor program came to a formal end on December 31, 1964, AWOC had established itself as the most likely labor organization to lead a new union drive in rural California.

Members of another organization, the Community Service Organization (CSO), believed in the empowerment of communities to place demands on elected officials to improve living conditions and social services. During the mid-1950s, the CSO used its momentum from the election of Edward Roybal in urban East Los Angeles to expand into farming towns throughout California. The organization worked on issues affecting Mexican Americans, but its expansion into rural communities forced it to contend with Public Law 78 and the displacement of local workers by braceros. By the late 1950s, a rift had developed between middle-class professionals who wanted the CSO to remain politically agnostic on contentious issues such as the bracero program and members who wanted to align with labor organizations.[24]

The preference for organizing farm workers fell in line with the efforts of CSO founder, Fred Ross, and his protégé, Cesar Chavez. Ross had begun his activism in Riverside and San Bernardino counties, working with black and Mexican residents of citrus *colonias* to create Unity Leagues, community organizations built on the model of Saul Alinsky's Industrial Areas Foundation organizations in Chicago. The Unity Leagues served as a testing ground for Ross's theory that one had to "organize people where they are, not where you want them to be." When his efforts produced an organized citizenry and improvements in their communities, such as streetlights and school buses, Ross felt confident about doing similar work in more urban neighborhoods under the banner of the CSO. In 1952, he met and recruited Cesar Chavez, a young veteran of the U.S. Navy and a former farm worker living in the San José barrio of Sal Si Puedes. Born in Yuma, Arizona, in 1927, Chavez understood the difficulties of rural life in the southern deserts. During the Great Depression, he had watched helplessly as the state took possession of his family's farm, forcing them into the stream of itinerant farm laborers traveling throughout California during the late 1930s and early 1940s. Chavez's wife, Helen Favela Chavez, also knew rural poverty; her family was dispersed throughout the Palo Verde, Imperial, and San Joaquin Valleys. Such intimate knowledge of rural California made Chavez sympathetic to the plight of farm workers and inspired him to move the CSO in the direction of farm worker justice.

As Chavez distinguished himself as a skilled organizer and became an officer within the CSO, he explored new solutions to the problems confronting rural communities. He began by recruiting members who shared his concerns and experiences, tapping activists in the many small towns familiar to him. Gilbert Padilla, who had been working part time as a dry cleaner and as a gleaner of onions and other crops grown in the Central Valley, was among his most important discoveries. Chavez found Padilla through his friend Pete García, a CSO affiliate who had invited him to a recruitment meeting at his home in Hanford. When Padilla declined out of a belief that the CSO was just another "social club," Chavez and García met him after work, and the three men ended up talking late into the evening about their shared goal of improving farm worker conditions. Padilla appreciated Chavez's desire to make community organizations more accountable to the needs of rural communities and agreed to become a member.[25] Padilla

FIGURE 2. Members of the Community Service Organization, ca. 1950s. Second from right, Cesar Chavez; front row center, Fred Ross Sr.; far left, Saul Alinsky; third from the right in back, Helen Chavez. ALUA, UFW Collection, 330.

and Chavez's relationship would ultimately serve as the foundation for a new farm worker movement.

In 1959 Chavez exhibited his affinities with agricultural workers and unions by accepting a grant from the Packinghouse Workers of America to study the effects of the bracero program in Oxnard, California. He succeeded in forcing the Farm Labor Bureau to comply with a provision in the bilateral agreement that required growers to hire local farm workers before contracting Mexican nationals. He also helped local farm workers secure state unemployment insurance benefits during seasonal downturns. Such actions deviated from the CSO's more familiar voter registration work and came closer to the services provided by unions.[26] When Chavez became the national director of the CSO, he assigned Padilla to the CSO service center in Stockton, a predominantly farm worker community, and encouraged him to pursue grants like the one he held in Oxnard. To his delight, Padilla succeeded in securing a grant in 1961 from the Bishops' Committee

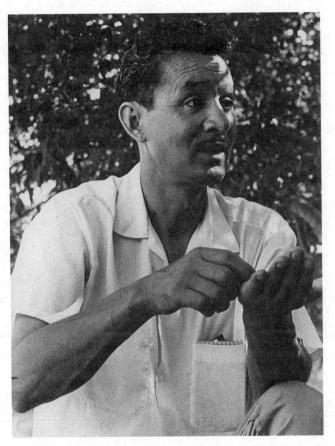

FIGURE 3. Gilbert Padilla, 1966.

on Migratory Labor in Chicago to study housing conditions for local farm workers.[27]

Padilla joined a growing team of rural recruits, including Julio and Fina Hernandez and Roger Terronez from Corcoran; Tony and Rachel Orendain and Gil Flores from Hanford; and a loquacious and fiery single mother from Stockton, Dolores Huerta.[28] Huerta had never worked in the fields, but she maintained a strong connection to labor unions and farm workers through her family. Her father had worked in the coalmines in Dawson, New Mexico, where she was born, and had belonged to the United Mine Workers.[29] When Dolores was an infant, labor unrest in the mines forced her father to seek alternative work harvesting beets in Wyoming, Nebraska, and California. The family eventually settled in Stockton, California, where her father worked in the asparagus fields among a predominantly Filipino workforce. In the 1940s, he participated in a strike on the Zuckerman asparagus farm alongside Huerta's future friend and Filipino activist, Philip Veracruz.[30]

Huerta clashed with her father over his "chauvinist" behavior and considered her mother, Alicia Margaret St. John Chavez, a stronger influence in her life. During the Great Depression, Alicia divorced Huerta's father and raised Dolores and her sister on $5 per week from wages earned at the Richmond-Chase canneries and a local restaurant. In 1937, Alicia participated in a strike of the canneries as a member of the United Cannery, Agricultural, Packing and Allied Workers of America, which forced her to depend entirely on her earnings at the restaurant.[31] In 1941 she opened a successful lunch counter with her second husband, James Richards. A year later the couple purchased a hotel from Japanese American owners who had to sell when the government relocated all Japanese Americans to internment camps. Alicia relied on her children to staff the restaurant and clean the hotel, providing Dolores with an invaluable cultural experience that strengthened her confidence and ability to organize in any community. She recalled the unique composition of their neighborhood and clientele: "The ethnic community where we lived was all mixed. It was Japanese, Chinese. The only Jewish families that lived in Stockton were there in our neighborhood.... There was the Filipino pool hall, the Filipino dance hall. It was [a] very colorful, multi-ethnic scene."[32] When the Richards' relationship soured and the couple divorced, Alicia lost the restaurant but held on to the hotel. Dolores continued to help her mother and became friends with many of the Filipino farm workers who were their primary patrons. Later her mother met and married Juan "Fernando" Silva, a former bracero, who conveyed to Dolores his deep feelings of bitterness over his treatment at the hands of growers.[33] These influences made her sympathetic to Chavez's appeals to join the local CSO, which she accepted in 1960. In time she too would be as important to the new movement as Padilla and Chavez.

The addition of rural chapters in the CSO and the new members' success in bringing attention to the plight of farm workers compelled Chavez to call for the creation of a farm labor committee. According to Padilla, the decision should not have been controversial because the CSO already maintained committees on housing and education, although some members questioned whether Chavez's new plan augured a more aggressive move toward labor organizing. Some members preferred to maintain a more nonpartisan image and believed that alignment with worker concerns would move the organization strongly to the left. Others objected to pursuing work that, they believed, duplicated AWOC's efforts. Opponents of Chavez's plan pointed out that AWOC, with funding from the AFL-CIO, had initiated the lettuce strike in Imperial Valley and made inroads in organizing Filipino workers in the Central Valley. Consequently, the CSO national committee chose to table the decision until the national convention in Calexico in March 1962, when they would discuss the matter in greater depth.[34]

In preparation for the conference, Chavez met with Padilla to share his plans. Padilla recalled, "[Cesar] said, 'I am going to propose to the convention that every chapter should have a farm labor committee, and that we should start doing something for farm labor. . . . If they don't approve this, I'm going to leave. I'm going to quit.'"[35] Chavez also communicated his intentions to a number of members on the CSO board of directors, but no one took him seriously, given his successful recruitment of new members, his ability to get outside grants, and, most important, his dependence on the director position as the only source of funding for his family. "I didn't believe him," Padilla recalled, adding, "because he's the one that built all the chapters." Like Chavez, Padilla also supported an entire family on his CSO salary, partially covered by the grant from the Bishops' Committee. Although the grant was set to expire in June, Padilla had hopes of applying for an extension and had already secured a promise from the local chapter to continue paying him.[36]

Chavez attended the Calexico meeting flanked by his new staff, including Padilla and Huerta, optimistic that a deal could be struck with his fellow board members. One of the founding members and his friend, Tony Rios, had been a member of the Electrical Union, and two other board members, Jay Rodriguez and Gil Anaya, had belonged to the Butchers Union and Steelworkers, respectively. In addition to these men, Chavez believed he could count on other board members who understood the power of a union and could see the value of his proposal. To his chagrin, however, they rebuffed Chavez. Those with union experience argued that AWOC's failed strike in the lettuce fields demonstrated the difficulty of organizing farm workers and recommended that the CSO leave the task to them. Padilla also recalled that many members with professional backgrounds objected to doing farm labor organizing altogether, signaling the degree to which the CSO had become a more conservative organization since its beginning. "We had really professional guys up there, not like in the fifties when you had those grassroots people." He added, "[The grassroots people] didn't speak English, [and] were awkward [when] speaking, but they had lots of balls and guts." In this case, neither union supporters nor professionals supported Chavez. At some point, Padilla recalled, the meeting turned "very nasty," with Chavez's opponents accusing him and his allies of betraying the original mission of the CSO. "I was attacked," Padilla recalled, "but I wasn't supposed to respond because I was staff."[37] Amid the insults, Chavez stood up and followed through on his threat to quit.

Chavez's resignation scared Padilla, who understood that Chavez's decision required him to leave the organization too. Padilla confronted Chavez outside the convention hall, but Chavez showed little remorse. "I quit! Fuck them! I'm not going to do it [any]more," he told Padilla. Chavez's response revealed his famous obstinacy and a willingness to risk everything to achieve his goals, two traits that would become the hallmarks of his leadership. In resigning from the CSO, however, Chavez considered the stakes quite low, given that they had not yet committed significant resources to the project. He also had great faith in his recruits to pursue their goals independent of the CSO. When Padilla asked Chavez, "What about me, what about us?," Chavez responded with typical brevity and confidence: "Let's go organize it ourselves."[38] Within three days of the meeting, Chavez left his post in Los Angeles for the small town of Delano, where his brother, Richard, and most of Helen's family lived. Padilla moved back to Hanford to work at the dry cleaner and prepared members of the local CSO chapters in anticipation of Chavez's call to action. On April 12, 1962, Chavez tendered his formal letter of resignation to the CSO from Delano and began making preparations for a new farm workers union.[39]

Chavez's ambition to start a new union took time and encountered more than a few skeptics. Organizing a union required faith that the bracero program would soon end and that farm workers could attain the same collective bargaining rights granted to industrial workers under the National Labor Relations Act. Galarza's activism created momentum for achieving the first goal, although the struggle against the program and the failure to sustain a labor movement among citizen workers made Galarza dubious of Chavez's chances. He gave him counsel and wished him well but had already begun to turn his attention to urban issues. Saul Alinsky remained supportive of Chavez during his transition from the CSO, but he too advised Chavez against the venture and encouraged him to organize in cities for his Industrial Areas Foundation.[40] Chavez's mentor, Fred Ross, remained optimistic, however, and helped channel IAF money to Padilla as he made important inroads in the labor camps.[41] Dolores Huerta moved from Stockton to

Los Angeles to become a staff member at the CSO's national headquarters while she awaited news from Chavez.[42] Meanwhile, Chavez's wife and the oldest of their eight children worked in the fields to support Cesar as he put together the union.[43]

Chavez succeeded in convening the first meeting of the National Farm Workers Association (NFWA), in Fresno in September 1962. At the meeting, composed mainly of former CSO members, the delegates adopted the black eagle logo as their symbol and red, white, and black as the official colors of the new union. They also adopted a dues structure that required each member to pay $3.50 per month. The initial death benefit insurance for members mirrored those of Mexican *mutualistas* familiar to many of the delegates. The delegates also selected officers, including Sanger resident, Jesus Martínez, as president; Hanford resident, Tony Orendain, as secretary-treasurer; Cesar Chavez as director general; and six others, including Gilbert Padilla, as board members.

Chavez dedicated the first year to building the organization CSO-style by holding meetings in the homes of Mexican farm workers and conducting registration drives and get-out-the-vote campaigns throughout the valley. Padilla participated in these activities and earned the trust of many local residents by organizing against police brutality and substandard public housing. He recalled that, although they brought many new members into the NFWA, neither the structure of governance nor the appointments worked out as well as Chavez and he had hoped. The work obligations of some officers and lack of shared commitment led to breakdowns in service. Chavez also found his role too vague and, ultimately, unsatisfying. As a result, he reshuffled the governing structure in 1964, taking over as president, a position that granted him the control he sought from the start. Orendain remained secretary-treasurer, and Chavez elevated Padilla to vice president. Chavez also recruited Dolores Huerta to return to the Central Valley to become a second vice president.[44]

The activities of other nonaffiliated activists operating in the San Joaquin Valley gave Chavez confidence that he had allies. Although rural poverty had become a distinguishing feature of life for most farm workers in California, the high rates of residency and the relatively weak influence of the bracero program in the valley provided farm worker activists a more stable local population with whom to work. Church groups set up operations in many of these farm worker settlements, often conducting relief work rather than organizing residents for political protest. Like the CSO, however, these groups contained members who wanted to go beyond the role of assisting field workers to form self-help organizations that approximated unions. The emergence of civil rights groups, such as the Congress of Racial Equality (CORE) and the Southern Christian Leadership Conference during the 1950s, also influenced the thinking of these religion-oriented groups. The audacious challenges by black civil rights organizations to Jim Crow laws and discrimination in the American South inspired many local activists to pursue a similar transformation in the rural West.

The California Migrant Ministry figured prominently among the religious organizations committed to serving rural communities. As a program within the Division of Home Missions of the National Council of Churches of Christ, the ministry had grown accustomed to working with immigrant populations. Like other organizations during the 1960s, including the CSO, the California Migrant Ministry felt the influence of youthful affiliates who had come of age after World War II and questioned the boundaries of what traditional community organizations could and should do.

The ministry's selection of Wayne "Chris" Hartmire as director, a twenty-nine-year-old father of three and a Presbyterian minister, demonstrated its willingness to embrace the leadership of a new generation. Hartmire sought to build on the work of a previous director who had secured a grant from the Schwartzhaupt Foundation to learn from CSO organizers' attempts to build new chapters in rural California. Upon his arrival, Hartmire met with Chavez, who recommended that he spend a month in Stockton working with Gilbert Padilla and Dolores Huerta to become familiar with the needs of the community. "I quickly became a CSO enthusiast," Hartmire remembered, attending all of the CSO conventions, including the fateful Calexico convention in 1962. "In retrospect," he remembered, "I . . . wondered whether Cesar wanted a 'yes' vote." Hartmire believed Chavez had already reached the conclusion that most of his CSO peers did not have the stomach for organizing farm workers and wanted an excuse to start his own organization.[45]

Hartmire took the lessons from Stockton and the CSO and immediately applied them to social work in the Central Valley. He recruited Jim Drake, a young New Yorker fresh out of Union Theological Seminary, to anchor the new rural projects for the ministry. Drake had finished his course work in December 1961, and his wife, Susan, had just given birth to their son, Matthew. As Jim remembers it, he pursued a place on Hartmire's staff "out of desperation" because he needed a job to be able to feed his family. At their first meeting, Hartmire quizzed him about what he knew of organizing. He lied to get the job. Immediately following their meeting Drake drove to the nearest public library to educate himself. He remembered, "In the card file was one book on organizing published by the United Nations. I stole it."[46] This would not be Drake's last act of improvisation to propel the movement forward.

In spite of their relative lack of experience and knowledge, the two embarked on organizing farm workers in the San Joaquin Valley from 1962 to 1964. Hartmire instructed Drake to move to rural California and consult with Cesar Chavez on how to get started. For Chavez, Drake's arrival provided a set of wheels and the ministry's gasoline money to take him around the valley and make local connections that would contribute to the formation of a new farm workers union. Drake benefited too, learning the lay of the land and meeting Gilbert Padilla in the process. Padilla was generous with information and gave Drake a history lesson on organizing.[47]

Padilla recommended Porterville, a small town thirty miles from Delano in the heart of grape country, where a county-owned labor camp known as Woodville housed three hundred families. Drake and another ministry representative, David Havens, followed Padilla's advice and used a small amount of money raised by Hartmire to rent an office behind the local barbershop for the Farm Workers Organization. Drake got the attention of residents by purchasing a large tank, filling it with gasoline, and inviting farm workers to pay a $2 annual fee for the privilege of purchasing fuel for $.20 per gallon—far below the going rate. Given workers' dependence on automobiles for transportation to local jobs, the plan worked, and the office flourished. News of their organization spread to the neighboring town of Farmerville near Visalia and attracted residents of another labor camp, Linnell, to participate in the program. The fueling station provided Drake and Havens an important base of operation, and the two began to run CSO-style house meetings with local farm workers to explore their needs.

Meanwhile, Padilla worked on behalf of the NFWA, using the last months of his grant to conduct a survey of farm workers' complaints. He began by recruiting members of Central Valley CSO chapters in Corcoran, Huron, and Selma who vowed to stay in the organization until Chavez set up his new union. "I had those guys organized doing the survey," Padilla recalled.[48] When the money ran out, he stayed on as a field laborer but soon picked up another grant through Ross to run a women's educational project in Hanford that included attention to reproductive rights and child care.[49] Drake and Havens shared an interest in making contraceptives available to women farm workers.

According to Padilla, Havens harbored the misconception that because most women farm workers belonged to the Catholic Church, they would be resistant to their message. "They go [to church] to look for their soul[s]," Padilla told Havens, "They don't pay attention to the priest!" To prove his point, Padilla accompanied Havens to the Woodville camp, where they quickly distributed a box of free contraceptives to four or five women who became their primary distributors to the rest of the residents.

The trips into the camp revealed the extent of the housing crisis among farm workers. "The labor camp was a very disgusting site," Padilla recalled. The houses amounted to windowless, two-bedroom tin shacks built in 1937 for dust bowl migrants that had been handed down several generations to the current residents. During the hot summer months, residents would place on the roof wet rugs recovered from the local dump in a futile attempt to get some relief from the heat. Padilla found that women resented having to share communal toilets and showers, where they encountered many single men who sat outside the facilities in an attempt to catch a glimpse of them naked. The conditions appalled Padilla, who encouraged Drake to join him in an effort to close down or reform the camp. Drake expressed some trepidation but agreed to look into the history of the facility, and Padilla agreed to do outreach among the residents.

In his research, Drake discovered that the federal government had designed the homes to last no more than ten years. After World War II, growers had taken over the camps and continued to use them for their workers throughout the 1950s, until they began to divest from housing projects in favor of working with labor contractors to acquire day-haul laborers. By the 1960s, the Tulare County Housing Authority had taken over the camps, but it did nothing to improve the conditions. Drake conferred about the tenants' rights with James Herndon, an African American attorney working on behalf of the poor in San Francisco. Herndon inspected the dilapidated facilities and informed Drake that the county was in violation of a 1947 law that restricted owners from raising rents on condemned dwellings. He recommended that they pursue legal action.[50]

Ever the organizer, Padilla encouraged Drake to take the bolder step of setting up a fund and asking tenants to pay their rent to them instead of the county. In return, Padilla and Drake promised to protect the tenants if the county attempted to evict them from the camp. Although not everyone participated, enough did, and county officials began to send eviction notices.

They also sent the sheriff to intimidate the residents, although Padilla reassured them that the county had no legal standing to force them to pay. "I said, '[The] County doesn't know . . . who's paying . . . so when they come to you to tell you to pay [your rent], screw 'em." According to Padilla, several residents followed his directions and lived in the camp for months, rent-free. They paid whatever they could to the fund set up by Padilla and Drake, which was deposited in the bank in case they needed it to take legal action against the county. Padilla also raised awareness of the problems in the camp by inviting the secretary of labor to visit; he also attracted the attention of the local press.[51]

The standoff between the residents and the county eventually erupted when the local housing authority chose to raise the rents to cover its losses. The action angered the newly empowered residents, who took to demonstrating against the county. Drake recalled the scene: "One day the Tulare County Housing Authority arbitrarily raised the rent on the condemned, tin shacks from $19 to $22 per month! I drove down to the camp not knowing this, and there was Gil under the water tank, standing and shouting on top of a car. By the time he got down, he had started a rent strike—300 families joined!"[52] Padilla, Drake, Havens, and a young college student, Doug Adair, counseled the Woodville families to join with residents of the nearby Linnell camp in Farmville to create one big march to the Tulare government office building. The protesters overwhelmed housing authority officials, who took cover in their offices until the marchers moved on to a local park for a celebration. In the months that followed, Drake and Padilla took the county to court, where they won a settlement that restored the original rent and forced the housing authority to build a new facility on the same property.[53]

The Tulare rent strike inspired many farm workers and a number of local organizers to join the NFWA. Among them was Brother Gilbert, a priest who had left his post as principal of the Catholic Garces High School in Bakersfield to help lead the march. "I wore my official Christian Brothers black suit, black silk vest, and a white starched collar somewhat similar to the clerical collar worn by the Catholic clergy." Brother Gilbert, later known by his birth name, LeRoy Chatfield, eventually left the priesthood to become a critical member of Chavez's team. During the rent strike, he carried a placard with a quote by the famous union organizer, Joe Hill: "Don't Mourn—Organize!" Chatfield got the idea from a Catholic anarchist friend, Ammon Hennacy, who ran a Catholic Worker hospitality house in Salt Lake City. "Even though I had never participated in a farm worker 'rent strike' march before," recalled Chatfield, "I thought Joe Hill's quotation was appropriate for the occasion."[54] Chatfield was not alone in his lack of experience. Many considered the rent strike an important opening salvo in a new movement to improve the lives of farm workers in the San Joaquin Valley.

A STRIKE IS NOT ENOUGH

While the National Farm Workers Association built its organization, Al Green and AWOC continued to work on a parallel track in the southern deserts and elsewhere in the San Joaquin Valley. Although disappointed by the failure to halt the use of Mexican nationals as scab labor in the Imperial Valley, AWOC kept the pressure on, believing that the national mood toward the bracero program had shifted in its favor. AWOC's national sponsor, the AFL-CIO, wanted to be organized and ready in the fields when the bracero program ended. To prepare for this moment, national representatives channeled funds to Green and Clive Knowles, who searched for the most likely workers to organize. The national office also pursued legal action against the U.S. Department of Labor to enforce ceilings on the employment of Mexican nationals who remained in the labor market. This move guarded against the replacement of domestic workers who, they believed, constituted AWOC's future.[55]

Green and Knowles reached out to many workers, including those within Chavez's fold. Padilla recalled that when he left the CSO, Green tried to persuade him to come work for AWOC. "I didn't like the program," Padilla said, "because they were organizing labor contractors."[56] This strategy circumvented organizing in the fields in favor of appealing to middlemen who maintained communication with several workers at a time. This was particularly true among Filipino labor contractors who stayed in contact with Filipino migrants as they spanned the entire West Coast, working in canneries, on boats, and on farms from Alaska to Arizona. As the Fresno State College study showed, however, these same men could be as exploitative as the growers for whom they worked, often retaining the greatest share of the money set aside for hiring field hands. The decision to organize contractors rather than the rank-and-file workers betrayed the organizing philosophy that Chavez, Padilla, and other CSO veterans had learned from Fred Ross. Chavez articulated the philosophy years later: "Fred used to say that 'you can't take shortcuts, because you'll pay for it later.' He believed society would be transformed from within by mobilizing individuals and communities. But you have to convert one person at a time, time after time."[57] Padilla and Chavez regarded AWOC's approach as the kind of shortcut Ross had advised them to avoid.

Chavez stayed true to his training even when workers themselves called on him to take stronger action. In March 1965, for example, a worker on a local rosebush farm, Epifanio Camacho, appealed to Chavez to organize a strike against the grower for repeatedly breaking promises of better pay. Chavez resisted, advising Camacho to have patience. By 1965, NFWA leaders had expanded its membership to approximately 1,200 through such painstaking methods that they believed would pay dividends later.[58]

In contrast, AWOC's approach garnered some immediate success, especially among Filipino workers. Larry Itliong, a veteran of the Pacific migration and a former labor contractor, epitomized the AWOC organizer. Born in San Nicolas, Pangasina, the Philippines, Itliong arrived on the West Coast in 1929 and worked in various crops throughout California and Washington, including a lettuce farm where he lost two fingers in a harvesting accident. He also canned salmon in Alaska and met many labor organizers along the way, some of them affiliated with the Communist Party. By the early 1950s, he had risen to the position of labor contractor in Kern-Tulare County while maintaining radical political views that made him an appealing candidate for membership in AWOC. In 1956 he joined the labor union organizing committee and began to assist Green, Knowles, and another organizer, Norman Smith, in attracting other Filipinos to the organization, including a young Peter Velasco and Andy Imutan. Along with Itliong, two other veterans of the fields, Philip Veracruz and Ben Gines, joined AWOC's organizing efforts and became key figures in AWOC's attempt to establish a foothold in the San Joaquin Valley.[59]

In spite of differences in their approach, AWOC and NFWA members had mutual respect and stayed in contact. Itliong was present and organizing among Filipino workers at the time of the Tulare rent strike, whereas Padilla maintained a positive but distant relationship with the Filipino organizers he encountered. Although exceptions existed, NFWA confined much of its organizing effort to Mexican field workers, a decision that mirrored the heavy Mexican influence in the CSO. AWOC had greater success among Filipinos, likely a reflection of its emphasis on organizing contractors, in which Filipinos played an important role.

In the summer of 1965 the tracks of these two upstart unions converged in the grape harvest. AWOC took on a more aggressive posture that season in anticipation of the end of the bracero program. When Lyndon Johnson reneged on the government's plan and revived the program to allow a limited number of Mexican nationals to work in the Coachella Valley grape harvest, AWOC pounced. It pointed out that domestic workers—many of them Filipino immigrants—earned 15 cents less than the braceros and instructed all AWOC pickers to vacate the field. Coachella Valley growers quickly resolved the matter by agreeing to a pay increase in an attempt to avoid a contract and the possibility of an extended battle.[60] AWOC's success on the wage increase, however, encouraged union officials to explore new opportunities as the harvest moved northward into the San Joaquin Valley, where the season lasted much longer and workers had an opportunity to take a much stronger stand. Larry Itliong moved to Delano and began organizing among the many *manongs* (fellow country people from the Illocano-speaking region of the Philippines) who participated in the local harvest. Throughout this period, he also maintained communication with Dolores Huerta, whose rapport with Filipino farm workers from her days working in her mother's restaurant and hotel made her the ideal liaison for NFWA in its communication with AWOC. Although the organizations maintained friendly relations, the question of which union would take the lead in the new union movement among field workers created a bit of a rivalry. In addition, AWOC had support from the AFL-CIO, while Chavez had been cultivating his own relations with Walter Reuther and the United Auto Workers (UAW). The nominal investment in the race to organize farm workers by two national unions raised the stakes enough for each organization to keep an eye on the other.

The NFWA's organizing model and attention to Mexican workers gave it a stronger influence in the San Joaquin Valley, where ethnic Mexicans dominated in the labor market. In addition, the rent strike served as an important training experience for new organizers. One of the camp residents, Paul Espinosa, went on to organize *Radio Bilingue*, a radio program in Spanish and English that fed the local populations important information regarding the union. Another resident, Ernesto Laredo, continued to organize tenants, along with a sixteen-year-old girl, Yolanda Barrera, who served as a translator and who eventually became a federal prosecutor. According to Padilla, Espinosa urged him to branch out into organizing on the local grape ranch,

J. D. Martin's Rancho Blanco, where many of the tenants worked. There, a foreman had agitated male workers by separating them from their wives. When the women relieved themselves in the fields, the foreman would follow to sneak a peek at them. Espinosa believed they could organize the workers to get the foreman fired or to arrange for adequate bathroom facilities on the job.

A lack of agreement on the next step and Chavez's health, however, initially delayed further organizing. The demanding schedule of house meetings and travel landed Chavez in a Bakersfield hospital with pneumonia that August. This setback and a preference for building the union one member at a time prevented him from moving aggressively. In addition, NFWA organizers wanted to respect the wishes of their allies. Unlike AWOC, which had been organized by union men and supported by the AFL-CIO, NFWA had started as a coalition of community organizers, religious leaders, and college students who did not always have a common vision for what the organization would become. Padilla, for example, recalled the moment Espinosa came into the Porterville office to ask him to organize at Rancho Blanco. "Jim Drake happened to walk in when I was talking to [Espinosa] and he [said], 'Don't go strike, you can't strike.'" According to Padilla, Drake worried about conservative funders from the Church who might withdraw their support if they learned that they were organizing a union. Padilla appeased Drake by promising to evaluate the situation on the ranch and not get involved in labor matters.[61]

Padilla's encounters at Rancho Blanco compelled him to take action. He witnessed several instances of abuse of workers on the job and heard from a number of employees who were ready to protest. He knew many of the workers from the rent strike and discovered that at least half the workers lived in Earlimart, a small town near Delano that had been fertile ground for recruiting new NFWA members. "So, one day," Padilla recalled, "I got up and I said, 'Ah, I'm going to pull them out.'" While Chavez lay in the hospital, Padilla directed the first labor strike of the decade in the San Joaquin Valley. When Chavez heard of the action, he called Padilla from his hospital bed, ribbing him for waiting to make the move until he, Chavez, was sick. Upon Chavez's release by the doctor, the two immediately hit the fields with picket signs and called all NFWA members to participate in the labor action. When Chavez called the owner of the ranch to reach a settlement, the owner refused to meet. Padilla recalled the grower's response: "Let [Chavez] rot; I don't care."

The unwillingness of J. D. Martin to settle the dispute signaled an important difference between growers in the San Joaquin Valley and those in Coachella. The longer seasons and a thriving day-hauler labor market gave San Joaquin Valley growers confidence that they could weather the storm.[62]

Chavez and Padilla viewed the strike as an impromptu action initiated by the workers rather than the beginning of a new movement. The strike came toward the end of the season and over issues not related to wages or a contract. In fact, as Padilla recalls, they did not even refer to NFWA as a union. In this regard, for Chavez the strike symbolized a flexing of NFWA's muscles and put the growers on notice that they could no longer mistreat their employees. For Larry Itliong, however, the strike represented a potential threat to usurp a union movement that he and AWOC members had been planning to take over. Padilla recalled his response: "Dolores told him that I was striking and I'm moving in, so he got scared." On September 8, 1965, Itliong pulled Filipino workers out of nine vineyards in Delano, initiating the grape strike.[63]

The AWOC action caught Chavez by surprise and forced upon him a decision about striking that he was not prepared to make. Padilla recalled his concern immediately following the news that Filipinos had walked off the job: "You better come; the world's coming to an end! There's 5,000 Filipinos on the street, [on] strike." When the two met, Chavez asked Padilla to attend an AWOC meeting in Delano at a community building known locally as Filipino Hall. He also instructed Bill Asher, a staff member on the newspaper *El Malcriado*, affiliated with NFWA, to join Padilla to document the historic meeting. Padilla and Asher sat in the front row in the mostly Filipino audience. For Padilla, the meeting revealed a diversity among Filipinos he had never known. "I didn't know what the fuck was going on," he remembered, because they were "speaking all their different languages." The meeting required several translators for the Filipinos alone to communicate among themselves, because members spoke at least three languages: Tagalog, Illocano, and Pangasinan. In spite of the language barriers, Padilla interpreted the sincerity of AWOC's commitment and received an appeal from Itliong for NFWA to join them. When Padilla returned with the news, Chavez arranged with the local priest to hold a meeting of NFWA members at the local church, Our Lady of Guadalupe, in Delano. He called on allies in the civil rights organizations, CORE and SNCC, to use their connections to draw in activists interested in supporting farm worker justice and told Asher to get the word out to the community of farm workers via *El Malcriado*. Meanwhile, Padilla took a sleeping bag down to Filipino Hall to live among AWOC members and discuss mutual interests.

Strategically called on September 16, Mexican Independence Day, the meeting of NFWA drew a capacity crowd that overwhelmed the small church built with money donated by many of the Catholic Slavic growers in the valley. Padilla conducted the meeting, which led many in attendance to confuse him with Chavez. He invited AWOC members to address the crowd to explain the reasons for their strike. Chavez, who waited patiently off to the side, had yet to decide whether he would ask NFWA members to join in the labor walkout. "Cesar was afraid to call a strike," Padilla remembered. When he finally spoke, however, he discovered a readiness for action among the people. He resisted shouts of "Come on, say it!" from people in the audience who wanted him to initiate the strike there and then, largely out of respect for the priest, who had asked Padilla and him not to call a strike that evening. Instead, he called a meeting for the following week at the American Legion hall. "That's where we called the strike," Padilla remembered. "The following day we went out and picketed, and the rest is history."[64]

Numerous scholars and journalists have documented the history of the Delano grape strike and the beginning of the modern farm worker movement. Many tell the familiar story of how a reluctant Cesar Chavez was drawn into the strike by the more radical, union-oriented AWOC members, especially Larry Itliong. This Filipino farm worker vanguard took the first brave steps toward the formation of a new multiethnic union. According to Padilla, the collaboration between AWOC and NFWA forced members to deal with cultural differences between Mexicans and Filipinos, as well as the very different relationships these two organizations had with the established national unions.

Early on, differences in resources brought the two closer together. The NFWA had not accumulated a strike fund or a permanent home, whereas AWOC had AFL-CIO money and Filipino Hall. The situation forced many Mexican families to rely on the generosity of Filipino workers to feed their families while out on strike. Many recalled strikers eating meals together in Filipino Hall, often sharing cuisines. "We [were] introduced to fish heads and bitter lemon and all that Filipino food," Padilla fondly remembered.[65] As the growers dug in and resisted a settlement, many of the men—both Filipino and Mexican—began to seek work elsewhere, testing the fortitude

FIGURE 4. AFL-CIO and AWOC members march in support of farm workers during the Delano strike, 1965. Left to right: Larry Itliong, AWOC; Walter Reuther, UAW; Cesar Chavez, NFWA. ALUA, UFW Collection, 362.

of the striking families. At these moments, Mexican women picked up the slack and led the picketing in the fields. The now famous photo of UAW president, Walter Reuther, leading a march, flanked by Cesar Chavez and Larry Itliong, in November 1965 conveys the multiethnic solidarity of the moment, although it obscures the significant role women played in sustaining the movement.[66]

The photo also hides the simmering tension that existed among the various labor factions that composed the movement at the beginning. AWOC struck, in part, because of worries that NFWA was about to take the lead in the race to establish a farm worker union. This misperception was fueled, in part, by Al Green, who had been active throughout rural California in search of the right formula for success. A mercurial figure, Green had belonged to the International Brotherhood of Teamsters before the organization was ejected from the AFL-CIO for corruption in the national office. He maintained connections to packinghouse workers organized under the Teamsters and advised Itliong and other AWOC members to be open to whatever affiliation gave them the best chance for victory. Meanwhile, the presence of the UAW's Walter Reuther at the November march and his gift of $10,000 to both AWOC and NFWA indicated more than just a helping hand from a big national brother. During the mid-1960s, Reuther locked horns with AFL-CIO president, George Meany, over a range of policy issues, including the role of the national union in the civil rights movement. That Reuther had an especially close relationship to Chavez spurred Meany to send Bill Kircher, an AFL-CIO representative, to shore up the national union's influence over the new movement. By August 19, 1966, Kircher had forged a merger of AWOC and NFWA under the name United Farm Workers Organizing Committee and brokered an agreement for Chavez rather than Itliong to become the president of the union.[67] The decision made sense, given that the majority of workers were Mexican; however, it also threatened to alienate the significant number of Filipino workers who still maintained allegiances to other unions, including the Teamsters.

By 1966, leaders had worked out much of the logistical issues related to who would guide the union, but many issues remained unresolved, including how this movement would succeed where others had failed. Although many noble efforts had been made over the previous sixty years, no organization or leader had figured out the right approach to earning collective bargaining rights for farm workers. The typical union strategy, the strike, had thus far failed. By the end of the harvest that year, growers showed their usual stubbornness in resisting negotiations and a confidence that they could outlast the poorly funded union. To succeed, Chavez would have to consider the boycott, a strategy that had lapsed since the NFLU used it in 1948 but that would have new potential in the era of the civil rights movement.

TWO

Capitalism in Reverse

AS JERRY BROWN HEADED FOR a meeting of the National Executive Board (NEB) of the United Farm Workers Organizing Committee in 1968, he pondered a future without the union. Accompanied by his wife, Juanita, Brown (no relation to the future California governor of the same name) had arrived in Delano in 1966 as a twenty-one-year-old graduate student in anthropology from Cornell University. Within a matter of minutes of their meeting, Cesar Chavez temporarily derailed Brown's dream of writing a dissertation on farm worker communities. Brown recalled Chavez's first words to him: "He said, 'Jerry, do you know who we hate more than social workers?'" Staring intently into Brown's eyes, Chavez answered his own question: "Social scientists." In the next minute, Chavez made a deal with Brown to open the Delano farm worker community to him if the couple vowed to serve the movement for at least two weeks. Now, two years later, Brown was heading for Filipino Hall as the co-coordinator of the international boycott to plead his case to the NEB for a major expansion of the campaign.

In his two years of service, Brown had put his love of data analysis to good use, studying USDA consumer and marketing reports for the top forty-one cities where California grapes were sold. Brown recalled, "I found out very rapidly that . . . the ten major North American cities—which also included Montreal, Toronto, and Vancouver —received 50 percent of the grape shipments."[1] Although the boycott had been a part of the farm workers' arsenal since 1965, the union had neither the resources nor the time to study the effectiveness of the tactic. Most of the union's boycott effort was intuitive, trying to stop the grapes as they wound their way through the market. Anecdotal knowledge of their success came from the front lines, where longshoreman, Teamsters, or restaurant and bar workers agreed not to convey grapes and wine to suppliers and customers. Occasionally the media covered an impressive demonstration in front of a supermarket, but the notion of how effective such campaigns were in changing customers' buying habits was a mystery. Now Brown's research provided material evidence of success and, more important, the prospect of improving the boycott. According to his statistics, only four of the cities had demonstrated meaningful declines in grape sales. Brown argued that by concentrating the union's meager resources on building effective boycott houses in the ten leading cities, the union could affect the majority of the North American market for grapes and bring the grape growers to the bargaining table in a way that neither the strikes nor the marches had been able to do thus far.

In spite of Brown's data, Chavez showed little enthusiasm for his research and privately upheld the primacy of the strike. "It was important in Cesar's and in many of the board members' [views]," recalled Brown, "to keep a big strike presence going on." Such a position ran counter to Brown's prescription for success: "I started realizing that we were never going to win the strike in the fields. You know, it was important for the media, it was important for the press, it was important for the farm workers' morale. Yes, you might get a few more [growers] to [capitulate to] the strike, but they could always replace the workers with workers from L.A., from Phoenix, from Mexico— using the poor against the poor. The idea started to form in my mind that unless we redeployed resources and got strong boycotts in ten of these cities, we were never going to win the boycott. And I started to argue this with Cesar more and more strongly."[2]

Rather than plead his case further to an obstinate Chavez, Brown appealed to two veterans of the movement, LeRoy Chatfield and Chris Hartmire, both of whom had the capacity to persuade Chavez to take the matter to the NEB. "We talked about democracy," Brown remembered, "but Cesar was very much in control of the union," and such a move was thought to be both audacious and politically risky. To his surprise, Brown received an invitation to speak at the next board meeting.

As Brown spoke, members listened patiently as he explained his charts and graphs, detailing changes in grape sales where the boycott had been most consistently implemented. His confidence growing with every word, Brown boldly challenged his audience: "I ended my presentation by saying if the board did not take immediate steps to strengthen the boycott, then I couldn't really believe that they were serious about winning. And I—Juanita and I— we're going to leave the union." He left the meeting with the impression that the members had finally grasped the importance of the data, though Chavez showed little sign of agreement and no intention of answering Brown's ultimatum. Three days later, the couple packed for Miami to visit Juanita's parents on their way to Mexico, where Brown planned to initiate research on a new dissertation topic. Just before departing, they received a call from Larry Itliong. Although Chavez would never speak with Brown of his decision, the labor leader and members of the NEB resolved to embrace Brown's ideas to redirect union resources toward an expansion of the boycott. Instead of heading to Mexico to jump-start his academic career, Brown traveled to Santa Barbara for a general meeting of the union membership, where he helped initiate a new phase of the movement.

Chavez's reluctance to embrace the boycott is understandable given the difficulty of maintaining such a campaign well beyond the primary site of struggle. As a product of an agrarian community, Chavez remained devoted to those who occupied similar spaces. This, in part, explained his withdrawal from the Community Service Organization in San Jose and Los Angeles in favor of organizing farm workers one house at a time in the San Joaquin Valley. The CSO experience, however, had opened him up to the possibilities of cultivating support for the farm worker movement among urban consumers, if for no other reason than to occupy union organizers' time during lulls in the harvest. A cadre of young, energetic, and intelligent college students willing to take a leadership role in this experiment made the effort all the more worthwhile. Their involvement would change the complexion and strategy of the movement and force Chavez to cede some of his control to youthful protesters in the marketplace. At the time, however, Chavez had limited options due to the grape growers' refusal to yield to the strike and a lack of resources to keep workers on the picket lines in the fields. Born of necessity, the boycott proved to be a stroke of genius that grew out of a period in which Chavez embraced creativity and independent thinking among the movement's many contributors.

THE NEW FRONT: BOYCOTT GRAPES!

The excitement caused by the impromptu strike by the Agricultural Workers Organizing Committee and the merger of AWOC and the National Farm Workers Association into one grand union produced an army of organized workers ready for battle. The seasonal nature of the grape harvest framed the period of conflict, concentrating the fight in the fields to the late spring and summer months, from May through August. As summer became fall, the struggle to stop the flow of scab workers onto Coachella and San Joaquin Valley grape plantations became less urgent, although the need to keep organized workers committed remained important to the survival of the movement. Gilbert Padilla recalled, "We talked about what the hell we were going to do in the winter." Leaders of the union worried that a lack of activity after the key summer months would deplete the organization of bodies and energy vital to its momentum.

These challenges confronted union organizers as early as the fall and winter after the initial 1965 strike. According to Padilla, the idea for a boycott was not the result of a grand plan, but originated in the community organizing experience of CSO veterans. "We learned in CSO," he recalled, "you don't organize people unless you have something for them to do; otherwise you lose them." In need of a task for the off-season, a core group of organizers, including Padilla, Chavez, Larry Itliong, Dolores Huerta, and Jim Drake, brainstormed about strategy. Now a seasoned twenty-eight-year-old, Drake had dropped his inhibitions about working with the new union and dove headlong into the fray. His commitment to social justice and Chavez's incorporation of Catholic and Christian symbols into the movement laid the foundation for a long and important relationship that kept Drake at the center of the union for more than a decade. According to Padilla, Drake proposed the idea of a boycott of grapes as a way of occupying the newly organized volunteers for service until the primary tool, the strike, could be employed again during the 1966 season. Years later, a more modest Drake claimed that Chavez had agreed to the boycott "figuring it was an easy way to get this young kid out of his way."[3] Whether or not he initially believed in the efficacy of the boycott, Chavez embraced the new strategy, assigned Drake to be coordinator of the national campaign, and asked fellow veteran community organizers to utilize their networks in the service of creating boycott drives in key cities.

Padilla and Huerta turned to their old CSO contacts in Los Angeles to build the first of many "boycott houses," as the location of operations in each city came to be called. Both had spent time building the CSO and developing relationships with numerous labor unions in East Los Angeles prior to organizing farm workers. Now, as members of the UFW, the two reached out to these same union leaders to kick-start the boycott. Padilla

FIGURE 5. Cesar Chavez at an unidentified event with Reverend Jim Drake, ca. 1970s. ALUA, UFW Collection, 3275.

recalled, "I went to the Central Labor Council, the restaurant and hotel labor union, the auto workers union—you name the union, we went to them." By appealing to fellow union members to boycott grapes, the United Farm Workers cultivated a beachhead. Padilla also brought in farm worker families from Delano in order to appeal to potential allies who might contribute their time to the cause. The appeals worked, as urban residents sympathetic to the farm workers left their jobs to serve the union.

Rudy Reyes, a veteran of the AWOC strike, joined Padilla and Huerta in Los Angeles, where they witnessed the evolution of the boycott from an off-season activity into an integral component of the movement. According to the twenty-three-year-old Filipino farm worker, the boycott unfolded intuitively:

> When truckloads went to L.A., we followed them, and our L.A. supporters tried to prevent the unloading of the grapes. If they got them unloaded anyway, we tried stopping any big buyers from buying them. If the grapes still got into stores, we set up picket lines to ask consumers not to buy the grapes and, if possible, not to buy in this store. Then our dozens or hundreds of supporters took turns calling up those stores, telling the managers that they were long-time consumers, and they wouldn't buy anything anymore until they promised not to buy and sell grapes from Delano anymore. After a while, we set up our boycott headquarters in L.A. to coordinate all our supporters into a cohesive army.[4]

The boycott slowly gathered strength through the winter of 1965 and spring of 1966 as the L.A. staff worked with local unions, followed the shipments, and appealed to store managers not to carry grapes.

Initially, the UFW directed its boycott indiscriminately, but the union eventually targeted two leaders in the industry: NFLU's nemesis, the DiGiorgio Corporation, and Schenley Industries, primarily a producer and distributor of liquor. Both were anomalies among grape producers, given their corporate structure and size of production. Although DiGiorgio held several acres in the San Joaquin Valley, the Borrego Valley in the southern desert near Coachella, and cropland in Florida, Robert DiGiorgio, Joseph DiGiorgio's son, began to diversify the company's interests soon after he became president of the corporation in 1962. In 1964, the company dropped "fruit" from its title and increased its nonagricultural business to 87 percent, on its way to 98 percent by 1967. The younger DiGiorgio also declared in his 1964 annual report that DiGiorgio Corporation was now "a publicly held, profit oriented processor, distributor and marketer of foods," moving further away from the production side of the business.

Schenley built a similar empire in the East. The company's name originated from Schenley, Pennsylvania, where a Jewish businessman, Lewis Rosensteil, produced and distributed medicinal whiskey during Prohibition. In the 1940s, Schenley expanded on 4,500 acres of premium land in the San Joaquin

Valley, but continued to draw most of its $250 million in annual income from the sale of such brands as Cutty Sark whiskey, Seagram's Seven whiskey, and Roma wines. In the 1960s DiGiorgio's main office was in San Francisco; Schenley operated out of Chicago, New York, and Delaware. Although both companies benefited immensely from the growth of agriculture in rural California after World War II, neither resembled the family-owned, immigrant-based, grape grower cliques that defined grower culture in California.

The distinctions between corporations and family-owned, immigrant growers became significant as the boycott wore on. Family-owned growers defended their turf as the ground on which they, as immigrants, had struggled to create a business and a way of life. For corporations, such as Schenley, DiGiorgio, and later InterHarvest—a New York–based company managed by Jewish mogul Eli Black—a commitment to business over culture made the corporations more inclined to settle labor disputes that crimped the flow of capital. Consequently, these corporations maintained an open mind about recognizing unions and signing labor contracts, whereas the old guard immigrant growers resisted such solutions.

Early on, boycotters did not perceive such differences; they pursued large targets such as Schenley and DiGiorgio because these companies depended on easily identified networks of unionized workers to deliver their products to market. In the case of Schenley, whose profits depended on the consumption of liquor in urban restaurants and hotels, the "jobbers," or middlemen between the producers and the businesses that sold the product, became the keys to the execution of the boycott. Once again, Padilla turned to a friend in the hotel and restaurant workers union, Herman "Blackey" Levitt, who served as the president of the joint council for labor unions in Los Angeles. Padilla recalled, "This guy Levitt said, 'Let me tell you how to do this.' And he got this book with all the jobbers. So we sent letters to all these jobbers we were going to boycott." Padilla's appeal to the wholesalers worked. In San Francisco, the union picketed the docks against the advice of AWOC leader, Al Green, who worried about embarrassing longshoremen, whom he assumed knew little about the farm workers. Chavez stood his ground, and, to the surprise of Green and other established labor leaders, the longshoremen aided the boycott by refusing to unload grapes. By April, Schenley was experiencing steep sales declines in Los Angeles and San Francisco, two key urban markets. The success proved that the boycott was useful to the movement, making it a permanent fixture in the UFW arsenal.[5]

The boycott worked in tandem with the evolving situation on the ground as rural communities prepared for the 1966 grape harvest. Throughout the off-season, the UFW conducted marches, challenged local law enforcement to manage the strike fairly, and reached out to established unions in hopes of maintaining momentum. The tenor of union events rose to the level of a religious revival, as songs, theater, and art developed to promote *la causa*. The movement inspired the creation of the theater group Teatro Campesino by a twenty-five-year-old native of Delano, Luis Valdez, who had graduated from San Jose State University but returned to the valley to be a part of the action. In addition to staging productions that presented growers, scab workers, and law enforcement officials as caricatures of themselves, Valdez penned something of a manifesto in *El Plan de Delano* that articulated the broad goals and cultural aspects of the farm worker movement. *El Plan* announced the arrival of a new social movement and its close affinity with the Catholic Church, whose symbols of sacrifice and piety became a part of the iconography of the UFW. The manifesto also announced a pilgrimage or *perigrinación* from Delano to Sacramento in which Chavez and UFW officials would march 280 miles through farm worker villages northward through the valley in anticipation of the 1966 harvest.

Drake and Chavez sent a handful of organizers out to unfamiliar cities across the country with the phone number of a sympathetic local contact, $100, and the charge of identifying and organizing volunteers to dedicate as many hours of their day as possible toward instituting the boycott in their assigned city. Organizers endured time away from home or school, and some boycott leaders occasionally moved their entire family to a location of the union's choosing. Unlike a march that came to many farm workers in their villages and demanded a finite amount of time from its participants, the boycott functioned like a full-time job with poor pay, usually in an unfamiliar environment. The strike demanded a similar level of commitment, although the fact that such battles took place near workers' rural homes among a community that shared a common language and culture made it slightly easier to organize, compared to the boycott.

Hijinio Rangel was one worker who made tremendous sacrifices for the boycott. Rangel worked in the Giannini packinghouse in Dinuba, California, in the San Joaquin Valley when Chavez recruited him. Although packinghouse workers received pay superior to that of most agricultural workers and enjoyed collective bargaining rights, Rangel chafed at the abuses suffered by field workers. As the movement matured, Rangel became loyal to UFW, recruiting field workers while driving a tractor and distributing water to pickers in the vineyards. He also hosted recruitment meetings at his home, where Chavez reached out to a small group of hearty farm workers willing to fight for the union. Rangel eventually earned enough money to buy a *tortilleria* (tortilla store) in Orosi, California, but maintained his commitment to the UFW, using his store as a base for organizing farm workers. In 1968, Chavez appealed to Rangel to work for the movement full time under the California Migrant Ministry. Rangel remembered, "I [had] to leave my job and my business and persuade my wife (which was not so easy) to move." That year, Rangel, his wife, and eight children committed their lives to the union, going first to Portland, Oregon, and eventually to Detroit, Michigan to oversee the boycott.[6]

College students imbued with a desire to make change also signed up in significant numbers. For some young people, such as Marshall Ganz, getting involved in the farm worker movement proved to be a homecoming. As a Jewish boy growing up in Bakersfield, California, during the 1950s, Ganz had developed a consciousness about the fight for civil rights in the South but had not yet recognized the relevance of this battle to his own backyard. "I grew up in the middle of the farm worker world," recalled Ganz, "but of course never saw it." Although his debate coach in high school tried to direct his attention to the farm workers, it took a trip to the Deep South while in college for him to discover the importance of civil rights activism back home. "I had to go to Mississippi and get [an] education about race and class and politics," Ganz remembered, "so that when I came back, I could see with what we call 'Mississippi eyes.'" Ganz acquired this new way of seeing during Freedom Summer, a Mississippi workshop in 1964 run by a coalition of northern black youths and southern black activists to train mostly white, northern college students to help in the fight to extend the franchise to African Americans in the South.[7] Ganz made his way to Mississippi that summer from Harvard University, joining such future leaders as Mario Savio from the University of California at Berkeley, who went on to lead the free speech movement, and Heather Booth from the University of Chicago, who later founded the Chicago Women's Liberation Union. The experience changed Ganz's life and made him more aware of the shared history of segregation and violence between African Americans in the South and people of color in rural California: "I mean, it was like seeing through a different lens, and it was like, oh, people of color, oh, no political rights, just like the South . . . marginal wages,

FIGURE 6. At a United Farm Workers rally, Cesar Chavez looks over
a binder with Marshall Ganz. Location unknown, 1971. ALUA, UFW
Collection, 3248.

just like the South. California's own history of segregation, racial discrimination, just like the South. . . . And so it was much more like an extension of the
movement than it was like, 'Oh, I'm going to work for a union,' which
wouldn't have occurred to me [before Freedom Summer]."[8]

Ganz belonged to the Student Nonviolent Coordinating Committee,
one of the primary recruitment and training organizations for Freedom
Summer. For SNCC, 1964 was a sobering experience, as their peaceful but
persistent protests went unheeded by the national Democratic Party. At the
Democratic National Convention that year, the party stalwarts, including
the Party's nominee, President Lyndon B. Johnson, refused to seat the Mississippi Freedom Democratic Party as the representative for the state even

after national media coverage brought the violence against civil rights protesters in Mississippi to public light. The murders of several civil rights workers, including three volunteers involved with Mississippi Summer—Michael Schwerner, Andrew Goodman, and James Chaney—proved to organizers that black and white activists could be killed with impunity. As a consequence, SNCC leaders contemplated a more confrontational politics but also embraced an expansion of the movement by placing SNCC representatives with social justice organizations operating outside of the South.

Ganz's path to the union came by way of the kind of diversity and intergroup dialogue that had lifted the farm worker movement in the early days and made the success of the boycott a possibility. Ganz, who had come back to Bakersfield at the end of 1964 in preparation for his return to Harvard in the fall of 1965, reconnected with an old friend, LeRoy Chatfield. By this time, Chatfield had abandoned the clergy to work with Chavez on the rent strike. Ganz had read about the strike while working for SNCC and accepted an invitation from Chatfield to meet Chavez. As with so many young people, Chavez persuaded Ganz to change his plans for the fall and instead appeal to SNCC leaders to make him a paid representative for the student organization within UFW. SNCC responded by approving Ganz's proposal and sent him and an additional representative, Dickie Flowers—or Dickie Flores, as the Spanish speakers in the union referred to him—to California. Eventually, Stokely Carmichael, the new leader of SNCC, came to California to meet Chavez in the fall of 1965 and made Ganz the sole representative of SNCC within the farm workers union. SNCC paid Ganz $10 per week, five more dollars per week than what the union could afford to pay its staff. Ganz recalled, "I was sort of a labor aristocrat there." This arrangement lasted until August 1966, when SNCC embraced the black power movement and chose a more unilateral, blacks-for-blacks-only approach to civil rights. According to Ganz, "I may have been the last white person on the SNCC payroll (laughter)."[9]

The early success of the boycott exceeded the expectations of Chavez and the leadership of the union. During the first two years, growers watched the "free on board" (FOB) price of a lug (box) of their grapes plummet from a high of over $6 in 1966 to approximately $5.50 in 1968, on its way down to $4.89 in 1969.[10] In addition to Drake, who served as the information director for Chavez, LeRoy Chatfield and a Bay Area ally, Mike Miller, communicated with boycott organizers located in key cities around the country. Indicative of the supplemental role the boycott played in this period, some of the communication came from Delano, where Chatfield and Drake spent much of their time, and some of the communication emanated from a San Francisco office convenient to Miller's location.[11] The union lacked so much in the way of infrastructure that Chavez had to rely on staff located throughout the state to carry out multiple tasks. Those involved in the boycott celebrated the moral victory of swaying the consumers in a given city or at a specific market but had little time to devise a system for charting their success. Tantamount to building a plane while flying it, Chavez and a small group of leaders constructed the union by stringing together public relations victories that gathered endorsements from a diverse set of supporters.

Securing well-positioned allies had been one of the early keys to Chavez's success. For example, when the AFL-CIO convened its annual meeting in San Francisco in 1965, the grape strike and boycott had piqued the interest of fellow unionists, but no one in organized labor formally endorsed the farm workers until UAW president, Walter Reuther, stepped out in support of the union. In the spring of 1967, Senator Robert F. Kennedy drew media attention to the struggle in a series of hearings by the Senate Subcommittee on Migratory Labor. Although the subcommittee chair, Senator George Murphy (R-California), staunchly supported agribusiness and hoped to sway public opinion against the farm workers, Kennedy's aggressive questioning of the Kern County sheriff, LeRoy Gallyen, on charges of false arrests of picketers exposed law enforcement officials' abuse of activists' civil rights and ignorance of the law. After the last hearing, Kennedy paid an unexpected visit to Filipino Hall, where he declared his support for the grape strike. Kennedy later joined a UFW picket line at DiGiorgio's ranch and was a close ally of the movement for the remainder of his life.[12]

The success of the boycott and the political events surrounding the Delano-to-Sacramento march placed Schenley and DiGiorgio on the wrong side of public opinion. Although grape growers dug their collective heels in against the union, Schenley's chief executive officer, Lewis Rosensteil, recognized the UFW campaign as a liability to the many products marketed by his company. Blackey Levitt's ability to deliver support from the bartenders union and the cooperation of the Teamsters in San Francisco not to load Schenley products worried the company brass, as Schenley's vice president James Woolsey later testified to the California Senate Subcommittee on Agriculture: "These reprisals and the publicity presented a threat of serious damage to our business on a nationwide scale. Our sales department felt that even more damaging than any decline in our sales was the adverse publicity that accompanied the boycott and the NFWA organizing activities."[13] Schenley was one of the four largest liquor distributors in the country, and its primary ownership of Central Valley grape vineyards had to do with wine production, not table grapes. Moreover, whereas the table grape growers had a tradition of not negotiating with unions, Schenley settled a strike by Galarza's National Farm Labor Union in 1952 by increasing wages, establishing a grievance procedure, and rehiring workers who had been locked out during the initial conflict. For a shrewd businessman like Rosensteil, anything that sullied the national reputation of his products had to be eliminated.[14]

Rosensteil broke ranks with other owners and called on attorney Sidney Korchak to broker a deal with Chavez. A mercurial man with assumed connections to the Chicago mob and a reputation for "fixing" labor problems in the liquor and film industry, Korchak summoned Chavez, Levitt, Teamster representatives, and AFL-CIO representative, Bill Kircher, to his Beverly Hills mansion on April 3, 1966. The meeting preceded the merger of the NFWA and AWOC in August; however, Kircher's presence provided representation for AWOC. According to Marshall Ganz, everyone at the meeting had an agenda, but Korchak recognized that "it was the NFWA that controlled the boycott." As a consequence, Korchak recognized the NFWA as the union to represent Schenley workers and agreed to an immediate 35 cents per hour increase in wages to $1.75, the creation of a union-run hiring hall, and the option for workers to join the NFWA credit union upon their affiliation. He also promised full contract negotiations to replace the temporary agreement in exchange for an end to the boycott against Schenley.[15]

News of the breakthrough reached the marchers in Lodi, California, on April 6, just four days prior to Easter Sunday and the culmination of the *peregrinación* in Sacramento. The next day DiGiorgio, the other corporate giant in the fields, announced its willingness to recognize a union, but without fully endorsing the NFWA. Rather, it expressed its support for a secret ballot election, with the NFWA, AWOC, and a company union, Tulare-Kern Independent Farm Workers, as options. When the press exposed the company's ties to TKIFW, DiGiorgio shifted tactics and appealed to the Teamsters to organize farm workers. Initially, DiGiorgio attempted to run an election at its Borrego Springs Ranch in San Diego County without agreeing to terms with either the NFWA or AWOC. When the NFWA appealed to workers to boycott the election and AWOC agreed, nearly half the 732 workers refused to participate, invalidating the results.[16]

To DiGiorgio's surprise, its attempt to divide the NFWA and AWOC had the reverse effect, driving the two unions closer and making it possible for Kircher to engineer their merger into the United Farm Workers Organizing Committee.[17] Fred Ross, who came to Delano to help with the DiGiorgio campaign, recalled, "Cesar learned as he went along; he knew he had to have money, and he had to have more strength." According to Ross, "He had to do it," but the decision to merge with AWOC did not sit well with many of the organizers who had hoped to maintain their independence. Chavez sympathized with these concerns, explaining, "I was worried that it would curb our style." Among his chief concerns, AWOC's tacit recognition of the government's restriction against "secondary boycotts" compelled him to push for terms that would allow for a continuation of its use. "I told them I didn't mind joining," Chavez told the reporter Ron Taylor, "as long as we got a good deal, but we had to have the right to boycott."[18] Ultimately, the two sides got what they were looking for: AWOC wanted a union supported by the Mexican workers who constituted the majority of the NFWA's rank and file, and the NFWA wanted the approval from the AFL-CIO that had been backing AWOC.

The formation of the UFW did not please everyone, and some from each organization defected to the Teamsters or left labor organizing completely. For most, however, Chavez adroitly navigated around conflict by honoring many of the Filipino organizers who initiated the 1965 AWOC grape strike. Larry Itliong became second in command of UFW, and Andy Imutan and Phillip Vera Cruz were named vice presidents. Veterans of the NFWA Dolores Huerta, Gilbert Padilla, and Tony Orendain also became vice presidents, while LeRoy Chatfield continued as an important manager of the new union's affairs from its base in Delano. Meanwhile, Chris Hartmire and Jim Drake continued to steer urban support and dollars toward the movement through Migrant Ministry.[19]

DiGiorgio attempted to protect the reputation of its national products, S & W Fine Foods and Treesweet fruit juices, just as Schenley had, by separating itself from the San Joaquin Valley growers' clique and pursuing peace with the union. Another company, Perelli-Minetti, a producer of quality wines and vermouth, pursued a similar solution when the newly formed UFW initiated a nationwide boycott of its products. Like DiGiorgio, Perelli-Minetti initially sought to have the Teamsters represent its workers rather than resist any union. The effectiveness of the boycott, however, compelled

Perelli-Minetti to back away from the Teamsters and accept the UFW as the bargaining agent for its employees. On July 21, 1967, the Teamsters reached an agreement to turn over all its contracts for field workers to the UFW in exchange for Chavez's recognition of the Teamsters' right to represent all employees working in canneries, packinghouses, and freezers. The next day, many of California's large wineries, including Gallo Wines and Paul Masson, followed Perelli-Minetti by agreeing to hold elections for their workers.[20] The wineries saw the virtue of this strategy because, like Schenley and DiGiorgio, they had made their money based on the quality associated with their brand names.

The solution of union recognition stood in stark contrast to the thinking of local table grape growers, who fought to maintain exclusive control over the hiring and labor processes. When Schenley caved to the pressure of the march and the boycott, for example, the California Council of Growers, a nonprofit public relations firm representing the majority of owners, issued the following statement: "While the NFWA and its religious cohorts were righteously preaching democratic processes and marching on Sacramento, the leaders were closeted elsewhere, working out a deal that denies workers any voice in the proceedings.... Schenley Industries, whose farm operations are incidental to their basic whiskey-making business, is not representative of California agriculture, where growers steadfastly refuse to sell out their employees and force them into a union which does not represent them."[21]

Unwittingly, the movement exposed the class cleavages among farm owners, prompting the local table grape growers to articulate differences between them and their corporate peers. The diversity of brands used by Schenley, DiGiorgio, and Perelli-Minetti made them more susceptible to the boycott and more inclined to settle the conflict quickly. In addition, the union learned that by toppling a leader in a particular industry, other companies quickly followed. This was the lesson of the Perelli-Minetti boycott, in which Gallo and Masson sued for peace immediately after Perelli-Minetti capitulated.

Table grape growers undermined the assumption that such a strategy worked in all circumstances. Rather than dividing and conquering all grape producers, the boycott had the unintended consequence of moving a diverse group of ethnic and family-based table grape growers toward greater cooperation. Forged in the crucible of class conflict, the South Central Farmers Committee (SCFC) became the leading self-help organization for growers.

The SCFC grew out of early affinities among Slavic pioneers, such as Jack Pandol and Martin Zaninovich, but it also included a handful of non-Slavic growers from the Delano area. By the 1960s, European ethnic growers had fully embraced Armenians as equals, but Japanese American small farmers remained conspicuously absent from the membership. According to the SCFC's first president, Martin Zaninovich, the organization incorporated on August 26, 1960, in anticipation of union organizing. When the union did come, the SCFC became more organized and leased an office in downtown Delano in early 1966. According to Zaninovich, "The primary function of the committee at that time was to serve as the public relations arm of the agriculture in the area."[22] Members also met routinely to plot strategy and strengthen their common bonds, if necessary through threats. In one case, a beleaguered grower confessed to having grown weary of constantly searching for workers and battling the union. "The next time you come, bring your pink slip," a peer responded, suggesting that he would buy him out rather than see his farm end production because of the unions. "Unionizing of farms was simply not accepted," Zaninovich remembered.[23]

Early on, the SCFC responded to the strike by denying its existence. The arrival of the boycott, however, generated bad publicity at the point of sale, hurting the grape growers' reputation with customers and forcing them to abandon their bunker mentality. In January 1966, the SCFC formed a speakers' bureau to circulate growers who were willing to make their case to urban consumers. It also reversed its position of refusing to communicate with the media and initiated a campaign through the Council of California Growers to win back the public. The Council channeled all inquiries through the SCFC office in Delano and hired a young ex-navy pilot, Bruce Obbink, to serve as the full-time director of education. Obbink had originally come to the Council in 1962 to help fight against the termination of the bracero program. With that battle lost, Obbink and the Council focused on the new challenge of defeating the United Farm Workers. He received a budget to hire an office manager for the SCFC, Eleanor Schulte, who coordinated communication among the Council, the growers, and the public.[24]

In spite of these efforts, the growers continued to lose the public relations war. Most of the growers attributed their losses to biased journalists who came to Delano with preconceived notions. "A lot of people who come here think they are experts on farm labor," Schulte observed. "They come armed with what they consider to be the facts, and this puts us in a defensive position right off the bat."[25] Rather than admitting the well-documented problems in farm labor housing and wages, the SCFC aggressively denied any discontent among workers. On behalf of grape growers, SCFC president, Martin Zaninovich, reported to a packed audience of journalists in San Francisco, "Over the years, we have developed and maintained a keen personal interest in each and every one of our employees. . . . Many growers provide superior housing free of charge." This flew in the face of popular accounts of the lives of farm workers depicted in programs like Edward R. Murrow's *Harvest of Shame*, broadcast in 1960, and the attention drawn to the problem by the union. Although some growers supplied better housing than others, the trend toward day-haul workers rather than the type of worker settlements described by Zaninovich undermined his paternalistic stance toward employees. The work of photo-journalists and documentary filmmakers transported images of unrest from the fields to urban consumers that served as visual rebuttals to Zaninovich's constant protestation that worker deprivation and discontent were a "myth."[26]

Unlike their corporate peers, the local ethnic and family-oriented growers refused to see the strike or the boycott as a business matter to be dealt with through negotiations. Of the corporate growers Ganz observed, "A lot of them had union contracts [in] other places; they weren't invested in their standing in the grower community; they weren't a part of that local scene; they didn't go to the Slav club and the Elks club and the same church."[27] Members of the SCFC, on the other hand, saw the union's campaign as a personal affront to their integrity that had to be resisted at all costs. For them, the struggle against the UFW was more than a business matter; it embodied a wider cultural struggle that threatened a way of life. Zaninovich, in particular, harbored deep resentment toward student volunteers, whom he characterized as "far left of left" and "very young, probably naïve, and obviously idealistic," who did not recognize that "they were being manipulated by a few unobtrusive but effective leaders." His dismissal of both these volunteers and Chavez placed him and his fellow growers on the other side of a new generation that now began to question the war, the treatment of racial minorities, and the responsibility of the educated class to society.

Buoyed by their defeat of the corporate growers, in 1968 Chavez and UFW leaders agreed to take the fight to table grape producers rather than consolidate their gains in the wine industry.[28] As in the battle with wine grape producers, union leaders decided to start with a campaign against the biggest producer. Giumarra Vineyards Corporation was the undisputed leader in table grape production, with $12 million dollars in annual sales from production on 12,170 acres of premium farmland.[29] This time, however, the leading company did not concede defeat, nor did its peers show signs of weakening in the face of pressure from the boycott. Unlike the corporate growers who cared about labels, table grape growers rarely marketed their products by brand names that were conspicuous to customers in supermarkets, thus making the boycott difficult to enforce at the point of sale. Table grape growers frequently used multiple brands to market a variety of grapes at different points in the season. When the union finally succeeded in distinguishing Giumarra's brands from those of other producers, fellow grape growers loaned Giumarra their labels to frustrate boycott organizers. As a consequence, rather than defeating the table grape growers during the 1968 season, the UFW found itself in a protracted war with the industry, no closer to winning the strikes on their farms or the boycott campaigns in the city. The union responded by declaring an industrywide boycott of all table grapes, extending the ban to include Arizona grapes, but the growers still did not budge from their position.[30]

To be successful, the UFW had to discover new cracks in the growers' armor. The failure to bring ethnic and family-oriented growers to the negotiation table through either the strike or the boycott signaled the long battle ahead. The union leadership discovered, however, that compared to the strike the boycott had made growers more uncomfortable about their position. "The whole strategic premise," Ganz remembered, "was ... that you didn't have enough power in the local labor market to win." The strike had drawn attention to the problem of farm worker wages and living conditions, but the union had a hard time maintaining a constant presence in the fields without a substantial strike fund to pay workers to walk picket lines or prevent growers from replacing them with scab labor. When Governor Pat Brown ordered investigators from the state department of employment to confirm the existence of a labor dispute, they had to rely on testimony from only forty-nine farm workers who remained in Delano long enough to confirm their participation. This number was far below the thousands of workers Chavez asserted had participated in the strike. Most farm workers moved on to seek work elsewhere in order to feed their families, thinning the picket lines in the fields.

The anemic display in the countryside forced Chavez to invest more time, money, and hope in the boycott. For all of their publicity, union officials had done little to stop the harvesting of grapes at the point of production. The secondary boycott, however, showed no signs of weakness, drawing new recruits in ever increasing numbers as the urban civil rights and antiwar movements became more violent and fragmented at the end of the 1960s. Although the boycott decentered the movement from its traditional base of power in Delano, where Chavez had more control, it also transferred the battle away from the stronghold of the growers and into an arena that gave the union a better chance of winning. According to Ganz, "By shifting the turf [to the cities] . . . we could successfully fight them."[31]

WORKING THE BOYCOTT

By 1968, as the union moved against the core group of table grape growers, the farm workers had three proven strategies in their arsenal: the strike, the march, and the boycott. Among the three, the boycott offered leaders the least control, given their dependence on other unions to block shipments and on consumers to avoid purchasing grapes. In addition, the boycott required organizers to move away from the cradle of the movement to live in far-flung cities with few connections to Delano. The union's standard compensation of $5 per week did not go as far in metropolitan areas, where it took organizers more time to locate allies who could offset their expenses with donations of food, shelter, and transportation. In some cities, such as New York, the union spent precious dollars to rent a boycott house where volunteers slept and worked. At the time, most in the labor movement thought these expenditures were risky since the boycott had long been regarded as a tool of last resort.[32] The success against Schenley, DiGiorgio, Perelli-Minetti, and Gallo, however, had encouraged union leaders to continue experimenting with the tactic.

The UFW built support for the boycott among urban consumers with the effort of a small but committed cadre of organized farm workers and youthful advocates. Drawing inspiration from Fred Ross and the CSO, Jim Drake applied the same approach to organizing volunteers for the boycott houses as he had in recruiting farm workers to the union. Drake shared the UFW philosophy: "If you try to spread yourself among all the workers . . . then you are going to do about 5% of organizing of maybe 20% of the workers. Forget about it, you are just never going to make it." Instead, the organizers put 100 percent of their time into organizing between 2 and 5 percent of the total population of farm workers. From this group came the "really organized [and] committed," argued Drake, who would "stick it out for 20 years" and "see to it that you win." For Drake and others, the number of farm workers involved was less important than the quality and commitment of those who carried the message of social justice to the general public. "We made it look like [there were] thousands of grape pickers out on strike," recalled Drake, "because we moved people around real fast." Once the boycott came into play, the UFW's central organizers applied this same tactic on a national scale. "[These workers] would think nothing of giving up their homes and everything to go to New York or Chicago for the boycott."[33]

As the boycott intensified in early 1968, Chavez asked his longtime friend and mentor, Fred Ross, to run a tutorial on organizing for fifty farm workers and volunteers in New York City, the largest and arguably most important market for grapes. Organizers ranged from teenage novices like Eliseo Medina to seasoned veterans like Gilbert Padilla and Dolores Huerta. Ross, however, treated everyone equally, employing a philosophy of "on-the-job" training, as Jerry Brown described it: "Ross never lectured about organizing. He believed that one could only learn to organize by doing it. He would point out that there was nothing romantic about organizing, and that it required mainly common sense, meticulous planning, hard work and a great deal of self discipline."[34]

From this group, Eliseo Medina, an eighteen-year-old native of the Coachella Valley, traveled to icy Chicago in the midst of winter with the usual $100 start-up funds, a handful of local contacts, and a bag of union buttons. Another farm worker, Marco Muñoz, established an effective house in Boston despite not speaking a word of English. In New York City, Dolores Huerta was called in to organize the boycott house on Eighty-sixth Street, while LeRoy Chatfield went to Los Angeles, and Gil Padilla started a house in Philadelphia. Meanwhile, Chavez made the boycott international from the beginning by assigning Ganz to Toronto and Jessica Govea, a twenty-one-year-old farm worker's daughter from Bakersfield, to Montreal.[35] The union also maintained houses in several big cities throughout the United States, including San Francisco, Detroit, Portland, Seattle, and Cleveland.

These were the boycott houses with which Jerry and Juanita Brown communicated in 1968. Chavez expected the couple to connect all spokes of the emerging network to the "pink house," a little, three-bedroom cottage on the outskirts of Delano that served as the headquarters for the union. There, Chavez introduced the Browns to the "boycott room," where he gave them minimal instructions. On a map of North America pinned to the wall, Chavez drew his finger down through Chicago and the Mississippi River and said, "Jerry, you take the East. Juanita, you take the West." Even then, Jerry and Juanita split their time by walking the picket lines in the fields in the morning and working the phone lines and writing letters to boycott organizers in the afternoon. Given Juanita's college-level Spanish skills, Chavez also had her translate depositions with immigrant farm workers acquired by the head of the UFW legal team, Jerry Cohen, to be used in cases against the growers. For an upstart union representing poor farm workers, such division of labor was necessary, although for the Browns, it also indicated that the boycott played a secondary role to the maintenance of the strike.[36]

Out on the front lines of the boycott, organizers had to be resourceful if they were to succeed. Jerry Brown recalled, "Each boycott organizer was like a brilliant campaign strategist that figured out what the key to their particular city was. . . . It was really, you know, on-the-ground organizations."[37] In New York, Ross's emphasis on community organizing gave way to establishing contact with labor unions that controlled the movement of produce in and out of Manhattan. During the spring of 1968, UFW vice president and chief negotiator, Dolores Huerta, appealed to the Central Labor Council, the Amalgamated Meat Cutters Union, and the Seafarers Union to establish a total blockade of California grapes. The unions agreed to cooperate in time to interrupt the first grapes of the season from making their annual trip across the Hudson River by barge. As the grapes rotted in New Jersey, grape growers filed an injunction against the New York and New Jersey unions for violating federal regulations against secondary boycotts and demanded $25 million in compensation for lost sales. Although the Taft-Hartley Act did not apply to farm workers, it did restrict the Seafarers Union from participating in such actions. It eventually released the grapes, but the pause in shipments had reduced the overall number of car lots for 1968 to a record low of 91, down from the industry norm of 418.[38]

In mid-July Huerta and the extremely efficient New York City house shifted to a consumer boycott, picketing stores throughout the city. Huerta pursued the same logic in organizing against supermarkets that the union had used in the campaigns against the corporate producers: the larger the organization, the greater its vulnerability. In the New York area, the A&P chain dominated the market, which made it the first target. Huerta described her strategy in a letter to Delano headquarters: "In each of the five boroughs, we organized neighborhood coalitions of church, labor, liberal and student groups. Then we began picketing A&P, the biggest chain in the city. For several months we had picket lines on about 25 to 30 stores and turned thousands of shoppers away. A lot of the managers had come up through the unions and were very sympathetic to us. In response to consumer pressure, the store managers began to complain to their division heads, and soon they took the grapes out of all of their stores, 430 of them."[39] By knocking off A&P, the richest market chain in the United States, the boycotters softened up its competitors— Bohack, Walbaum's, Hills, and Finast—for the kill. One by one, the stores became the exclusive target of the New York boycott house until all except one—Gristedes, an expensive delivery service market for wealthy clients— stopped selling grapes in the city.

Although Huerta's tactic became part of a larger strategy used in the boycott, it did not always work elsewhere. In Los Angeles, for example, LeRoy Chatfield and a former farm labor contractor, Joe Serda, led the boycott against the second largest supermarket chain in the country, Safeway. Chatfield and Serda's initial approach mirrored that of Huerta's campaign: topple the largest chain, and the others will follow. To their chagrin, however, the large, boisterous demonstrations they staged in front of markets just upset a conservative clientele. Serda could not believe the response: "I was shocked. Most of the people would roll up their car windows and gun their motors right by us." These responses differed from those in New York City, where many working-class consumers belonged to unions and declared their allegiance to the UFW. In his report from Los Angeles, Serda told Brown, "Even many of the union members here are conservative and racist." In front of some stores, customers occasionally spit at picketers and yelled at Mexicans on the picket line "to go back to Mexico."[40]

Safeway's own business practices contributed to the sentiments of its customers. The company—referred to derisively by some employees as "Slaveway" for its treatment of workers and union-busting politics—fought the boycott vigorously and took out full-page ads in the *Los Angeles Times* challenging the legitimacy of boycotters to speak for workers in the fields.[41] In the summer of 1968, during the key months of the table grape harvest, Chatfield, Serda, and volunteers at the Los Angeles boycott house shared little of the momentum enjoyed by Huerta in New York.[42]

Farther up the coast, in Portland, Oregon, the boycott team used Huerta's approach against the supermarket chain Fred Meyer, but also discovered new strategies. Lead by a former Giumarra picker and Migrant Ministry member, Nick Jones, a small number of volunteers "introduced the highways [or] human billboard idea." The idea involved placing several volunteers on highway bridges adorned with body-length signs promoting the boycott. Jones admitted to balking at the tactic initially, although he encouraged those who wanted to experiment to try. "It's one of those times ... that I really blew it. I [said], 'it's bullshit. Nobody's going to respond to that, it's just a waste of time.'" Within five minutes of taking to the freeways, however, Jones discovered how wrong he was. "People were letting loose of their car wheels and looking up at us and giving us the fist and the 'V' and the finger. I mean we were getting a real definite response out of everybody ... to the point where they were looking and they had to hit their brakes to keep from hitting the car in front of them." In time, the human billboard strategy traveled across the country, where volunteers in Boston used it to great effect.[43]

In Toronto, Marshall Ganz adopted a slightly different approach, a combined strategy of appealing to unions for cooperation, picketing, diplomacy, and, when necessary, acts of civil disobedience. He began by making overtures to the Amalgamated Meat Cutters Union for support, but the union could promise only to make the boycott an issue in future negotiations with Canadian markets. Union organizers experienced far greater success appealing to Toronto consumers, who showed much sympathy for the farm workers' struggle and responded favorably to Toronto media coverage of the boycott. Consumers tended to show greater support for the boycott in locations where chain stores rather than independents dominated the grocery market landscape. Toronto was one such place, with more than 85 percent of food sales concentrated in four stores: A&P, Loblaw's, Dominion, and Steinberg's. Unfortunately for Ganz and the boycotters, Canada also maintained laws against picketing in store parking lots, a lesson they learned when police arrested the president of the Canadian Labor Council for trespassing when he attended a public rally for the UFW in front of one of the chains. The law forced Ganz to make a decision: either engage in civil disobedience in an attempt to change the law, as he had done in Mississippi several times, or pursue a different approach. Based on his experience in the civil rights movement, Ganz understood that the former often took many years to achieve results. Changing the law was not the primary goal; applying economic pressure in the service of the farm workers and achieving victory in the fields of California were. Consequently, Ganz had to devise an approach that did not squander the goodwill of the public while avoiding becoming embroiled in a legal battle on foreign soil.

Ganz adapted to local conditions through a combination of diplomacy and creative protests that played on public sympathies. Rather than approach the most obstinate storeowner first, he made a private appeal to Sam Steinberg, an owner who had a reputation for being fair with his employees and had already stated his support for the grape strike. Ganz reminded

Steinberg of upcoming contract negotiations with the Amalgamated Meat Cutters Union, whose president had expressed his displeasure at handling scab grapes from California. Deciding to observe the boycott, Ganz argued, would give Steinberg an advantage in dealing with the union representing his workers and competing with other markets that showed no signs of complying with the boycott. To convince Steinberg of public opinion in support of the UFW, the local boycott committee directed Ontario residents to send letters or visit the market personally to express their intentions not to shop at his store as long as he continued to sell grapes.

Unlike his competitors, Steinberg and his legal advisor, Irving Levine, showed respect for the union. During the negotiations, Steinberg turned to Levine for guidance. Levine had recently returned from a trip to California to inspect the fields for himself and reported, "Conditions are feudal." According to Brown, this information moved Steinberg: "He [told] us, 'We are not going to handle grapes anymore. In fact, we're going to put color signs of the fields up at our empty grape bins to explain to our customers why we're supporting the grape boycott.'"[44]

Other stores, however, resisted such appeals. Dominion, the largest of the Canadian chains, openly flaunted its disdain for the boycott by refusing to meet with Ganz while defending customers' "freedom to choose" whether to buy grapes. In response, the boycott committee bypassed the parking lots for the interior of the stores. Once inside, boycotters engaged in "creative nonviolence" by filling their basket, wheeling it to the front of the store, then leaving without making a purchase. The stunt upset store managers who had to assign workers to reshelve merchandise.

In another action reminiscent of the theatrical protests by the emerging Youth International Party, or Yippies, boycotters carried helium-filled balloons into the store with the message "Don't Eat Grapes" written on them, and distributed them to children while letting others float to the ceiling. When managers ordered employees to pop the balloons, confetti carrying pro-UFW messages rained down upon the store, causing another mess and infuriating store managers. In response to the protests, Dominion executives questioned the legality of such actions and publicly labeled Ganz and his merry group of pranksters "union goons." The press, which had been called in anticipation of the theatrics, covered the balloon incident in a sympathetic tone that swayed public opinion toward the union. On one Toronto radio broadcast, a local deejay composed and delivered the following poem:

If all the goons popped toy balloons
And sprayed us with confetti
Then cops and crooks would use dirty looks
And guns that shoot spaghetti.[45]

Soon after that broadcast, Dominion retracted its denunciation of the boycotters and agreed to suspend the sale of California grapes indefinitely.

Volunteers celebrated such victories but also valued the day-to-day excitement of building a movement within a given city. Nick Jones, for example, recalled the difficulty of adapting to the cold and rainy Northwest but found it manageable because of the relationships he developed in Portland. "We conceived it as one big committee and we took probably about 25 or 30, maybe as many as 50 people and really worked with them for months, bringing them into committee meetings and movies . . . working with them to get the boycott work done." Picket line volunteers eschewed intimidation and assumed most consumers possessed a moral responsibility critical to the success of any consumer activism. This approach earned the respect of their adopted community and drew in many new recruits to the campaign. "We got together regularly and did pot lucks," recalled Jones. "We became a pretty tight community." The cramped quarters of many houses meant that people often slept on floors and clashed with one another, although the spirit of camaraderie in the early days of the boycott shaped the culture of most boycott houses. Service on the front lines of the boycott best represented what many in the union called "missionary work," seemingly impossible tasks that, when accomplished, drew people closer to one another.[46]

The work of boycott volunteers in cities also paid dividends in shoring up political support for the Migrant Ministry among Protestants at a time when it drew fire for supporting the UFW. Although Chavez drew on Catholic symbols and rituals to appeal to a mostly Catholic workforce, it was Hartmire and Drake, Protestant ministers, who were the first religious leaders to get behind the movement. When members of the rural denominations discovered that their donations had been funding the Migrant Ministry's activism, many of them passed a resolution demanding that the Ecumenical Ministry of the Protestant Churches terminate Hartmire's budget. The conflict initiated a "two-year war" among Protestant churches in California as to the fate of the organization. "The rural churches wanted us gone, out, or dead," Hartmire remembered. "Fortunately for us, the urban churches' membership outnumbered the rural membership." The boycott played a significant role in educating urban Protestants about the stakes of the farm workers' struggle and convinced many urban congregants to encourage their ministers to fight for the preservation of the Migrant Ministry. The moral dimensions of the battle also persuaded many urban Protestants to contribute time and money to the boycott.[47]

As the examples of New York City, Los Angeles, Portland, and Toronto illustrate, boycott strategies varied from city to city, but overall the boycott seemed to be working. By mid-1968, under the auspices of Jerry and Juanita Brown, the UFW began to chart the progress of boycott houses by the changes in the quantity of car lot shipments to major North American cities. In New York City, for example, shippers delivered 801 fewer car lots than they had in 1967; in Chicago and Boston, the totals were down by 360 and 327, respectively. Although these numbers signaled success and overall shipments declined by 2,254 car lots in North America, the Browns also noticed increases in nontraditional cities: Miami was up 57 car lots; Atlanta up 16; Houston 36; Denver 12, Kansas City 11; Fort Worth 7. These numbers revealed the growers' strategy of circumventing the boycott by marketing their table grapes to new markets, particularly in the South, West, and Midwest. In addition, although the UFW had established a presence in Canada, 1968 market reports suggested that shippers had redirected a number of car lots north of the border: Montreal was up 57 car lots, whereas Toronto climbed by 44.[48] These were the trends that compelled Brown to challenge the union leadership to make a decision: either continue to treat the boycott as a supplement to the strike or place greater emphasis on it by embracing an approach that gave them a greater chance for victory.

COMMITMENT DAY

By midsummer of 1968, the struggle had turned nasty, with threats against Chavez's life and palpable anxiety among civil rights activists everywhere. In April, Martin Luther King Jr., an important ally of the movement, had been assassinated in Memphis, precipitating a rash of violent reactions in urban centers throughout the United States. Growing tension in the country mirrored that of the city, as picketers on the front lines of the grape strike experienced physical attacks, first by Teamster affiliates and then by law enforcement officials, who employed rough tactics in dispersing union demonstrations. Chavez, who had observed the effectiveness of King's peaceful protests and

FIGURE 7. Jerry Brown (front right) on a grape strike picket line, Delano, California, ca. 1968.

read Gandhi's philosophy on nonviolence, suppressed movement advocates' appetite for retaliation by practicing long fasts that took a toll on his mind and body. The physical challenge of the fasts further weakened his aching back, making travel of any sort painful. Jerry and Juanita Brown, who owned a Westphalia Volkswagen van with a fold-down bed, provided Chavez with a vehicle ideal for traveling up and down California. Accompanied by Chavez's two German shepherds, Huelga and Boycott, he, Jerry, and Juanita made the trek up California Highway 1, followed by an entourage of farm workers trained to provide security. "There'd be security cars in front of us, and one in back of us," recalled Jerry Brown, "all connected by walkie-talkies."

As they entered Santa Barbara, Chavez ordered a quick diversion to the California mission to reflect on the battles ahead and pray for the success of the retreat. From the beginning, Chavez regarded the Catholic Church as an important influence on the movement and derived great personal inspiration from the example of Christ and His sacrifice. During the Giumarra campaign, the association grew stronger as the U.S. Council of Bishops moved from a position of neutrality to being an advocate for the farm workers. Although some local priests in the San Joaquin and Coachella Valleys remained partial to the growers, a number of Catholic and Protestant clergy willingly sacrificed time and occasionally their bodies for the movement.[49] Chavez's hour-long visit to the mission refreshed the embattled leader and gave him time to think about the message he would deliver to movement participants later that day.

Jerry Brown chose a much more secular form of preparation for the retreat. Brown believed Chavez's initial apathy for the data he had collected was a consequence of his poor style of presentation. Brown recalled, "I was very intense, very fast-talking, [and] very impatient. . . . I did the most horrible job one could imagine." Brown turned to the experienced LeRoy Chatfield for guidance. Chatfield understood what inspired the rank and file, and he embodied the calm but deliberate approach Chavez valued. Together, the two men shared their vision of the boycott's future with the entire membership, while Chavez watched intently at the back of the room.

Brown and Chatfield argued for a much more systematic approach to the campaign, taking into consideration the data collected by Brown and drawing on the experience of leaders in some of the most effective boycott cities to date. First, the two argued for an approach that concentrated on building strong boycott houses in ten of the top forty-one cities where more than 50 percent of California table grapes were sold. Those cities were New York, Los Angeles, Chicago, San Francisco, Philadelphia, Boston, Toronto, Detroit, Montreal, and Cleveland. They replaced the anecdotal reports for judging the success of the boycott with a clear and measurable goal of reducing shipments in every city by 10 percent or more over 1966 totals.[50] Although growers had begun to show signs of redirecting shipments elsewhere to soften the blow of the boycott, Brown and Chatfield calculated that such a shift could not make up for the substantial losses in growers' traditional markets. As growers sent grapes to other ports, Jerry and Juanita would respond by working with volunteers in those cities to open up new boycott houses.

Second, Brown and Chatfield provided an analysis of Huerta's successful campaign in New York City and proposed that every leader strive to implement a similar strategy in his or her city. The brilliance of Huerta's strategy, Brown concluded, was her insistence on changing the marketing habits of the entire A&P chain rather than settling for victory at individual A&P stores, one at a time. According to Brown, Huerta had built strong boycott committees in neighborhoods where union membership was high and volunteers were plentiful, enthusiastic, and committed to stopping the sale of grapes in their neighborhood. "Once [these individual A&P markets] started to capitulate," Brown told the retreat participants, "[Huerta] wouldn't call off the picket lines until they agreed to take [grapes] off the entire division [of A&P markets]." Brown explained the logic of what he called the "tactic of the hostage stores" by way of his own research on supermarket chains across North America:

> [I had acquired] one of these wonderful documents that showed every super-market in the country, every chain; what its divisions were; what cities, counties, and areas were under each division; who the management was of that division. So I was able to say, you know, you've got this many stores in that division. And, you know, we recognized [that] the whole chain in the whole country wasn't going to take it off, but that the profit and loss for that division, that manager [would]. And as you know, food stores, chain stores, operate on high volume, very thin profit margins. So if you start turning away two, three, five percent of their customers, you're going to send that store negative.[51]

According to Brown's research, supermarket sales in chain stores were $22.7 billion out of the total $68.3 billion spent on groceries in North America, an amount that constituted 33 percent of all grocery sales. In the eight of the top selling cities for table grapes, chain stores controlled over 50 percent of grocery sales. Brown and Chatfield argued that by taking a few key stores in the largest chains in the United States and Canada hostage, they could influence sales more quickly than if they targeted independents. Given that the boycott had already moved into the peak harvest months of July through November, when 71 percent of all table grapes entered the market, use of the "hostage stores" tactic became crucial to salvaging an effective effort for 1968. Huerta had pursued this strategy intuitively; the boycott coordinators now had worked up a rationale for its success and a justification for its use elsewhere.

When the duo finished, Chavez walked to the front of the room, convinced of the boycott's importance to achieving overall victory. Offering his own interpretation of the strategy, he referred to the idea of targeting chain stores as "capitalism in reverse." "We will picket the stores," Chavez announced, "until we turn enough customers away to make the management realize that it is more profitable to stop selling grapes than to sell them."[52] On the question of how to do this, neither Chavez nor Brown nor any of the veterans of the boycott had a definitive answer, but examples abounded around the room. Marshall Ganz, who had flown back from Toronto for the meeting, shared both his diplomatic approach with cooperative owners as well as his acts of "creative nonviolence" against those who remained stubborn. Marco Muñoz, back from Boston, generated a laugh from the room when he reported on how his house held a "Boston Grape Party," in which they dumped cartons of grapes into Massachusetts Bay in order "to liberate the farm workers from the tyranny of the growers."[53] Chatfield and Serda shared their experiences in Los Angeles as a way to learn from mistakes made in cities where a more hostile climate prevailed. Through it all, the group developed a sense of camaraderie, forming a bond that would inure them to the difficulties that awaited them as they moved forward, now with a clearer sense of their mission.

Chavez announced a redeployment of boycott workers to the cities, sending his best organizers to the front lines and accepting volunteers to lead boycott houses. Jerry Brown, who had remained in Delano in hopes of eventually launching his Ph.D. research, now set aside the dissertation indefinitely for an assignment to coordinate the boycott from Toronto. "They had given a lot to us," he remembered. "They were accepting [our challenge to] really put in place a strategy to win." Within the month, Jerry and Juanita moved into a four-story brownstone in Toronto with Chavez's compadre, Manuel Rivera, and began orchestrating the new, improved boycott network from there.

Before adjourning the meeting, Chavez asked everyone to answer a straightforward, yet until now deceptively difficult question: "What is the key to the boycott?" Going around the room, participants offered a variety of answers: effective picket lines, raising money, countering the propaganda of the Teamsters and the growers, and getting the churches involved. "All of these answers have some truth in them," Chavez responded, "but the key to the boycott is people." In a tone that instilled confidence in every volunteer sitting in the room, he elaborated: "You're building an army of supporters, and you need to find a way to get the people on your side. An organizer will find a way to do the boycott. You can tell me the boycott's difficult. You can tell me they're spitting on you in L.A.; that they're telling you to go back to Mexico, that they're calling you a Communist. You can tell me it's cold in Toronto. I understand that. But don't tell me it can't be done. 'Si se puede!' Your job as an organizer is to find the key."[54] Chavez's endorsement of the boycott signaled an important turn of events, even if he had not indicated as much prior to the meeting. More than the convincing argument put forth by Brown and Chatfield, the results of the boycott spoke for themselves, demonstrating that the tactic could instill fear in the growers in ways that the strike had not. Whether it could actually bring the most stubborn of them to the bargaining table remained to be seen, although Chavez's support gave volunteers the confidence to try. His encouragement of a free exchange of ideas also contributed to their collective knowledge, making the group a more effective team. As they embarked on their new assignments, each volunteer carried the belief that he or she was about to make history.

THREE

Workers of the World, Unite!

ELAINE ELINSON HAD NEVER VISITED the headquarters of the United Farm Workers union, nor had she ever met the president of the organization, Cesar Chavez, despite having served in the movement for more than a year. Yet in 1969, as soon as she stepped onto the stage at Filipino Hall in Delano, California, the mostly Mexican and Filipino audience greeted her as a long-lost sister. Farm workers and activists alike honored her with the traditional farm worker "clap" that started slowly and built rapidly to a crescendo and cheers of "Viva la Huelga." Elinson, like many boycott workers, had skipped a process of initiation in the trenches of the grape strike in favor of serving where she was needed most: on the front lines of the consumer boycott in urban centers around the world. For her, the notion of an *international* boycott became a reality on the docks and in the union halls of London, Copenhagen, and Stockholm, where she combined asking consumers not to buy grapes with the more traditional appeal to fellow unionized dock workers not to unload them. She recounted her experience that evening in Delano after the long battle abroad:

> And as I stood there before this huge, curious, and open-hearted crowd, I realized I was one of the luckiest people in the world. I had been the link between the courageous, tenacious, spirited farm workers of the UFW and the committed, internationally minded transport workers of Britain and Scandinavia. Though they didn't know each other, they were ready to fight together for *La Causa*. Together, they had pulled off an amazing feat of solidarity. The cheers that I heard in the Filipino Hall mixed with the cheers I had heard on the docks at Tilbury, Malmo, Birmingham, and Liverpool. So this is what they mean by "Workers of the World, Unite!"[1]

Relying on a London pay phone and the advice of the boycott coordinator Jerry Brown, Elinson had stopped grapes from reaching the European market. For those on the ground in Delano, this achievement earned her a degree of respect equal to workers and picketers in the fields and in front of markets in the United States. Her success proved to the faithful in the movement that consumers and workers around the world had the capacity to care for farm workers in rural California.

Events in Europe also provided evidence that the union's investment in the boycott at midharvest 1968 had been a wise one. Growers disputed the effectiveness, but the shift in sales of table grapes away from traditional markets to smaller cities, rural areas, and overseas signaled an industry in crisis. Table grape growers repeatedly pointed to the increases in their production—up 19 percent in 1969 from 1966 totals—while ignoring the fact that use of these grapes for table consumption had declined by 12 percent. Increasingly, growers designated grapes for crushing to salvage any value from their crops.[2] The Grape & Tree Fruit League attempted to disguise losses in sales of the popular Thompson seedless grapes by announcing the record sales of other varieties, while ignoring that growers earned between 50 cents and a dollar less per box than in 1968. Such media efforts failed as desperate Coachella growers, dependent on the substantial profit margins created by being the first on the market, publicly disputed the rosy picture painted by the league. Among them, Lionel Steinberg, owner of the David Freedman Ranch, worried aloud about falling grape prices, rising production costs, and the declines in Thompson sales that threatened to put him out of business. "We are not selling in normal quantities in major markets such as Chicago and New York," Steinberg complained, "and prices for Thompson seedless grapes have already broken and are down to $5 a box, compared to about $6.50 last year." Predicting, "Many of us will show red ink this year," Steinberg's admissions disclosed two uncomfortable truths: the UFW was winning, and the growers lacked the power to stop it.[3]

The substantive data flowing from the nerve center of the boycott confirmed the momentum experienced in the field. Whereas Brown and LeRoy Chatfield had established the goal of having effective boycott houses in ten of the forty-one leading cities, by early 1969 the union had established boycott houses in thirty-one cities and was about to open new ones in the South and Mountain West, places formerly thought to be impervious to farm worker appeals. In the traditional markets, organizers stepped up their efforts to overcome impediments to the boycott, while news of their success encouraged volunteers elsewhere to implement boycotts of table grapes in their cities. Through it all the UFW maintained no budget for publicity, relying exclusively on coverage from eager journalists.

Yet despite this success, the union struggled to make ends meet. Beleaguered growers maintained the economic advantage by hiring a San Francisco–based public relations firm, Whitaker and Baxter, to counter union claims of worker exploitation and pesticide use.[4] Members of the South Central Growers Association also began to see beyond their ethnic divisions to organize twenty-six growers into a new coalition. The growers' group secretly financed the Agricultural Workers Freedom to Work Association, a parallel labor organization that failed to attract meaningful support among workers. The UFW quickened AWFWA's demise by exposing the organization's general secretary, Jose Mendoza, as an anti-Chavez labor contractor on the growers' payroll.[5] Still, countering the growers' moves depleted resources as the union stretched its budget to meet the commitments made to the boycott during the July 1968 retreat. Chavez, who privately worried about "the tremendous drain on the [union's] treasury," saw 1969 as a critical year to the overall success of the movement. "At this point," he told Ganz as the union prepared for its fourth and most serious year of the boycott, "it's either them or us."[6]

SUCCESS IN NORTH AMERICA

The game plan prepared by Jerry Brown and LeRoy Chatfield produced results as boycotters returned to houses across the country for the remainder of the 1968 season and through the 1969 harvest. Chatfield, for example, adapted to the conservative environment of Southern California. In October 1968, seventeen Los Angeles stores, led by Safeway, successfully sued to limit to four the number of picketers outside the entrance of their markets. Rather than resist the new laws with civil disobedience and boisterous protests, Chatfield chose a more labor-intensive approach that involved well-dressed union representatives working ten hours a day, six days a week. Each representative adopted a calm, business-like demeanor and made appeals to shoppers on an individual basis. Chatfield recruited sixty new, full-time volunteers and concentrated their efforts on thirty stores in the Arden-Mayfair chain, a major competitor of Safeway. "It was grueling work, but it did the trick," Chatfield reported to Brown. "At first, people didn't pay much attention to us. But after they saw us several times, they'd stop to talk. Eventually, many of them agreed to shop elsewhere. The ones who did really understood the issue and would often talk to the manager and tell him why they were switching to another store."[7] By the end of the 1969 harvest, Chatfield's tactics had succeeded in convincing Arden-Mayfair to remove table grapes from their stores. Although Los Angeles continued to be a challenge, the boycott reduced overall shipments to the second largest market for table grapes in the United States by a respectable 16 percent.[8]

The boycott swept over the continent, garnering support from consumers and politicians alike. In Toronto, the mayor declared November 23, 1968, "Grape Day" and announced the city government's decision not to buy grapes in recognition of the farm workers' struggle. In Chicago, Eliseo Medina organized a boycott campaign that persuaded the leading supermarket chain, Jewel, to stop carrying table grapes at every one of its 254 store locations. For this feat, Mayor Richard Daley, a pro-labor Democrat, recognized Medina as "Man of the Year" and endorsed the boycott. Similarly, in Cleveland, Mayor Carl Burton Stokes, the first African American to be elected mayor of a major U.S. city, ordered all government facilities to cease serving table grapes. Mack Lyons, the only African American on the National Executive Board of the UFW, made the appeal to Stokes and organized one of the strongest boycott houses in the network. In San Francisco, five major agribusiness organizations canceled their annual meetings in the city in response to the San Francisco Board of Supervisors' endorsement of the boycott. At the annual meeting of the National League of Cities, the mayor of Delano, Clifford Loader, tried to stem the tide of city governments' support for the boycott by introducing a resolution requesting mayors not to take sides in the grape dispute. To Loader's dismay, his peers soundly defeated his proposal.[9]

Support from religious leaders extended the appeal of the boycott to patrons ordinarily more reluctant to weigh in on labor matters. From the beginning individuals from a range of organized religions supported the movement, volunteering their time to the union, occasionally in defiance of their church's orders. By 1968, however, organized religion began to see the moral dimensions behind the farm workers' modest demand for collective bargaining. That growers resisted this basic right shared by many working-class churchgoers permitted men of the cloth to take a position in favor of the union.

New reports of farm workers suffering from exposure to pesticides also moved religious and secular consumers alike. Jessica Govea, working in the new union Service Center, received complaints from many women who experienced dizziness, nausea, and sweats after working in the fields. As a former field worker in Bakersfield, she knew the symptoms associated with exposure to pesticides and immediately appealed to Jerry Cohen to see what could be done about the problem. When Cohen asked the agricultural commissioner, C. Seldon Morely, for reports of pesticides use on grapes, the growers went to the courts to block access. When the matter finally made it to a Kern County court, the judge blocked access to the records on the grounds that the union would use it in the boycott. Eventually, Cohen succeeded in winning access to several "little green booklets" listing the days in which growers sprayed, but limited information on what exactly had been used. The lack of clarity on the subject inspired the union and Senator Walter Mondale, a Democrat, to aggressively pursue a farm worker's right to know the contents of the pesticides, and provided boycott volunteers another talking point on the picket lines.[10]

The momentum of the boycott carried it north, where shipments of California table grapes arrived at a fruit terminal in Detroit before being distributed throughout Michigan, Ohio, and Canada. The UFW initially tried to shut off the corridor by targeting the fruit terminals run by a director known only as "Mr. Andrews." During the 1968 campaign, the Detroit boycott house, managed by a Catholic nun, Sister Lupé Anguiano, and an L.A. boycott veteran, José Serda, appealed to Andrews to cooperate with the boycott, but the terminal director showed little regard for the union. Appearing to have reached a dead end in Detroit, Chavez shuffled the leadership by bringing in Hijinio Rangel to run the house.

Rangel moved his entire family to the Motor City from Portland, Oregon, in December 1968. Within a few weeks, the Rangels mobilized a group of 5,000 volunteers composed of students, religious leaders, and fellow unionists to march from Ann Arbor to Detroit. The former Delano labor contractor and *tortilleria* owner followed this show of force with quiet but persistent appeals to Andrews to rethink his opposition to the boycott. As Rangel recalled in his memoir, Andrews responded with disdain, boasting, "I sent José Serda and Lupé Anguiano back to California, and the same is going to happen to you. You will go back on your knees."[11]

Rangel accepted the insult as a challenge to devise a successful strategy. Rather than continue his appeals to Andrews, he took his case to Detroit's leading supermarket chain, Kroger's. Flanked by nuns on one side and a priest on the other, Rangel asked store managers not to carry California table grapes. When these efforts failed, he directed volunteers to enter the markets with their protest, provoking managers to call the police to arrest them. As protesters filled the city jail to capacity, court officials quickly arranged arraignment hearings on a Saturday to deal with the deluge of cases. Rangel recalled, "[The] judge arrived still in his shorts because he had been cutting his lawn." In advance, Rangel made contact with local leaders in the AFL-CIO, UAW, and steelworkers, carpenters, and electrical workers unions, who lent their legal counsel to the boycotters in their moment of need. As the courtroom filled with more than a thousand arrested protesters, the judge dismissed the charges and sent UFW volunteers flowing triumphantly into the streets of Detroit. On Monday morning, Kroger's acquiesced and announced its decision to stop selling grapes at all of its twenty-five Detroit-area locations. Rangel complemented these actions by engaging in an eleven-day public fast to draw attention to two other markets, AM-PM and Farmer John's, both of which eventually fell into line with the boycott.

The campaign against Detroit-area markets did not immediately break Andrews, given that the fruit terminal served as a transfer point for table grapes going to markets beyond the city. Rangel ordered 150 volunteers to picket the terminal around the clock and sent another 500 to picket independent stores still receiving table grapes. Picketers met Andrews every morning at seven, first in front of the terminal as he came in for work, then quickly moving to his office to create the illusion that the union had 300 boycotters working the picket lines. On the ninth day, Andrews agreed to negotiate, offering to discontinue the sale of California grapes after the arrival of the last trainload. Rangel recalled the conversation: "I said, 'This is not acceptable, Mr. Andrews. Send a telegram to Mr. Giumarra requesting he take the grapes back. I want a copy of the telegram. Also I want permission to inspect your terminal every day until further orders.'" A beleaguered Andrews conceded to Rangel's demands and stopped selling grapes immediately. A few days later, when Rangel sent his son, Manuel, to inspect the terminal, Andrews asked the young man to convey a message: "Tell your father that I have much respect for him."[12]

The success of the boycott significantly disrupted the grower community as differences among them became more pronounced the longer the boycott wore on. Coachella growers, who had a reduced capacity to withstand the pressures of the boycott given the shortness of their growing season, felt the pinch earlier and more acutely than their San Joaquin Valley peers. They increasingly resented the messages from the Grape & Tree Fruit League that growers were impervious to the boycott. Lionel Steinberg, the unofficial spokesperson for Coachella growers, broke with the league's practice of focusing on production totals from one year to the next by making broader and longer range comparisons that took into account production costs and consumer spending on groceries. For Steinberg, the differences between 1952, when consumers spent 30 percent of their income on food, and 1969, when they spent only 17 percent, provided a more accurate portrait of the changes in the market. The doubling of wages from $1 to $2, increases in the cost of containers from 25 cents to 70 cents, and the cost of tractors up from $1,800 to $6,000 over this same period gave them reason to worry. The prospect of losing 20 percent of their market to the boycott weighed heavily on Steinberg and other Coachella growers who had had enough by 1969. "Farm workers and growers both have problems," he opined, "and it does not do any good to try to fool anyone about the additional problems presented to growers by the boycott."[13]

Steinberg responded to these conditions by resigning from the Grape & Tree Fruit League and organizing ten of his fellow Coachella growers to sue for peace with the union. In his letter of resignation, Steinberg accused E. Allen Mills, the league's executive vice president, of sweeping the problem of the boycott under the rug. "When you keep insisting everything is rosy and we should keep our chins up," Steinberg angrily wrote, "I sincerely feel you are doing a disservice to the growers." Steinberg now laid bare to the public a rift within the industry. San Joaquin Valley growers viewed Coachella as a relative newcomer to the business, constituting only 10 percent of the total market for grapes. Steinberg, an entrepreneur who had invested in farmland after the arrival of federal water in 1948, stood outside a well-developed grower culture in the San Joaquin Valley. Although Marshall Ganz thought it more than a coincidence that Jewish owners of farms were often the first to settle disputes with the union, the breakdown in the grower coalition during the 1969 harvest appeared to have more to do with market share and regional differences among California growers than with anti-Semitism.[14]

Trying to work out a settlement with the union proved to be as difficult for Coachella growers as getting their San Joaquin peers to care about them. Caught up in the momentum of the boycott, union officials pushed hard once they arrived at the negotiation table. The union's delegation, which many growers deemed "the circus," offended the majority of Coachella growers, who abandoned Steinberg and vowed to fight on. A year later, Monsignor George Higgins of the National Catholic Conference reported the sentiments of the growers in the aftermath of the failed negotiations: "They said the union had 20 or 30 people in the room, workers and what not. They said the union didn't negotiate; it made demands." Whether the UFW overplayed its hand mattered less than that the union had opened up yet another schism among the growers.

. The absence of a settlement with Coachella growers did little to dampen Chavez's excitement for the boycott. By the end of the 1969 season, the union had achieved most of the goals set during the summer retreat a year before, namely the organization of effective boycott houses and the reduction of table grape sales in nine of the ten most important cities in North America. The union relied on two sources of information that indicated progress: the reports flowing from the boycott houses to Jerry and Juanita Brown and the hard evidence present in USDA reports regarding the changes in grape sales from year to year. The poor growing conditions in 1967 that led to unusually low crop yields caused the union, growers, and the government officials to rely on 1966 as the more appropriate benchmark for the 1969 season. USDA reports confirmed Steinberg's complaints and the unions' claims of progress. Shippers posted a decline of 24 percent in grape shipments to the ten leading cities and provided evidence of extremely effective boycott operations in Chicago (down 42.8 percent), Boston (down 41.8 percent), Detroit (29.6 percent), and New York City (27.6 percent). In fact, only one city among the top ten, Montreal, posted an increase in car lots of California and Arizona table grapes from 1966 to 1969, whereas the other nine major boycott houses hit their target of reducing shipments by 10 percent or more.

Growers attempted to circumvent the boycott by redirecting table grapes to other major North American cities, especially those in the South, including Atlanta, Memphis, Miami, and New Orleans. The UFW built new boycott houses in thirty-one of these cities to meet the challenge, including twenty-one supported by a paid organizer and the other ten staffed entirely by volunteers. Among these houses, the twenty-one with paid organizers reduced shipments by 13 percent, whereas the ten with no organizers still managed to reduce shipments by 12.6 percent. Growers also experienced a dramatic decline in profits as the glut of unsold grapes on the market forced brokers to lower the prices to offload their inventory. These declines hurt Coachella growers the most because their profits depended on the bump in prices that accompanied being the first on the market. By placing their grapes in cold storage in anticipation of finding new markets, Coachella growers experienced more competition and lower prices as the season wore on and San Joaquin Valley table grapes became available. In a market made uncertain by the boycott, grape growers could anticipate a poorer return on their investments.

TABLE I. Car Lot Unloads of All California and Arizona Table Grapes in Ten Major North American Markets, 1966 and 1969 Seasons Compared*

City	1966 Unloads	1969 Unloads	1966-1969 Difference	% of change
1. New York	2,733	1,979	−754	−27.6%
2. Los Angeles	2,360	1,983	−377	−16.0%
3. Chicago	1,275	730	−545	−42.8%
4. San Francisco	932	749	−183	−19.2%
5. Philadelphia	818	650	−168	−20.5%
6. Boston	764	449	−315	−41.2%
7. Toronto	737	570	−167	−22.6%
8. Detroit	735	517	−218	−29.6%
9. Montreal	729	754	+25	+3.4%
10. Cleveland	472	406	−66	−14%
Total:	**11,555**	**8,787**	**−2,768**	**−24%**

SOURCE: Compiled from U.S. Department of Agriculture, Consumer and Marketing Services, *Fresh Fruit and Vegetable Unloads in Eastern, Southern, Midwestern and Western Cities by Commodities, States and Months, 1966, 1967, 1969, 1970, passim.* In Jerald Barry Brown, "The United Farm Workers Grape Strike and Boycott, 1965-1970: An Evaluation of the Culture of Poverty Theory," (Ph.D. dissertation, Anthropology, Cornell University, 1972) 212.

*May through January shipments

The enthusiasm of volunteers to staff more effective boycott houses and the mostly sympathetic press coverage the union received convinced Cesar Chavez of the centrality of the boycott to the movement. Over a four-year period, the boycott moved from an activity undertaken by the union to keep farm workers and volunteers inspired between harvests to a year-round tactic. According to Jerry Brown, when farm workers from other crops and workers from Oregon, Texas, Florida, and Ohio appealed to the UFW to send organizers, Chavez declined such invitations not only because the union had been stretched to its limits, but also because he now believed it would be "foolish" to initiate a strike without the backing of a boycott.[15]

Growers refused to concede defeat, however, believing that their tactic of shifting sales to underdeveloped markets had not been fully explored. As bad as USDA shipment reports for traditional markets appeared, growers succeeded in rerouting one-third of their shipments to rural areas and smaller cities where the UFW had no representatives. The diverted shipments amounted to a 20 percent increase in these areas, which left growers' total shipments for the entire North American market down by 9.2 percent for the year. Given their ability to adjust to the adversities caused by the boycott, most growers held on to the idea that an organized rerouting and strategic marketing of grapes could wear down the union. Moreover, the failure of the UFW to create a viable boycott in Montreal suggested the possibility of beating the union in the international marketplace, where cultural distinctions and different labor and picketing laws made it more difficult for the union to establish effective boycott houses. By moving grapes across borders and offshore growers hoped to finally expand beyond the reach of the UFW and break free of the power of the boycott.

THE INTERNATIONAL ARENA

Across the Detroit River in Canada, Marshall Ganz and Jessica Govea worked to consolidate the gains made in the United States by enforcing the boycott in the provinces of Ontario and Quebec. Although laws restricted the union from staging storefront protests, Ganz's uses of creative nonviolence played on the sympathies of customers. The enthusiasm of local volunteers affirmed the beliefs of the Toronto boycott staff, as did the support from Canadian unions and the decidedly favorable coverage by Toronto media. These attitudes reflected not only the presence of a strong pro-labor sentiment among Toronto residents, but also the ability of boycott workers to communicate the stakes in the grape strike taking place in the fields of California. That both boycott house workers and residents of Toronto spoke English was significant, allowing them to speak a common language— literally and figuratively—when it came to discussions about workers' rights.

During the 1969 season, Govea worked with Ganz to organize the entire Canadian campaign from the Toronto office.[16] Born in Bakersfield, California, into a farm-working family, she spent every summer from the age of four to fifteen picking cotton, grapes, and plums in the San Joaquin Valley. Her father routinely demonstrated against grower injustice toward workers and inspired the young Govea to organize farm worker children to petition and protest for change. In 1966, she left college to work for the UFW in Delano, then accepted an assignment from Chavez in July 1968 to join Ganz in Toronto. The two worked well together and over time developed a personal and professional relationship bound by their service to *la causa*.

In addition to Govea and Ganz, the Toronto staff included Mark Day, Hub Segur, and Jim Brophy from the United States, and Linda Gerard and Keith Patinson, both natives of Canada. Gerard came by way of a "donation" from the UAW regional office in Windsor, where the twenty-one-year-old

FIGURE 8. Supporters of the grape boycott demonstrate in Toronto, December 1968. Jessica Govea is in the center, front row (wearing poncho). ALUA, UFW Collection, 303.

secretary had served the union for the previous two years. The UAW continued to pay her full-time salary, while the union covered the cost of her food and paid her the usual $5 per week allotted to every volunteer. Patinson also served the boycott full time at the will of the UAW, which covered all of his expenses. In addition, the Delano office assigned Mike Milo to work out of Windsor, to organize "secondary Ontario cities," although eventually Ganz incorporated him into the Toronto house to centralize his staff.[17]

The growth of the Canadian campaign through the summer and fall of 1969 required the union to split up Govea and Ganz for strategic purposes, placing Govea in Montreal while Ganz remained in Toronto to build on his success. At the end of 1969, Chavez expressed a desire to have Ganz and Govea return to Delano in case growers again showed interest in negotiating a settlement with the union. Ganz's success in convincing all but one of the presidents of Toronto's grocery chains (Leon Weinstein of Loblaw's) to discontinue sales of California grapes distinguished him as a talented negotiator; Chavez valued Govea for her authentic voice that lent credibility to any potential negotiating team. The importance of the Canadian boycott, however, forced Chavez to delay their return until their presence was absolutely necessary.[18]

Throughout 1969, Govea and Ganz concentrated on creating a national campaign, organizing volunteers, arranging conferences, and reporting on the progress of the boycott well beyond their base in Ontario (Toronto, Windsor, and Ottawa) and Quebec (Montreal) to the northeast, and cities to the west in the provinces of Manitoba (Winnipeg), Saskatchewan (Saskatoon, Regina), Alberta (Calgary, Edmonton), and British Columbia (Vancouver). In the central and western provinces, Ganz relied on volunteers to staff boycott houses, while he and Govea coordinated with allies from the Canadian labor movement to generate support for the boycott. One of the union's staunchest foes, Safeway, dominated the grocery store landscape in the West, making the fight even more difficult. Still, Ganz reported progress in Winnipeg and Manitoba, where strong boycott committees picketed stores and the provincial governments agreed to halt the purchase of table grapes.[19]

Ganz and Govea focused most of their attention on Windsor, Toronto, and Ottawa in Ontario and Montreal in Quebec, but the distance and cultural differences between the two regions made operations difficult. When the two attempted to bring together volunteers from Toronto, Ottawa, and Montreal for an annual weekend planning conference in a central location, Ganz found it "not really practical because of tremendous differences in Ontario and Québec and the distances involved." A seven-hour drive separated Toronto and Montreal, a distance not easily bridged until the boycott house purchased a second car, a 1966 Ford Galaxy, for $1,000 with the help of a dealer in Detroit and money donated from the Canadian Labour Congress, the UAW, and the steelworkers union.

The expense of maintaining contact over such great distances perpetually challenged the boycott house and made money a constant concern for the organizers. "Our budget of $590.00," Ganz wrote Juanita Brown in January 1970, "was predicated on two full-time people at the time it was drawn up." Although the amount constituted a significant sum for the union, their overwhelming success at recruiting local volunteers generated new expenses, including food and a weekly stipend of $5 per volunteer that stretched the annual budget beyond its limits. The house also had to pay for rent increases, phone bills, and office expenses, including gas, often on one union credit card passed from volunteer to volunteer. Although these problems confronted every boycott house, the exchange rate and the miles the Toronto house volunteers had to cover and the cost of long-distance and international phone calls complicated their situation. "Jessica wrote repeatedly asking that a budget adjustment be made," Ganz wrote, "[but] it was never made." As a consequence, the house lost volunteers when Ganz, Segur, and Govea returned to Delano between seasons.[20] Ganz recommended the creation of a full-time staff in Toronto and suggested moving Govea to Montreal long enough to remedy the situation. He also recommended funds to support a separate office in Ottawa, about five hours away, but the request exceeded the capacity of the union to pay for it. "The whole Canadian [boycott] is about a year behind the major American cities," Ganz reported, but he believed such changes would produce a campaign "stronger than ever this year."[21]

In spite of their late start, Ganz's work with Steinberg's and Dominion in 1969 laid an important foundation for the house to build on in the winter of 1969 and the spring and summer of 1970. Loblaw's remained the only holdout, which allowed volunteers to concentrate on it. Ganz and Govea made a concerted effort to strengthen their relationship with supporters in the Canadian labor movement and the Canadian government. The endorsement of the Canadian Labour Congress contributed not only good publicity to the boycott, but also local union members who staffed picket lines in the toughest of conditions. Beginning on December 20, in the midst of a typical Toronto winter with temperatures falling to 2 degrees, more than three hundred volunteers participated in a five-day, 110-hour continuous vigil in front of Loblaw's largest downtown location. Volunteers, local aldermen, and members of the provincial parliament sang Christmas carols, staged candlelight processions, and held an ecumenical midnight Christmas mass while Ganz and five others fasted in solidarity with strikers in California. Boycott organizers also targeted professional athletes and sporting events, such as the Toronto Maple Leafs' hockey games, which drew 16,000 people two nights a week. The house printed thousands of leaflets with a lineup of the teams and special commendations to those stars who endorsed the boycott. "Passed out 6,000 leaflets in about 35 minutes," Ganz reported to Delano. At the games, volunteers collected signatures on a petition asking Loblaw's to stop selling grapes.

The effectiveness of the boycott through the 1969–70 winter produced concern among Coachella growers who, once again, desired to settle the strike in advance of the upcoming table grape season. In anticipation of negotiations, Ganz moved back to Delano. Meanwhile, Jerry and Juanita Browns' move to Toronto supplied the Canadian campaign with two proven leaders to sustain the momentum while Ganz was away.[22]

Upon their arrival, Manny Rivera and the Browns made contact with Loblaw's owner, Leon Weinstein, who invited the leaders and Manny's wife and three children to his office. Born in the back of his father's neighborhood grocery store in Toronto, Weinstein had taken over the family business as an adult and expanded it into a successful chain built primarily on good customer relations. Although politically conservative, Weinstein prided himself as a fair-minded entrepreneur with the power to disarm those who questioned his business practices. Jerry Brown recalled, "He [told] us how he would not have grapes in his home, how he supports the farm workers' cause, but he is the president of a large chain, and the consumers have to have free choice, so he cannot publicly support the boycott." Weinstein also made a peace offering of Cuban cigars to Rivera, who accepted the gift and came ready to reciprocate. "He hand[ed] Leon a farm worker calendar," Brown remembered, "every month of which ha[d] a picture of the travails in the fields—you know, hungry children, child labor, tired workers." "I'm going to give you . . . our calendar," Rivera told Weinstein, "and I hope you'll put it on the wall, so that every day you look at it, you'll be reminded of the suffering you're causing our people by carrying grapes in your store."[23]

A few days after the meeting, Mrs. Rivera found out about a Loblaw's party at which Weinstein would be honored for his leadership of the company. Typically, the house would picket such an event, but this time Mrs. Rivera proposed something different: "We're going to turn this into a funeral procession." For the night of the celebration, the union created cards that, at first glance, appeared to be a program for the evening. Once guests opened the cards, however, they discovered information about the unfair labor practices of grape growers and their use of pesticides in the fields. Volunteers also brought to the event makeshift caskets made of used grape cartons covered in black paper and photos of farm workers toiling in the fields. The union recruited several priests and nuns to accompany them to the event, creating a public relations nightmare for Weinstein. Brown remembered, "He almost broke out into tears at the celebration." Two weeks later, Weinstein announced his decision to remove table grapes from all twenty-six Loblaw's locations and resigned from the company.[24]

In Montreal, Jessica Govea worked to replicate the success in Toronto. In January, Ganz wrote of Montreal, "We have not had a particularly effective boycott here." He attributed the problems to three causes: "1) lack of effective organizing work; 2) lack of French-speaking staff; 3) the nature of Quebec itself." Govea's move to the city on a full-time basis helped turn the situation around. She began by recruiting a staff with some capacity to speak French, including Peter Standish, a twenty-something who had served in the highly successful New York City boycott house during the 1969 season.[25] A visit by Cesar Chavez in late 1969 lent legitimacy to the movement in the province and gave Govea a foundation for coordinating with local unions. She cultivated a relationship with Louis LaBerge, president of the Québec Federation of Labour, and worked with the farmers union in Quebec, L'union de Cultivateurs Catolique, which publicly endorsed the boycott.[26]

Yet for all her efforts, the creation of an effective boycott equivalent to those in other cities eluded Govea. The union's appeal to a society embroiled in a secessionist crisis made the boycott, at best, a secondary consideration. For many Québécois, the embrace of the boycott by English-speaking Ontario made the movement suspect. "Not only is the boycott an 'American issue,'" Ganz wrote Larry Itliong, "but we have to deal with a foreign country in a foreign language, which makes the boycott doubly distant." The difference in reception from English-speaking and French-speaking Canadians was manifested most acutely in the varying level of support the union received from organized labor. "We are particularly concerned about the fact that we are not getting the kind of co-operation that we need from the two Quebec labour movements," Ganz wrote. "It is a bit as if the Quebec apple pickers were on strike and sent a representative to Delano and expected us to go all out [on] behalf of their problem." In spite of Govea's relations with LaBerge, he withheld his endorsement of the boycott until Chavez requested it.[27]

Govea appreciated Chavez's assistance, but the need for "man-to-man" communication to gain the respect of a fellow unionist must have rankled her. In addition to her frustration with LaBerge, she tussled with the younger Standish, who challenged her authority within the Montreal boycott house. Although Standish had worked under Dolores Huerta in New York City and lauded her leadership, he demonstrated a lack of respect for Govea and undermined her leadership by questioning her strategies, maligning her organizational skills, and engaging in *tonterías* (stupid behavior) that influenced the morale of the house. In a letter to Chavez, Govea explained that Standish had come to Montreal with the expectation that he would be put in charge of the house. When that did not happen, he began to work behind Govea's back to undermine her credibility with the staff. Govea's meetings with Standish confirmed her impressions but also revealed a level of disrespect reserved especially for her. "He also believes that I am extremely incompetent," Govea disclosed to Chavez, "[and] that if he could go to a city where there was someone like Gilbert Padilla or someone important like that, then he would." Standish gave Govea the impression he was telling her, "You go, or I go," a sentiment she deeply resented and equated to blackmail. Ultimately, she recommended that Chavez not give in to Standish's wishes: "Either he stays here where he is needed and works well with this group, or he goes [leaves the union] altogether."[28]

Standish, in fact, did circumvent the chain of command by writing to Chavez directly, requesting a transfer and telling his side of the story. For him, the question came down to a personality conflict and contrasting philosophies of organizing. He objected to Govea's attitude toward him, which he saw as "increasingly defensive and combative." Undoubtedly, Standish's organizing against Govea influenced the tenor of her communication with him, yet his own "ghastly feeling" that he was being "horribly under-used" smacked of arrogance and even insubordination. Moreover, Standish openly expressed hostility toward the "shop-in" used to great effect by Huerta in New York City and Ganz in Toronto because it promoted "an element of play-acting or pretense, which is repugnant to me." He objected to the insincerity of the act and worried that if the boycott house ever faced severe internal crisis, members would not trust each other in their attempts to resolve differences. Oddly, Standish advocated a "top down" approach in which the house leader instructed volunteers to stay focused on recruiting customers one shopper at a time, asking them to keep their receipts from markets not carrying table grapes, and sending them to managers of stores that did. Although Standish credited Govea with inventing the "receipt-saving campaign," he faulted her for not following through on it. "If well carried out," he wrote Chavez, "it could enable the boycott to sink its roots quite deeply into the population of a city, and could get thousands of people more concretely and directly involved than if they simply signed a pledge not to buy scab grapes and not to shop in stores which sell them."[29] He asked Chavez to consider moving him to Cleveland to replace Dixie Lee Fisher, who, it was rumored, wanted to return to school full time.[30]

The lack of results in Montreal pointed to weaknesses in the campaign that Standish sensed and both Ganz and Govea admitted. Standish's observations, however, discounted the complexities of organizing in a foreign country and missed the trial-and-error process used by even the most successful leaders. In Los Angeles, for example, LeRoy Chatfield had to employ both raucous demonstrations and painstaking appeals to customers before learning that the latter worked better in a conservative climate. An underlying conservativism and anti-union sentiment did not shape the attitudes of Montreal shoppers; indeed, Quebec, like Canada as a whole, was more pro-union than most of the United States in 1970. Rather, the union had to overcome not only language barriers but also cultural differences inflamed by the UFW's early coordination with English-speaking unionists in Ontario. Govea employed a range of tactics in Montreal and worked to build personal relationships with labor leaders, an approach that Standish neither appreciated nor excelled at. Ganz, in his assessment of Standish's strengths and weaknesses, characterized his approach as "very systematic and organized" and credited him with speaking excellent French, but faulted him for his "lack of experience [in] working with organized groups, especially labour." Standish's proposed solution to Montreal's problems mirrored the disciplined and patient approach taken in Los Angeles; however, by 1970, the union felt the pressure to produce results more quickly as expenses mounted on both sides, and some growers again sought resolution to the conflict.

Standish's impatience with Govea also signaled the unique difficulties women faced as leaders during late 1960s and 1970s. For example, Govea took exception to Standish's preference to work with other men or on his own. She told Chavez, "Feelings with respect to titles and importance are his, not mine."[31] Standish made known to both Govea and Chavez his ambition to pursue community organizing as a career. He wrote to Chavez, "I was initially attracted to the struggle by my desire to learn to organize under your leadership so that I could prepare myself to participate in other non-violent struggles which I believe will have to be organized in America."[32] That these skills could be acquired only through mentorship from Chavez and Padilla, or that his break as a leader would come at the expense of a woman—either Govea in Montreal or Dixie Lee Fisher in Cleveland—apparently did not trouble him. Govea refused to accept his behavior, first calling him to a face-to-face meeting to reprimand him. When this failed, she used her clout with Chavez and her authority as the house leader to recommend drawing Standish into line or cutting him loose. Although the record does not show how Chavez responded, Govea's insistence that Standish remain in the boycott house as a dutiful member under her demonstrated her determination to receive respect on a par with male leaders in the movement.

No story better illustrates the challenges and triumphs that women in the boycott experienced than Elaine Elinson's. As an undergraduate student at Cornell University in the mid-1960s, Elinson served on the boycott in New York City during summers between her job at the Natural History Museum and acting in "off-off-Broadway" plays. In time, her service expanded well beyond a part-time commitment in Manhattan to a consequential piece of the worldwide boycott puzzle.

Elinson's background as the granddaughter of Russian Jewish immigrants predisposed her to serve a movement on behalf of immigrant workers. "I was told never to cross a picket line," she remembered, "and that all people are equal." Her grandmother came to the United States in 1905, but returned to Russia in 1911 to participate in the Russian Revolution. Elinson remembered her grandmother as a very political person whose grandparents shipped her back to the United States in 1916 to save her life. According to Elinson, her grandmother never fully got over leaving Russia before the 1917 Revolution: "She said, 'All my friends had gotten killed, I was so depressed . . . I could have killed myself.'" Elinson's father reinforced these politics as a professor of public health who looked beyond medicine to social factors such as racism and poverty as reasons for illness among people of color.

Her family cultivated a strong sense of social justice, which manifested itself early in her life. During a trip across country at the age of twelve, she remembered being kicked out of the Alamo for objecting to the sale of Confederate flags in the gift shop. "The woman said, 'If you don't like it, you can just leave.' And I said, 'Well, I'm trying to leave, but this state is so big, I can't get out of it!'" After graduating from high school in New Jersey in 1964, Elinson attended Smith College, but the elitism of the school troubled her family. In a questionnaire distributed to all incoming freshman, the college wanted to know, "Will you need a place for your horse?" Elinson recalled, "My dad [said], 'Oh my God, where are we sending you?'" When some of her classmates took exception to her dating an African American student from Amherst, Elinson sought a transfer to Cornell, a bigger school with a more diverse student body and a wider range of studies.

At Cornell, she studied abroad in the Philippines and pursued a major in Asian studies and Chinese, but also traveled to Honduras to teach literacy and build schools. In general, Cornell provided a broad spectrum of opinions and experiences, including those from the antiwar movement. She considered membership in Students for a Democratic Society, but ultimately found the organization too "white male dominated." The UFW had much greater appeal because of the bold leadership of Dolores Huerta, whose success in New York she discovered while serving on UFW picket lines and participating in the successful boycott campaign of 1967. During her first year in the movement, Elinson never met Huerta but saw the reverence fellow volunteers had for her: "Dolores was like the great mother of that house on Eighty-sixth Street."[33] When she graduated in 1968, Elinson considered becoming a full-time organizer for the union, but she remained conflicted about pursuing a career as a professor or committing herself to activism. She ultimately decided to serve the boycott house in New York during the summer of 1968 before moving to London to start a graduate program at the School of Oriental and African Studies in the fall.[34]

The contrasts between the two experiences could not have been more decisive in determining the course of Elinson's life. The solitude of research in London made her feel somewhat removed from the major conflicts of the day. "I'm sitting in the basement of the British Museum copying characters off Ming dynasty vases," she recalled, "and [I was] thinking, the Vietnam War is raging, and what am I doing this for?" When she wrote Jerry Brown in Delano to see if she could come back to the United States to work for the union, Brown instructed her to remain in England. By 1968 the growers had begun to transfer shipments overseas in an attempt to circumvent the boycott in North America. "If necessary you could come back right away," Brown told her, but added, "In as much as you are in London and we are trying to internationalize the boycott, Cesar asked if you couldn't hold on to your means of existence and do some ground work for us there."[35] Although he knew it would be a long shot, Brown realized that keeping Elinson overseas gave the union a chance to establish its presence in Europe and put the growers' on notice that the UFW could move with the grapes.

Given the size of the boycott effort, Elinson did not initially stand out for Brown until he saw a photo of her in a file of potential volunteers in Delano. He remembered his reaction: "I saw that she was this cute girl in a mini-skirt with those big glasses that were so popular, kind of Jimi Hendrix glasses . . . and I said, 'This girl is perfect for the longshoremen.'" In a letter to Elinson instructing her of her duties, Brown reminded her, "No labor leader can resist a pretty girl," and offered her the following "side note": "Sorry to mention this tactic, and [I am] fully aware that liberation begins [at] home, but let's face it[,] when women want to be completely equal they lose their most powerful advantage over men."[36] European and American journalists also took note of her attire, especially the miniskirt, which Elinson described: "It was a chartreuse mini-skirt dress with a big white pointed collar . . . and big white buttons."[37] She often wore long white stockings and flat loafers, and accessorized with a red and black UFW badge and a UFW scarf with the union eagle on it. During the winter months, she donned an orange coat.

FIGURE 9. Elaine Elinson distributes flyers on the London docks, ca. 1969. Private collection.

Elinson's dress sharply contrasted with the work clothes of dockworkers and the black and gray tweeds of union officials. Brown believed she cultivated this look to her "advantage," although, as Elinson remembered, she had little choice in the matter: "I literally had no money to buy a suit, or something to look sort of presentable." Moreover, what appeared alluring to Brown did not seem excessively so to the average Briton, who had grown accustomed to such short dresses in shops along Portobello Road, the fashion district of London.[38]

Fashion decisions aside, the problem of sexism confronted every woman activist who dared to become a leader in the United States or Europe. In a period when women's liberation occupied a place alongside the antiwar movement and civil rights movements, women such as Jessica Govea and Elaine Elinson had to manage men's perceptions of them as merely sexual objects. Govea, for example, wrote of her discomfort during a trip to Shreveport, Louisiana, where she encountered the twin challenges of racism and sexism. "Personally, it was a very bad experience as racism still has the upper hand in that area," she wrote Chavez, "and if you think that things are bad for black men in that area they are even worse for black women and, in the South, I am a black woman." She reported receiving "all kinds of invasions and propositions" from men in the International Brotherhood of Pulp, Sulphite and Paper Mill Workers until she rose to speak on behalf of the grape boycott. "I was really scared," she admitted, "but I played it 'cara palo cool'" (cool faced) and in the end decided that her trip was "a good experience, I suppose."[39] Similarly, Elinson remembered Britain as "a very sexist society" and the problem of discriminatory behavior toward women "rife in the trade union movement."

Elinson did not struggle with the problem of racism; however, as Brown's comments signaled, her age and gender presented both challenges and opportunities. What Brown labeled her "powerful advantage" made her a novelty for readers of union newspapers but also placed her in a potentially precarious position with trade union members. "These guys, in fact, were in some of the roughest trades," Elinson recalled. "They were people who had grown up with very set ideas about the woman's roles." Yet, in spite of their backgrounds, trade unionists in England treated Elinson "very respectfully" and helped her whenever she asked for assistance. She theorized that her outsider status as an American made her nonthreatening to the union bosses and ingratiated her to the rank and file in the United Kingdom.

As Elinson established herself in England, British and American union officials introduced her to male union leaders who showed less respect toward women. In Sweden, for example, she attended conferences and communicated with unionists who paid more attention to her hemline than her message. She recalled, "There were a lot of guys who thought, 'Okay, let's just let her give her talk, and then take her home' I didn't feel that comfortable sometimes going to weekend conferences."[40] When Elinson requested Brown's recommendation on how to handle such advances, he sought the help of Chavez and offered his own remedy. Chavez had "no words on the subject," whereas Brown replied with practical, if not sympathetic advice: "I think it requires a combination of good humor and firm will—we don't expect total sacrifice for the cause."[41]

Elinson drew on her family experience and the example of other women in the movement to overcome such awkward moments. The sister of three brothers, she felt comfortable dealing with men and believed herself their equal. Her parents had instilled this confidence and rejected the idea prevalent among some of their generation that women went to college primarily to find a man to marry. "There were a lot of my contemporaries like the bright women who went to Smith," Elinson remembered, "who really were taught by their parents or their cultural milieu [to] study art history, and then you're going to marry a nice guy who's going to be a doctor, or something, from Harvard." Her parents, on the other hand, raised her to be self-sufficient and empowered her to think that she could achieve the same level of independence as her brothers. The example of Dolores Huerta weighed heavily on her mind as she began to work with leaders who viewed her presence with a jaundiced eye. Huerta, who negotiated the first labor contracts with Schenley, gave Elinson a powerful role model to emulate: "I was drawn like a magnet to Dolores. . . . She was one woman in the midst of all of these men. And she was way gorgeous . . . but she just forged ahead with all of her political passions and commitment and smarts, and you know, the fact that she may have been totally attractive to half of the people around her was not what got her going, you know?"[42]

Jerry Brown also treated Elinson as an equal—comments about her looks notwithstanding—and dispensed advice, support, and contact information without equivocation. Their frequent correspondence provides an impressive record of the evolution of the European boycott and evidence of Elinson's intuition and independence.

Brown's early advice to Elinson demonstrated a faith in the consumer boycott that was based on the union's success in North America. Because England was the fifth largest importer of grapes and a market where growers could move unused shipments, Brown felt an urgency to educate the British public through "a one-shot provo[cative] publicity stunt against importing US grapes on the theme of helping the poor in America (which ought to appeal to British students)." In addition to students, Brown advised Elinson to target union members and government workers, who "might move to either stop grape imports (unlikely) or make a public display of displeas[ure] (likely)."[43] Among his many suggestions for action, Brown amusingly advised Elinson to unfurl a "don't buy grapes banner" from Big Ben or convince the Beatles to write a protest song, going so far as to suggest the title "Sour Grapes" before concluding, "This I leave entirely up to local imagination."[44]

Elinson had to overcome a lack of resources to educate herself and the union on which strategy should be used in England. She felt the union's notorious lack of funds and meager weekly stipend of $5 per volunteer more acutely than most leaders, given the exchange rate and the cost of communication. Although Chavez permitted a modest increase in her stipend and allowed Brown to send a bit more money as needed, the UFW relied on her to raise money, secure donations, and budget wisely—including using much of her own money set aside for education—to fund her activities. Elinson lived in less than ideal conditions, sharing a flat on the third floor of an old row house with three other graduate students. She remembered, "The place was rundown and damp; when it rained, the kitchen floor was crowded with buckets and bowls to catch the leaks, and the whole flat was heated by a rickety gas stove that had to be constantly fed shillings." When she needed to use the phone, she had to rely on a pay phone shared among all the residents of the house in the hallway of the bottom floor.[45] At the height of the British campaign, one phone bill between Brown and Elinson reached $40, prompting Brown to caution, "Don't worry about it; but let's try to avoid that kind of thing."[46]

Cut off from immediate contact with Delano, Elinson relied primarily on her own instincts to build a campaign in London and beyond. In talking to her peers at school, she found a sympathetic group of English students and community activists steeped in the politics of anticolonialism in the former European colonies of Zimbabwe (Rhodesia), Namibia, Mozambique, and Angola. In addition, British peace activists demonstrated against the U.S. war in Vietnam and endorsed boycotts against products that supported apartheid in South Africa. All of these friends served as allies at a time of great upheaval, providing her encouragement and occasional resources in an otherwise foreign land. Yet in spite of these efforts, Elinson recognized the limitations of building an effective consumer boycott.[47] Although her fellow students and friends in the peace movement and expatriate communities understood the stakes in the farm workers' struggle, the average English consumer had a rather steep learning curve when it came to U.S. domestic politics, making it virtually impossible to generate the kind of mass support for a boycott that had been achieved in North America. Moreover, the absence of a British bill of rights with an amendment protecting free speech for individuals made Elinson and other potential volunteers vulnerable to prosecution (and in her case deportation) for telling customers not to buy grapes.[48]

Elinson quickly figured out that social justice for farm workers could flow more easily through the collective action of unionized laborers. Unlike in North America, where labor laws restricted allied unions from helping the UFW execute a blockade of shipments, in England unions had greater freedom to assist other workers. British labor leaders and union officials were particularly scandalized by the denial of collective bargaining rights to farm workers, a right guaranteed and defended by U.S. law for most other American workers. In this regard, Britain resembled Canada, where Marshall Ganz and Jessica Govea had cultivated alliances with leaders of organized labor who expressed their objections to the exclusion of farm workers from the National Labor Relations Act. Elinson's goals differed from those of Ganz and Govea, however, in that she appealed to British dockworkers to create a blockade against grapes reaching English shores rather than to participate in storefront picket lines.[49]

Elinson made it her business to become familiar with the Transport and General Workers Union (TGWU), the union representing dockworkers responsible for unloading ships carrying California table grapes. Given the presence in Delano of AFL-CIO representative, Bill Kircher, Elinson assumed she could obtain introductions to TGWU members through the European office of the AFL-CIO, the official sponsor of the UFW. In Europe, however, Elinson found the AFL-CIO icy; her attempts to contact either Irving Brown, the European representative, or Jay Lovestone, the international labor director, were futile. "My feeling is that the AFL-CIO might try to keep you from working with the radical anti-certain-aspects-of-American-policy-elements," Brown explained, "[because the] foreign AFL-CIO is lined up with all the conservative right wing forces and not with the people who are going to help us."[50]

Brown recommended working with Victor Reuther, Walter Reuther's brother, because of the UAW's historic support of the UFW. Reuther's frequent trips to Europe also gave the UAW credibility with both the TGWU and the more radical members of the Trade Union Congress (TUC), the umbrella British labor organization to which the TGWU belonged. "Our goal in London," Brown wrote Elinson, "is to have the dockers or the Transport Workers (TGWU) or the entire TUC refuse to handle a major shipment of U.S. grapes bound for England."[51] Postwar increases in U.S. imports, combined with consumers' growing rejection of South African grapes in protest against apartheid, made U.S. grapes prevalent in British markets and an appealing target for the union.[52] After a couple weeks, Brown secured Chavez's approval for Elinson to contact TGWU officials directly to circumvent the sticky labor politics that were holding up her progress.

Elinson's own initiative in contacting members of the TGWU proved to be the most important act in establishing relations with English dockworkers. Rather than start at the top of the organization with the general secretary, Frank Cousins, she appealed to Freddy Silberman and Reagan Scott, two writers in the Communications Department of TGWU responsible for reporting labor struggles within the union and beyond. Silberman wrote most of the stories for the union newspaper, *The Record*, and Scott served as editor. Elinson remembered, "Freddy was the first person to invite me into that building, which to me was like the fortress that I had to get into." Silberman was a Holocaust survivor, making his way to England with his family by way of South Africa. As a young adult, he had attended Cornell University, giving him an instant connection to Elinson. Silberman and Scott interviewed Elinson for a feature article on the UFW—the first of its kind to appear in the British press—that led to others about her and the farm worker movement in the *London Times, Manchester Guardian,* and *Telegraph.*[53]

Elinson simultaneously worked with fellow graduate students on labor issues, eventually making contact with Terry Barrett, a dockworker from the Isle of Dogs on the River Thames and a member of the Socialist Workers Party who organized demonstrations committed to achieving peace in Ireland and an end to the U.S. war in Vietnam. Barrett invited Elinson down to the docks to share the story of the farm workers and introduced her to fellow dockworkers at West India, Millwall, and Tilbury. A fiery speaker, he concluded every meeting with a pledge to Elinson: "The scab California grapes would be blacked [blocked] by the British unions—and we're going to start here and now!"[54]

Eventually, these dock appearances led to a formal invitation from William A. Punt, the fruit and vegetable markets section officer of the TGWU, to address a gathering of dockworkers at the main union hall in Covent Garden Market in the center of London. At a meeting of the general membership, Elinson stood before hundreds of dockworkers on "lunch" break at 7 A.M. as they cradled steaming hot cups of tea on a cold fall morning. Elinson's stories of child labor, poverty, and high rates of tuberculosis among farm workers evoked comparisons to *The Grapes of Wrath* familiar to some of the members. That the National Labor Relations Board in the United States did not recognize farm workers especially shocked the membership, who saw government recognition and the right to collective bargaining as fundamental to their own health and well-being. In response, Punt secured a unanimous vote from the floor to send a resolution to the TGWU and the TUC headquarters endorsing the strike and boycott, and a letter to the U.S. Embassy announcing their intention of cooperating with the UFW. The dockworkers also made a collection of funds to support Elinson and offered to take her out for a pint when the meeting concluded, but she graciously declined.[55] Elinson carried this momentum well beyond the London docks to other ports in England, including those run by longshoremen represented by the global union federation, the International Transport Workers Federation

(ITWF). In every case, dockworkers expressed a deep sense of solidarity with the farm workers and their intention to help Elinson enforce a blockade of California grapes throughout England.

Media coverage of Elinson's organizing and the TGWU's actions finally grabbed the attention of both AFL-CIO leaders and the U.S. government. Her growing influence over British transporters compelled U.S. Labor Attaché Thomas Byrne to contact AFL-CIO president, George Meany, to find out more about the twenty-one-year-old organizer working out of a dreary cold-water flat in North London. Given the European office's neglect of Elinson, however, Jay Lovestone could not attest to her character, forcing Meany to contact Bill Kircher in Delano. "The day your letter regarding the ITWF [support] arrived," Brown wrote to Elinson, "Bill Kircher received a call from George Meany asking who the hell you are." Brown's report to Kircher that Elinson was "a 'solid citizen' (read: not new-left)" allayed some of Kircher's fears and permitted him to communicate Elinson's good intentions to Meany.

Thomas Byrne conducted his own investigation, eventually inviting Elinson to the U.S. Embassy for a chat. Although a neutral party to the conflict, the embassy had tipped its political hand by working with the U.S. Department of Agriculture to distribute bulletins advertising California grape sales in Britain. TGWU porters responsible for work onboard ships responded to Elinson's appeal for cooperation by refusing to appear in publicity photos tied to the USDA campaign. Although the porters showed greater caution than the dockworkers in their endorsement of the boycott, their unwillingness to appear in the advertisement caused Byrne and USDA officials to worry about the extent of Elinson's organizing.[56] At their meeting, Byrne revealed the contents of a letter from Punt on behalf of Covent Garden transporters regarding Elinson's involvement in British affairs. Punt's statement of "hope that the members of our organization are not *obliged to use their industrial strength* to assist their American brothers and sisters" alarmed Byrne; he held Elinson accountable for this thinly veiled threat of labor action not sanctioned by Punt's superiors.[57] Although the meeting with Byrne indicated a level of surveillance by the U.S. government that made Elinson uncomfortable, the meeting also demonstrated progress in her efforts and gave her confidence that the "blacking" of all grapes from England was an achievable goal.[58]

Byrne's message of doubt regarding the TGWU's official position on the boycott signaled to Elinson and Brown the importance of securing a formal resolution from the union's governing council. Although porters and dockers demonstrated an inclination to cooperate, a contact within the union, identified only as "Willis," informed Elinson that the TGWU, by law, could not call for a blockade directly. Rather, he advised Elinson to push for the TGWU general council to "pass a resolution strongly endorsing the [UFW] strike and making the membership aware of it." This approach worked. By early December, Elinson's work with union officials, backed by formal appeals from Chavez and Reuther, produced an agreement by President Frank Cousins of the TGWU to bring the issue before the full body. "The job you are doing," Brown told Elinson, "really needs a 20-year diplomat, only you're doing better than that."[59] On December 22, 1968, Cousins released the official position of the TGWU: "The Transport and General Workers Union is advising its 1 1/2 million members to operate a consumer boycott of California grapes, and has written to the TUC suggesting that affiliated unions be encouraged to do likewise." According to Jack Jones, the executive secretary of the union, the TGWU chose to support the UFW because "they were not included within the legal protection that requires American employers to recognize a representative union, and we certainly want to do what we can to help them."[60]

News of the resolution thrilled the UFW back home and inspired collaboration with members of the International Longshoremen Workers Union (ILWU) in the United States. Although ILWU president, Harry Bridges, refused to endorse the strike and the boycott, many rank-and-file longshoremen showed their allegiance to the farm workers by deducting money from their monthly paychecks to support the UFW and conducting food and clothing drives for unemployed workers walking the picket lines. Two ILWU clerks, Lou Perlin in Los Angeles and Don Watson in the Bay Area, went a step further by sharing information from manifests of ships that were leaving the West Coast. "We are now working closely with the ships clerks," Brown wrote Elinson, "who are systematically checking at both San Francisco and Los Angeles [for the location of grapes]."[61] Brown also clarified the objectives for Elinson: "Our friends in the shipping industry here inform us that if we can stop one shipment (and cause all the legal, international, political problems that would involve), these shipping lines would simply refuse to take grapes to any European ports—it's as simple as that."[62]

In Britain, the resolution did not make the blockade a fait accompli, but it gave Elinson a powerful tool for organizing one. Resolutions and public speeches notwithstanding, the execution of the blockade depended on reliable dockside leadership and accurate information regarding the whereabouts of grapes located in ladings on the ship. Once again, Elinson turned to her rank-and-file allies along the docks to make the blockade a reality. At Covent Garden, she met Brian Nicholson, the head of the London docks and a member of the executive board of the TGWU. A veteran of the docks, Nicholson used his authority and imposing physical presence to bring the hustle and bustle to a screeching halt for Elinson to do her work. Elinson described the typical scene:

> With the bill of lading in hand, I went down to the London docks with Brian. We would approach the team of dockworkers working on that particular ship and that particular hold. The workers would put down their ominous looking dockers' hooks (a pointed piece of iron attached to a strong wooden grip, used to pull cargo off ships before containerization), and gather round this odd pair. Brian, a third-generation dockworker, 6'3", in a thick sheepskin coat and cloth cap, orange sideburns, and a booming Cockney voice, would introduce me. I came up to his shoulder, had a ponytail and big mod glasses. They could hardly understand my American accent. We both wore red-and-black UFW buttons on our jackets.[63]

Holding the bill of lading Brown had acquired from Watson and Perlin in Oakland, Elinson scoured the contents of ships with the "walking boss" of the dock to determine the exact location of the grapes. Such transatlantic solidarity between ILWU and TGWU members transcended the political posturing of union leaders and completed a network that effectively blocked 95 percent of the grapes from reaching British shores.[64]

In response, growers reacted as they had before: moving the grapes to another market, this time to Scandinavia. The union had anticipated this move, given Brown's extensive research on the quantity and location of exports, which showed that a majority of the 15 million pounds of U.S. grapes going to Europe went to the United Kingdom, the Netherlands, Sweden, Norway, Denmark, and Finland in 1966.[65] The line of communication with West Coast clerks helped update the destination and location of grapes not only for ships going to Liverpool and London, but also those headed directly to Scandinavia. In January, Brown learned that three ships—the *Brasilia*, *Aconcagua Valley*, and *San Joaquin Valley*—were now bound for Stockholm, Goteborg, and Malmo in Sweden, and another, the *Bolinas*, was en route to Norway.

Brown promptly dispatched Elinson to Sweden. She recounted the harrowing trip across the North Sea and her arrival in Stockholm during the dead of winter: "I threw my warmest socks and sweaters in a bag, bundled up a big batch of UFW literature, and bought a pocket Swedish dictionary and a second-class ticket to Stockholm. The trip by bus, train and ferry took 48 hours. It was January, and a heavy snow blanketed the Swedish land-scape. I was invited to stay in the home of an American war resister and his Swedish girlfriend who taught labor history at the university. I slept on the couch in their living room, and a floor-to-ceiling ceramic furnace kept us warm when the daily temperatures outside fell way below zero."[66] Elinson's host, Victor Pestoff, who had fled the United States to avoid the draft, now worked part time with the International Federation of Plantation, Agricul-tural, and Allied Workers (IFPAAW), a global agricultural workers' union in which the UFW maintained membership. With Pestoff's help, Brown managed to have his allies in the ILWU telex the ships' manifests indicating the location of the grapes to the IFPAAW office in the Netherlands, which then forwarded the information to Sweden.[67]

The union prepared for Elinson's arrival by calling in favors from new and old labor friends at home and abroad. Chavez sent a letter to Victor Re-uther, requesting his help in securing a proper welcome for Elinson from Swedish labor officials. "One of the problems we face in Europe," Chavez explained to Reuther, "is being recognized as a legitimate union that is sup-ported by the major unions like the UAW and the AFL-CIO in the United States." Chavez's message, of course, alluded to the ongoing trouble with the AFL-CIO European office and its failure to recognize Elinson as a represen-tative for the union. The UAW's departure from the AFL-CIO over politi-cal differences between Walter Reuther and George Meany in 1968 had given Reuther an opportunity to accentuate the union's leftist credentials among European unions that tended toward socialism, especially in Swe-den. Although Jay Lovestone courted more conservative leaders in Europe on behalf of the AFL-CIO, not everyone within the union agreed with him, especially Bill Kircher, who increasingly influenced Meany's thinking about the farm workers as the popularity of the boycott swelled on both sides of the Atlantic. For the UFW, UAW assistance in Europe could prompt a more committed response from the AFL-CIO, which had to worry about its pub-lic image and protecting its turf. At worst, the AFL-CIO would continue to neglect Elinson and offer only lackluster support for the boycott abroad.

Chavez's gamble worked. Victor Reuther responded by sending cables to his allies in the International Transport Workers Union in Sweden to request their cooperation in an extension of the blockade.[68] Reuther also directed

Virger Viklund, a representative for the Swedish Metalworkers Union attending a UAW meeting in Los Angeles, to visit Delano during his trip. Brown reported to Elinson, "Viklund was very interested in the strike and boycott and told me how Sweden had made a 100% effective boycott of South African grapes [to put pressure on the apartheid government]." Before leaving California, Viklund communicated his interest in supporting the UFW to Lars C. Carlsson, vice consul to the Swedish Consulate in Los Angeles, who called the Delano office to offer his help. Carlsson honored Brown's request to secure a formal invitation from the Swedish Trade Union Federation for Elinson and gave Brown contact information for transport workers responsible for unloading grapes throughout Scandinavia.

Elinson received a hero's welcome in Sweden. "The Swedish unions," she recalled, "were even more anxious to help—if that is possible—than the British ones."[69] The success of organized labor in Sweden to secure health care, pensions, educational funds, and job security produced a pro-labor public that was open to the appeals of the UFW. A burgeoning oil industry in the North Sea accounted for much of Sweden's collective wealth, and a spirit of generosity pervaded Swedish society that was manifested in a general willingness to participate in movements for social justice. "In a country as homogenous, liberal, and tight-knit as Sweden," Brown advised, "I don't think that we should discount the possibility of an effective consumer boycott."[70] The leading role Swedish consumers played in the boycotts against South African products to protest apartheid and peace demonstrations in the streets of Stockholm against the war in Vietnam informed Brown's advice. Chavez and Brown made overtures to the Swedish Food Cooperative, Kooperative Foerbundet, where 30 percent of Swedes did their shopping. They sent stories regarding the unsanitary conditions under which field workers labored to the Swedish Consumer Cooperative journal and magazine editors in hopes of spurring a boycott of California grapes.[71]

Yet for all the potential of a consumer boycott in Sweden, Elinson discouraged such talk, focusing primarily on work with the unions. The absence of a ready army of volunteers and the need for Elinson to manage several fronts from a foreign location made pursuing such a strategy impossible. Although Elinson spoke English, Spanish, Russian, Chinese, and French, she had little grasp of the Swedish language and depended on sympathetic journalists to communicate her message. When given the opportunity, she used newspapers to communicate directly to dockworkers. "Two boats, the Aconcagua

Valley and the San Joaquin Valley, have just been forced to change course and are now en route to Sweden," she told one reporter. Placing a finer point on her message, she added, "You must do the same thing as the English have done; otherwise things will never get straightened up back home."[72] Elinson reinforced her message by focusing her activities on convincing the Swedish transporters to support the blockade of grapes. She immediately made contact with Reuther's friends in the Swedish Trade Unions and the Transport Workers Union, securing an official tour of the main ports and the assistance of a translator. In response, the Swedish Trade Unions hosted a press conference to announce their support for the boycott, and the transporters directed her to Malmo, Sweden, in anticipation of the arrival of the grapes.

Ever conscious of both practicality and style, Elinson boarded the train for the southern port of Malmo, dressed in a brand-new pair of reindeer-skin boots—courtesy of the Swedish farm workers' union—heavy stockings, and a long wool skirt covered by a floor-length shawl. When she arrived, trade unionists, port officials, reporters, and TV cameras covered the docks. The lading crew had already taken the position that they would not unload cargo until Elinson could board the ship to ensure that the dockworkers did not remove boxes of grapes with the rest of the freight. The captain stood at the bow of the ship, arguing with the shop steward that all of the grapes had been unloaded in London. "Well then," the steward responded, "we are going on the ship, and you are going to show us there are no grapes in there." By union contract, the captain could not refuse the shop steward entry to the vessel, but he insisted that Elinson not come on board. Neither side would budge from its position.

As the standoff grew increasingly tense, snow began to fall on the port and families of the dockworkers refreshed the crowd with hot coffee and bread. National television captured the drama for all of Scandinavia to see, dividing time between scenes of the dock and a documentary film about the farm worker movement made by a Swedish filmmaker, Christian Stannow, two years earlier. Finally, with few options left and other cargo in jeopardy of not being unloaded, the captain conceded to Elinson's inspection of the refrigerated container. With the ILWU manifest in hand, she quickly located the grapes and set them aside for transporters to work around as they went about their business unloading the rest of the ship.

The events in England and Sweden had a ripple effect through northern Europe. True to ILWU predictions, the hard-fought victories on the docks of Liverpool and London led to a quicker public defeat of the growers in Sweden. News of Elinson's triumph spread ahead to the next potential ports of disembarkation for the grapes. Trade unions in both Finland and Norway issued public statements of their intentions to enforce the blockade too, while strong union ties in the Netherlands and Denmark suggested the futility of redirecting the rotting cargo to those countries. Finally, the ship sailed on to Hamburg, Germany, in late January in an attempt to salvage any profit from the much diminished shipment. Victor Reuther, who had played a role in her success, marveled at Elinson's ability to make the most of his contacts and invited her to meet with him during an international labor conference in Denmark. He honored Elinson by flying her to the conference from Sweden, a rare treat, given her meager budget and humble living quarters throughout the campaign. Elinson remembered her short time with Reuther fondly: "He was a wonderful teacher. White-haired and bearded, he had a patch over one eye, an eye he had lost to a policeman's gunshot at the great General Motors strike at Flint, Michigan in 1936. He tutored me in American labor history and introduced me to union representatives from all over the world."[73]

Elinson's success impressed union members back home, perhaps none more than Jerry Brown and Cesar Chavez, who used the news of the blockade to motivate strikers picketing California farms and boycott volunteers demonstrating in front of North American stores. "We can't begin to tell you how big what you are doing is," Brown reported to Elinson, "and how important it is at this time. You are single-handedly making a major contribution to winning this strike."[74]

For Elaine Elinson, such words of encouragement mattered in the darkest hours, when AFL-CIO leaders refused their assistance. She complained of the "sad and lonely business" of union politics and wondered out loud whether her time would be better spent back home. Brown empathized with Elinson, noting his own frustrations with AFL-CIO bosses: "Sometimes I wonder who our real enemy is." In the midst of the Swedish campaign, for example, the AFL-CIO refused to vouch for the validity of the farm workers union or its boycott, even after Elinson's success in achieving the blockade in Britain, precipitating letters from Reuther and Chavez to Arne Geijer, president of the Swedish Trade Union Federation. "It is better in Delano," Brown admitted, "more supportive and friendly and warm, so warm at times that you could cry to see how the strikers have sacrificed." Brown balanced such depictions with a sobering note to Elinson: "It is frustrating too, to realize that they are all just people with many selfish goals and petty jealousies."

Brown may have used such "grass is not always greener" messages to persuade Elinson to stay and fight in Europe. Following a tumultuous year in which the murders of Martin Luther King Jr. and Robert Kennedy and the police riot against demonstrators at the Democratic National Convention in Chicago challenged some activists' faith in nonviolence, Brown may have reached his own existential crisis. He wrote to Elinson, "Civil rights and the decennium of non-violence and brotherly marchers fade into the dusty song books of camp history and America is coming face to face with the hypocrisy of its own myths and untold realities." For him, service to the union was his small attempt to "act out a life with some dignity," although he wondered aloud how consequential, ultimately, their work might be. "Here we sit making the most anachronistic revolution of all," he confided to Elinson, "unionizing farm workers in the quicksand of a disappearing rural dream that will be gone tomorrow."[75]

Success in Europe showed organizers that victory was within their reach. Elinson returned to Delano in the spring of 1969, but the TGWU remained loyal to the UFW and the blockade the following year. Freddy Silberman maintained a file cabinet dedicated to the blockade in the TGWU office, allowing Elinson's replacements, Vivian Levine and Donna Haber, to pick up where she left off.[76] Haber cultivated a relationship with Dan Gallin, the general secretary of the International Union of Food and Allied Workers' Association in Geneva, Switzerland, who helped extend the blockade in Europe during the winter of 1969 and 1970.[77] Elinson remained close to her contacts in England, eventually moving back to London in 1974 to work for the UFW on another boycott. Her service on the front lines of the boycott changed Elinson's life. "It definitely was pivotal for me in terms of my political outlook, in terms of my ability to organize around issues that I really care about," she stated.[78]

WINNING BATTLES, BUT NOT THE WAR

The success of the boycott challenged the growers' strategy of a moveable feast, demonstrating that grapes could not be marketed beyond the reach of the union and the consciousness of consumers and allied workers. Jerry and Juanita Brown's new system, backed by Jerry's extensive research and the on-the-ground intuition of boycott house leaders, surprised the industry and catapulted the movement into an international spotlight. As the European campaign wound down for the season, Jerry prepared Elaine Elinson for a possible assignment to Venezuela, while the union made attempts to expand to Puerto Rico and Hawai'i.[79] The union also began to collect records of international sales in anticipation of the growers' attempt to reach beyond untapped markets in Latin American and the Pacific for the 1970 season.

Boycott workers also received important assistance from Jerry Cohen, who continued to pursue the names of pesticides used by growers. He appealed to two volunteers, a Protestant minister, Reverend Boutitier, and Mark Vasquez, to purchase grapes at Safeway and submit them to C. W. England Laboratories, the same one used by the supermarket chain for testing. During the boycott campaign in 1969, Cohen revealed the findings as part of a U.S. Senate hearing led by Senator Walter Mondale from Minnesota. The lab found evidence of aldrin, a toxic substance known to cause cancer in mice at levels exceeding the limits permitted by the government. Growers argued that sulfur, a nontoxic substance used in the fields, had triggered the positive reading. The ambiguity of the findings, however, raised suspicions among consumers, as did the growers' refusal to cooperate with the testing in the first place. When a pro-grower senator, George Murphy (R-California), accused Cohen of intentionally submitting false evidence, Mondale backed the union by sharing a letter from Safeway confirming the source of the test. Although the question of pesticides remained a contentious issue from that point forward, the union won the public relations battle in 1969 and boosted the confidence of those working on the front lines of the boycott.[80]

The stress of the boycott in 1969 and 1970 finally ruptured relations between Coachella and San Joaquin Valley growers. Once again, Lionel Steinberg took the lead, appealing to Monsignor Higgins to act as a mediator in talks with the union. In April, the two sides signed a contract covering all workers at Steinberg's David Freedman Ranch, the largest table grape farming operation in Coachella. Steinberg's neighbor K. K. Larson employed many of the same workers and asked the local Presbyterian minister, Reverend Lloyd Saatjian, to oversee a vote to unionize on his ranch. The results were overwhelmingly in favor of the UFW: seventy-eight to two. "Had the workers voted 'no' and the boycott been continued," Larson commented, "we'd have been out of business, and I think the workers knew that."[81]

The idea of ending the boycott for a select few while maintaining it for the vast majority of grape growers initiated a risky shift in strategy that threatened to undermine total unionization of the industry. The absence of labels on most table grapes made it difficult to enforce a selective boycott. In addition, the mixed message of continuing a boycott for some and not for others could potentially confuse consumers, who had an easier time observing a boycott of all table grapes. In Europe, Elinson's difficulty in locating grapes on ships among a diverse cargo proved taxing enough; adding the task of segregating union from nonunion grapes complicated things even further. "We were very nervous about signing with Steinberg," Ganz recalled, "because it wasn't clear that you could boycott some grapes and not others."[82]

These challenges required the now experienced hand of Marshall Ganz, who returned from Toronto to work with Steinberg and Larson's salesman, Steve Volpey, in the refrigerated warehouses run by Tenneco Corporation in Coachella. Rather than sort union from the nonunion grapes at the point of reception, as Elinson had done, they managed storeowners' demands for union grapes from the point of distribution. Ganz worked closely with Steinberg and Volpey, learning the grape market from the point of view of the grower. "We understood who was ordering grapes [and] we picked up information about who was ordering nonunion grapes [through] the grapevine, so to speak." This knowledge allowed the UFW to control the boycott through its network by punishing markets that carried nonunion grapes with picket lines while encouraging consumers to shop at stores selling union grapes. Steinberg and the union collaborated to the point of renting a room and adding a phone bank at the Stardust Motel in Coachella to serve as their headquarters. These strange bedfellows effectively split the market into union and nonunion grapes, producing a price differential that rewarded Steinberg and Larson, while punishing the holdouts in Delano. "In the union market," Ganz remembered, "it was like $1.50 or $2 a box more than in the nonunion market."[83] This distinction was also manifested in inventory, as Ganz recalled in vivid detail: "It was one of the most exciting moments in the union for me because I remember going into the Tenneco cold storage and Tenneco was shipping for a couple of the growers who had signed, but then others who had not. . . . And the nonunion [grapes were] stacked to the fucking ceiling, and the union [side] was empty. And it was like, 'Holy shit, this sucker's really working!'"[84] Along with his work on the boycott, Ganz served as a negotiator for new contracts, as Coachella growers, one by one, came to the bargaining table. By mid-July, the UFW had signed contracts with most of the Coachella growers, allowing the union to shift its efforts to the north.[85]

In the San Joaquin Valley, Ganz and the union worked the ethnic and class divisions among the growers to secure new contracts. As Ganz became more involved on the negotiation team, he began to recognize "both the growers' end and the workers' end; the whole industry was ethnicized." The union exploited this self-segmentation, as Ganz explained: "You really have to understand that about the industry to appreciate a lot of the dynamics, because on the growers' side, what it meant was there were these very tightly knit clumps, and they were very closed off and insulated from a lot of the world, which turned out to be a huge advantage for us."[86] These clumps also tended to be insulated from one another, a condition that became much more pronounced as the negotiation teams moved up the valley. Armenian Americans predominated in the south, around Arvin, and also shared the region around Fresno with Italian Americans. The Slavic American growers controlled much of Delano, although one Italian American, John Giumarra, owned the largest and most profitable ranch in the area. Other Italian American growers, such as Bruno Dispoto, maintained semiautonomous ranches, whereas most Japanese American farmers had small, independent farms thought to be inconsequential to the overall industry.

A team of union negotiators, including Dolores Huerta, Jerry Cohen, Gilbert Padilla, and Marshall Ganz, each assumed responsibility for a tile of this ethnic mosaic. Ganz followed the harvest, moving to Arvin first and securing contracts with the Armenian American growers. When the harvest started in Delano, the union used a combined approach of appealing to an outsider while respecting the importance of ethnic difference. "In Delano," Ganz remembered, "it was a Slavic deal." Yet Giumarra's success commanded the respect of the Slavic Americans and made him "so big, nobody could ignore him." After failed negotiations with all Delano growers in mid-July, the union ignored the tight-knit Slavic American growers in favor of working out a model contract with Giumarra that would bring most of the industry in line. "The deal with Giumarra," Ganz recalled, "was that we wouldn't sign with him unless he brought the whole industry."[87]

The union's strategy worked. In a predawn negotiation session at a Delano motel one week after the breakdown in talks, Cesar Chavez, Jerry Cohen, and Dolores Huerta worked out a final agreement with John Giumarra Sr. and John Giumarra Jr., who quickly called a special meeting at St. Mary's School in Delano to share the news with their peers. All twenty-six of the growers signed the historic pact on July 29, 1970, ending the five-year-long

Delano grape strike. The contract increased wages from $1.40 to $1.80 an hour and set field-packed box rates at 20 cents, down from 25 cents in 1965. The union secured the creation of the Robert Kennedy Health and Welfare Fund by extracting 10 cents an hour from the growers; they also deducted another 2 cents an hour for a new social service program. Finally, the union assumed control of the hiring process by establishing a hiring hall located at UFW headquarters in Delano; they also added protection against pesticides through new safety regulations.

Workers and allies of the farm workers union celebrated all over the world, thanks, in part, to the strong network that the Browns and the volunteers built. "All I can say," Jerry proudly remembered, "is that I think Juanita and I brought systematic support, research, and what turned out to be a winning boycott strategy." The strain of this work sent Jerry and Juanita into retirement from the union and Jerry back to graduate school, where he completed his Ph.D. dissertation. But the success of the boycott was a welcome departure from assassinations, police riots, and a turn toward violence by some activists that drained much of the hope away from the counterculture of the 1960s. In this respect, the boycott restored some faith in peaceful collective action and the viability of a social justice movement that brought rural workers and urban consumers together.

Yet for all its success, what the union had won was not entirely clear at the start of the new decade. The continued hiring of nonunion workers by small independent growers operating in the shadows of the table grape industry prevented the union from covering all workers on grape farms in California. Capturing the remaining 15 percent of the industry not covered by the contracts would have to wait, however, given the challenges of servicing the contracts. In truth, by 1970 the United Farm Workers Organizing Committee more closely resembled an "organization" rather than the "union" it now declared itself to be. The contracts required leaders to institutionalize the movement, establishing systems for managing the hiring halls, health clinics, and social services that members relied upon. With the acceptance of unionization, growers expected a level of professionalism that mirrored their own. Growers also learned that they needed to get beyond the ethnic and regional cliques that had defined the industry prior to the boycott. This new consciousness led to an expanded role for the California Table Grape Commission. It also led to new strategies in labor management that depended on unions but avoided complete subservience to them. Finally, although the contracts did much to inspire workers in other crops—most notably lettuce workers in the Imperial and Salinas Valleys—they also attracted greater scrutiny from disapproving politicians and competition from the Teamsters. These would be the challenges that awaited the United Farm Workers in the 1970s as the ground beneath the industry continued to shift.

FOUR

Stuck in the Middle

ON MARCH 30, 1972, the president of the International Brotherhood of Teamsters, Frank E. Fitzsimmons, entered the Oval Office to meet with President Richard Nixon. In a meeting arranged by the White House assistant Charles Colson, who would later do time in prison for his part in the Watergate scandal, the two men fell quickly into a freewheeling conversation lasting more than an hour. Captured on Nixon's now famous running recorder, the conversation included discussions of the president's pardon of Fitzsimmons's predecessor, James "Jimmy" Hoffa, the economy, and a shared philosophy of governance. Offering his vision of effective leadership, Fitzsimmons confided in Nixon, "Only one principle [has] carried me through all these years. . . . I never won an argument standing on the outside throwing a brick [and] I never represented my people properly by being on the outside when I couldn't be [on] the inside."

Nixon, experiencing a rare moment of trust in a labor leader, expressed gratitude toward "Fitz" for his candor and assured him that he understood how "[Fitzsimmons] must have caught hell from a lot of [his] colleagues" for his decision to meet. "Your decision [will] prove to be a good one," Nixon promised the Teamster boss. "I'm going to do my very best in our shop to see that this comes true."[1] Through the remaining months of Nixon's troubled presidency, Fitzsimmons enjoyed an open line of communication, which afforded him unparalleled influence on labor and economic policy. Such access proved decisive not only in determining the fortunes of the Teamsters, but also in shaping the direction of the farm worker movement and the new economy of the 1970s.

At first glance, Fitzsimmons's presence in the Oval Office seems unusual, given Nixon's notorious rants against organized labor. The spring of 1972, however, was no ordinary time for either man. The Vietnam War had severely compromised U.S. credibility in the world, while domestic protests had placed Nixon in a precarious position going into his reelection campaign. To make matters worse, Nixon had entered office at a moment of mounting economic turmoil that had reached a peak in 1971, with U.S. exports shrinking, unemployment climbing, and prices of food and durable goods at an all-time high. Economists used the term *stagflation* to describe the dilemma: price inflation without continued growth in the economy. The weakened state of the nation seemingly played into the hands of organized labor leaders, who looked for ways to mobilize the righteous indignation of the working class against a pro-business Republican president. No one wanted to unseat him more than Cesar Chavez and the United Farm Workers, who had fought Nixon during the 1968 campaign and tussled with him throughout his first term.

Frank Fitzsimmons, however, felt no solidarity with his labor compatriots, least of all Chavez. Although the farm workers counted the Teamsters as early allies of the movement, the relationship had turned progressively sour the more success the farm workers enjoyed. As early as the fall of 1970, the Teamsters attempted to expand their contracts covering employees in food processing and warehouses to include field workers in Salinas, California. These actions preempted the UFW's plans to move from grape workers in Coachella and the San Joaquin Valley to the new challenge of organizing lettuce workers in the salad bowl of Salinas. George Meany, president of the AFL-CIO, successfully averted all-out war between the two by convincing Fitzsimmons to leave field workers to Chavez. Fitzsimmons, however, flouted the agreement in 1972 and invited grape growers to sign with the Teamsters, effectively replacing UFW contracts set to expire the following year. Taking advice from Nixon's undersecretary of labor, Laurence Sibelman, Fitzsimmons addressed growers at the annual convention of the American Farm Bureau Federation on December 12, 1972. In a speech in which he chided Chavez for leading a "revolutionary movement [that] is perpetrating a fraud on the American public," Fitzsimmons called for an alliance between the Teamsters and the farmers.[2] During the 1973 spring harvest, Fitzsimmons followed through, signing contracts with grape growers and initiating a fight that plunged California rural communities into two years of bloody conflict.

The Teamsters' actions illustrate one of the major ironies of agricultural unionism in California: the union that proves it can organize farm workers invites more, not less competition from competing unions.[3] The rise of the National Farm Workers Association on the heels of the AWOC strike represented a similar phenomenon, but with a much more amicable solution that produced the UFW. Unlike AWOC and NFWA, however, inequality in size, wealth, and experience distinguished the Teamsters from the fledgling UFW. The Teamsters represented the largest number of employees in the country during the early 1970s, whereas the United Farm Workers confronted the daunting task of converting a protest movement into a bona fide union. Chavez and his young organizers also had to manage the expectations of field workers in other crops and other states who appealed to them to organize their workplaces. For a well-oiled machine like the Teamsters, adding such tasks constituted a relatively minor challenge that promised to pay dividends in the form of more dues-paying members. Ironically, by signing grape contracts in 1970, the UFW became a victim of its own success.[4]

Labor theories and unrealized union dues notwithstanding, Fitzsimmons's move on the UFW at such a crucial moment in the history of California farm labor organizing represents an especially divisive act that defies easy explanation. The level of violence alone that Teamster representatives committed against UFW organizers signaled Fitzsimmons's extraordinary dedication to destroying the United Farm Workers at any cost. Through outright physical intimidation, the Teamsters attempted to quite literally beat the UFW into submission. That was the experience of Alicia Uribe, a committed *Chavista* (UFW supporter) who picketed against the hiring of scab workers in Coachella Valley during the 1973 season. Reporting for *Rolling Stone* magazine, journalist David Harris shared Uribe's story: "'Los Teamsters,' the woman next to [Alicia] said. As the word jumped from ear to ear, the pickets began shouting and waving their red and black flags. . . . Making a sudden skip on the loose dirt, the car swerved right and one of the [men] in the back window leaned out and laid a pair of brass knuckles along the side of Alicia Uribe's head. Ever since, her face has had a little dent to it. The blow fractured Alicia's cheek, broke her nose and dug a scratch across her right eyeball."[5] As such violence became the norm, Cesar Chavez used his now famous hunger strikes to quell the urge for retaliation among his followers, although nothing and no one seemed to quell the Teamsters' rage. As Chavez fasted, solidifying his reputation as a paragon of nonviolent protest, local families endured a decade of trauma. Meanwhile, within the union, debate raged about how best to repel the Teamsters and capitalize on the momentum of the grape boycott.

The roots of such chaos reside in the seemingly cosmic convergence of events that worked against the farm workers during the first half of the 1970s from forces within and outside of the union. The unique economic circumstances inherited by Nixon inspired a Faustian pact with Fitzsimmons that made the UFW's goal of organizing all California field workers under the banner of the black eagle more difficult, if not impossible. Yet to say that the actions done *to* the union, not *by* the union, precipitated such struggle ignores important errors in judgment by UFW leaders, especially Cesar Chavez. Chavez grew increasingly frustrated with the dissonant advice coming from all corners of the union, as some of the most seasoned organizers came home from the front lines of the boycott to negotiate contracts, manage hiring halls, and organize new workers. Rather than draw valuable lessons from the learning community that the union had become, Chavez began to show signs of addiction to the boycott and his own power.

THE GREAT TREASON

In the years prior to the grape contracts, the Teamsters had shown faint interest in organizing field workers. Their one success story came before the founding of the UFW in 1961, when the union included field workers in contracts covering packers and haulers working for lettuce grower, Bud Antle. An anomalous arrangement, the contracts turned out to be an excuse for the Teamsters to invade Salinas in 1970. Before the ink had dried on the grape contracts in Delano, the Teamsters built on this unlikely beachhead by arranging contracts with sixty other growers. The move by the Teamsters put a damper on the UFW celebrations and required Chavez and other union officials to relocate to Salinas immediately. Speaking to a sea of angry lettuce workers, Chavez called the Teamsters' moves "a great treason against the aspirations of men and women who have sacrificed their lives for so many years to make a few men (growers) rich in this valley."[6] Chavez punished the growers by reprogramming the network of forty-two boycott houses to wage a new campaign against lettuce.

The Teamsters' decision to move into the fields after 1970 grew out of a number of circumstances, not the least of which was that the United Farm Workers had proven that farm workers were worth the time and effort it took to organize them. By August 1970, the United Farm Workers claimed 12,000 grape pickers in its membership and garnered a considerable number of donations and positive publicity from the success of the grape boycott. Still, the size of the membership paled in comparison to the Teamsters' 1.9 million members. The West, however, constituted an important area of growth in the United States as people and industry continued to relocate from the industrial Northeast to the warm weather and the right-to-work states of the Southwest. The rise of the Sunbelt promised a shift in the balance of power in the Teamsters' empire. Not a union to miss out on any opportunity, no matter how meager the spoils, the Teamsters' representative Bill Grami eventually negotiated contracts covering 9,000 lettuce workers with 170 growers from Santa Maria to Salinas without surveying the wishes of employees.[7]

The campaign by the Teamsters to usurp the farm workers' momentum failed as a consequence of poor planning and ill-tempered behavior on the part of Teamsters representatives and skillful political maneuvers on the part of Chavez and the UFW leadership. The Teamsters tried to bully their way into the lettuce fields, at one point beating Jerry Cohen unconscious and attacking Jacques Levy, a writer who would later document the farm workers' struggle in his book *Cesar Chavez: The Autobiography of La Causa*.[8] Newspapers captured the brutal act on camera, creating a public relations nightmare for the Teamsters and establishing their reputation for violence.

Even when the UFW lost in court, Chavez still managed to find a way to capitalize on his popularity. In December 1970, Bud Antle won an injunction against the boycott, which forced Chavez to appear before Judge Gordon Campbell to answer how he intended to end the boycott. At the hearing, Chavez defiantly refused to call off the picket lines and inspired a local crowd of 3,000 supporters to "boycott the hell out of them" as authorities took him away in handcuffs. His incarceration touched off several days of continuous protest in Monterey County, including a twenty-four-hour vigil in front of the jail, prayers and a mass held in downtown Salinas, and public visits to Chavez by the recently widowed Coretta Scott King and Ethel Kennedy. The barrage of negative publicity and the chaotic conditions in the county finally persuaded Judge Campbell to release Chavez on Christmas Eve, twenty days after putting him behind bars.[9]

The struggle in Salinas proved to be a prelude rather than an apogee in the fight against the Teamsters. Cohen succeeded in convincing the courts that the Teamsters had created a "company union" to preempt the UFW from organizing lettuce workers. In their decision, the six California Supreme Court justices acknowledged that a precise number or percentage of field workers favoring the UFW could not be reached, but agreed that a majority preferred the United Farm Workers to the Teamsters.[10] The court order cleared the injunction against the boycott, and public opinion swayed Fitzsimmons in mid-March 1971 to leave the organization of field workers to the UFW. George Meany, who had been lukewarm in his support of the Salinas campaign, brokered the deal in Washington, far from the front lines of the battle. In California, however, the UFW's difficulty in building an effective infrastructure continued to fuel Teamster hopes of one day replacing the farm workers union.

In the days following the grape contracts, the task of fending off the Teamsters competed with the UFW's need to establish control over the hiring process of field workers, a responsibility that the young union now assumed. During the grape strike and boycott, Chavez frequently inspired farm workers and activists to think beyond the constraints of the seasons, encouraging them to organize for social change because "the wheels of justice do not move as fast as nature grows grapes."[11] Chavez's observation is useful for understanding why the union placed so much importance on establishing hiring halls in the 1970 contracts. By the time pickers organized in a given location, the grape harvest had moved on to another location, allowing growers (and their foremen) to dictate who would work and under what conditions. The United Farm Workers created hiring halls with the belief that a network of union-controlled clearinghouses for selecting workers would lead to a more just system of employment. The UFW attempted to end the cycle of migration that challenged workers' ability to sink roots into local communities and develop year-round networks that union officials presumed would strengthen the hand of labor at harvest time across multiple growing regions of the state. Under such a system, grapes could grow at any rate nature and modern agricultural science dictated; in theory, the workers would be organized and ready to deal with the harvest on their own terms.

This type of labor organizing, however, butted up against deep-rooted and, in some cases, culturally bound practices among a significant portion of the workforce. Many workers adapted their lives to a cycle of migration that not only spanned the area of the grape harvest in California but, in some cases, extended across state and national boundaries. In addition to field workers who followed the grape harvest from Coachella through the San Joaquin Valley, some workers came from surrounding states. Filipino workers, in particular, established migratory patterns that involved work in the fishing industry in Alaska, traveling down through Puget Sound and into Washington, then taking field work in apple orchards in Washington, and eventually harvesting a variety of crops in California during the summer and fall. For example, before serving as the first vice president of the UFW, Larry Itliong traveled up and down the Pacific Coast, working on ships and in docks in the fisheries of Alaska and in a variety of crops, including asparagus, lettuce, and grapes in Washington, Oregon, and California. Such migrations were common among Filipino migrants, many of whom came from Luzon, in northern Philippines. Frequently referred to as Ilocano, based on their ethnolinguistic group, these migrants came from a heavily agricultural region that helped define their identity. As in much of the early Mexican and Chinese migrations, single men dominated the initial Filipino migration to the agricultural districts of California.[12] Similarly, Mexican immigrants with experience in agriculture traveled across the U.S.-Mexican border; some had even participated in the bracero program from 1942 to 1964. Joining these populations were a sprinkling of Yemeni immigrants, Puerto Rican migrants, and Texas Mexicans (Tejanos), whose expertise in agriculture came in handy in the fields of California. All of these migrations complemented—and at times competed with—the settled Mexican American, black, and poor white populations that dominated the inland valleys of California.

In the wake of the 1970 contracts, the United Farm Workers confronted the challenge of managing this heterogeneous and far-flung population of workers. The rhythms of the harvest and the entrenched practices of acquiring labor assignments complicated social relations, producing tension among workers who sought solidarity across cultural divides. Although Filipinos and Mexicans found themselves in a similar position in terms of the hierarchy of class and race in California society, they maintained different approaches to organizing labor and migration. As the union settled on the formation of hiring halls to act as clearinghouses for labor on the grape plantations, it encountered difficulties that threatened its ability to sustain the movement.

Philip Vera Cruz, vice president of the UFW from 1966 to 1977, later acknowledged the struggle over the hearts and minds of the Filipino workers: "The Filipinos have been used and pulled back and forth by the UFW, the Teamsters, and the growers for many years."[13] To his dismay, Vera Cruz witnessed the departure of several Filipino leaders from the organization, including Ben Gines, who belonged to AWOC in 1966 when it merged with the mostly Mexican National Farm Workers Association to create the United Farm Workers Organizing Committee. Vera Cruz recalled: "At the time of the merger, I counted about seven Filipinos who went with Ben [Gines] over to the Teamsters. Of course, it was like the tip of an iceberg.

You see, later on, when the UFW made mistakes in the Hiring Hall about dispatching jobs, and some Filipinos felt they weren't being treated fairly, many of them switched over to the Teamsters."[14] Gines ultimately found the Teamsters equally incompatible and left union organizing altogether to pursue a career in watch repair.

The resignation of Larry Itliong on October 15, 1971, was the most painful defection from the UFW, given the timing and his position in the union. Itliong had served as the leader of the original 1965 AWOC strike in Delano and maintained the closest contact with the AFL-CIO representative at the time, Al Green. Perhaps the most experienced and radical labor organizer among the leaders, Itliong conceded the leadership of the United Farm Workers Organizing Committee to Chavez largely because the majority of the farm workers were Mexican. Itliong assumed the position of assistant director of UFW but never settled comfortably into his role. During his tenure, he offered his resignation or threatened to resign several times over disputes concerning the union's failure to reimburse his expenses, the growing distance between UFW leaders and the rank and file, and the union's unwillingness to address issues related to Filipinos, especially the lack of support for aging Filipino farm workers.[15] In the wake of his resignation, Itliong explained his decision to his friend Bill Kircher: "I left at my own accord because of many reasons. But my biggest disappointment is that the Organization I participated in to fight for Justice and Dignity is not turning [out] as planned. So I had to go in order to save my reputation (insignificant as it may [be]) and my conscience. Do you know that since my leaving[,] the Delano office has lost its appeal ... its liveliness and that people working in the offices seem to be doing their work only because they are told that's what they should do and not because they wanted to do it. ... Many of the workers around here, Filipinos and Chicanos, are very unhappy on how the Union is being operated."[16]

Vera Cruz and Itliong disagreed privately on the issue of strategy, and the two maintained a tense relationship throughout their years together in the union.[17] Yet for all their differences, they shared many of the same concerns. Both worried about the aging population of Filipino workers and where these men would live once their time as farm workers had passed. They both vigorously advocated for the construction of Agabayani Village, a retirement home for UFW workers; Itliong worked on behalf of this population through the Filipino American Political Association, a bipartisan organization created

FIGURE 10. Dolores Huerta and Larry Itliong, ca. 1970s. ALUA, UFW Collection, 197.

to lobby on behalf of Filipinos among lawmakers in Sacramento and Washington, D.C. Both also felt the sting of being a minority within a union run by minorities.[18]

The complaints of Mexican dominance, however, constituted just one of many factors that shaped the Filipino defections. For a worker interested in the ability to feed himself and send money back home to his family, the issues of contract management and fairness in work assignments loomed even larger. Vera Cruz, Itliong, and Gines understood this, and all commented on problems of managing the contracts, with Vera Cruz specifically citing problems with the hiring halls. These complaints resulted less from ethnic rivalries than from management concerns that skewed the hiring process in favor of settled, mostly Mexican American farm workers living in the San Joaquin Valley. These biases developed in part out of a desire to curb itinerancy in farm work, but they also reflected a degree of inexperience that plagued the union in the months immediately following the signing of the grape contracts.

Cesar Chavez had little experience running a union, and the mismanagement of the hiring halls, in particular, became an issue not only among growers who scrutinized every move of the young union, but also among some of the rank and file who expected fairness in work assignments. Doug Adair, a longtime UFW farm worker and a veteran of the Philadelphia boycott, worked at the Freedman and Tenneco plantations in Coachella at the beginning of the contracts. Adair recalled the difficulty in getting the halls started: "The first contracts, we didn't know what we were doing. We'd never been there before. We had no idea."[19] Although a seemingly mundane issue, how the hiring halls operated became the Achilles' heel of the UFW when it came to fending off the Teamsters.

The UFW organizer Reymundo Huerta arrived in Coachella in 1971 from the front lines of the grape boycott in Los Angeles amid disputes regarding work assignments and the management of the local grape contracts. A small but vocal minority sought to establish local control over the new hiring system, whereby workers showed up at the tiny hiring hall in Coachella to receive their work dispatches. Chavez reassigned Huerta to assist Marshall Ganz, who was trying unsuccessfully to quash the rebellion and shore up local support for the union. Although Huerta arrived thinking he would serve Ganz for a "few days," he soon discovered that he, not Ganz, would remain in Coachella to manage the hiring halls.[20]

Conflict developed when the workers themselves resisted the UFW organizers. According to Huerta, "We had to enforce the contracts not only with the companies, but also with the workers because they didn't know too much about contracts either." These efforts included tutorials on the requirements of the contract and translation of documents into Spanish. Although this helped allay the concerns of many Mexican workers, Filipino workers continued to show resistance to the new system. Referring to these workers as "disgruntled," Huerta explained the Filipino reaction: "In the process of us enforcing the contracts, a lot of the Filipino workers were offended because they didn't hold any seats of power in the union, although there were Filipinos in the union. There was a whole bunch of them. These guys didn't want to accept that, a lot of them. So they kind of resisted."[21] According to Adair, the union elections, which eventually took place in 1973, proved the Filipino dissatisfaction with the UFW: "The Filipinos began peeling off. And then I think in the elections here, probably 70 to 80 percent of the Filipinos voted against [the UFW]."[22] The feeling of losing ground within a union dominated by Mexican workers contributed to their discord.

In Huerta's opinion, these conditions predisposed the Filipinos to supporting Teamster overtures, which, in turn, led to their defections from the UFW.

A coworker of many Filipino farm workers, Doug Adair believed that the radical transformation in the Filipinos' working and living conditions under UFW contracts accounted for much of the discord among them. Under AWOC in the 1960s, prior to the formation of the UFW, foremen controlled the hiring of their pickers, and some, especially Filipino foremen, managed their crews like a family. Adair recalls the conditions under the first contracts: "In the first contracts, the Filipino foreman was part of the unit. Many of these crews were very tight around the foreman. They were relatives. They were from his province. They were like his family. They moved from the grapes to the asparagus and from here to there as a unit. And the foreman would loan them money."[23] Prior to 1970, workers had to pay dues year-round because the union paid insurance annually. Consequently, workers accumulated substantial debts in the off-season as a result of unpaid dues that some foremen covered for their employees when workers traveled back home or moved on to work in other regions. Filipino workers established significant ties to the Northwest, whereas Mexican workers traveled in all directions, including east to Texas and south to Mexico, for work or to visit family. In either case, a good relationship with the foreman allowed for a degree of job security, as Adair recalls: "The foreman, if he was a good foreman, gave them a little bit of benefits that they could be sure of. If they'd gone to Seattle or somewhere and they got back a little late, he made sure there was a bed in the camp for them. He got them into the crew."[24]

The UFW, however, insisted on the formation of hiring halls as an equitable solution to a system that frequently favored growers over workers. For the Filipinos, an aging, mostly male minority population in a labor pool dominated by Mexicans, the loss of power among the foremen gave them some cause for concern. Under this new system, Filipino foremen could no longer hold jobs for co-ethnic workers who came to expect such privileges. Adair observed, "To get their jobs, instead of going to . . . whoever had given them a job before, they had to go to the union and stand in line with all the Mexicans and they finally get to the window and there aren't any jobs, or not at *that* company." Their disappointment drove many to support the Teamsters. According to Adair, "There were reasons—good reasons—why they preferred the Teamsters' system."[25]

The Teamsters exploited this tension by imposing a system that returned power to the foremen. The restoration of hiring and firing privileges to the foremen reestablished a sense of continuity for mobile workers from one season to the next. The hiring halls, on the other hand, tended to benefit the local, sedentary populations of workers, which did not sit well with more itinerant laborers. Adair explained how the system worked: "You had a friend of your neighbor, a cousin of your *compadre*, and the word would get around: 'There's going to be dispatches tomorrow.' You are here. You are local. You are there in line; you get them. And the guys from Texas come in and [the hiring hall worker would say]: 'No, you're a day late. We gave that to the dispatches yesterday.'"[26]

For many migrant workers who lived hand-to-mouth and often traveled with a family, the irregularity of the dispatches made it impossible to wait around for the next assignment. The growers and foremen complained because they had grown accustomed to hiring workers as they needed them, with no regard for the structure of a union. Foremen demonstrated an immediate preference for the Teamsters' approach and shared this sentiment with migrant workers dissatisfied with the new system. Adair again: "The worker would go in and if he didn't get the job, then the foreman would say: 'I would have hired you but the union doesn't [allow it].'" In addition to Filipinos, a significant number of Mexicans traveling from Texas opposed the system, because they too found it difficult to negotiate work assignments in California from a distance.[27] These problems cut across racial lines, although, because of the unique relationship many Filipinos had with Filipino foremen and because Filipinos constituted a minority within the union, their defections drew more attention from growers who wanted to point out the waning support for the UFW.[28] Mexicans who traveled from Texas and, increasingly, Mexico also expressed frustration with the UFW's system of hiring.[29]

This disgruntled minority continued to give the Teamsters a reason to plot against the United Farm Workers. Although in 1971 Fitzsimmons agreed to leave these workers alone, the Teamsters held contracts with warehouse workers, packers, and haulers in California agriculture, placing them in close proximity to farm workers. As a consequence, the Teamsters continued to agitate against the UFW, flaunting the benefits of belonging to the strongest and richest union in the nation. In appealing to potential members, Teamster officials liked to point out that the union's benefits package rivaled that offered by the farm workers union, including fewer limits and costs related to medical procedures, a greater range of services, and no age or amount limits in payments to survivors of fallen workers.[30] For some, the

Teamsters offered superior services that served as a reminder that alternatives existed.

Cesar Chavez also contended with serious complaints from within the movement, including criticism of his decision to relocate union headquarters to a mountain resort in Keene, California. Although initially Chavez treated the former tuberculosis sanitarium rented to him by a wealthy movie producer as a place of respite, by 1971 a deal was struck to purchase the 280-acre plot and its buildings and rename the site La Nuestra Señora de la Paz, or La Paz. Soon after, Chavez moved most union operations off the valley floor and into the Tehachapi Mountains, where former farm workers and volunteers alike could learn to become "union professionals." Chavez converted the decrepit facilities into the nerve center and training ground for the union and reduced "Forty Acres" in Delano to a field office.

Chavez cultivated a commune-like atmosphere at La Paz, which appealed to many volunteers invested in the counterculture, although it did not sit well with some union stalwarts. The population at La Paz fluctuated between 100 and 150 mostly white or Mexican residents who came for a month to a year to be a part of the experience. Residents lived in drafty and occasionally cramped living quarters, but few felt they could complain given the terrible conditions farm workers had to endure.[31] For white volunteers like Melanie Coons working the picket lines in Los Angeles, going to La Paz was like a "journey to Mecca" and produced a reverence for Chavez that overshadowed other leaders: "The minute you meet [Chavez], you just know he's special, he's so patient and forceful at the same time."[32] For those like Itliong, who preferred that the union stay in touch with farm worker families in their communities, La Paz placed unnecessary distance between the leaders and the rank and file in and around Delano.

As white boycotters moved to La Paz to work and live, the changing ethnic composition of the movement fueled additional anger. For Itliong, the aging of the mostly male Filipino population within the UFW, coupled with his years of service to a mostly Mexican and Filipino membership, accentuated his feelings of betrayal. He publicly questioned Chavez's reliance on what he derisively referred to as "the Anglo Brain Trust," particularly the service of young white (and Jewish) volunteers such as Marshall Ganz and Jerry Cohen. Although these people had no connection to the corporate world, their participation in the union as managers of contracts and service centers signaled for some a move away from the grassroots. The presence of the Teamsters, who employed salaried, professional organizers, introduced a model

FIGURE 11. Jerry Cohen, head of the legal department for the United Farm Workers, testifies before the U.S. Senate Subcommittee on Labor, Washington, DC, date unknown. ALUA, UFW Collection, 3365.

that contrasted sharply with a UFW volunteer system dependent on the dedication of many young activists. The increased reliance on attorneys and doctors also ignited a debate within the UFW about whether this system could adequately compensate those who had more lucrative, "professional" opportunities outside of the union. Regardless of the National Executive Board's decision to pay some and not others, competition from the highly experienced Teamsters required the UFW to become more organized in their delivery of services.

As the UFW moved toward greater professionalism, Chavez made no excuses for the trend away from "a minority-oriented union." His position remained constant, even when questioned about his loyalty to the ethnic Mexican base of the movement. "Now the union has a Chicano thrust," Chavez admitted to a reporter, "but that will change as we spread to other areas." For him, the struggle constituted "an economic movement by poor workers" that transcended issues of race and ethnicity. In making this point, Chavez, perhaps unwittingly, promoted a class-first, color-blind philosophy, proclaiming, "A poor black worker in Florida hurts me as much as a poor Chicano worker in Texas." His inclusion of and dependence on middle-class white volunteers, however, complicated his claims of leading a movement "by poor workers," a fact his critics were only too happy to point out.[33]

Conflicts over boycott strategy signaled a more immediate danger to unity within the movement. The first wrangling about strategy occurred between the UFW and the AFL-CIO, over a campaign against Heublein Inc., a wine and liquor company based in Hartford, Connecticut. From the UFW's point of view, Heublein's incorporation of United Vinters, a subsidiary invested in smaller California grape growers not under contract with the farm workers, made them fair game for a targeted boycott. George Meany disagreed. The number of farm workers working for Heublein subsidiaries paled in comparison to the overwhelming number of unionized distributors in the AFL-CIO–affiliated Brewery Workers Union employed by the company. As a consequence, Meany refused to back the boycott and made his displeasure with the UFW well known in the media. Although it took the union and Heublein less than two weeks to reach an agreement, the conflict over the use of the boycott demonstrated that not all in the UFW's corner agreed with the strategy.[34]

Chavez's commitment to the boycott also altered the union's philosophy regarding the inclusion of workers under the National Labor Relations Act (also known as "the Wagner Act"). In the years leading up to the 1970 contracts, advocates for UFW, including Chavez, used the exclusion of field labor from the NLRA as evidence of the federal government's neglect of farm workers. This argument more than any other compelled dock workers in Europe to execute the blockade requested by Elaine Elinson. As Chavez realized the power of the boycott, he privately shifted his position regarding farm workers' inclusion in the NLRA. He was particularly concerned about the restrictions against secondary boycotts for workers covered by the NLRA as a result of the Taft-Hartley Act of 1947. For these reasons, he publicly lamented the exclusion of farm workers from collective bargaining rights but privately relished the freedom to use the boycott whenever and wherever he saw fit. Chavez's true feelings became public once the UFW had gained legitimacy and growers, legislators, and competing unions had become much more serious about extending the act to cover farm workers after

1970. As growers and politicians began to warm to the idea of extending collective bargaining rights to farm workers, in part to limit the UFW's use of the boycott, Chavez became protective of the tactic and more skeptical that recognition from employers and the state would be the panacea everyone imagined.

Lettuce farmers were the first growers to advocate for the inclusion of farm workers in the NLRA. They had watched with horror how the boycott had devastated the grape growers' profits and feared that the new boycott against lettuce would have the same effects on their product. Mike Schultz, an El Centro lettuce grower and vice president of the Western Growers Association, offered the first signs of change among growers who had famously fought against the Wagner Act during the 1930s. In 1971, Schultz secured a commitment from his peers to seek federal legislation to bring farm workers under federal labor laws and added that they would also support a state-level "little Wagner Act." "We have just decided to be realistic about the situation," Schultz announced, "and [will] try to bring our industry into the 1970s."[35] In truth, growers understood that the laws governing labor organizations, if extended to farm workers, would deny Chavez the boycott, the tactic they feared most. The Teamsters, who had learned to thrive within the parameters set by the Taft-Hartley Act that included a restriction against secondary boycotts, also endorsed the inclusion of farm workers under national or state labor legislation and went to great lengths to highlight Chavez's change of heart on this matter.[36]

Growers and the Teamsters demonstrated that they had become wise to what fueled the movement by adopting a strategy that would potentially short-circuit the UFW's growth. These tactics included the Teamsters' use of the boycott *against* the UFW during their failed struggle in 1971 to sign lettuce workers in Salinas to Teamsters contracts. As with the large corporate grape growers (like DiGiorgio and Schenley) who had agreed to contracts long before their family-owed peers, United Fruit Company's Inter-Harvest division and S. S. Pierce Company's Pic N' Pac sued for peace with the UFW by agreeing to contracts on their lettuce farms in Imperial Valley during the 1970–71 season.[37] The deal with InterHarvest, in particular, precipitated the Teamster boycott, as Ganz remembered: "We were striking in Salinas, and we were boycotting Chiquita [another subsidiary of United Fruit Company], and after a week, [InterHarvest] signed." United Fruit's president, Eli Black, the liberal Jewish mogul who would become famous for his 1975 suicide plunge from a Manhattan skyscraper after being exposed for corruption and bribery in Honduras, became a supporter of the union, attracting the ire of the Teamsters and growers alike. Ganz recalled that Black's agreement in the midst of the lettuce boycott "blew the growers away in Salinas" and produced, in Ganz's words, "anti-Semitic shit that came out for a long time."[38] To punish both Black and the UFW, the Teamsters appealed to wholesalers in Los Angeles and San Francisco not to unload "boycotted" lettuce coming from InterHarvest farms in an attempt to sway the company to cancel its contracts with the UFW. Although the Teamsters had limited success, the act contributed to a growing confusion among consumers about which products to boycott. The UFW's decision to start and stop boycotts in grapes and lettuce and its many threats of boycotts against melons, grapes, lettuce, and citrus growers, not to mention wine and liquor producers, began to confuse consumers.[39]

Growing tension with Governor Ronald Reagan and President Richard Nixon, both Republicans, posed perhaps the most serious check against the UFW's strength. Although Reagan and Nixon had a competitive relationship, they shared a pro-grower position when it came to farm labor politics. During their election campaigns, both politicians took a strong position against the UFW and openly advocated for growers' rights to market their products free from the constraints of a secondary boycott.[40]

Reagan campaigned against the boycott in New York City during the development of Dolores Huerta's "hostage store" strategy and used the power of the podium to deny the existence of a boycott even in the face of substantial evidence to the contrary.[41] When the boycott's reality could not be denied, Reagan famously took to the television airwaves to eat grapes in a show of solidarity with growers.[42] As the clock ran down on the industry after Steinberg and his Coachella peers agreed to sign contracts in 1970, Reagan reversed his opposition to unionization by advocating for secret ballot elections on each farm in hopes of stalling the movement. The governor failed in this and his advocacy for California Senate bill SB40, which, if passed, would have instituted secret ballot elections and restricted unions from using the secondary boycott. Reagan repeated this act in 1972 by supporting Proposition 22, an initiative heavily funded by the growers to place limits on the secondary boycott. The union campaigned against the initiative, and voters responded by soundly defeating it, 57.9 to 42.1 percent.[43]

Reagan also used the power of the purse to punish farm worker families by scaling back on social programs, such as California Rural Legal Assistance (CRLA), an organization designed to alleviate inequalities within the countryside. Founded in 1965 as part of Lyndon B. Johnson's War on Poverty, CRLA provided poor farm workers free legal assistance in labor disputes. Although the nonprofit agency was nonpartisan, the cases it accepted skewed toward support of a farm worker union. In fact, Jerry Cohen, the head of the UFW's legal department in Salinas, left the agency in 1967, ironically because he found it too tepid in its support for the downtrodden.[44] When Imperial Valley growers criticized CRLA for giving the UFW an unfair advantage in labor disputes, Reagan pulled the plug on the agency's funding, vetoing its $1.8 million budget in 1971.

For the most part, however, Reagan distinguished himself by not intervening during moments of conflict in the war between the UFW and the Teamsters. The California secretary of state and Reagan's Democratic successor, Edmund "Jerry" Brown, criticized him for allowing a "bloody civil war" to rage in rural communities by not resolving the legal "no man's land" farm laborers found themselves in: exempt from federal and state labor laws regulating labor relations. Reagan's inaction in rural California contrasted sharply with his campaigns to end antiwar demonstrations and violent rebellions in urban California, most vividly illustrated during his terms as governor by the kidnapping of Patty Hearst and the bank robbery by the Symbionese Liberation Army in Berkeley, the bombings by the antiwar group Weather Underground in San Francisco, and the gun battles between the Black Panther Party and police on the streets of Oakland. Reagan failed to take a similar interest in protecting the rural poor from violence, even when it resulted in the death of farm workers. However, his message "to clean up the mess in Berkeley" and "send the welfare bums back to work" struck a chord with a suburban, white electorate worried about the violent turn in the counterculture and the cost of urban social programs.[45]

As president of the United States, Richard Nixon found himself dealing with a greater range of economic problems that denied him the luxury of seeking refuge in issues-oriented politics that fed Reagan's popularity. Unlike his California Republican contemporary, to remain in office Nixon could not depend solely on white homeowners' resentment of the urban poor and anger toward radical youth. A member of a national Republican Party still committed to a degree of bipartisanship, Nixon had not fully embraced an emerging, conservative ideology promoted by those on the right who laid the problems of the United States primarily at the feet of those who advocated for government programs. The vagaries of a slowing economy, not to mention the continuation of the Vietnam War, required Nixon to engage labor organizations and experiment with economic policies in an attempt to solve the growing trade imbalance between the United States and the world while creating a foundation for his reelection in 1972. His maneuvers to dismantle the United Farm Workers and empower agribusiness in the name of economic recovery demonstrated how far he would go to achieve his goals.

TAKING CARE OF BUSINESS

Nixon assumed office during a period in which U.S. economic stability had begun to falter for the first time since the Great Depression. During the immediate postwar period, the relative strength of the U.S. economy helped the world economy back to health. By the 1960s, however, U.S. consumers' taste for imports diminished a balance of trade surplus enjoyed by U.S. manufacturers, eventually leading to a trade deficit in 1971, the first time in the twentieth century. The trade imbalance put less money into the federal budget as manufacturers' profits stagnated or declined even as prices on goods continued to rise.

The new trade imbalance and the failures of U.S. manufacturers to improve efficiency tempered the Nixon administration's expectations for an economic recovery completely, or even primarily, based on manufactured goods. By 1971 the United States needed to generate a $13 billion turnaround in the balance of payments to eliminate the trade deficit. The rise of Japan and West Germany, however, augured a new world order in which the United States would have to exploit all of its advantages in order to reignite its economy and maintain the value of its currency. Agriculture constituted an area of nearly unparalleled strength in global markets and a sector of the economy that could be expanded through exports. Although not a new idea, the context and purpose of agricultural exports changed in the 1970s. In the past, the United States shared its bounty with the world to help win wars and nurse allies and conquered nations back to health. Now agriculture would be used to return the United States to economic supremacy.

As the first president from California, where food production played a prominent role in the state's economy, Nixon understood the profit-making potential of agriculture. In 1973, agriculture accounted for one-third of the jobs in California and better than half of the Golden State's accumulated wealth.[46] Nixon confirmed the importance of agriculture nationally in the Flanigan Report, a 1973 Council on International Economic Policy task force study headed by his friend and trusted advisor Peter Flanigan.[47] In the report, Flanigan vigorously argued for a significant expansion of farm exports by lowering government subsidies for wheat and feed grains, allowing the free market to dictate trade. He believed that such a policy would lower the cost of these items and increase their export to countries such as the Soviet Union, China, and Japan. The reduction in trade barriers, Flanigan argued, would pressure trading nations to import more U.S. agricultural goods, raising U.S. farmers' incomes by approximately $4 billion. In negotiations of new trade policies with Europe, Japan, and Canada in 1973, Flanigan's report figured prominently in the position advanced by the United States. "From our point of view," Flanigan reported, "it is especially important that these negotiations include trade in agriculture. Our goal needs to be the fullest possible liberalization of policies with regard to agricultural trade."[48]

Nixon sought to achieve his goals under a New Economic Policy (NEP) that included a government freeze on prices and wages and tax cuts for businesses and individuals.[49] For big agriculture, NEP exempted unprocessed agricultural commodities and inputs in the production of farm products from price regulation. Such conditions allowed profit margins to rise on raw agricultural goods and led to the administration's goal of expanding agricultural output faster than domestic consumption of food. The new surplus in agricultural products could now be traded internationally. As an incentive, food processors and retailers were restricted from passing along price increases to American consumers, but they did not have to abide by these same regulations on exports. Consequently, NEP encouraged domestic food producers to sell in foreign markets where higher profit margins could be realized. U.S. agribusiness quickly took advantage of these favorable terms by selling more of their products abroad, improving the trade surplus on agricultural goods from $1.56 billion in 1972 to $10.53 billion in 1974.[50]

The administration's plans depended on the containment of labor unions. Some advisors within Nixon's administration predicted that the freeze on wages would invite criticism from labor groups and precipitate organized demonstrations. George Shultz, one of Nixon's chief economic advisors and secretary of labor in 1971, predicted, "A freeze will stop when labor blows it up with a strike." Nixon tried to head off such criticism by establishing the Pay Board and inviting labor leaders such as AFL-CIO president, George Meany, and Teamsters president, Frank Fitzsimmons, to participate. Meany declined the invitation, although he initially acceded to the popularity of the price-and-wage freeze. The administration's decision to deny raises negotiated before implementation of NEP to 1.3 million workers eventually moved Meany and two other prominent labor leaders, Harry Bridges of the International Longshore and Warehouse Union and Leonard Woodcock of the United Auto Workers, to publicly oppose the president's wage-and-price-control program.

Nixon took an especially aggressive posture toward the United Farm Workers. During his first term in office, as the boycott began to gain strength and inspire new legislation in Congress, Nixon stymied liberal reforms in 1969 at the last minute by working with the pro-grower senator from California, George Murphy, to submit an alternative proposal that would have limited harvest-time strikes, prohibited secondary boycotts, and instituted a three-person farm labor relations agency to oversee union representation elections and monitor labor relations generally.[51] Nixon accompanied these maneuvers with a dramatic increase in U.S. military purchases of table grapes for soldiers fighting the war in Vietnam. The Defense Department's purchase of grapes rose from 7.5 million pounds in 1966 and 1967 to 16 million pounds in the first year of Nixon's presidency. The federal government also encouraged South Vietnam to import more fresh grapes, increasing their consumption from 350,000 pounds per year in 1967 to 2.8 million pounds in 1969. Such purchases elevated Vietnam to the world's third largest importer of grapes and inspired union criticism of Nixon for artificially creating "a market of last resort" for struck grapes.[52]

In 1972, at a time when the UFW threatened to go national, it signed a contract with the Coca-Cola Company to represent Florida citrus workers picking fruit for use in its Minute Maid orange juice. The Nixon administration responded by suing to place the union under the restrictions of federal labor statutes, including restrictions against secondary boycotts. UFW supporters responded by flooding the National Republican Committee office with more than one million protest letters. Although the administration eventually backed down in response to negative press, Nixon's actions secured his reputation with farm worker advocates as an enemy of the farm worker movement.

Nixon attempted to counter the negative press and neutralize labor's opposition by courting the favor of Teamsters' president Frank Fitzsimmons. As the union representing more workers than any other in the nation, the Teamsters constituted a primary target for Nixon's divide-and-conquer strategy. He began by commuting the jail sentence of ex-Teamster president, James "Jimmy" Hoffa, on December 23, 1971. Nixon assuaged Fitzsimmons's concern that

Hoffa would try to regain the presidency of the union by making Hoffa's release conditional on his agreement not to participate in the union for ten years. Fitzsimmons benefited from the perception that he had negotiated Hoffa's release, while the restriction on Hoffa's involvement in the Teamsters strengthened Fitzsimmons's hand in the fight to maintain control. Nixon's preferential treatment of Fitzsimmons solidified his loyalty to the administration and forged a mutually beneficial relationship. The frequent meetings with the president earned Fitzsimmons the reputation among Nixon's advisors as "our man" on matters pertaining to labor. Their relationship enabled Fitzsimmons to contain the farm worker movement that threatened to derail Nixon's plan to increase agricultural profits.[53]

Fitzsimmons's investment in Nixon was both political and self-serving. He had risen to the Teamsters' presidency with the approval of Hoffa, who, according to union insiders, "treated [Fitzsimmons] like a gopher or a servant."[54] Six years Hoffa's elder, Fitzsimmons had allied himself with the charismatic labor leader while working as a truck driver and serving as a shop steward for two dozen fellow workers at CCC Trucking Company in Detroit. In 1937, Hoffa, recently elected president of Teamsters local 299 in Detroit, embraced Fitzsimmons as a member of his cadre of loyal supporters. Fitzsimmons's deferential nature may explain why Hoffa chose Fitzsimmons to replace him when he went to federal prison in 1967. Hoffa apparently confused style with substance and assumed that his old friend would do his will until he completed his sentence and returned to the union presidency. Fitzsimmons, however, surprised many by choosing to ignore Hoffa's instructions from behind bars. Instead, he consolidated his power as president of the Teamsters by assigning more autonomy to his vice presidents, hiring staff on the basis of nepotism and political patronage, and cooperating with the president of the United States in exchange for influence and favors. These favors included not only the restriction against Hoffa's involvement in the union, but also a pullback on federal investigations of Teamster-mob schemes under Fitzsimmons's watch.

The investment in Nixon paid its greatest dividends during an FBI investigation into possible relations between the mafia and Fitzsimmons. The controversy became known to the public on April 29, 1973, when the Justice Department rejected an affidavit by FBI director, L. Patrick Gray, to continue electronic surveillance of People's Industrial Consultants, a shell business for mafia operations in Los Angeles. The FBI believed that members of the Los Angeles and Chicago crime syndicate had negotiated a deal with Fitzsimmons to siphon $10 million a year from the union's pension fund. Between golf tournaments in Palm Springs and La Costa, California, Fitzsimmons met with mafia figures, including Chicago mobster, Lou (the Tailor) Rosanova, on February 12, 1972. According to an anonymous FBI agent, Fitzsimmons approved of the scheme during this meeting. The following morning, Fitzsimmons drove the short distance from the Teamsters-supported La Costa Country Club in Carlsbad, California, to El Toro Marine Air Station near San Clemente, where he boarded Air Force One and accompanied Nixon on the six-hour cross-country flight back to Washington. No record of what Fitzsimmons and Nixon discussed exists. Within months, however, the FBI surveillance of the Teamsters-mafia relationship ended, and on July 17, 1972, Fitzsimmons announced the Teamsters' endorsement of Nixon for reelection.[55]

The suspension of wiretapping demoralized the FBI and ended an investigation of the mafia and Fitzsimmons, allowing Fitzsimmons to escape prosecution and leaving unanswered many questions regarding the scheme and the motivation of the Justice Department.[56] The decision of Attorney General Richard Kleindienst so angered FBI agents working on the case that someone in the Bureau leaked the contents of the investigation to the *New York Times* reporter Denny Walsh. Although Walsh and other reporters pursued the case, the nation's preoccupation with the events of Watergate forced the story from the headlines and eventually out of public consciousness. Walsh labeled the scandal "the lost story of Watergate," but media and government attention became so overwhelmed by the Watergate break-ins that neither pursued an investigation of the affair.[57]

Fitzsimmons also contributed gifts of cash to Nixon and his aides, both directly and indirectly. Along with the 1972 endorsement, Fitzsimmons asked all Teamsters vice presidents and organizers to give $1,000 to Nixon's campaign, while he personally gave $4,000. According to Steven Brill, author of *The Teamsters*, sources close to Allen Dorfman and Tony Provenzano, both Teamsters officials convicted of corruption, revealed a scheme in 1973 to have approximately $1 million siphoned off from Las Vegas casinos—a growing area of influence for the Teamsters—and redirected to Charles Colson, Fitzsimmons's primary sponsor within the White House. Colson allegedly approached Fitzsimmons first in 1971 about the transaction in hopes of securing funds for the 1972 campaign.[58] *Time* estimated that the Teamsters ultimately contributed $1 million dollars toward Nixon's reelection campaign.[59] In 1974, as the Watergate scandal intensified, Fitzsimmons contributed $25,000 from Teamsters' coffers to an anti-impeachment group. By that point,

Colson had left the White House but had not yet been indicted for his role in the cover-up involving the Watergate break-ins. That year, Fitzsimmons moved the legal business of the Teamsters, worth approximately $100,000 per year, from the law firm of Edward Bennett Williams, the prosecuting attorney in the lawsuit against the Watergate burglars, to one employing Colson.[60]

Nixon and Fitzsimmons's collaboration came at the expense of the Teamsters' rank and file, whose dues not only financed the extravagant lifestyles of union officials but also funded the third and most serious breach of an agreement to leave the organization of field workers to the UFW. The replacement of UFW grape contracts in 1973 initiated a bloody war in rural California, as farm worker volunteers attempted to defend their turf with picket lines in the fields. Although Coachella growers, Steinberg and Larson, chose to renew their contracts, most of the other grape growers defected to the Teamsters. The Teamsters prepared for UFW challenges by funding a mercenary army that carried baseball bats, knives, and whatever else they could put their hands on to drive *Chavistas* from the field.

The "Battle of Coachella" opened perhaps the most tumultuous season in rural California since the 1933 cotton strike in the San Joaquin Valley and the 1913 wheatland hop riots in Northern California. The assault on Alicia Uribe on April 16, 1973, was followed by scores of violent attacks that traveled with the harvest. In Coachella, growers such as the Gimmian brothers and Milton Karahadian aided the Teamsters by supplying grape stakes, clubs, baseball bats, and pieces of irrigation pipe to use against UFW picketers. These attacks spilled into places of business, where Teamsters encountered picketers such as Father John Banks, who had come to the desert to show his support for the farm workers union. Teamster, Mike Falco, recognized the Catholic priest and punched him in the face, breaking his nose. In nearby Mecca, another Teamster, Johnny Macias, recognized farm worker, Silverio Torres Madrid, in a local market, followed him out, and beat him with a two-by-four. Throughout the valley, Teamsters patrolled the lonely rural highways, looking for familiar UFW faces. On one particularly violent day, June 26, 1973, Teamsters found and beat Marshall Ganz unconscious, ran down UFW representatives, Bill Encinas and Alfredo González, and punched them through their car window, forced a carload of picketers driven by UFW volunteer, Michael Drake, off the road, and attacked a UFW picket line at a grape ranch, sending several UFW volunteers to the hospital. At one point, the Teamsters became so indiscriminate in their violence that they mistook allies for enemies. Riverside County sheriff's deputies arrested two Teamsters, Guadalupe Tamez of Santa Ana and Guadalupe Sausedo of Salinas, when they mistook Israel Guajardo, a foreman at Maag Citrus Company, for a UFW member. Tamez and Sausedo were charged with attempted murder and kidnapping for running Guajardo off the road near Mecca, pulling him from his car, and stabbing him six times with an ice pick. In another embarrassing case, Teamsters accosted Murray Westgate, a Las Vegas publicist who had been hired to improve the image of the Teamsters. The Teamsters physically removed him from the Morocco Motel in Indio, kicked him into the parking lot, and told him to "get out of town."[61]

Violence occurred on both sides, with UFW supporters burning down storage facilities and cars and, at one point, striking Western Conference Teamster representative, Bill Grami, in the head with a rock during one of his visits to Indio. Manuel Chavez, Cesar's cousin who had done hard time in prison, encouraged aggressive behavior by UFW affiliates by ordering them to work with INS agents to stop undocumented immigrants from entering the labor pool and block the flow of scab laborers into the fields. Yet the occasional acts of arson or the apprehension of undocumented immigrants did not compare with the daily incidents of violence committed by the Teamsters. To ensure that UFW actions did not escalate, Cesar Chavez fasted and encouraged volunteers to participate in civil disobedience by resisting a new grower injunction against picketing. "We had over 3,000 people arrested that summer," Jerry Cohen recalled, "because you could get arrested in this state by violating an unconstitutional injunction."[62] Although these acts played well in the media, they did nothing to deter the Teamsters.

Neither did the UFW's actions please the AFL-CIO, whose leader, George Meany, had grown cold toward Chavez. In addition to his opposition to the campaign against Heublein, Meany questioned directing the boycott at supermarkets that employed AFL-CIO–affiliated meat cutters and retail clerks whose livelihoods suffered as a consequence of the UFW picket lines. Chavez's shifting position on the inclusion of farm workers in the NLRA also baffled Meany, leading to a deafening silence from the national labor leader as the battle raged on in the desert. When asked by the media whether the AFL-CIO would support the UFW in its time of need, Bill Kircher, a longtime farm worker supporter and liaison for the AFL-CIO, responded, "No. We can only subsidize organizing committees."[63]

The cost of maintaining the strike and boycott during the first two months of the 1973 grape harvest forced Chavez to seek an infusion of cash from the AFL-CIO, an organization that had granted the UFW an independent charter the year before. In anticipation of the harvest in the San Joaquin Valley, Chavez made an overture to Meany that was followed by a formal invitation to Washington, D.C. to discuss the role of the AFL-CIO in the battle with the Teamsters. At the meeting, Chavez defended his commitment to the hiring halls and the boycott but focused his attention on securing strike funds for the ongoing struggle against the Teamsters. Meany took umbrage with Chavez's go-it-alone approach, but ultimately decided to provide monetary support for the farm workers. At a news conference, Meany announced, "The Council voted in the next three months to give Mr. Chavez $1,600,000 to try to help him conduct an effective strike against the most vicious, strike-breaking, union-busting effort that I've seen in my lifetime on the part of the Teamsters." For this support, Meany expected Chavez to accept a legislative solution once the struggle had ended.[64]

The continued threat of violence and the AFL-CIO's renewed support brought Chavez back to the negotiating table with grape growers in an attempt to avert a blood bath as the season moved north. The new boycott of grapes did little to shame the Teamsters, but it remained a powerful tool against growers. Although the AFL-CIO remained dubious about the tactic and the union now juggled several tasks along with maintaining a network of boycott houses, the boycott managed to force wholesale prices down and move more table grapes into cold storage or to raisin and wine production. The lettuce boycott never really succeeded in getting off the ground; however, the experience of boycotting grapes and the public's memory of the first grape boycott allowed the union to achieve a degree of success.[65] For example, the new grape boycott did not quite achieve the low price of $3.19 per lug of grapes in 1969, but it did succeed in knocking it down from $7.44 in 1972 to $4.60 in 1973. Coachella growers not carrying the union label took the brunt of the losses, from a total profit of $3,705,000 for all varieties in 1972 to a deficit of $3,322,000 in 1973.[66] Both the losses and the violence in Coachella foretold a possible scenario in the San Joaquin Valley, one growers wished to avoid if at all possible.

Once again John Giumarra Jr. became the primary negotiator on behalf of growers in a new round of talks with the UFW. Giumarra had become extremely disenchanted with the hiring halls, at one point bringing his own crew down to Delano, jumping behind the counter, and dispatching his own workers to his farm.[67] His frustration with the process led him to the contracts with the Teamsters, but the violence brought him back to the bargaining table with the UFW.

Jerry Cohen, who oversaw the negotiations with Giumarra, believed that, despite his problems with the hiring halls, "Giumarra was ready to sign with [the UFW]."[68] According to Cohen, the growers—especially those who had learned from the first boycott experience—saw the union as "an economic problem" that they wanted to remove as quickly and efficiently as possible. Giumarra entered negotiations in 1973 looking for two things: to resolve the hiring hall problems effectively and to avoid a repeat of the 1969–70 public relations nightmare. On the hiring halls, Chavez and his team negotiated in good faith, admitting that the struggles with the Teamsters in lettuce and the newness of being a union had caused them to make mistakes. Privately, the union acknowledged that their dependence on one staff member, Richard Chavez, to administer the contracts had been "a huge factor" in creating disorder in Delano and displeasure among grape growers in the San Joaquin Valley. "When you look at the administration of the grape contracts," Cohen explained, "you've got to look at where the talent went." Chavez shifted the most skilled organizers to Salinas, leaving a vacuum of leadership in the grape fields of Coachella and the San Joaquin Valley. As a consequence, most of the negotiating team offered convincing remedies to the hiring halls and reached a tentative agreement on reform of the system without scrapping it. As Cohen remembered, however, "Cesar never bought into [the agreement]" forged by his negotiating team.[69]

Chavez's doubts about the agreement crystallized into open hostility when he introduced another issue: sexual relationships between Filipino male workers and prostitutes. On the verge of a settlement, Chavez surprised his colleagues and Giumarra by breaking into a rant against "whores in the camps" that derailed the negotiations. Chavez had heard of prostitutes frequenting Filipino men in their off hours and demanded that Giumarra do something to prevent it as a prerequisite for signing a deal. Giumarra pleaded ignorance, which enraged Chavez, who became intransigent despite appeals from his negotiating team to relax. "That's one of the first strange things Cesar does," Cohen remembered, "when he jump[ed] around and said, 'we have to deal with whores in the camps!'" Cohen called for a break in the negotiations to calm Chavez down and get him to refocus on the issues at hand, but Chavez refused to listen to reason. Cohen recounted the conversation: "[I said] 'What the hell was that?!' And, you know, [he] started bitching, 'You don't understand this, Jerry. I do. We have to deal with whores in the camps.' I said, 'These are single, old Filipino guys; leave them alone. Leave them alone! What the hell does it have to do with us?'"[70] Chavez never offered an explanation for his tirade beyond the cryptic assertion that he knew best, and others, such as Cohen, did not. Perhaps he thought the new strike funds from the AFL-CIO would lead to a better deal with the growers if he prolonged the strike. Perhaps he had become obsessed with the trouble of retaining and controlling Filipino farm workers within the union. Regardless, his position sank the deal with Giumarra, extended the strike, and led to a long, hot, murderous summer in the Central Valley.

UNION SUBSTITUTION

The grape contracts of the 1970s were a wake-up call for lettuce growers, who became the first growers to switch from union-busting tactics to a new strategy of "union substitution," replacing the United Farm Workers with the Teamsters as the union representing their employees.[71] Although the negative product identification with lettuce was a harder sale to the public, the UFW's success in popularizing unions as a solution to injustice on California farms neutralized the old tactics of aggression against labor organizing in the fields. Lettuce growers dealt with the stigma of being anti-union by embracing a union that would do business with them: the Teamsters. Unlike the UFW, the Teamsters looked at field workers as new dues-paying members who would contribute to the wealth of the union. The Teamsters' rejection of hiring halls appealed to growers weary of turning over such responsibilities to a union bureaucracy.

Union substitution succeeded in shifting the struggle from the UFW versus the growers to a battle between two unions. In this context, the growers appeared to the public as hapless victims of an internecine labor war that had little to do with them. To the general public who had participated in the early boycotts, the announcement of victory in 1970, coupled with growers' acceptance of unions, made it appear as though the farm workers had won their battle. Few consumers distinguished one union from another, even with the negative publicity generated by the Teamsters. With Hoffa out as president, the problems of the Teamsters appeared to be behind them. The new boss, Fitzsimmons, had been embraced by Nixon, a president who, in 1972, won an election in a landslide and still had credibility with the public prior to full exposure of the Watergate scandal. Moreover, the public understood little about the virtues of hiring halls versus foreman selection in the hiring process, nor did they see the purpose of boycotts that seemed to start and stop within a period of several months in 1972. Like the Stealers Wheel's hit song of that year, growers seemed to be stuck in the middle between the UFW and the Teamsters, who were unable to work out their differences for the benefit of the workers.[72]

The success of the union substitution strategy among lettuce growers quickly spread to grape growers, especially in the wake of the failed negotiations with Giumarra. Rather than renew the contracts, grape growers substituted the Teamsters for the United Farm Workers just as the lettuce growers had done earlier in the season.[73] By 1973, the United Farm Workers, despite its success in 1970, had lost a majority of its contracts and teetered on the brink of collapse.

For their part, Fitzsimmons and the Teamsters saw the success of the farm workers as yet another opportunity to usurp the momentum of the grape boycott and take over representation of farm workers. This approach to labor organizing was not aberrant behavior for the Teamsters, but rather a long-standing organizational strategy for growth. From the 1930s through the period of Hoffa's leadership in the 1960s, the Teamsters had demonstrated a commitment to expansion into sectors of the economy that adjoined their base of short-haul drivers. In the 1930s, they expanded from organizing drivers in the cities to cross-country haulers. Under Hoffa, the Teamsters branched out to cover warehouse workers, forklift operators, and packing shed employees, whom Teamster drivers encountered in storage facilities. The contact between Teamster packers and warehouse workers and nonunion field workers encouraged the next phase of their expansion. Similarly, employers, although resistant to unions in general, were partial to the Teamsters when push came to shove over the unionization of their field workers because they knew the Teamsters through their presence in packing sheds.[74]

Why Fitzsimmons broke his pact with the UFW can best be explained by the changing economic conditions, his friendship with Nixon, and the politics within the Teamsters. Nixon's New Economic Policy, with an emphasis on increasing agricultural exports, signaled the expansion of the agricultural workforce. The Teamsters saw in these developments an increase in the number of possible dues-paying members, a fact that was not lost on Einar Mohn, head of the Western Conference of Teamsters, who infamously commented in 1973, "We have to have them in the union for a while. It will be a couple of years before they can start having membership meetings, before we can use the farm workers' ideas in the union. I'm not sure how effective a union can be when it is composed of Mexican-Americans and Mexican nationals with temporary visas. Maybe as agriculture becomes more sophisticated, more mechanized, with fewer transients, fewer green carders, and as jobs become more attractive to whites, then we can build a union that can have structures and that can negotiate from strength and have membership participation."[75] Mohn's comments reveal the cold business logic of the Teamsters. The merits of the farm workers union as a social movement were minimal; the real value in their success was the potential for an organized (and white) workforce as agriculture matured with NEP. In the short term, the mostly Mexican workforce under Teamster control would cost the union little in the way of services, while bringing in $8 per member in dues each month. Such dues contributed to the wealth of the Teamsters under Fitzsimmons. The very public drive to organize new workers and contributions to the Western Conference of Teamsters promised to shore up Fitzsimmons's strength in the West and counter any threats among loyal followers of Hoffa in the Central and Eastern Conferences.

Chavez's refusal to reach a settlement with Giumarra played into the hands of the Teamsters. When the fight came north, the violence escalated, given the heavy-handed approach of law enforcement officials in the Central Valley compared to Riverside County sheriffs in Coachella. On June 28, Kern County sheriffs arrested twenty to twenty-five Teamster members for attacking a UFW picket line at the Kovacavich Ranch. The assault sent four UFW volunteers and farm workers to Kern General Hospital, including sixty-two-year-old Juan Hernández, who suffered a fractured skull. Such occurrences happened with greater frequency and involved firearms, as growers began to feel the effects of the strike and boycott. On August 1, an unidentified assailant shot UFW striker, Joe Moncon, in the right shoulder at Tudor Vineyard in Delano. Just ten days later, another unknown gunman opened fire on a UFW picket line at Missakian Ranch in Kern County, wounding two. Kern County sheriffs did not make an arrest in either case. Finally, the conflict turned deadly on August 14, when a striker, Nagi Daifullah, an immigrant from Yemen and a UFW member, suffered a fatal beating at the hands of Kern County sheriffs as law enforcement officials scuffled with UFW protesters on a picket line in Lamont. Two days later, on August 16, an armed strikebreaker shot and killed Juan De La Cruz, a sixty-year-old veteran of the movement from Arvin who was picketing at Giumarra's vineyard. The carnage of the summer spurred the National Executive Board of the union to call a halt to the strike while Chavez engaged in another fast to draw union members' attention away from acts of retaliation. The murders also triggered an impromptu funeral march by 7,500 UFW members and supporters, which was covered by reporters and filmmakers from across the nation.[76]

Although the march inspired new volunteers to join *la causa* and garnered public sympathy at a critical time for the union, the missed opportunity to achieve a new contract with Giumarra earlier in the season must have weighed heavily on the conscience of those involved in the failed negotiations. If Chavez had used the excuse of "whores in the camp" to squelch a deal with the grape growers in an attempt to capitalize on the economic pressure of the strike and boycott, the death of two farm workers and numerous injuries suffered by scores of volunteers must have led him to doubt his own tactics. Whether Chavez acknowledged these links, others within the union did, prompting some to question his executive abilities. As the fight with the Teamsters wore on and the decision to accept a legislative solution to achieving collective bargaining rights for farm workers loomed in the near future, such questions continued to grow.

In 1974 the Teamsters engaged in their most aggressive and expensive assault on the United Farm Workers. Fitzsimmons set aside more than $100,000 a month to fight the UFW and an additional $1 million for the establishment of a new local in Salinas Valley. On the ground, coordinators from the Western Conference of Teamsters in Burlingame, California, worked with farm workers in Salinas to organize lettuce workers. In typical Teamster fashion, the union usurped the name of a successful but short-lived movement of local workers associated with the AFL-CIO in 1965: the Agricultural Workers Organizing Committee. The new AWOC hoped to attract the support of workers for contracts already negotiated by the Teamsters. Even before the campaign began, the union had 308 contracts with growers who hired about 50,000 workers in the peak season. Conversely, at the beginning of the 1974 season, the UFW had fewer than a dozen growers still under contract and fewer than 10,000 members.[77]

The tumultuous years of 1973 and 1974 brought results in the farm labor battle that neither group expected or perhaps wanted. The Teamsters' naked aggression against the UFW in Coachella discredited the organization in the eyes of both workers and the public. Moreover, their attempt to change their image from a union that had contempt for Mexican workers to one that valued them proved to be too steep a curve. Within a year, many of the original Mexican American organizers hired by the Teamsters were fired, and the union lost credibility with the rank and file, never to be regained.[78] For the United Farm Workers, the conflict stretched their budget beyond its limits and confused consumers about the purpose and target of the boycott.

That the Teamsters never fully succeeded in organizing field workers mattered little to Fitzsimmons or Nixon. In spite of their personal failures as leaders, both men succeeded in achieving the goals each set for himself at the beginning of their relationship. Nixon succeeded in strengthening the hand of agribusiness over laborers and winning Fitzsimmons's support for his economic policy. Although Nixon's forced resignation due to the Watergate scandal denied him an opportunity to see the full implementation of his policies, the decade witnessed a decisive expansion in agricultural exports. In 1983, the Congressional Budget Office reported, "Today, two of every five [U.S.] acres produce for world markets, making exports a critical part of U.S. agricultural sales."[79] For his part, Fitzsimmons successfully neutralized Hoffa's challenge to his presidency, avoided prosecution for schemes to rob the pension fund, and consolidated his power in the union through expansion in the West.

For Cesar Chavez and other UFW leaders, the conflict with the Teamsters precipitated a reevaluation of strategy that would make the union less dependent on the boycott. With membership in precipitous decline and volunteers dying in the line of duty, Chavez was forced to consider working with friends in government who might be able to deliver an agricultural labor law worthy of their sacrifices. Such a change in strategy would, of course, require a reversal of Chavez's opposition to government regulations of labor disputes. It also demanded his acceptance of a much more bureaucratic approach to solving the problems that confronted farm laborers. In a world dependent on lawyers and union field organizers to win union elections, Chavez would have to learn how to share the spotlight and decision-making powers, something that had become foreign to him by 1975.

FIVE

A Bitter Harvest

THE REGIONAL OFFICE of the new Agricultural Labor Relations Board (ALRB) in Salinas, California, opened on a typically cool morning, September 2, 1975. The union had planned for this day for months, collecting membership cards and preparing petitions for elections on farms. The Salinas office covered farms over a wide swath of the state, from the coastal growing regions just north of Los Angeles to the fertile lands of Monterey County. Union organizer, Jesus "Chui" Villegas, and a law student interning for the farm workers had driven all night from Oxnard, nearly 300 miles away, carrying seven petitions to file with the ALRB on its first day of operations. Sandy Nathan, a young cause lawyer who had joined the UFW team in 1973, met Villegas at the farm workers' office before dawn to go over the petitions and combine them with cards collected from local ranches and fourteen petitions prepared over the previous hours.[1] Nathan embraced the new law as an opportunity to prove that the union could achieve justice through the system. Many rank-and-file members of the union shared this optimism, congregating in front of the office a day before, on Labor Day, to hold a mass at 5 o'clock in the afternoon, followed by an all-night vigil to pray for the success of the new law.

At a quarter to eight on the morning of September 2, Nathan and Villegas arrived at the board office, met by throngs of farm workers and television reporters waiting with great anticipation. The office director, Norman Greer, and members of his new staff began to move supplies in and out of the building in anticipation of the big day. Nathan, Villegas, Marshall Ganz, and the rest of the workers remained close to the front door, though each time a staff member needed to pass, the courteous but anxious crowd made way for him. "We were kind of standing off to the side of the door," Nathan remembered, "and presumably they were going to say, at some point, that they were ready to go." That moment never came. Instead, as Nathan and Villegas looked on, Greer and his regional attorney, Ralph Pérez, cut a path to the parking lot. Nathan recalled what he witnessed next: "What had happened, it turned out, a couple of the Salinas cops told me that José Charles [a Teamsters representative] and one of his companions from the Teamsters were out in the parking lot and they asked the cop to go inside and tell Greer they wanted to talk to him. They didn't want to walk through the UFW line, so Greer and Pérez went out [to them]. The next thing we see, here's Greer leading the Teamsters into the office ahead of us. So I said, 'Let's go!' And all the people went in, and I went in."[2]

Within minutes the scene turned chaotic, as Villegas insisted that he be the first to file a petition after traveling all night and having fellow farm workers hold his place. With television cameras rolling and Villegas, Ganz, Nathan, the Teamsters representatives, and about ten farm workers crowded into the small office, Greer began shouting, "This is a mob! There's an unruly mob in here! I'm not going to take these petitions until you get them out of here!" Greer directed most of his ire at Nathan and Ganz, whom he assumed had staged a publicity stunt. In the heat of the argument, Greer also uttered a racially tinged concern about getting his "pocket picked," inflaming tensions even more. Nathan opined later, "It was just incredible that after all this—I mean it was like a festive occasion—suddenly this guy was hitting his hand on the counter, saying they're not going to take any petitions until this mob gets out of here."[3]

This inauspicious beginning to the labor board tempered union members' expectations and, in many ways, confirmed their worst fears. In the months that followed, insensitivity toward farm workers, internal rivalries between young and old government agents, and general mismanagement from the top down plagued the board and inspired challenges to the new law from those most concerned about delivering justice to farm workers in California. In the years leading up to the passage of the Agricultural Labor Relations Act, Cesar Chavez had resisted a legislative solution to farm worker troubles. After receiving funds from the AFL-CIO in 1973, however, Chavez shifted his position, asking Jerry Cohen to propose the most liberal, pro-union labor relations act that would extend collective bargaining rights to farm workers without compromising the union's most coveted strategy: the secondary boycott. The time seemed right given that the staunchly anti-union governor, Ronald Reagan, had concluded his second and last term in

1974 and California's electorate had replaced him with the young, ex-Jesuit seminarian, Edmund G. "Jerry" Brown. As the attorney general under Reagan, Brown had watched his predecessor's willful neglect of the farm workers, frequently entreating him to take a more active role in the resolution of the conflict. Now, as the governor of California, Brown promised "to extend the rule of law to the agriculture sector and establish the right of secret ballot elections for farm workers."[4] These were the circumstances under which the ALRA was born; however, the results on September 2, 1975, looked far different from those that Cohen had negotiated or Brown and his legislative partners had intended.

The failure of the ALRB to live up to its expectations surprised union officials who had worked diligently in the years and months since the battle of Coachella to get a "good law."[5] Chavez sent Cohen and Nathan to the state capitol during the preceding months to work closely with sympathetic lawmakers, California's secretary of agriculture and services Rose Bird, and Governor Jerry Brown on legislation that they thought gave them the best chance to succeed. The UFW lobbying group in Sacramento succeeded in improving upon all the rights afforded to industrial workers in the NLRA for agricultural workers, including securing the right to a secondary boycott with limited restrictions. Although the law remained irritatingly vague on eligibility to vote and how to recognize workers' interest in an election, the final version, passed on May 29, 1975, required elections to be held at the peak of the seasonal harvests. The law's promise to "[ensure] peace in the agricultural fields by . . . [bringing] certainty and a sense of fair play to a presently unstable and potentially volatile condition in the state," simultaneously acknowledged a tumultuous past and present while casting a hopeful eye toward the future.[6] In describing the law to the union members after its passage, Cohen assured them of their right to boycott, but reminded everyone that the bill's implementation still required their hard work. "We have the solution," Cohen proudly reported, "now all we need is to work out the details."[7]

The difficult first months of implementation, however, produced new doubts about the efficacy of a legislative solution and renewed suspicions that the state government was ill-equipped to manage the fight in the fields. Although journalists hailed the passage of the law as the "dawn of a new era for farm workers," and Jerry Brown later proclaimed it "the greatest accomplishment of my administration," those who struggled to make it work found it less effective as a tool for justice.[8] Indeed, Chavez strained to defend the law after two months of frustration, while members of the UFW legal team debated whether the law was, in fact, truly good for the workers. Jerry Goldman, a veteran UAW attorney working on loan to the UFW legal team, rendered his verdict after just three weeks on the job: "I think this is one of the most anti-union laws I have ever seen."[9] Nathan believed it was "the administration of the law, not the law" itself that produced the anti-union bias.[10]

Chavez, Nathan, and Cohen had little choice but to be optimistic. In addition to the promise Chavez had made to George Meany to pursue such a solution, the UFW approached the formation of ALRA in its weakest state since its founding, with only twenty union contracts and 15,000 members during the peak harvest season.[11] In this context, the union had few options other than to enter into a Faustian pact with Brown and the state for its survival. In embracing the challenge to work within the confines of the new law, the union set out, once again, to prove that it could adapt to the changing dynamics of the struggle and stay one step ahead of its rivals.

THEY'RE FOR THE STATE

The Agricultural Labor Relations Act, at least on paper, gave UFW organizers reason to be hopeful, although it also offered the Teamsters and the growers a chance to win in union elections. At a basic level, the ALRA recognized farm workers' rights to organize and join labor unions. The law also set up provisions for filing unfair labor practices against growers and competing unions who interfered with this process or impinged on the free will of workers to determine their own fate. In cases where the board affirmed claims involving unfair termination of employment, the law instituted a "make-whole" remedy, whereby the employer would have to pay the worker the difference between what he received and what he would have been paid if the employer had bargained in good faith.

Although Teamsters officials opposed these new regulations during the legislative process, they softened their position over time. The ALRA allowed the Teamsters to retain their existing contracts, which totaled some 467 farm labor contracts and covered approximately 65,000 members at the time of its signing.[12] The Teamsters stood to lose in the upcoming elections, but the head of the Western Conference of Teamsters, M. E. (Andy) Anderson, remained confident that they could hold on to their advantage, given the presumed superiority of their contracts. The legislation applied strictly to agricultural field workers only, thereby protecting the employees covered by the Teamsters in warehouse and hauling from UFW infringements.

For the growers, the law implemented stricter guidelines for picketing and boycotts; specifically, it forbade the "hard boycott" (also known as a "traditional boycott"), in which unions asked employees not to handle a particular product, and restricted the right to boycott to labor organizations currently certified as the representatives of the primary employer's employees.[13] The law restricted use of the secondary boycott if the union lost an election, though loopholes remained for the UFW to continue its campaigns against grapes, lettuce, and Gallo wine. The grower newspaper, the *Packer*, initially declare an end to the boycott; however, within a week it published a retraction.[14] The growers successfully petitioned for restrictions on the use of recognitional strikes, which would have allowed employees to select a union as their bargaining representative by having a majority of the unit walk off the job.[15] Instead, the law provided for the expeditious creation of secret ballot elections to determine representation—or no representation—by a union for those ranches where 50 percent of the employees exhibited a "showing of interest." In short, the law gave something to everyone, although most regarded the ALRA as more favorable to unions than the federal NLRA.[16]

A week after Brown signed the ALRA into law on June 5, 1975, Cesar Chavez announced to a group of union field officers, staff, and the full executive board, "The decisions we make today—or fail to make today—will have a profound effect on the future of the union."[17] Members discussed what approach they would take to secure elections on ranches across the state and tackled the thorny issue of whether to organize undocumented workers, whom Chavez referred to as "illegals" in the common parlance of the day. Cesar's cousin Manuel upheld the importance of illegal aliens as "economic strikers" whose eligibility should not be challenged and expressed the sincere belief "that illegals can be organized just like all other workers." Jerry Cohen, who tried to remain agnostic on the question, admitted that the new law did not deal with the issue, but he offered his legal opinion that "it would be unconstitutional to prohibit illegals [from voting]."[18] Seeing an opportunity to strengthen his point, Manuel Chavez observed, "Illegals [were] no longer afraid of the migra [federal immigration officials]" largely because enforcement had grown lax and most members of the union had undocumented relatives in their families. Ben Maddock, a Delano organizer working in the Central Valley town of Lost Hills, shared that although most of the members with whom he had spoken did not want undocumented workers to vote, he agreed that "some of the members have illegals at home, so there's a contradiction." The Fresno area organizer agreed with Manuel Chavez, adding, "[We] will lose without them." In response, Manuel offered to travel to the Fresno area to have undocumented workers sign cards and to push for residency for those who chose to work with the union and labor in the fields. Displaying Machiavellian reasoning, however, he also suggested that such actions could be used to the benefit of the union: "[We won't] ask whether the worker [is] illegal or not, but if [we] lose [the] election, then [we will] blow [the] whistle on him!"[19]

Cesar Chavez and Gilbert Padilla took the opposite position. Chavez offered a response consistent with the standard industrial union line: "Meat cutters, UAW and Steel Workers all have lost elections because of the illegals." Padilla, who had worked closely with members of established unions in building the boycott, shared the position that "unions are weakened if illegals are allowed to be members." Most union leaders believed that the lack of citizenship made undocumented workers vulnerable to expulsion and therefore much more pliable and less inclined to speak out against injustice when it happened. The use of undocumented workers as scab laborers to replace striking workers during the early days of the union suggested to Chavez and Padilla that undocumented workers could never become equal members and would ultimately only hurt the union if included. Both rejected the idea that the ALRA and the filial loyalties among union members gave the union cover to organize among the undocumented. Chavez cited the upswing in growers' hiring of undocumented workers as evidence that they would "use [the] same work force to break elections as they did to break strikes." "We don't want chattels as members," he announced at the meeting. "Even if we win elections with them, we don't win." In his most extreme interpretation of the problem, Chavez saw the flood of undocumented laborers into the fields as a "CIA operation" designed to serve multiple political objectives, including the restoration of the bracero program and an attempt to alleviate Mexico of radical farm workers who, if allowed to stay in the United States, would foment a communist revolution south of the border.[20]

Chavez's desire to exclude undocumented workers from the union sharply contrasted with the union's advocacy for a state labor relations act that accounted for the unique conditions of agricultural workers. That the new law accounted for their vulnerabilities—for example, insisting on elections during the peak of harvests—opened the door for the UFW to make enormous gains among this mostly Spanish-speaking group of laborers. Chavez, however, rejected the advice of some of his field organizers, including his cousin's, in favor of a traditional union philosophy that held the line between documented and undocumented workers. He suggested that the state should address the problem by stopping the "coyote" from transporting the workers in the first place rather than focusing on the labor contractor who hired the workers at the work site. Cohen found this position disingenuous given that the law now held growers accountable for the contractor's actions. But this too had become another unenforced provision within the law that would grow in significance as growers tried to increase their distance from the hiring process throughout the late 1970s. On this day, however, the members could not reach an agreement on an approach and ultimately agreed to return to it after two weeks of study.[21] When Manuel returned from Fresno with news of progress in organizing undocumented workers to vote for the union, Cesar remained doubtful, claiming, "Illegals, not Teamsters, are our biggest problem."[22]

The union upheld the relevance of the boycott, but the majority of the union's efforts would now go toward confirming the desire of documented workers to have ALRB-sanctioned elections. The union's lawyers also took on a new watchdog role, filing unfair labor practice charges against growers who sought to curb the influence of the United Farm Workers by firing employees who demonstrated an inclination to vote for the union. The union remained committed to a range of activities, including managing the boycott and a number of social services, although during the summer of 1975 the UFW redirected most of its resources toward making the most of the ALRB.

The unfortunate incidents in Salinas, however, represented just the beginning of problems within the board that kept it from becoming a full partner for justice. In the weeks that followed the opening of the ALRB office, lawyers working for the union complained that former NLRB operatives dominated the staff of the new agencies and failed to implement the law. According to Sandy Nathan, "They [brought] all the NLRB notions with them and under the NLRB, after you file for an election it takes a number of months before it actually happens."[23] The ALRA stipulated that elections must be held within seven days of a valid showing of interest, and the UFW insisted on such a provision because of the itinerant status of field laborers. But coming mostly from industrial sites, many of the ALRB agents did not appreciate the need for timeliness. The agents dragged their feet on enforcing the provision to hold elections during the peak harvest, and the board ultimately failed to offer an acceptable remedy when UFW lawyers complained.[24]

Board agents tended to be too trusting of the employers, accepting at face value the list of employees submitted to the office. According to Nathan, employers often "inflated the number of people," which had a detrimental effect on the union's ability to prove that at least 50 percent of the employees wanted an election. Nathan explained, "If we claim there's 200 and the growers claim there's 300, [and] if we have 140 cards thinking we're well over what we need, we in fact are short."[25] When the lawyers challenged the list, agents refused to examine the grower's payroll, arguing that they either had "no time" or "no reason" to doubt the grower's claims. In one case, where the union compelled a sympathetic agent to evaluate the payroll in Calexico, the grower submitted an address on Airport Boulevard for 300 men, women, and children who worked on the ranch. When the union conducted its own investigation at the site, they found a single men's camp housing approximately forty men, but the board office in the region refused to verify their findings. "It's common," Nathan shared, "that the lists contain twenty-five per cent inflations in most of the big places."[26] In some cases, UFW lawyers found evidence not only of blind trust in the employers, but of actual communications between board agents and growers in which the two worked out the final version of the list.[27] According to Nathan, "The first week we spent fighting because they kept trying to throw us out of elections. . . . I was in that office day and night, just screaming all the time."[28]

When the board finally held elections, they often failed to provide a transparent process that assuaged workers' fears of employer and Teamster retribution for supporting the UFW. Since elections were new to most workers, the board held preelection conferences with employees to explain the process. Such conferences, however, occurred at the whim of the employer, usually after hours at the ranch, making it inconvenient for most workers to attend. Although UFW lawyers insisted that board members conduct the conferences in both Spanish and English and translate all documents into Tagalog, Spanish, and English, the agency refused. Nathan recalled, "[The agents would] say, 'why don't [you] translate the important stuff into Spanish?,'" and he would respond, "'We'll conduct the thing in Spanish and translate the important stuff into English for the employer.'"[29] Needless to say, the agents declined. On the day of elections, growers often provided transportation to the polls only for workers who supported their position. Growers also covered the air travel of board agents charged with the task of monitoring elections and often treated board agents to extravagant lunches and luxurious transportation while in the field.

During the counting of the ballots, myriad problems arose. Often, non-Spanish-speaking agents threw out ballots of voters whose last names they could not read. In other instances, agents assumed Spanish surnames that appeared to be similar were repeat voters and invalidated those ballots without consulting with the union.[30] Growers and Teamsters also engaged in downright intimidation of workers who they knew preferred the UFW. Nathan recalled, "People are getting fired, threatened, pushed around in all kinds of ways, and if they'd only gone out after one grower, maybe taught somebody a lesson, maybe there would have been a fair atmosphere in those elections." During the first three weeks of the law, the UFW filed twenty-two unfair labor practices; the board neglected to act on a single one.[31]

Confidential reports from within the Salinas ALRB office confirmed the biases that the union lawyers perceived from the outside. During the first few weeks of the agency's operation, a young Salinas agent, Ellen Greenstone, disclosed her frustrations with the management of the office. "Probably the most characteristic thing about our office," she explained to Chavez biographer Jacques E. Levy, "is how racist it is." Greenstone worked with thirty-nine colleagues in Salinas and nine field agents in Ventura. "A lot of agents won't even listen to UFW people," she reported. "They discount them totally." Greenstone attributed such treatment to a lack of familiarity with workers and a prevailing attitude of noblesse oblige among her colleagues. According to Greenstone, many of the agents assumed a significant level of ignorance among the farm workers and rejected the importance of talking to them. When Greer's actions on the first day elicited strong reactions from the farm workers, many agents were "taken aback" and "shocked" at the stridency of the UFW representatives. "Part of it was [the agents] thought they were being involved in a paternalistic, benevolent helping of workers," Greenstone opined, "and they didn't realize that all of these people were in a total uproar and had been battling it out for years." When farm workers and UFW representatives challenged the agents, most of Greenstone's colleagues became incredulous, asking, "How can these people act this way?" and "Why don't they take our help?" "In reality," she added, "the board agents didn't know anything about what was going on."[32]

To convey the level of danger, UFW representatives invited witnesses to accompany them into the fields. Esther Padilla, a longtime member of the UFW and the wife of the union's cofounder Gilbert Padilla, likened the conditions in rural California to Selma, Alabama, in 1965, during the height of the civil rights movement. She remembered, "[The growers] had the dogs, and the bats, and everything else waiting to beat the hell out of us . . . and intimidating the workers." Although the ALRA included a provision for union access to farms during elections, this was honored more in the breach than in the observance. The union tested the law by sending representatives to the farms during lunch hour and after work. During one of these trips, Esther Padilla and three other members entered the Metzler farm in the small town of Del Rey, just outside of Fresno. Anticipating violence, the UFW team invited the local television station, Channel 30, to accompany them. "The growers were absolutely livid," Padilla recalled, but the presence of the media forced them to temper their response. When the same group went back at the end of the day, this time without the television cameras, a grower pulled a rifle on Padilla. At the nearby Guerrero farm, another team of union officials encountered similar hostility from gun-toting growers.[33] Elsewhere in San Joaquin and Tulare counties, ranchers formed a citizens "posse" that threatened to plunge rural communities back into the violence of the previous two years.[34] When the union reported these incidents to the ALRB office, agents tended not to believe them.

Much of the agents' ignorance stemmed from their poor training on farm labor issues. The Sacramento office, run by Walter Kintz, hired retired members of the NLRB to staff the training sessions in the state capital before dispersing the agents to the field offices. The NLRB veterans imparted useful knowledge about how to run a union election, but demonstrated a profound lack of appreciation for the likelihood of violence in the fields. Greenstone found that retired NLRB members "couldn't at all anticipate reality" and failed to prepare ALRB agents for the intensity of the conflict. When the Sacramento office arranged a field trip for the would-be agents to get acquainted with the work, members of the grower-oriented Farm Bureau escorted the group aboard National Guard buses. The Bureau used the visit as a public relations opportunity, allowing agents to speak only to labor contractors and giving what Greenstone regarded as a "false picture of what it was like in the field." When the agents relocated to their field office, the local office manager maintained distance from the farm workers. According to Greenstone, Greer and her colleagues "never saw workers until they showed up to file petitions in our office."[35]

Kintz's decision to hire mostly veteran state bureaucrats as agents rankled UFW representatives and produced tension with some of the younger ALRB staff members, many of whom had come straight out of law school. Several older agents had served in state civil service agencies prior to joining the ALRB and assumed a balance of power in agriculture between workers and employers that existed in industrial settings. The media coverage of the strikes and boycotts in the years leading to the passage of the ALRA created an illusion of power for the UFW. Jerry Goldman, for example, complained about a "lack of sensitivity . . . and not knowing anything about agriculture" among agents, and "the presumption that UFW is a radical, trouble-making organization and the employers are good and honest and the Teamsters are good and honest."[36] According to Greenstone, the unfamiliarity with "the sophistication of all of this struggle and the fight that has been going on" led many of her senior colleagues to underestimate the potential for chicanery on the part of growers and Teamsters and anger on the part of the UFW. "The attitude, 'well, I'm the board agent and I decide' is really disturbing," Greenstone told Levy, "because they don't have any feeling for what goes on out there."[37]

Greenstone attributed much of the insensitivity to "older people" within the office, revealing a generational and gender divide among government agents. Whereas many of the older agents joined the office as permanent members of the team, given their years of experience, younger agents like Greenstone received "temporary" jobs and inferior assignments. In the Salinas office, for example, Greer broke the agents into teams of three to conduct elections and selected team leaders based on seniority. As a consequence, older members stymied the opinions of younger agents who spoke Spanish and possessed a fresh interpretation of the conflict untainted by biases developed over years of bureaucratic work in state agencies dealing with mostly white, English-speaking industrial laborers. In some local offices, younger members included former farm workers whose experience and concerns older colleagues discredited. Greenstone recalled one incident in which a former farm worker was branded as pro-UFW simply for arguing that agents should take migration patterns into account when scheduling elections.[38] Greenstone also found most of the leaders resistant to translating documents and holding bilingual meetings. When younger agents complained, the heads of teams assigned them to secretarial duties. The disproportionate number of men to women in senior leadership positions added a gender dimension to this tension. Greenstone, a younger bilingual agent, felt "a lot of sexism" within the board office and believed her "downgraded" assignments to be a consequence of "more men than women in [the] office."[39]

After weeks of UFW complaints and internal discord, Kintz finally replaced Norman Greer with Paula Paily in the Salinas office, but only on a temporary basis. Greenstone had a much higher regard for Paily's leadership, especially because Paily paid greater attention to complaints from women and younger agents. Paily put an immediate end to agents accepting chartered flights from growers and stopped employers from bussing in workers to participate in union elections. Her reasons for ending these practices, however, had more to do with restoring a "sense of fair play" and less to do with acknowledging a culture of disregard for farm workers among her own staff. She told the Salinas agents, "These elections are not for the growers, they're not for the UFW, they're not for the Teamsters; they're for the state."[40]

This new approach stopped the most egregious manipulations of the new law, but Paily and the majority of her staff remained ignorant of the intensity of the battle and did nothing to address attitudes favorable to the growers and the Teamsters. Her reasoning also conflicted with the sentiments among a majority of governor-appointed board members in Sacramento, who saw the law as an opportunity to bring social justice to the fields. Governor Brown appointed LeRoy Chatfield to the ALRB and tapped Catholic bishop Roger Mahoney to be chair. Another pro-labor appointee, Jerome Waldie, articulated the sentiment among the board's majority: "I make no bones about my belief that the law was enacted to protect farm workers in their effort to organize for collective bargaining."[41] Yet the prevailing attitude among agents in the field undermined this interpretation.[42] For Greenstone, who came of age during the boycott and had joined the ALRB with the intent of becoming an agent of justice rather than a career bureaucrat, such interpretations did not sit well. Within the year she left the board, deciding to work for the UFW before moving to private practice.[43]

The failures contributed to a growing skepticism among UFW lawyers that the law would become a solution to farm worker problems. Jerry Goldman became utterly exasperated with the process: "I am so totally frustrated. Because these acts can work, and all my life I've been saying that, in the private sector. If you engage in obfuscation, if you are not empathetic, if you are not understanding, if you do not communicate, if you do not treat everybody on a fair basis, these fucking acts aren't going to work, and if that is what they want, for it not to work, they're sure as hell doing a damn good fucking job of doing it. And I want to tell you my feeling is that they don't want it to work."[44] Most union lawyers shared Goldman's frustration, if not his pessimism. Nathan and Cohen, however, insisted that if the union could enforce sections of the law that required elections within seven days of a showing of interest by workers, they could turn the tide in their favor.[45]

UFW lawyers also demanded better access to workers. During the AL-RA's creation growers had vehemently but unsuccessfully resisted a provision to allow unions to campaign on their property one hour before work began and one hour at the end of the day. Once the legislation became law, growers tested the ALRB by impeding the UFW. For example, when UFW representatives attempted to enter fields and labor camps, grower-paid security guards chased them off the property, forcing board agents to weigh in on the matter. The UFW filed numerous unfair labor practices to address the situation, yet often the regional directors claimed to have their hands full with staging elections. In some regional offices, directors did not regard providing equal access a part of their job description. According to Greenstone, Greer told the agents in Salinas "it was not [their] business to enforce" the access rule, inviting growers to violate the law at will.[46]

In the courts, the South Central Farmers Committee successfully obtained an injunction against the UFW, blocking labor union representatives from entering the fields without grower permission.[47] Cohen and the UFW lawyers appealed to a higher court to suspend the ruling, but the problem of enforcement of the access rule continued to plague the UFW. According to one report, the UFW could have won 15 to 20 percent more votes in elections if the ALRB had enforced the law and policed distortions in lists of eligible voters.[48]

During the elections, the UFW kept growers honest and consumers informed by maintaining a strong boycott of Gallo wine, California grapes, and lettuce. Given the volunteer nature of the boycott, many of the activists who made the first boycott successful had moved on, although some veterans remained to show new devotees how to build a campaign. Among them, Eliseo Medina excelled as he had in Chicago. Besides organizing workers in the California fields during elections, Medina managed a staff of twenty-eight volunteers in Chicago who, at one point, drew a crowd of 1,100 people to march on Jewell Market. The Chicago boycott house garnered 20,000 signatures asking Jewell's ownership to divest from Gallo and raised $26,000 at a screening of the film *Fight for Our Lives,* documenting the 1973 battle for Coachella. Some of the money went toward a campaign started by members of the community to elect Medina chairman of Jewell's board of trustees. In his reports to La Paz, Medina wrote that support in Chicago was "far stronger than before."[49]

Elsewhere old hands such as Gilbert Padilla, Jessica Govea, and Pete Velasco contributed their experience. Like Medina, they balanced service on the National Executive Board and work on elections in California with orchestrating boycott houses far from La Paz. Gilbert and Esther Padilla managed a staff of fourteen volunteers in Washington, D.C. and Virginia. Pete Velasco, one of two Filipinos on the executive board, traveled to Baltimore to lead the boycott and succeeded in securing support from the city's mayor and Maryland's governor. Govea returned to Canada, now charged with managing a staff of forty-one volunteers spread throughout Ottawa, Toronto, Montreal, and other cities. Although the infrastructure she and Ganz had put in place during the run-up to the 1970 contracts allowed her to plug back in and manage the houses from Toronto, her value as a credible voice among farm workers during elections required her to divide her time between California and Canada.

Chavez and members of the executive board recognized that these assignments removed effective labor organizers from the elections at a critical moment, yet attachment to the boycott made backing away from the campaign unacceptable. Chavez held firm to the belief that contracts could be attained only in tandem with an effective boycott, and he continued to channel funds toward a reduced staff of volunteers in 150 cities across the country, including five in Denver, thirteen in Detroit, three in Minneapolis, seven in Pittsburgh, fourteen in St. Louis, fifteen in Philadelphia, four in Seattle, three in Houston, two in Portland, Oregon, and two in Atlanta. These numbers were far smaller than the boycott in its heyday; however, the existence of a boycott house kept growers on their toes.

The network also included more boycott houses abroad. Victor Pestoff, who had assisted Elinson during the 1969–70 season, became the European director of the boycott and moved between Norway and Switzerland securing the support of Scandinavian labor organizations and cooperative markets. The Council of Nordic Trade Unions gave $7,500 to the cause, and two Danish and one Swedish co-op voted not to carry California grapes on their shelves. Elinson, who had gone back to graduate school in the United States after 1970, once again found academic work tedious and contacted Chavez's brother, Richard, to see if she could assist. Her timing turned out to be perfect since the Teamsters had begun to counter the UFW campaign in 1975 by putting pressure on their fellow transporters in England not to cooperate. As members of the International Transport Workers Federation, the Teamsters and the Transport and General Workers Union belonged to a common international union, which made support of the UFW much more difficult.

Richard Chavez sent Elinson to England in hopes that her connections with the TGWU could break through Teamster opposition and again forge a strong alliance with the English dockworkers. In spite of the Teamsters' activities, Elinson found the work much easier compared to 1969. "This time," she recalled, "the union had much more of a name and much more of a presence." The BBC aired documentary films about the UFW in Britain, and union journalists knew of Elinson from her previous stint, making her a familiar face in both England and Ireland. The success of the union and Elinson's modest celebrity also earned her office space at the World Peace Council in central London, a far cry from the tenement apartment she had worked out of in 1969 and 1970. Elinson also quickly reestablished relations with Freddy Silberman and Brian Nicholson in the TGWU, the latter having advanced to president of the union between the two boycotts. Nicholson had recently divorced, and he and Elinson fell in love and married. Her familiarity with the British public, the trade unions, and old friends like Silberman and Nicholson helped her overcome the Teamsters' resistance. Of the work, Elinson recalled, "We were doing a lot more kinds of newspaper articles, meetings, and speaking at conferences, and speaking at the Labour Party conferences and things like that rather than tromping around on the docks, looking for grapes."[50]

The international component of the boycott also included Asia. In Japan, the UFW made contacts with dockworkers to support a blockade, while in Hong Kong a committee of fifteen, including GIs stationed in the area, worked on behalf of the union to boycott Gallo wine. The great distance from the center of the boycott, however, created the potential for deviations from the nonviolent strategy advocated by Chavez. In Hong Kong, for example, three organizers were found guilty on eleven counts of arson for burning down a storage facility holding grapes. The judge sentenced the three to eleven months in jail, and the image of the union overseas was temporarily tarnished.[51]

Closer to home, the union diversified its use of the boycott in California by threatening to use it against the state if either the general counsel or the governor did not enforce the new labor law. Although most observers saw Governor Brown and the ALRB as allies to the farm workers, union officials worked hard to bend the governor and the board their way by threatening to withdraw from the legislative solution in which both had become deeply invested. Brown, for example, had staked his political future on the success of the Agricultural Labor Relations Act (ALRA) early in his first term, and

ALRB directors and agents had jobs only as long as the union agreed to use it as a tool for achieving their objectives. "The situation is already bad and getting worse as the growers and Teamsters see they can get away with their coercive tactics," Dolores Huerta told a reporter. Turning to the familiar tool of the boycott, Huerta threatened, "If those tactics are not stopped, we will have no choice but to boycott the whole election process."[52] Although the union refrained from ever calling a formal boycott of the ALRB, it picketed both regional offices and the main Sacramento office to bring attention to the agency's deficiencies.

In response, the governor appealed to Sam Cohen, a respected attorney with a lucrative private practice in San Francisco, to head a special task force to deal with the backlog of unfair labor practice complaints and organize the field operations of the state agency. Cohen's guidance had an immediate effect in the Imperial Valley, turning what had been seen as a regional office in crisis into "a whirlwind of efficiency."[53] The regional board director in El Centro, Maurice Jourdane, pulled back from the brink of quitting when Cohen came to the office and imposed a "sense of dedication and determination to make the law work." As in other regional board offices, the workload overwhelmed the staff, turning the office into a "sit-back-and-wait agency" that usually reacted to violations of the law long after the workers had given up hope in the process. "When I first began working with the agency," Jourdane told a reporter, "I was appalled by what I saw in the fields. . . . Workers were frightened."

After Cohen arrived, agents took a proactive approach, fanning out into the Imperial Valley to inform employees of their rights and ensuring their ability to vote without fear of reprisal. Unlike Greer or Paily in Salinas, Jourdane, a thirty-three-year-old attorney, embraced the law as an opportunity to bring justice to the farm workers. Growers and Teamsters routinely attacked Jourdane, accusing him of being pro-UFW whenever he tried to enforce the law. Contrary to Paily's position, Jourdane believed the "specific intent of the law . . . was to give workers the free, un-coerced right to choose a union, or no union, by secret ballot." Thanks to the reforms instituted by Brown and implemented by Cohen, Jourdane now felt "that is what we are doing at last."[54]

The threat of a boycott and the aggressive action by Cohen and the UFW legal team helped the union win far more elections than it lost. By the end of December 1975, the state had managed to hold a remarkable 354 elections without one strike or the defections of the union from the process. Of these

354 elections, the UFW scored victories in 189 of them, representing 26,956 workers, or 50.2 percent of voters. The Teamsters, on the other hand, won 101 elections representing 12,284 workers, or 23 percent. Among these totals, fifty-eight ranches involving 8,228 workers switched from the Teamsters to the UFW. In the contest to win elections where either the UFW or the Teamsters held contracts already, the UFW fared much better than its rival. The UFW won all of its elections where it held contracts, whereas the Teamsters lost 58 percent of the workers they had held under contract on 177 ranches prior to the elections in 1975. Finally, in spite of the growers' vigorous campaign against unions among employees, only six ranches involving 938 workers switched from either the UFW or the Teamsters to no union at all. In fact, growers succeeded in convincing only 4 percent of the workers to vote for no representation in twenty elections.[55]

Union officials had their hopes tempered, however, by a number of ominous trends that continued to threaten the new law. A victory in an election won the union the exclusive right to negotiate a contract but did not ensure one. The difficult work of negotiating with their adversaries lay ahead. Growers, Teamsters, and UFW officials continued to challenge the results of more than 75 percent of the elections, which delayed certification of the results. Indeed, the UFW legal team led all parties in the submission of unfair labor practices, triggering a series of hearings to settle the matter against eighty-five growers. The level of activity far exceeded the expectations of the state, forcing the board to spend its entire budget of approximately $1.3 million within the first two months of operation. By the end of 1975, the ALRB had spent $5,268,571, requiring the state to consider a special appropriation of $3,795,034 just to keep the board's doors open for business. The appropriation needed the approval of two-thirds of the state legislature and the signature of the governor. In addition, the board predicted a similar volume of activity in the 1976–77 season and requested a budget of $6.6 million, approximately five times the total approved for its initial operation.[56]

The success of the union and the cost of operation placed the ALRB in jeopardy as the legislature approached a February 1 deadline to approve the funding.[57] Growers used the crisis as an opportunity to either push for reforms that would tip the scales back in their favor or dismantle the board altogether. Among their complaints, growers demanded the removal of Walter Kintz, whom they believed worked "in conspiratorial fashion with the UFW to assure victories for Chavez's union." Growers insisted on amendments to the law that mirrored conditions present in the National Labor Relations Act. Don

Curlee, a spokesperson for the South Central Growers Association, petitioned for a provision available to employers under the federal law that allowed a company to seek decertification of a union when company officials believed the employees no longer wanted to be represented by a union for which they had voted in a previous election. Curlee also opposed the requirement under state law to hold an election within seven days. Joe Herman, attorney for the association, added the objections of most growers to the "make-whole remedy," which required the agency to determine the pay for a worker when the employer was found to have bargained in bad faith. An Imperial Valley grower, Jon Vessey, voiced the common complaint among growers that the law failed to distinguish year-round employees from temporary workers in determining the eligibility of voters in union elections. Vessey complained, "That means that a few hundred people, working for me for just a few weeks, can, by majority vote, decide which union, if any, my year-round workers want, even though the year-round people are those on whom we are most dependent." Although the association demanded that such procedures be changed, the majority of their efforts went toward lobbying state senators to block funding for the ALRB rather than to reform it.[58]

In spite of appeals by board chairman Roger Mahoney and general counsel Walter Kintz to pass an emergency appropriation to keep the agency open until the next legislative cycle, a coalition of Republicans and farm-area Democrats voted against it. At the time of the vote, the UFW had won 55 percent of the ALRB elections, compared to 34 percent for the Teamsters, 5 percent for other unions, and 6 percent for no union at all. In addition, as the harvest and voting moved to the Imperial Valley, the UFW had built momentum, putting together a string of eleven victories compared to just one for the Teamsters since December 1. The failure to pass the appropriation bill stopped the UFW from accumulating more victories and forced the agency to lay off all but thirty of its 175-member staff.[59] By February 6, the ALRB had all but ceased to exist.

Cesar Chavez responded to the crisis by turning to the trusted strategy of picket lines in the fields and in front of markets. "[This is a] day of infamy for farm workers," he declared. "Our only recourse is to take our cause to the people of California and return to strikes and boycotts."[60] As the reality of the agency's closure hit rural California, the labor situation returned "to the law of the jungle." Predicting that the violence had just begun, Chavez made the tactical move of exporting the struggle to the urban marketplace, announcing a boycott of Sun Maid raisins, Sunsweet nuts and processed fruits, and products backed by eight Fresno packinghouses that had played a significant role in defunding the ALRB.[61] "We'll beat them with the boycott and pin them to the wall," Chavez angrily told reporters, predicting, "They'll come back to Sacramento crying for the money (to reactivate the board)."[62] This time, however, the growers stood firm, aware that the union had directed many of its resources away from the boycott toward elections. Whether Chavez and the union admitted it, the hard-fought victories in secret ballot elections had shifted their priorities from pressuring growers in the marketplace to achieving collective bargaining through the farm labor law. As the defunding crisis prevented the UFW from making gains during the 1976 harvest, the union focused on a new strategy: reviving the ALRB through the California initiative system.

A TOUGH GAME OF CHICKEN

At the same time Chavez announced the renewal of the boycott, the UFW also filed an initiative proposal for the fall ballot in California. During the early twentieth century, progressive reformers in the Golden State had added three revolutionary electoral procedures—the recall, the referendum, and the initiative—that provided a degree of direct democracy to voters. By a majority vote, the electorate could recall an elected official, invalidate an established law (referendum), and circumvent the state legislative process and create a new law (initiative). These measures had come about as a reaction to the excessive influence of railroad moguls during the Gilded Age. By the mid-twentieth century, however, these progressive reforms had become the tool of powerful interest groups who achieved a variety of goals, especially through the use of the initiative (more commonly known as the proposition). By the 1970s, conservative groups had gained the upper hand in controlling an initiative system in which qualifying a proposition became more challenging.[63] Between 1970 and 1976, only fifteen initiatives out of ninety-six proposals received enough signatures to make it on the ballot. Of those fifteen, only four passed, with only two considered by the UFW executive board as consistent with their political beliefs. During the board meeting to discuss the decision, Chavez acknowledged, "Many people vote no on an issue because they feel that is the safe thing to do." Unfortunately for the union, they would be asking the public to say yes when statistics showed that a no vote had an 8 percent advantage among voters. Such history and statistics notwithstanding, the initiative system provided a well-organized union such as the United Farm Workers the possibility to achieve its legislative goals through popular vote. Chavez expressed confidence in their ability to obtain at least a 60 percent margin of victory if they appealed to the California electorate to create a new, improved farm labor law more to the union's liking.[64]

The situation in the fields and on the board went from bad to worse, as new disputes broke out on Imperial Valley farms and three of the five members on the ALRB resigned. In April 1976, LeRoy Chatfield quit the board to work on Governor Brown's presidential campaign. Two other board members, Joseph Grodin and Joseph Ortega, both seen as appointees favoring the UFW, resigned, leaving its chairman, Bishop Roger Mahoney, and the growers' representative, Richard Johnsen Jr. Within ALRB offices, a skeleton crew held on without pay in hopes that legislators would reach a compromise to fund their operations. As the growers dug in and the UFW adopted the initiative strategy, hopes of a legislative solution dimmed, and government agents began to peal off. By mid-April, the embattled general counsel, Walter Kintz, announced his resignation, calling the ability of a small minority of senators to kill funding for the ALRB a "travesty of justice." "Emotionally and professionally," Kintz reported, "I could not tolerate sitting around any longer while the Legislature debates all over again whether or not it wants a farm labor bill." He threw his support behind the UFW initiative, which garnered enough signatures by May to make it onto the November ballot as Proposition 14.[65]

Proposition 14 dealt with the immediate problem of funding, although the union also sought to change the farm labor law in ways that strengthened its ability to win more elections. Advocates of the original law complained about the ability of one-third of the senate to block funding; as a consequence, the initiative proposed to mandate that the legislature provide appropriations necessary to carry out the purpose of the act without interruption. The initiative would replace the current law with another that mirrored the ALRA by setting up a government-supervised election system that would allow farm workers to decide by secret ballot which union, if any, they wanted to represent them. The initiative also added a few key changes, which drew the ire of the growers and support from labor unions, including the Teamsters. Under the ALRA, unions and employers frequently disputed the number of employees eligible to take part in an election largely because the employer dictated when and how a list of employees would be submitted to the agency. Surprises in the size of the workforce and challenges

FIGURE 12. Cesar Chavez at an unidentified United Farm Workers rally, 1971. Behind him stands a man in a United Steelworkers of America jacket. ALUA, UFW Collection, 3223.

to the list from unions often resulted in unfair labor practice claims that delayed the results of elections. The initiative would empower the new ALRB to decide under what circumstances a union could receive a list of workers from the employers. The new law would increase the punitive powers of the ALRB, allowing the agency to impose triple damages against a grower or a union found guilty of unfair labor practices. It would also require those opposed to an already certified union to get 50 percent of the workers to sign cards saying they no longer wanted such representation before an election could be held. Finally, the initiative addressed the thorny issue of union access to workers on California farms during elections. The initiative sought to write into the law an "access rule" that required growers to permit union representatives on their property one hour before work, one hour after work, and at lunch time.[66] The director of the "Yes on 14" campaign, Marshall Ganz, simplified the union's argument for the rule change as "an access to information" issue. "If you are going to have free union elections," he explained, "the workers must be fully informed."

Chavez believed the boycott and the positive press during union elections would translate into support for the UFW at the ballot box. Although some members had doubts about the ALRA's effectiveness, Chavez, union organizers, and the UFW legal department had succeeded in turning the farm labor law into a political coup. By the time the ALRB shuttered its doors, the United Farm Workers had won a majority of elections and enjoyed momentum in the Imperial Valley in anticipation of the 1976 harvest. Negative stories in the media regarding labor strife in the fields once again focused on Teamsters' acts of treachery or growers' resistance to farm worker justice. The continued observance of the boycott by consumers showed the UFW's appeal to the general public and the potential for the union's urban network to deliver a "Yes on 14" message to California voters. Some members questioned the strategy. Esther Padilla remembered, "There had been a lot of discussion within the executive board [about not pursuing the proposition] because you're talking about making people in the cities think we're going to invade their private property."[67] Chavez, however, insisted that they could win and ordered all resources to be directed toward the "Yes on 14" campaign.

In his announcement of the union's initiative strategy, Chavez anticipated the considerable cost of the campaign for both sides. "The Farm Worker Initiative campaign will be difficult and expensive," he anticipated, forcing the growers to spend millions to defeat it and requiring farm workers to "sacrifice themselves and their time" to achieve victory. "We will match their millions," he promised, "with our bodies, our spirits and the goodwill of the people of this state."[68] Within a week of his announcement, Chavez had redirected most of the funding and staff from the boycott houses to an all-out effort to pass the initiative. Walter Kintz, in his assessment of the strategy, called the decision a "tough game of chicken," suggesting that the initiative drive challenged growers, the UFW, and ultimately the voters to resolve the funding of the ALRB once and for all.[69] In the interim between exhausting the ALRB budget in February and the start of a new fiscal year in July, the governor replaced Kintz with Harry J. Delizonna and named three new members to the board, but could do nothing to provide long-term funding. UFW leaders maintained a high level of confidence in their ability to persuade voters to resolve the matter by supporting the initiative.

The union's position underestimated the growers' ability to adapt. Growers had become wise in their previous battles and made a number of key decisions to strengthen their appeal to voters, perhaps the most important of which was to mobilize and unify their community into an organization of thirty-two farm groups representing both large corporate farms and small family farmers. Chaired by a fifty-three-year-old Japanese American farmer, Harry Kubo, the Ad Hoc Committee discussed the best way to combat the farm workers' initiative and began a fundraising effort.[70] Don Curlee, spokesperson for the South Central Farmers Association, spoke glowingly of the ability of the agricultural community to raise money for the new growers' organization, commenting, "I am flabbergasted at [their] eagerness to respond financially." Fred Heringer, president of the California Farm Bureau, shared his goal of raising between $2 and $2.5 million, and Les Hubbard of the Western Growers Association used his organization's newsletter to gather a minimum of $100 to a maximum of $10,000 from each of his readers. In addition, the Associated Produce Dealers and Brokers of L.A. Inc. and the Council of California Growers broadcast their appeal for contributions to the committee's war chest through their members-only monthly newsletters. In the end, Kubo and his colleagues garnered donations from a who's who of the California business world, including Southern California Pacific, Superior Oil Company, Pan American Insurance Company, California Farm Bureau, Irvine Land Company, Newhall Land Company, Weyerhaeuser Paper Company, the Western Growers Association, and Tenneco. This coalition gave growers the resources to challenge the "Yes on 14" campaign with a barrage of television and radio ads.[71]

At the first few meetings of the Ad Hoc Committee, Kubo distinguished himself as a credible voice on farm labor issues. "[Kubo's] not polished and he's not a professional," one unidentified leader of a statewide farm group told a reporter, "but he knows what he's talking about and he knows how to tell it to the people." The local newspaper took note of Kubo's rags-to-riches story, deeming him "the ineloquent speaker-turned-spokesman" for all farmers.[72] His handle on labor issues that confronted a wide spectrum of the agricultural community, from large-scale farmers to small family farmers like himself, provided useful cover to corporate entities who had become easy targets for derision in the David-and-Goliath struggle. Seeking greater organization and a more sustained campaign, the Ad Hoc Committee chose to form a "No on 14" organization, Citizens for a Fair Farm Labor Law, and named Harry Kubo as their president.

Growers' organizations understood that economic superiority constituted only half the battle, given their defeats during the 1970 boycott. The ability of Citizens for a Fair Farm Labor Law to craft an appeal that resonated with voters behind a credible spokesperson showed a degree of savvy in a decade-long struggle to control labor conditions in rural California. At first blush, Kubo was an unlikely representative for growers. Like many Japanese American farmers, he had spent much of his life in rural California as an outsider to the European American–dominated grower networks. The Kubos' family farm in Parlier in fact was their second after Harry, his parents, and his siblings were placed in an internment camp at Tulare Lake in Modoc County, California. After leaving the camp, the Kubo family worked in Sanger, California, as field workers for 75 cents per hour. In 1949, they pooled their earnings and purchased a forty-acre grape and tree fruit ranch. While the family worked the homestead, Kubo and his brothers continued as farm workers to pay off the mortgage and raise money to buy an additional sixty acres. By the mid-1950s, the Kubos had accumulated 110 acres in the Parlier-Sanger section of the San Joaquin Valley and eventually acquired 210 acres by 1976.[73]

Kubo's entry into the battle owed as much to UFW tactics as it did to the vision of wealthy growers. After the UFW had signed contracts with most San Joaquin Valley grape growers in 1970, a small group of independent family farms constituting 15 percent of the market remained outside of the grower-union accord. In an initial effort to corral these farmers into contracts, the United Farm Workers picketed eight packinghouses handling their fruit and approximately seventeen farms throughout Tulare and Fresno County. Japanese Americans owned fourteen of the seventeen fields picketed, including the Kubos' small farm.[74] During the conflict, tension erupted into occasional acts of vandalism, including slashed tractor tires, nails and spikes in driveways, arson-caused fires, and yearling trees cut down at the trunks. Larry Kubo, Harry's son, remembered one incident in which a number of young UFW picketers entered the Kubo farm at night: "I was fourteen, and they ran on to our property and started screaming and yelling at us, and they were not much older than me." In their exuberance, the group vandalized the Kubo tractor. Through it all, Harry kept his family inside and told his son to "stay where you're at" until the group passed.[75]

Such encroachments on their property inspired Harry Kubo to action. "In 1971," he told a reporter, "I saw fear in the farm workers' eyes and I thought it was unjust." When he shared his concerns with workers and fellow Japanese American farmers, both gave him the same message: "Why don't you do something about it?" Reflecting on the moment, Kubo recounted the impetus for his activism: "The general thinking was that the entire government is built on equality, yet we weren't doing anything to preserve these basic rights for ourselves or our workers. We felt something should be done and someone should help the unassuming farmer and those who don't like to speak out."[76] Together with fellow Japanese American growers Abe Masaru and Frank Kimura, Kubo organized the Nisei Farmers League and became the organization's first chairman. The league began with twenty-five neighboring farmers; under Kubo's leadership, it grew to 250 members within a year. By 1976 the league had swelled to more than 1,400 members, of which, surprisingly, only 43 percent were of Japanese descent.[77]

Chavez and the "Yes on 14" advocates viewed Kubo's involvement as a cynical ploy by wealthy growers. Throughout the campaign, Chavez emphasized the $2.5 million budget of his opponents, which they used to hire "experienced manipulators of public opinion" who tried to "persuade a lot of people that passage of Proposition 14 will give the right to Mexican farm workers to enter their homes without permission." Such allusions to fears of home invasion never directly entered into Kubo's vocabulary, but growers employed Janice Gentle, president of the Central Valley Chapter of California Women for Agriculture, to make them. Gentle articulated the familiar concern of "allowing union organizers uninvited entry onto farm property three times a day" without explaining the context of their visits. She went further by asking the question "Why is it that a person who grows our food should be denied the same rights to his property that you and I currently have simply because we or our spouses work in construction, in a financial institution, or in a factory?"[78] Gentle's conflation of rural agriculture with industries that employ mostly white workers conveniently ignored the racial fault lines in rural California that were well known to the public. Such a conflation invited urban and suburban voters to imagine their homes or workplaces being overrun by Mexican workers, a specter that benefited the anti-14 forces.[79]

Kubo, however, remained focused on the consequences of the rules change to farmers and farm workers. He worried, "You kick an organizer off the farm for being disruptive . . . and the next day the guy is back on your farm and you have to let him enter and he can disrupt things all over again." Kubo believed, "Under '14' the worker would just about lose his right to work or not work under a union contract. The union could bring such pressure on him . . . he'd have to join even if he didn't want to."[80] In his rebuttal, Chavez ignored nuances in the anti-14 position, inserting a not so subtle jibe at Kubo's credibility by asserting that agribusiness had "already started a slick campaign...using a small grower as a front, presenting Proposition 14 as a violation of property rights."[81] Kubo rarely if ever criticized Chavez's character in public, but in his oral history, he shared his impressions of the labor leader after they met in 1974. "My first impression of him," he told his interviewer, "was a person that was very arrogant...but I also found that he was a very intelligent man, a person with total dedication to the cause that he was pursuing." Kubo maintained an abiding respect for Chavez, acknowledging that their "roots are the same" and that they shared a commitment to improving farm workers' lives.[82]

Although advocates for Proposition 14 refused to acknowledge it, Kubo's concern for private property rights stemmed from his experience in World War II. Like other Japanese Americans, Kubo saw the internment as "a black mark in the history of the United States" and vowed to "do everything in [his] power to disseminate and tell the people what happened in 1942" so that "it will never be repeated."[83] For Kubo, allowing the ALRB to dictate the terms of workers' access to private property harkened back to a dark period for him, one that included the interruption of his education at a community college, the undoing of eighteen years of hard work as a sharecropper, and ultimately the dispossession of private property that the family had worked hard to acquire. In his 1978 oral history, Kubo painfully recounted how local whites whom he referred to as "vultures" offered to buy appliances at severely discounted prices from his family when they were evacuated to an Assembly center in Arboga, California. "It took a lifetime to buy those things," he explained, "and they were offering my parents for the refrigerator and the washing machine two dollars, a dollar and a half, five dollars, and my father said, 'well, even if we had to throw it away, we wouldn't give it to them.'"[84] Fortunately for the Kubos, the Leak family, which owned the property they sharecropped, safeguarded most of their possessions and sent the family's portion of their earnings to them at the Tulare Lake in Modoc County, California where they spent the remainder of the war in an internment camp.

The kindness of the Leak family notwithstanding, the traumatic experience made Kubo distrustful of the government and vigilant about protecting his rights. For Kubo, the loss of appliances symbolized a loss of freedom associated with a life of farming, an occupation common among many Japanese Americans living in the Central Valley and the primary vehicle for achieving economic success for Nisei in California.[85] The position of "Yes on 14" advocates who saw the private property rights argument as disingenuous failed to appreciate how, for Kubo at least, such concerns were based in an experience of state oppression.

The cities became the battleground for Proposition 14, with both the UFW and Citizens for a Fair Farm Labor Law investing much time and money into winning the war of ideas among these large blocks of voters. Kubo traveled more than 30,000 miles and organized highly visible "No on 14" rallies in Los Angeles, the San Francisco Bay Area, and San Diego in the week prior to the election, drawing as many as 4,000 participants at each event.[86] He orchestrated successful door-to-door campaigns that rivaled the UFW's supremacy in grassroots outreach and conducted media events, complete with a country-western music concert that inspired supporters to attend rallies throughout the state. He honed the position of the growers to an easily digested message, "Protect Private Property—No on 14 Committee," that the public understood and editorial boards of several urban newspapers and television and radio stations picked up and incorporated into their opinions on the subject.[87] These efforts gave the growers an unprecedented voice in the cities and helped raise political contributions that supported an increased presence of campaign ads on the airwaves.[88]

The union countered these events with an aggressive grassroots campaign of its own. In Los Angeles, for example, the community organization Coalition for Economic Survival worked on behalf of the union to challenge the private property argument as "the old 'big lie' campaign." "They have poured millions into a demagogic 'vote no' campaign," its steering committee wrote to its members, "using the phony 'private property' slogan."[89] As the election neared, Chavez's attack on the validity of the private property argument became more urgent. In a speech to 800 supporters in National City, he implored the partisan crowd not to take victory for granted and urged everyone to assume individual responsibility for challenging the growers' attempt to confuse voters. "We've got to tell the people that [the private property argument] is a phony issue," he warned, "or we're in trouble."[90] In many posters and fliers throughout the months leading up to the election, the UFW routinely drew attention to Kubo's private property argument as "the Big Lie" and republished articles identifying the wealthy growers who had contributed to Citizens for a Fair Labor Law.[91] The union also highlighted the many politicians whom they counted as allies, including President Jimmy Carter, Governor Jerry Brown, Mayor George Moscone of San Francisco,

FIGURE 13. Governor Jerry Brown of California visits with Cesar Chavez and members of the United Farm Workers at LaPaz, Keene, California, 1976. ALUA, UFW Collection, 292.

and Mayor Tom Bradley of Los Angeles. In return, the UFW endorsed the candidacy of any politician who supported Proposition 14, including a very public endorsement of Jerry Brown for president when Cesar Chavez introduced him as a candidate at the Democratic National Convention in New York City.[92]

In the end none of these endorsements helped the union. Voters handed the UFW a crushing defeat, rejecting Proposition 14 by a better than three-to-two margin on November 2, 1976. The "No on 14" forces garnered more than 2 million more votes than advocates for the initiative and carried fifty-six of the fifty-eight counties in the state, with Alameda and San Francisco the only two counties voting in favor.[93] Although the growers' newsletter interpreted the outcome as "a repudiation of the naked power grab of Cesar Chavez" and "a major defeat for Governor Gerald Brown," Kubo offered a more sanguine evaluation, highlighting the importance of the organizing drive: "[It was] amazing to see the grassroots response from agriculture. People we didn't know were out there came to the front and pitched into the effort to defeat this bad initiative. It was this all-out support that made the victory possible. . . . Every grower—all of agriculture—can be proud of this accomplishment."[94] Union organizers tried to attribute the outcome to the growers' $2.5 million budget, but in the end the UFW spent $1.3 million of its own. To add insult to injury, the "No on 14" campaign ended the year with a surplus of $29,750, whereas the United Farm Workers showed a deficit of $218,448.[95]

The defeat forced Chavez and the union to reevaluate their assumed influence on the public. The appeal of the boycott to citizens had built an expectation that the union could always paint its opposition as exploitative and that consumers would always side with the farm workers. Indeed, the decision of the executive board to redirect the boycott network in the service of promoting Proposition 14 signaled such faith. Their defeat might be explained by the substantial media budget raised by growers, although the magnitude of the loss suggests other reasons for the one-sided victory by the "No on 14" campaign.

Support for Kubo's message manifested common ground between him and voters on the sanctity of private property in California. The electorate's decision was consistent with an entrenched preoccupation with the rights of property owners, clearly articulated in the repeal in 1964 of the fair housing law known as the Rumford Fair Housing Act. During the civil rights movement, the California Assembly had passed the law named for William Byron Rumford, the first African American elected official in northern California, that prohibited discrimination in most privately financed housing and outlawed racial discrimination by home lenders. In response, a coalition of the California Real Estate Association, the Home Builders Association, and the Apartment Owners Association organized a successful campaign to overturn the law by way of an initiative—coincidentally, also Proposition 14—that passed by a two-to-one margin. Racism clearly played a role in the vote, but many voters also expressed their opposition to what they perceived as the state interfering in the management of private property.[96]

Kubo's role also signaled an important turn in the political strategy of the growers. Prior to their victory, they had attempted to discredit Chavez as a false prophet, the UFW as a social movement rather than a union, and the Teamsters as the superior choice for workers. None of these strategies worked. In Kubo, however, they found a sympathetic character whose life story successfully countered the appeals of the UFW. By 1976 much of the public accepted the internment of Japanese Americans during World War II as an injustice and saw Kubo as a victim of the misguided Executive Order

9066, which initiated the government action. Indeed, within two years, the Japanese American Citizens League believed it had enough of the public's sympathy to launch a reparations movement.[97] Kubo's history gave him increased credibility with the public and enabled him to articulate a political position that questioned the state's right to determine who could enter private property. One of the most effective images of the "No on 14" campaign was a poster of Kubo standing in front of his home with the following message in bold letters: "Thirty-four years ago, I gave up my personal rights without a fight...IT WILL NEVER HAPPEN AGAIN."[98] This evocation of internment paid tremendous dividends for growers who, ironically, now relied on an act of racial injustice to stem the UFW's momentum.

UFW officials tried to draw attention to the inconsistencies between Kubo's life and the growers' position; however, the fact that voters bought Kubo's story made all the difference in the defeat of Proposition 14. The failure of the initiative ended the union's dream of rewriting the labor law and securing full funding for the ALRB, even though the California legislature continued to earmark funds for it. Indeed, workers continue to clamor for elections, and the growers braced for another contentious year in 1977. In response, some UFW organizers and executive board members prepared for elections. Eliseo Medina, for example, set his sights on addressing citrus workers' desires for an election in Ventura, while Marshall Ganz and Jessica Govea strategized on how to organize lettuce workers in the Imperial Valley who were denied elections as a result of the funding crisis.

The real cost of the ballot measure's defeat lay in the changes the campaign wrought on UFW strategy and Cesar Chavez's psyche. Chavez's decision to suspend the boycott in the service of the "Yes on 14" drive interrupted what had been an effective tool for the union. In the wake of the defeat, the union confronted a morale problem that rippled throughout its ranks, from Chavez to the many volunteers who campaigned for Proposition 14. In anticipation of the vote, Chavez characteristically started an eight-day fast to influence voters. When the news of Proposition 14's defeat broke, he ended his fast abruptly, eating so much at an election-night party that he made himself sick. On the drive home, he asked his assistant, Ben Maddock, to stop the car, got out, and sobbed on the side of the road for more than an hour. "It was a most awful time," Maddock recalled. "We were not used to having an election and losing like that."[99]

Those closest to Chavez remembered that he took the defeat personally and began to descend into erratic behavior. Esther Padilla believed that "Cesar lost

FIGURE 14. The "No on 14" poster, featuring Harry Kubo, 1976. UCLA Political Collection.

it after Prop 14": "I think he had a break down. He just couldn't believe that Cesar Chavez, this icon he had become, would lose an election." Ganz, who had been in the fields campaigning for Proposition 14, came back to find Chavez "really shaken up about [the loss]" and beginning to get "into some strange stuff." Ganz remembered, "He's doing mind control, he's doing healing, he's starting to talk about conspiracies."[100] During the "Yes on 14" campaign, Chavez made many trips to Los Angeles, striking up friendships with a number of Hollywood actors, including Valerie Harper from *The Mary Tyler Moore Show* and *Rhoda*. According to Gilbert Padilla, Harper introduced Chavez to mind-control experts, including "mentalist," Bruce Bernstein, and Tejano parapsychologist and author, José Silva, who espoused a belief in extrasensory perception, the ability to communicate without speech or physical gestures. Padilla witnessed Chavez's "shift in personality" and raised the issue quietly among friends, but at the time union members and volunteers were so involved in their own tasks that few noticed the change.[101] According to Esther Padilla, Chavez had a difficult time owning his decision to channel the union's resources into a losing battle. She remembered, "He had to blame somebody for the failure of Proposition 14."

In the past, the union had approached setbacks as an opportunity to learn from its mistakes and improve its strategy. This time, however, Chavez chose not to convene his usual meeting of the executive board to make recommendations on how to move forward. Instead, he left the postmortem to youthful volunteers, whom he summoned to La Paz. A crestfallen seventeen-year-old, Sharon Delugash, recalled how she and her fellow volunteers "look[ed] forward to that series of meetings so that we could commiserate and lick our wounds together." When they arrived at the North Unit for the meetings, volunteers were told by La Paz staff that Chavez would not attend in order to give them their privacy to be completely honest. Delugash and her fellow attendees, however, resented his absence and saw it as Chavez "not want[ing] to hear any criticism about what had gone wrong." Or so the group thought. As the meeting began, volunteers shared their opinions, including criticism of the leadership. Delugash recounted what happened next: "Suddenly Cesar climbed in through the window and was yelling, 'Bullshit!' We were stunned at how angry he was, and defensive. Maybe we who were not in leadership were terribly naïve, but this seemed completely in contradiction with how the union ran. We were used to singing every morning and talking about highlights and lowlights, not blaming ourselves for things, many of which were completely out of our control."[102] Chavez's actions and abusive words in this moment manifest alterations in his personality familiar to Gilbert and Esther Padilla, Marshall Ganz, and the few people who had witnessed his collapse in the days following the loss of Proposition 14. Tom Dalzell, a member of the legal team who helped pull the ALRB out of the fire, offered his interpretation of Chavez's state of mind at the end of 1976: "Prop 14 was not our first defeat (the summer of 1973 comes to mind), but it was a public and political defeat, which could not be turned to good. Cesar's faith in his ability to take his case to the voters was shaken, adding to his growing lack of confidence in a new world."[103] Although that new world still included a functioning ALRB, negotiations with the Teamsters, an effective legal team, and an army of experienced labor organizers ready to reach out to eager farm workers in Imperial Valley, Ventura, and Salinas, Chavez, for the first time, turned inward and dark, focusing on how he had lost control and obsessing about how to get it back.

SIX

Busy Dying

ON JULY 24, 1976, Nick Jones sat down with his old friend Bill Taylor to reminisce about the early days of the movement and reflect on the future ahead for the United Farm Workers. Taylor had worked for the union in 1967 and 1968, participating with Jones in the establishment of the boycott house in Portland, Oregon, until personal issues and differences with Jerry and Juanita Brown compelled him to leave. "I would have played it a whole hell of a lot different[ly]," Taylor admitted. "I was tired, frankly, and I used to runoff at the fucking mouth and call people names."[1] Taylor admired Jones for seeing it through and wanted to record for posterity how his friend had endured ten years in the movement. The two acknowledged frustrations, at one point hitting "pause" on the recorder to talk off the record. Now the future looked bright for both Jones and the union. In February, Cesar Chavez honored Jones's service by naming him national boycott director and entrusted him with more responsibility at La Paz. Jones embraced the promotion and engaged in a restructuring of the network that brought more volunteers and money to the union.

By September Jones could brag of a boycott department with more than 300 volunteers in thirty-four cities around the country. The increase in staff strengthened boycotts against Dole, Sunsweet, Sun-Maid, and Diamond companies and helped produce a contract with Dole's subsidiary, West Food's mushroom plant in Ventura, California.[2] The promotion had been gratifying to Jones, who, along with his wife, Virginia, lived and breathed the union. "We made our life out of it," Jones told Taylor, adding, "I will live and die in the movement." Taylor remarked on the potential in the summer of 1976, given the presence of a sympathetic governor in office, a likely Democratic president on the way, and the addition of new recruits. "It's like an earthquake waiting to go off," Jones predicted. "We're going to make that leap and very soon."[3] Little did he know that the tremors he felt beneath his feet came from a dramatic shift in Chavez's thinking and personality, one that would soon open up the ground, swallowing the new boycott chief and the future of the union.

Over the next four months much of the goodwill between Chavez and Jones disappeared. Tension between the two began when Jones questioned the diversion of his staff from the boycott to the "Yes on 14" campaign in California. Jones had placed an enormous amount of faith in the efficacy of the boycott and lamented a break in the action. Worse, the shift in strategy undermined his newfound authority and forced him to work under Marshall Ganz, the "Yes on 14" director. Since Jones had recruited much of the new blood, especially those in the all-important New York City and Boston houses, recruits sided with Jones and, according to some, took their time getting across country. Years later, in an essay documenting his experience, Jones recalled hearing "rumblings [among the leadership] about the boycott staff taking too long to leave their cities."[4] In spite of his misgivings, Jones honored Chavez's instructions to "clear the decks in the boycott dept.," relocating a total of 262 staff to California and leaving behind a skeleton crew of thirty-nine volunteers in boycott cities around the nation.[5] Still, the slowness of Jones's response and the alleged leftist orientation of some of his recruits unsettled Chavez, who became increasingly manic as the union's tremendous advantage in the fight to pass Proposition 14 began to evaporate.

A dispute over the reintroduction of the union newspaper *El Malcriado* amid the initiative campaign in September exacerbated tension between Jones and Chavez after the reluctant editor and Jones recruit, Joe Smith, ran afoul of the labor leader and some members of the National Executive Board. Chavez hired Smith on Jones's recommendation to oversee the revival of the paper following a hiatus from publishing for more than a year. Smith held an English degree from St. Ambrose College and exhibited considerable talent as a writer but had no experience as an editor. To compensate, Chavez also hired Bob Neff, a veteran of Students for a Democratic Society and an experienced editor. Although Chavez assured the two he would exercise only a light touch in overseeing the newspaper, his response to the first edition on September 15 betrayed his promise. At the next meeting of the National Executive Board, Chavez used the forum to attack Smith and Neff for seemingly minor transgressions: the omission of an article about board member, Mack Lyons; the inclusion of a story about the International Longshore and Warehouse Union rather than one concerning fellow AFL-CIO union workers at a rubber plant; and the absence of Chavez's name on the masthead. Although these were relatively small offenses, Chavez excoriated the two for deliberately misrepresenting the union and later fired Smith.

During the meeting, Chavez redirected his ire at Jones for bringing Smith into the union. When Jones agreed to meet with Chavez about the incident in October, Chavez surprised him with an expletive-laden assault on his character, accusing him of being a communist conspirator and recruiting several "spies into La Paz" to sabotage the union.[6] "For ten years," Jones sorrowfully recounted, "there had not been a hint of mistrust towards me because of my politics."[7] Now, on November 14, 1976, Nick and Virginia Jones saw no other choice but to resign from the United Farm Workers.

The Joneses' resignation alarmed UFW volunteers and devotees and confirmed fears that Chavez had initiated a purge of people perceived as being disloyal. The recriminations, accusations, and terror inflicted by Chavez and his followers marked the beginning of the end of a period in which feelings of collegiality dominated relations among UFW volunteers, the executive board, and farm workers. In the months following Jones' sacking, Chavez accused members of the extended network of betraying his orders, losing Proposition 14, and intentionally "fucking up" the union in the name of communism. Such charges, of course, obfuscated his responsibility for pursuing a risky initiative strategy. In the past, these failures would have been used as lessons to learn from; now Chavez sought to hold others accountable for their mistakes and look for ways to remove them. Rather than embrace a diversity of viewpoints, he widened his witch-hunt over the next two years to include targets within La Paz, the legal department, and the National Executive Board itself, at one point turning to the methods of a drug-rehabilitation expert cum cult leader, Charles Dietrich, to ferret out the "assholes."

Why Chavez engaged in such destructive behavior became the subject of much debate among UFW volunteers in later years.[8] For many who dedicated a substantial portion of their youth to the union, respect for their collective success has tempered much of the criticism, as have ongoing attempts by members within what remains of the union to control the narrative of Chavez's life. During the purges, volunteers and UFW sympathizers tempered their objections to Chavez's decisions with a healthy appreciation for the ways enemies might use such internal discord to their advantage. The few who witnessed the madness from the inside realized too late what was being lost in these moments, as questions of loyalty, sacrifice, and the identity of true believers cowed those who might have stopped the organizational tailspin.

PURGING THE BOYCOTT

In spite of the loss of Proposition 14, the union still had ample reasons to be optimistic as 1976 came to a close and the union prepared for a new year. The failure of the initiative ended the dream of revising the labor law and continued to ensure only a shoestring budget for the Agricultural Labor Relations Board, but the campaign laid the groundwork for a permanent peace between the Teamsters and the UFW. The Teamsters' endorsement of the initiative ended up being more than just an olive branch. The day after Proposition 14's defeat, Jerry Cohen received a call from Teamsters lawyer, Jack Ormes, on behalf of the western regional director M. E. Anderson, offering to work out an agreement to end hostilities between the unions. On December 1, 1976, the two sides agreed to a moratorium on filing suits against each other, and on March 10, 1977, Cohen and Ormes brought together Chavez and Frank Fitzsimmons, the Teamsters president, to sign a formal agreement to leave field workers to the UFW while granting the Teamsters primacy in organizing truck drivers, cannery workers, and other nonfield workers. The jurisdictional pact ended the six-year war between the two unions and created a clear path for the UFW to organize all California farm workers.[9]

Anticipating this agreement and the re-funding of ALRB, Chavez called a special organizing meeting of key staff members, executive board officials, and veteran organizers at La Paz on November 24, 1977, to discuss the future direction of the union. The meeting came at a critical time as workers prepared for the vegetable harvest in the Imperial Valley, with the grape harvest to follow in Coachella in the spring. Opportunities to capitalize on the union's momentum in elections the previous year had been lost amid the ALRB funding crisis, and Chavez hoped to regain some of the UFW's luster by claiming victory in these two critical areas. Unfortunately, the union faced a funding crisis of its own, having accumulated a debt during the Proposition 14 campaign while trying to maintain full service in a number of programs, including the Robert F. Kennedy Medical Plan, the Juan De La Cruz Pension Plan, and the Martin Luther King Service Center. Although UFW organizers had convinced approximately 28,000 workers to vote for the union during the first year of ALRB elections, UFW negotiators had secured contracts covering only 6,000 new dues-paying members. Failure to follow up on these victories meant dues constituted less than 22 percent of the union's income, a total that made the union dependent on donations and contributions from outside sources. Eliseo Medina, who headed the contract administration department, responsible for converting ALRB victories into union contracts, acknowledged the problem, complaining that his staff had been overextended during the previous year by the union's inability to concentrate resources on winning elections and securing contracts on larger ranches. Chavez agreed, noting that, although the union enjoyed great popularity, "it is a movement without members."[10]

The meeting produced a new plan of action that included three major changes. First, the union would concentrate its efforts to increase revenues by converting certified election victories into contracts. This strategy would require the union to streamline its procedures for negotiations, including giving more autonomy to field negotiators to sign contracts without constantly seeking final approval from Chavez. Second, the union had to cut back on services at campesino centers and clinics that generated filial-like loyalty but drafted away important resources from the union. Chavez argued pointedly, "The best service we can give workers is a contract."[11] By downplaying services, the union hoped to shift volunteers from centers and clinics to the front lines of organizing workers and negotiating more contracts. Third, Chavez reorganized leadership around regions rather than functions and identified six key locations throughout the state. Although Chavez detested the formation of locals, the union had already invested heavily in the creation of ranch committees, which generated a meaningful base of power in some areas around the state.

Chavez thought it worthwhile to risk facilitating greater autonomy at the ranch committee level for more effective organizing at the grassroots. The new regional structure encouraged competition among organizers, imposing a degree of accountability on staff members. While skilled organizers like Ganz welcomed the challenge, he also acknowledged that competition threatened "to create certain kinds of divisions in the leadership" that festered just below the surface.[12] For the time being, however, the new structure allowed the more accomplished UFW organizers to sink deep roots into the local culture and develop a passion for the union. Medina, for example, could now be freed from the tyranny of bureaucracy in the contract administration department to focus on organizing workers in Coachella and Oxnard, areas familiar to him. Chavez also established the goal of having 100,000 workers under contract by December 1, 1978, to motivate his team.[13]

By and large, union officials agreed with Chavez's recommitment to winning new members, especially Ganz, who had spent substantial time with vegetable workers in the Imperial Valley and Salinas, studying the potential for securing a permanent presence in the industry. Ganz welcomed Chavez's seriousness about organizing, in large part because it signaled a reversal in the leader's behavior that had given Ganz cause for concern. During the ALRB battles in 1976, Chavez had inexplicably withdrawn from the weekly brainstorming that took place among the active leadership and instead drifted across the state in what he called a *caminata* (long walk). "It was weird," Ganz recalled, "because the *caminata* was sort of like his own sort of act of sacrifice on his part, but it was curiously disconnected from the organizing."[14] Ganz did not pause to psychoanalyze Chavez, choosing instead to work with thirty-seven local farm workers and members from other allied unions to put together a string of victories over the Teamsters in Salinas. Occasionally Ganz became stern with Chavez in order to initiate deployment of experienced coordinators to the front lines of the battle. "He [eventually] agreed [to send] a team and then we were able to kick ass," Ganz remembered, "but it was like he was on another wavelength."[15] For 1977, Ganz anticipated between fifteen and twenty more contracts in the vegetable industry and the addition of 4,000 new workers in Calexico.

Chavez's plans also included a major reorganization of the boycott network at a time when volunteers were still settling back into their houses across the country. The order proved to be yet another challenge for the boycott department, even without the controversy of Jones's forced resignation, given that it had undergone a number of changes throughout 1976, including a major reorganization in the spring and the halting of the boycott during the fall in order to campaign for Proposition 14. In spite of these disruptions, the boycott network continued to raise money, bringing in approximately $258,000 during the months of May, June, and July before most volunteers came to California. When members of the southeast team returned to Florida and Atlanta, they picked up where they had left off, raising an average of $80 per day.[16]

Many in the East had grown comfortable working in a departmental structure where house leaders in a particular section of the country reported to division directors on their operations in a given city. For example, although separate houses existed in Boston, New York City, and New Jersey, each reported to the division director Charles March, a veteran boycotter located in New York. Similarly, in the Southeast, houses in Miami, Tampa, and Atlanta reported to the southeast division director, Jon Heller, also a veteran of the boycott, who had served time in Boston and Providence, Rhode Island, during the previous three years before relocating to Atlanta. Like most volunteers, both March and Heller identified as politically left, and each had a relationship with Nick and Virginia Jones. In Heller's case, during a conflict with a local labor leader in Rhode Island, Nick Jones inquired about Heller's political affiliations to rule out rumors that he maintained ties to the Communist Party. "We watched him closely," Jones reported to Chavez in 1975, "and never caught him promoting any ideology in his work."[17] Jones's private correspondence with Chavez demonstrates the scrutiny the union applied to its directors; it also suggests the importance of each one's job, given his influence over numerous volunteers. The new emphasis on organizing workers in California now threatened to dismantle this structure, because Chavez demanded the consolidation and regrouping of houses that removed division leaders and required those remaining in positions of authority to report directly to La Paz.[18]

Chavez assigned the reorganization of the network to a new national boycott director, Larry Tramutt. Tramutt met Fred Ross Sr. in Salinas in 1971 while pursuing a graduate degree at Stanford University and was inspired to follow the veteran organizer into community service. Ross took Tramutt under his wing, offering typically blunt advice. "To be successful," he told Tramutt, "you have to sting people into action."[19] Tramutt got his first opportunity to apply these lessons as the director of the boycott in Santa Clara County, California. Chavez appreciated his dedication to the union and saw Tramutt as the antithesis of Nick Jones: a loyal soldier who had come by way of his own mentor and who had performed his duties without incident. As the national boycott director, Tramutt received a number of delicate tasks from Chavez, including relocating staff to California to fortify organizing efforts in the fields, removing leaders whom he suspected of conspiring with Jones, and consolidating the Atlanta and Florida boycott houses into one house in Tampa.

Chavez, however, underestimated the response from volunteers to the Joneses' forced resignations, nor did he account for Tramutt's lack of subtlety in handling the emotions of people deeply affected by their departure. Virginia and Nick Jones had not gone quietly, choosing instead to write a letter to the National Executive Board that, in December, circulated widely across the boycott network. In it, they expressed their deep sadness at Chavez's accusations and offered details of the one-on-one meeting between him and Nick.

The letter depicted Chavez at his most paranoid, exposing his claim that Nick had misled him by sharing information about "splinter" groups but intentionally failing to report infiltration by "mainliners" (communists). The Joneses also protested the dismissal of Joe Smith and stood up for a number of volunteers suspected of disruptive behavior in the boycott network, especially Charles March, the northeast division director, whom Chavez claimed had sent five volunteers to undermine the Proposition 14 campaign. The Joneses singled out Larry Tramutt as a possible source for such rumors and challenged the board to assess each volunteer's value based on his or her work, not on "*chisme* (gossip) and cheap accusations."[20]

Letters soon flowed into La Paz from boycott houses in New York, Boston, Miami, Atlanta, Tampa, and Seattle, protesting the relocation and consolidation orders and expressing a deep concern about the red-baiting of valuable members of the boycott network. The strongest and earliest letters to arrive came from the Southeast, where the changes promised to dismantle the Atlanta house and overburden Tampa. Members of the three houses influenced by the consolidation vigorously protested the orders, citing their belief that "political motives" lurked behind several staff changes, most prominently the proposed transfer of Jon Heller from Atlanta to the Coachella Valley. Atlanta members praised Heller's leadership and appealed to Chavez to reconsider the move on the practical grounds of maintaining strength in growing markets. Offering Chavez a lesson in the geography of the new U.S. economy, volunteers argued, "Atlanta is the undisputed new commercial center of the nation." In proposing to move all operations to Florida, the union, they believed, had not taken "into account the critical importance of Atlanta as a grocery market, population center, and regional headquarters for labor, church, and civil rights organizations." These observations conformed to shifts in manufacturing and demography that placed a new emphasis on urban centers in the South. Holding on to the dream of creating a national farm workers union, the volunteers argued, "To attempt to organize farm workers in Florida will require far-flung urban support, not only in Florida, but in the entire Southeast."[21]

Jon Heller wrote to Chavez on his own behalf. He objected to the decision on three grounds: his transfer was politically motivated because of his friendship with the Joneses and their shared left-wing political views; it was part of a wider and, to his mind, misguided move by the union to dismantle the boycott; and he had neither the Spanish-language skills nor the same level of personal commitment to working in Coachella as he did to serving the boycott. Like many volunteers serving in houses across the country, Heller had developed an appreciation for the "delicate web of relationships" among churches, organized labor, and the grocers. To him and other volunteers, the strategic decision to dismantle the boycott had been "made in a vacuum," without any consultations from those, like himself, who had built and maintained the network and knew its power. "My experience over the past four years on the Boycott in Boston, Providence, and the South," Heller pleaded, "has enabled me to be of use to the union in the cities." Citing the relocation of fellow division directors Sue Sachen and Charles March in the Southwest and Northeast, respectively, Heller argued, "The leadership has made a series of decisions which threaten all of the progress our [boycott] Dept. has made in the past six months."[22]

Heller also strongly objected to the manner in which Tramutt communicated his reassignment. According to Heller, when Tramutt called him to share the order, he showed little respect for fellow division directors, whom he disparaged. Tramutt also gave notice to Heller's replacement, Richard Cook in Tampa, before consulting Heller. Adding insult to injury, when Tramutt learned of Heller's romantic relationship with an accomplished boycott volunteer and colleague, Claudia Shacter, he instructed Heller to tell the other member of his "pair" that "the assignment goes for her too."[23] Tramutt, anticipating trouble after his conversation, wrote Heller a letter reasserting his position without giving any ground. Embracing Ross's advice "to repeatedly prod [volunteers] to get off their butts," Tramutt acknowledged Heller's reservations and misgivings but coldly listed a timetable for him to carry out his orders.[24] In closing, Tramutt ignored Heller's request for a moratorium on the restructuring of the boycott and told him that having "first hand contact with workers [in Coachella] will . . . give [Heller] an added dimension."[25]

The callous nature of Tramutt's communication did not go over well with volunteers, especially Shacter, who had been in the union for two and a half years, including at the Tampa house since early 1976. She wrote to Tramutt and copied it to Chavez, expressing her belief that "the persecution of staff members in the union" had occurred "for no real reason at all except *chisme*, conjecture, and fantasy." In her recounting and judgment of Tramutt's method of reassigning her, Shacter pointed out that such behavior signaled a serious weakness in the union on the issue of the treatment of women. Chastising Tramutt for treating her as a "tag along" to Heller "with no consideration of her own work," she stated her belief that the union needed "to fight for the equality of women as well as the fight against racism."[26]

Susan Sachen, a five-year veteran of the boycott and the former southwest division director, shared similar complaints. Sachen had participated in the spring reorganization of the boycott in 1976 and weathered most of the tumultuous changes associated with the Proposition 14 campaign. In the run-up to the election, she worked to the point of exhaustion. After the defeat of the initiative, she took a two-week leave and moved back to her home in Kansas City to see her doctor and convalesce near her family. When she returned, Sachen expected to serve as the Los Angeles director; instead, she found her position given away to a male staff member with considerably less experience.[27] Like Shacter, she found Tramutt to be dismissive of her opinions and uninterested in her contributions. Prior to Tramutt's promotion, Sachen had played a leadership role in shaping strategy; now "at this time when the need is the greatest," she wrote Chavez, "I find myself more excluded than I have ever been from offering and implementing a program." She attributed this change primarily to the behavior of Tramutt, who maligned her in an address to the Los Angeles house and accused her of organizing to sabotage the union. Like the Joneses, Sachen resigned from the union.[28]

Collective letters challenging Tramutt's leadership and Chavez's decision came in to La Paz, especially from New York City and Seattle, where Nick and Virginia Jones had spent years in the struggle and recruited many volunteers. Both houses expressed outrage at the rash of transfers and dismissals as acts "reminiscent of McCarthyism." From Seattle, volunteers found the Joneses' letter "too believable . . . to dismiss" and alluded to Tramutt as one of the "individuals in the union who would not be above using unfounded charges, in bad faith, as a means of realizing [his] own ambitions for power within the union."[29] From New York, staff members expressed similar dismay over the apparent purge of leaders in the boycott, commenting, "Now many of us no longer feel trusted, no longer feel respected; we see many brothers and sisters being 'relieved' from their positions, and we are asking for a straight and personal explanation from you for what has happened in recent weeks." Echoing a request made by other houses, the New York City staff responded to Tramutt's cold orders with three sharply worded, bulleted demands of their own: a meeting with Tramutt and Chavez in the East to explain the dismantling of the boycott; evaluation guidelines for staff hires, transfers, or dismissals; and an end to politically motivated demotions and transfers.[30]

Several individual members from these houses wrote letters to Tramutt and Chavez separately. In his letter to Tramutt, Charles March acknowledged that the staff letter "most likely has not set too well with you or Cesar," but reassured him, "We are not out here planning an overthrow of the union."[31] Dale Van Pelt, a volunteer and leader in the Seattle house, assumed a similar tact with Chavez, reminiscing about Nick and Virginia's service in Seattle before expressing regret at "the part [the Joneses] perceived [Chavez] to have played in [their forced resignation]." Others took a much more aggressive approach, such as Mary Dynes and Dave Shapiro, former members of the New York City and New Jersey boycott houses, who questioned Chavez's commitment to nonviolence, given his attack on Nick Jones. Still others, such as Bill Ferguson of the Seattle house, told Chavez bluntly, "I do possess enough information to determine that something is terribly amiss within the union." Susan Sachen wrote Chavez to convey her belief that a boycott conference among division directors when Tramutt first took over the department would have smoothed the leadership transition and made all the volunteers less anxious. In wondering aloud why this did not occur, Sachen queried, "Did you trust our commitment so little?"[32]

Chavez refused to answer any of the letters and allowed Tramutt to handle the rebellion. Tramutt upheld the orders from his office and accepted the resignations from numerous disgruntled volunteers who took the union's silence as a sign of disrespect. When news of the Joneses' resignation became the subject of a *Los Angeles Times* article, the media-savvy Chavez uncharacteristically offered, "No comment," and directed all inquiries to a newly appointed public relations director, Marc Grossman, who answered questions from the confines of La Paz. In his response, Grossman corrected the impression that the Joneses had been fired and deflected allegations of red-baiting by suggesting that Chavez had disagreements with them on the basis "of incompetence, not ideology."[33] Such characterizations of the Joneses deepened feelings of resentment among boycott volunteers who knew them to be the hardest working members of the network.

The airing of differences exacerbated a moment of crisis for Chavez. The public's abandonment during the Proposition 14 campaign had been the first blow; now volunteers who had been the foot soldiers in the boycott appeared to be rejecting his leadership. Chavez's decision to surround himself with loyalists created a barrier between him and a network he had counted on over the previous ten years. Volunteers' reactions against transfers may have come from a fear of the unknown in their new jobs in California or unease about the prospect of leaving a tight-knit community of young people who shared similar politics and backgrounds. Yet the absence of transparency in the decision-making process and the assertion that "spies" lurked among the ranks of volunteers undermined whatever credibility Chavez and his lieutenants might have had with boycott staff. Although Chavez never offered an answer to Sachen's question, "Did you trust our commitment so little?," his silence spoke louder than words. In their collective letter to Chavez, Seattle boycott staff members acknowledged that organizations often deal with such problems with silence and encouraged him not to take that route. "We would have to interpret [the] failure [to respond] as an invitation to accept the Joneses' letter as accurate." To their chagrin, Chavez never responded.

Privately, Chavez fumed, seeking affirmation and loyalty from friends and staff close to him and enforcing order over the departments in the union where he believed he still had control. Among the few people to whom he listened, the advice of his longtime friend and donor Charles "Chuck" Dederich figured prominently during these critical months of transition. Dederich, a portly, white, former Gulf Oil sales executive from Toledo, Ohio, founded the drug rehabilitation center Synanon, which, by 1977, had treated thousands of addicts and developed retreat locations throughout California. The organization had evolved from Dederich's own battles with alcoholism and drug addiction and his dissatisfaction with Alcoholics Anonymous's restriction against admitting drug users into the group's fellowship meetings. Believing AA's public confessional approach to rehabilitation could help all addicts, in 1958 Dederich broke from the group, rented a storefront office in Venice, California, and convened a cadre of twenty drug world missionaries that grew into Synanon.

Dederich's emphasis on developing self-reliance caught on, especially with members of the jazz and performing arts world in and around Los Angeles. According to one contemporary observer, Dederich "achieved success at controlling addiction through habituating new ways of talking in order to channel new ways of thinking."[34] During the 1960s and early 1970s, this new way of thinking included an embrace of progressive ideas, such as interracial marriage and a practice Dederich called "hustling": encouraging the donation of products, food, and clothing to sustain the foundation. Synanon's success in attracting gifts led to surpluses that he shared with allied organizations, a process he deemed "anti-hustling." He saw the work of Chavez and the UFW as worthy of help and directed much of the group's "anti-hustling" to the union in times of need.[35] The donations created an enduring bond between the two men and opened Chavez to the possibility of incorporating some of Synanon's management practices into the union.

Chavez saw Synanon as an unqualified success story for the financial independence it had achieved and the strict obedience Dederich inspired from his followers, who lived on residential communes located across California. Dederich and his African American wife, Betty, lived with several other "lifestylers" on a sprawling 360-acre ranch he called "Home Place" in Badger, in the Sierra Nevada foothills.[36] Although residential treatment had been a feature at other Synanon locations, including in Santa Monica and Tomales Bay, Home Place marked an important departure for Dederich, from the open-door policy he extended to all addicts and a willingness to accept whatever they could pay, toward a materialistic lifestyle among a select group that emphasized comfort at the price of residents' personal wealth and privacy. In 1974 Synanon dramatically expanded beyond drug rehabilitation in favor of promoting an alternative, "intentional" community based on communal living.[37] Dederich encouraged several Synanites to abandon their careers, donate all of their worldly possessions and money, and work as staff.[38] To avoid paying business taxes, he declared Synanon a religion and began to promote specific diets for residents. He also played tapes of him reading "scriptures" over an FM transmitter called "the Wire" that was broadcast throughout the compound.[39]

At the heart of Synanon's practices was "the Game," a group encounter that one observer commented "is to their religion as the Mass is to the Catholic."[40] Inspired by AA's fellowship meetings and Dederich's reading of Ralph Waldo Emerson's essay "Self-Reliance," the Game involved eight to fifteen people engaged in an aggressive encounter in which participants were encouraged to publicly indict, or "game," one another for behavior detrimental to the maintenance of the group and destructive to the individual. Dederich believed that addicts, and indeed most people, wasted their energy by trying to cover up character traits that they should confront and abandon. The Game relied on the power of peer pressure. By confronting one another, Dederich argued, participants would confront their weaknesses and empower each individual to "detect and watch that gleam of light which flashes across his mind from within."[41]

In practice, the Game was very confrontational. Dederich encouraged participants to yell, curse, and scream at each other, and even suggested that people lie about another's behavior just to provoke an argument.[42] He also encouraged the use of obscenity and blasphemy, which he believed made sessions more engaging and entertaining.[43]

Initially, Dederich applied the Game to the treatment of addicts, but eventually he developed a belief in its powers to ameliorate tension and address destructive behavior among people in any group, be it an organization, a team, or a commune such as Home Place. Dederich never adequately explained how or why the Game worked in a communal setting, but swore that relationships became more harmonious and workers became more efficient in the execution of their duties. He diagrammed the place of the Game in communal life, depicting the community as a triangle and the Game as a circle.[44] The triangle represented the work organization structure that placed the leader alone at the top, a decidedly nondemocratic system that gave him complete authority over Home Place. The circle representing the Game, on the other hand, was a place where, in theory, everyone was equal and ordinary members could offer new ideas and disagree with him.

Although Synanon had success with the Game among drug addicts and recovering alcoholics, its ability to export its benefits to other organizations happened in fits and starts over eighteen years, until Chavez tried to incorporate it at La Paz in 1977.[45] Chavez maintained a close relationship with Dederich and considered "the old man" (as he was often referred to) brilliant for his ability to realize his dream of a communal living environment where he enjoyed complete power to pursue whatever course of action he thought best. Dederich maintained the illusion of democracy at Home Place, where residents resided in two worlds simultaneously: the everyday community of followers who lived and worked together to maintain successful drug and alcohol rehabilitation centers, and the space within the Game where people could say just about anything to anyone as long as it did not result in physical violence.[46]

At Home Place, Game rooms resided in a prominent place on the commune's grounds, and residents were expected to respect the separation of conversations within and outside the Game. Indeed, once inside the Game, an outside observer could be taken aback by the level of vitriol expressed among residents who, in their daily lives, asserted their love for their brothers and sisters. A judge in Detroit who witnessed one of the Games to determine whether to send juvenile delinquents to Synanon for treatment wondered if he "had been transported to Dante's Inferno where its inhabitants were half-human and half-demons." Although he walked away with serious reservations about subjecting youths to such methods, he recognized in the experience "a renewal process for many of those who play it."[47] During a visit to Home Place in 1966 to take advantage of Synanon's dental care for his children, Chavez exposed his own family to the Game. His wife detested the practice, and one of his children told him, "Daddy, I've never seen anything like it. . . . They're so mean!"[48]

Chavez showed no such ambivalence. During the restructuring of the union and the rebellion of boycott volunteers, he maintained an open line of communication with Dederich, although the content and extent of their conversations remain a mystery. Gilbert Padilla, who distrusted Dederich, believed "the old man" had advised Chavez to work toward the removal of movement veterans who challenged his authority. "If your people don't follow you," Padilla recalled Dederich saying to Chavez, "get some new people."[49] Dederich advised Chavez to use the Game among union members to expose those who disagreed with his authority and cultivate a new generation of loyal union officials among the youth at La Paz, including his son Paul ("Babo") and Dolores Huerta's daughter, Lori. Chavez's focus on youth mirrored Dederich's own emphasis on shaping young minds at Home Place, where Synanites' average age was between twenty-two and twenty-three.[50]

While away from La Paz, Gilbert Padilla began to openly question whether Chavez had "gone crazy." He prepared for an intervention, but no one wanted to believe him. Esther Padilla initially counted herself among the disbelievers, although eventually she came around to her husband's position. "[Chavez] wanted a group that he could dominate," Esther recalled, "[one] that would [convey] one message." According to the Padillas, Chavez privately advocated for a new philosophy—"one policy, one mind"—and shared his belief that "anybody who differed with that was out to fuck the union."[51] Tempered by loyalty to the union and his responsibility as a member of the National Executive Board, Gilbert Padilla withheld judgment, while Dederich moved more aggressively to establish a formal relationship with Chavez and La Paz.

In early February 1977, Dederich sent a forty-foot tractor-trailer full of food, clothing, and building materials to La Paz to improve conditions among residents. During this same period, he offered his helicopter and eventually sent his limousine to drive Chavez the ninety miles from La Paz to Badger.[52] At Home Place, Dederich impressed upon his friend the benefits that came with communal living, where residents pooled resources, regularly played the Game, and respected the authority of the leader. Obedience included the "containment" of residents that sealed them off from the outside world from time to time. Male residents voluntarily had vasectomies en masse in accordance with Dederich's teachings on the need to address overpopulation in the world.

Women voluntarily began shaving their heads in 1975 to effect a message of equality, but the custom quickly evolved into a symbolic act of allegiance to the Synanon lifestyle.[53]

Although these practices signaled an increasingly authoritarian bent to Dederich's rule, Chavez saw only harmony between the leader and his followers. At one point, Chavez and Dederich brought a handful of Synanites together with union members for a meeting in the North Unit of La Paz. Dederich instructed his followers to set up the stage in preparation for the event, while Chavez and a number of staffers looked on. One La Paz resident, Cynthia Bell, recounted what she saw: "All of the sudden these bald-headed people (men and women) poured in with their white outfits. They worked in silence and in unionism setting up within minutes the sound system/stage. Cesar was smiling and also observing in silence; then they left as quick[ly] as they came. I was just sitting there and all these mixed emotions going through my mind trying to figure out what this was leading to. Not once did these people make eye-contact with us."[54] After Dederich and his group departed, Chavez informed La Paz residents, "This is how I want you all to be!" Privately, Bell and others expressed reservations about Synanon but did not make their concerns public. In the meantime Chavez made plans to work more closely with Dederich's team, inviting one of Synanon's Game masters, Matt Rand, to prepare for experimentation with the Game at La Paz.[55]

Most leaders on the National Executive Board chose to ignore the changes in Chavez's character and priorities. The reassignment of organizers to regions meant that Marshall Ganz stayed focused on organizing vegetable workers in the Imperial Valley and Salinas; Eliseo Medina concentrated on making gains among grape workers in Coachella and citrus workers in Oxnard; and Dolores Huerta, Richard Chavez, and Gilbert Padilla worked in the traditional stronghold of grapes up and down the Central Valley. Others, like Mack Lyons, remained focused on their particular projects with farm workers outside of the state, whereas Peter Velasco and Philip Vera Cruz continued their work with farm worker retirees in Delano. Jessica Govea, the youngest member of the board, struggled to maintain health clinics in the field, including across the border in northern Mexico. Among organizers, Ganz and Medina made the greatest gains throughout the winter months of 1976 and 1977 and began to see the promise of further organizing in their respective regions, if only the union could decide where to direct its collective energies.

FIGURE 15. Members of the National Executive Board, June 10, 1976. Standing, left to right: Marshall Ganz, Philip Vera Cruz, Richard Chavez, Pete Velasco. Sitting, left to right: Mack Lyons, Cesar Chavez, Gilbert Padilla, Eliseo Medina, Dolores Huerta. ALUA, UFW Collection, 252.

Ganz dedicated himself to total victory in the vegetable fields of the Imperial Valley and touched base with Chavez only when necessary. Chavez's son-in-law, Arturo Rodríguez, worked with Ganz to educate eighteen inexperienced organizers transferred from the boycott to El Centro to pursue victories in a dozen ranches across the Imperial Valley involving approximately 2,100 workers. Under Ganz, the UFW team managed to achieve significant gains in dues-paying members outside of Calexico, maintaining a favorability margin of nine-to-one among workers in asparagus crops, and a 97 percent approval rating from all farm employees in the Imperial Valley. As the UFW team ramped up its offensive, growers struggled to counter their momentum.

The retreat of the Teamsters as a viable alternative to the UFW led one grower to the familiar option of creating a company union. At the Royal Packing Company, owners converted the employees association into the Agrupacion Independiente de Trabajadores and entered it on the ballot. When the new general counsel for the ALRB, Henry Delizonna, refused to remove the company in response to demands from the United Farm Workers, Ganz and a team of picketers descended on the ALRB office in El Centro, where they allegedly ripped paper from typewriters, took over telephones, and prevented a car containing five agents from getting to a preelection conference. Police arrested Ganz and twenty-seven picketers, touching off a public showdown with the new general counsel, whom Ganz referred to as "Dirty Harry."[56]

Although he publicly challenged the owner's actions that later resulted in the decertification of the company's victory, privately, Chavez questioned Ganz's aggressive behavior. Chavez felt compelled by Ganz's actions to unleash a vicious attack on Delizonna, calling him a "liar, racist, and union buster," but he admitted to the board, "I didn't feel too good afterward."[57] The assault on the ALRB office generated bad press, especially at a time when the union enjoyed an advantage in elections as long as it worked with the general counsel.[58] Equally annoying to Chavez, the disturbance had drawn him out of his cocoon at La Paz, where he had been dealing with the fallout from the Joneses' resignations and the news of rebellion from across the boycott network.[59] Chavez's decision to call a meeting of the National Executive Board in late February at Synanon's Home Place cheered Medina and Ganz, both of whom anticipated a serious discussion about strategy and establishing a set of priorities for organizing.[60]

The distractions in the Imperial Valley also troubled Medina, who wanted more attention paid to Coachella and Oxnard. Between trying to quell the rebellion in the boycott department and forging closer relations with Dederich, Chavez tried to put pressure on Delizonna to resolve the Imperial Valley conflict at Royal Packing Company. Medina disapproved of the idea of having Chavez fast and labeled his decision to conduct a vigil with 2,000 farm workers in front of Delizonna's office in Sacramento a "mistake." "How can it be that our job is to organize workers and I've got to be picketing the ALRB?" Medina complained.[61]

Ganz, of course, believed the attention on the Imperial Valley worthwhile, although he welcomed a clarification of priorities and believed, along with Medina, that too much time and money had been directed at what had increasingly become a losing cause in the grape fields around Delano.[62] Although the new regional structure pitted the two organizers against each other in a struggle for resources, Ganz and Medina agreed on the need to organize where the likelihood of adding more workers to the union showed the most promise. "Organizations are either growing or dying," Ganz believed, and the union had reached a period of stasis. "It's like the Bob Dylan song [It's Alright, Ma (I'm Only Bleeding)]," Ganz recalled, "you're either busy being born or you're busy dying." "And," he added, "we had a whole lot more being born to do."[63]

PHILOSOPHY

Most members of the executive board arrived at Badger with high hopes. Jerry Cohen, who had delayed his arrival to work on the Teamsters pact, anticipated a productive few days. Although he had to give up an antitrust suit against the Teamsters and lettuce growers in Salinas to get the agreement, Cohen believed he had put the union in a position "to clean the table" in the next few months by removing the main impediment to UFW organizers. He sided with Ganz in moving more aggressively into vegetables, recalling, "If you look[ed] at the election stats to understand . . . the strength of the union, you'd see that after the law passed, [Salinas and Imperial were] the base."[64] He welcomed the opportunity to debate the union's priorities and favored a shift away from organizing among grape workers.

Officially Cohen was not a member of the board, but he attended most meetings as the head of the legal department, especially when decisions related to the department had to be decided. For this meeting, he prepared to discuss a proposal submitted to the board by members of his paralegal team requesting that they move from a volunteer system to a wage-based staff. The team proposed that staff receive a base salary of $450 a month in addition to benefits and that a personnel review board to hear grievances be established. In the lead-up to the meeting, Chavez had dismissed the proposal and instead encouraged Cohen to move to La Paz. "Cesar offered me to come here and stay," Cohen recalled, "but [he said] 'I can't afford Sandy [Nathan] and all these people.'"

Cohen declined Chavez's invitation and argued for paying union lawyers based on simple economic terms. "If you have Sandy at 12 or 10 grand a year," he argued, "and the Teamsters' and growers' lawyers were going at $300 or $400 an hour, it's economic pressure." Cohen knew that it was this pressure that had brought the Teamsters and the growers to the bargaining table and thought that Chavez would be "whacko" to give that up to save a few dollars. He also argued that having the legal team in Salinas, closer to the base of power in vegetables, made sense.[65] Like others, Cohen had heard rumors of Chavez's quirky behavior at La Paz and was loath to relinquish the autonomy that distance afforded. By 1977 La Paz, in fact, had become a running joke among board members, a reputation about which Chavez had grown increasingly sensitive.

Early on, the meeting produced conflicts between Chavez and board members, starting with differences over the agenda. To begin, the group constructed a list of discussion topics. Eliseo Medina wanted to talk about organizing priorities and strategy; Mack Lyons raised the question of paid staff versus volunteers; Marshall Ganz wanted to address how they would deal with "Dirty Harry" and the ALRB; someone else mentioned the need for planning outside of California and inquired about the future of the boycott. Chavez, however, channeled all suggestions into the broad and amorphous topic of "philosophy." "I think we are at a crossroads of our philosophy," he announced. "I think we're confused." "Where are we going?" he asked the members. Ganz, who sought to make sense of his direction, offered a number of interpretations until he landed on an idea that Chavez approved of: "[The issue of philosophy] is the whole question of *community* and where that fits in in the whole scheme of things and whether we're serious about it or not serious about it."

The comment enlivened Chavez. "Exactly right, exactly," he told the group, "that's *the* word," referring to *community*. Yet the exchange proved to be a foreshadowing of future disagreement rather than a moment of common understanding. Chavez leapt to define Ganz's thought, offering, "We're growing two heads at the same time." For Chavez, who had grown increasingly committed to cultivating a community in the likeness of Synanon's Home Place, the union threatened to formalize relationships in a way that would deny his dreams for La Paz. Ganz stood on the other side, but for now he responded with the vague comment, "A lot of us feel two different ways about it." Chavez avoided conflict and simply repeated his belief that they would work it out in a discussion of "philosophy" throughout the day.

As the meeting dragged on, Ganz and Medina, both frustrated, joked among themselves, needling Chavez for his failure to rebuild the boycott and his aversion to strikes.[66] At one point Ganz encouraged the board to consider the financial health of the union and identify sources of funding, but Chavez ignored him, choosing instead to clarify the terms of the discussion: "The crossroads right now is, is it a movement or is it a union?" "We're at the stage," he elaborated, "where we need to make a decision because we are neither right now." Crosby Milne, who had been hired as a management consultant to create structure for the board, agreed, adding, "We're being managed by the law." The words rang true for Chavez, who worried aloud about how ALRA had changed the union for the worse. He told the board, "The law has changed us completely." Whereas the act of striking had defined the movement before 1975, "the strike is now the fight with the [Agricultural Labor Relations] Board." The law, he lamented, "has become the center of power."

Ganz and Medina seemed ready to engage that reality, but Chavez redirected the discussion toward more existential questions, including who should belong to the union, on what terms, and what should be their motivation for belonging. The questions reflected concerns on the minds of many board members regarding recent resignations and the legal team's proposal to pay staff rather than to continue the volunteer system. Several members of the legal team had come straight from law school to work for the union instead of pursuing lucrative careers in private practice. Chavez, however, measured their commitment solely by their willingness to adhere to the volunteer system. In the absence of Cohen, who had yet to arrive, Chavez stated his preference against paying people and declared "community" as the "next thing." "We try to build community," he asserted, "but we don't really have community." Addressing the recent departures, he stated, "We're not asking them to leave, but we should have." For him, the only people of value were those who came seeking community and who were willing to adhere to the volunteer system. Given these "facts," he saw the task of defining community as the key work of the board over the three days in Badger.

Taken on their own merit, none of Chavez's concerns were considered frivolous by those in attendance. Most agreed that the union had to reestablish an underlying philosophy, given that the law had forced a degree of institutionalization unfamiliar to most veteran members. Many on the board worried about the inadequacy of the current staff—in terms of quantity and quality—to meet the challenges before them. Medina complained that the union had not made "a real effort to attract *the people*," by which he meant farm workers. Others, such as Peter Velasco, shared the opinion that the union had forced out volunteers unfairly, which had produced fear among those who remained. Velasco waxed nostalgic about the early days, when a general feeling of "love" had pervaded the entire movement and people joined, went away, and then brought back their friends, offering food, money, clothing, and their time. "I think we've lost that love," he lamented. Both Velasco and Philip Vera Cruz were troubled by the purges in the boycott network after Proposition 14 and wanted to correct what appeared to be an arbitrary process of firing staff. Vera Cruz recommended that volunteers "have equal rights to express themselves" similar to those given to workers in the ranch committees. Velasco focused more on the poor conditions at La Paz, citing a lack of hot water, the "shaggy" mattresses, and the deteriorating facilities as reasons for low morale among volunteers living at the union's headquarters. "When it comes to our volunteers, we don't give a fuck," he stated bluntly. Velasco and Vera Cruz expressed a desire to increase stipends to address some of these ills, but both stopped short of recommending that the union pay its staff.

The question of abandoning the volunteer system for salaries was a serious one, given that most of their AFL-CIO peer institutions paid wages. Many confessed having trouble feeding themselves, let alone organizing workers on $10 per week, the stipend for NEB members. "Let's be honest here today," Richard Chavez complained, "you can't fucking eat on $10 a week anymore!" Clearly affected by his deprivation, he added, "It would clear my goddamned mind if I could get $10 to eat!" Throughout the meeting, he exhibited flashes of anger on the subject, at one point pushing the group to think about their future and wondering aloud about the value of their lives. "What's going to happen to me when I am 65?!" He urged the group to think about their worth to the movement if for no other reason than that it shaped the consciousness of staff who would later take over the union. "Someone might come into the administration and take over," he worried, "and say, 'ah, you old fucks . . . You've done your things for free . . . [now] get the fuck out of here, and we're going to take over and do things different[ly!]'" When his brother told him to stop worrying, Richard pressed the point: "I have to know how much I am worth to this movement . . . each one of us!" His concern shed light on just how alienated from the staff some members of the leadership had become. Several members expressed agreement with Richard, and some even began to calculate how their labor would translate into wages, but the majority refused to let go of the volunteer system.

Medina returned repeatedly throughout the meeting to his desire to recruit farm workers and people of color as an answer to the problem of a dwindling staff. "The fact that we don't pay is our strength," he shared, "but also our weakness because we attract every Twinkylander around." His comments revealed his discomfort with the predominance of young, white idealists who had come to La Paz often with very little connection to life in the fields. Alluding to the need to fire unwanted staff, he told the group, "We know what to do with them, but we don't do it." Yet in making the suggestion to get rid of more people and aggressively recruit farm workers for service, he acknowledged a conundrum: the more they improved wages in the fields, the less incentive they created for farm workers to become part of the volunteer staff. "I go out there and talk to a worker," he shared, "and

I say: 'You're making $3.40 per hour . . . come and work for *cinco pesos [por] la causa* [five dollars for the movement].' [They say] *'Ay, Chingada!* You're *loco, Cabrón* [Oh, fuck! You're crazy, asshole]!'" "We're making farm work so goddamned attractive," Medina alleged, that the workers had no interest in sacrificing their emerging "middle-class" existence for the poverty associated with union work.[67]

Medina's frustration with recruitment tapped into a growing resentment among many on the board toward farm workers who reaped the benefits of the union but contributed little to its maintenance. The disparities between their well-being and the struggles of union officials grated on members, producing a litany of complaints. According to Chavez, because of the union, "fifty percent of the farm workers are getting unemployment insurance, and another ten percent are getting welfare . . . food stamps . . . shit, they qualify for all the goodie-goodie programs!" Jim Drake reminded everyone that the union supplied farm workers with tax preparation services free of charge and suggested that they cut them off. Medina complained that irrigators represented by the UFW made $15,000 a year while he earned just $10 per week. Mack Lyons half-seriously joked, "Let's consider California liberated and move somewhere else!" Gilbert Padilla recommended Florida, where Lyons had hoped someday to organize black farm workers. When Crosby Milne tried to refocus the discussion on goals rather than complaints, by asking what the original intent of the movement had been, Chavez answered, "We've been so successful [in the fields], that we're having problems here [in the union]." Medina agreed, reminding everyone that wages had tripled in the eleven years since he had joined the union. Velasco, who had a longer view of these trends than Medina, shared that he had entertained the thought of returning to the fields rather than continuing to take the vow of poverty that working in the union required.

Chavez seized on the simmering resentment as an opportunity to direct the board's attention toward building a disciplined community. He admired Dederich for his ability to turn dope fiends, alcoholics, and criminals into productive members of a community that revered its leader. By encouraging the board to dwell on their material deprivation relative to farm workers and by casting recipients of union largesse as ungrateful, Chavez prepared the board to accept his new target for organizing: the people to whom he referred as "the *really* poor": "I think secretly all of us are really [feeling] a lot of pull in rural areas still with people who are not farm workers. They don't have jobs. And I think that, probably, that's one of the things that bothers us because we know that we're not reaching [the] *other* people who are unemployable. They're wretched. They got one eye this way, and one leg. They're old, they haven't got a job. Nobody likes them." His willingness to turn away from farm workers revealed his true intention of pursuing a vision similar to Synanon's.

While most pondered Chavez's suggestion, Ganz challenged it, asking Chavez and his fellow board members to consider what was at stake. "I am not sure where I came in on this," Ganz exploded. "You're talking like we have 80 percent of the farm workers organized. We have maybe 5 percent?" Trying to pacify Ganz, Chavez responded in a quiet, condescending voice, "Marshall [long pause]. It's just a matter of time." When Ganz proved not to be persuaded by his entreaty, Chavez added, "It just means doing it." As the first day came to an end, Ganz responded, "That seems to be presenting a pretty big problem." He wanted to get into "that problem," but just as he began, Matt Rand interrupted the meeting to invite the board to dine with Chuck Dederich and observe a session of the Game in another building.

The following day, Ganz grew more insistent on dealing with the problems of managing the union to its maximum potential. When Chavez attempted to channel the board along the same false dichotomy of paying wages versus building community, Ganz pounced. "I think there are much more options than the extremes," he told the board. Not keen on Chavez's intent to imitate Synanon at La Paz, he tried to nip the discussion in the bud by highlighting the differences between the two organizations. Reflecting on the board's communal meal with Dederich the night before, Ganz set up the scenario: "When it is vitally important to be at the meal time at that place and time, so that you can share with everybody in the community, or the gaming, or whatever it is, and then over here you've got someone who has been thrown in jail that you got to get out of jail ... are you going to choose yourself or are you going to choose the guy in jail?" Chavez refused to answer the question and insisted that Synanon's model was more similar to the UFW than Ganz recognized. "Yeah, but they're not involved with people out *there*," Ganz retorted, hoping to draw attention to the insular nature of Synanon. Chavez resorted to claiming that he knew better than everyone. "I know more than most of you," he told the board, "because I am at the eye of the storm at La Paz." Richard Chavez disagreed with his brother, arguing that La Paz had become nonrepresentative of life in the union. "It's isolated," he complained. "You can't work up there." Richard recommended that they convert

La Paz into a training center rather than maintaining it as the headquarters where people lived and worked. The idea precipitated an angry response from Cesar, and the two descended into an argument unique to siblings.

Realizing that the board was on to him, Cesar Chavez dispensed with all pretense of impartiality and launched into a defense of his community-building idea. "The way we are going," he intoned, "we're not going to make it." The board, he argued, could decide to start paying wages, but the numerous financial obligations of the union made such an option nearly impossible. The existing resources would require a much leaner staff and a reduction of services to which, he predicted, most board members would not agree. To this Chavez added a prophesy of obsolescence for farm workers and, by extension, the union: "No sooner than we will have it built than we're going to be faced with other forms of poverty... with mechanization and things coming up, it's going to be a small percentage of workers working, very well paid, a large majority of people in the rural areas still poor, you know, former farm workers, the rural poor." Under such a scenario, the detritus of a mechanized world—including both farm workers and their union representatives—would become the social outcasts for the new UFW to organize. Rather than wait to become obsolete, Chavez suggested that the board anticipate this change by organizing into collectives ahead of the apocalypse. "The way for me to go," he finally admitted, "is to have a community like Synanon or close to that and start truly cooperative ventures." "In other words," he added, "we start taking over the land."[68]

Chavez revealed the depths of his convictions by acknowledging that he had given this plan deep thought. In addition to his visits to Synanon, he expressed his admiration for Sunburst, a commune established in 1969 by Norman Paulsen, a disciple of Paramahansa Yogananda, the archetypal self-help guru who had emigrated from India to Los Angeles in 1920 to spread his message of "self-realization" in the West. Although Chavez remained loyal to Dederich, Paulsen impressed him as a man of vision who espoused the principles of high thinking and simple, natural living. "They used to live in wigwams, tepees, and abandoned cars, *really poor*," he told the board. Yet in spite of these humble beginnings, Paulsen inspired a small group of followers, some of them quite wealthy, to give up their worldly possessions, live communally, and begin farming 300 acres outside of Santa Barbara. Paulsen "had a vision in a dream to own a million acres." Within a short time, Sunburst had a yacht and airplanes at their disposal and had built a compound and cultivated an organic farm on 50,000 acres that provided for all the needs of the spiritual community. In addition to Sunburst and Synanon, Chavez had personally re-searched the Hutterites, another religious group living communally in North Dakota, and had asked Chris Hartmire, the head of the National Migrant Ministry, to research similar groups in Europe.[69]

Chavez shared his sincere belief that such "land cooperatives are going to come." The rise of other religious groups, such as Jim Jones's Peoples Temple and the Reverend Sun Myung Moon's Unification Church, yet to be discred-ited by homicidal tendencies and bizarre behavior, proved the popularity of communal living organized around one leader and inspired Chavez to see such models as viable options. "All the pressure that we have of getting out of the city," he told the board, "are pressuring people to go back to the middle ages." "Going back to the land," sharing resources, and producing their own food, he predicted, would make the UFW self-sufficient and "solve the prob-lem of machines by making the machines work for us." For him, unions such as the United Auto Workers missed an opportunity in the 1930s and 1940s to take over the factories and own them cooperatively, retaining most of the profits for the union. Realizing that his arguments were beginning to slide toward the Marxist theory he had accused troublemakers of espousing in the boycott network, Chavez asserted, "I am not talking about Communism; I am talking about cooperativism."[70]

As board members struggled to make sense of these new ideas and Clyde Milne encouraged Chavez to explain Synanon's relevance to the UFW, Ganz seethed. When Chavez dismissed the work of the union as secondary to the new challenges of organizing a commune, he erupted: "But there's a lot of real struggle ahead in California! We shouldn't be counting those chickens so damn easy. I remember we did that once before." Chavez rejected Ganz's im-plication that they were falling into the same mistakes they had committed after signing the 1970 contracts, when the mismanagement of hiring halls led to widespread trouble maintaining members. Instead, he chastised Ganz for seeing things through his "personal experience" in the Imperial Valley and encouraged him to "look at the whole union." When Chavez suggested that the real "missionary" work for the union existed in building community at La Paz, Ganz shot back, "But most of California is still missionary," suggest-ing that the aim of organizing and negotiating contracts had to take prece-dent in order to reach their goal of 100,000 new members before the end of the year. Admitting just how much he had shifted his priorities, Chavez re-sponded, "But we're not doing that anymore." "No kidding," Ganz sarcasti-cally retorted. "Let's deal with that! Most of the workers aren't organized!"

Rather than move the meeting toward a discussion of how best to add dues-paying members, Chavez and Ganz's confrontation descended into a debate over the exact meaning of "missionary work," a concept bantered about among board members that harkened back to the harrowing days of building the union. When Chavez argued that winning elections was the true "high" and suggested that negotiating contracts did not interest him, Ganz responded, "Then we should make it like missionary work." Ganz tried to put in perspective the work of converting elections into dues-paying members: "We have a couple thousand workers organized in the state, and we're talking as if we had 200,000 workers organized here and [in] the whole country, and now we're ready for a case of the hardening of the arteries. . . . I mean, shit!" When Ganz explained that negotiating contracts with those farm workers not covered by the UFW constituted "90 percent of what's left to do," Chavez accused him of being too absorbed in his work in Calexico. "But that's where the action is!" Ganz protested.

As the meeting wore on, it became clear that Chavez wanted the unconditional approval of the board to rebuild La Paz in the likeness of Synanon and other communes. "The road is open," he told the members, "and we ran out of gas." He saw the current work of the union as a dead end. He complained, "If we had 100 more organizers, we could go out there and get the goddamned job done, but we don't, see?" He explained that organizing for more victories would just produce the need for more negotiators of contracts; in turn, more contracts would require new people to administer to the new members. Inexplicably, Chavez attributed the failure to climb this ladder of tasks on "a very badly construed plan for a community" that dated back to 1962, when they began to think about forming a union. "We're trying to make it work, but it doesn't work because it's got to be remodeled."

The board returned to a discussion of paying or not paying staff, once again without a conclusive result. Medina agreed with Ganz that greater focus had to be placed on organizing rather than on retreating to La Paz. He preferred going after "more and more contracts," he told the board, so that the union would "attract less and less of the idealistic young people from the cities." He admitted, however, that such a scenario would earn farm workers "so much goddamned money" that they would not be attracted to volunteer service. Medina worried aloud, "We're going to shrink." Although Philip Vera Cruz and Richard Chavez expressed a desire to provide some form of material compensation for people's service to the union, including their own, no one could bring himself to endorse the payment of wages. Most did not understand how Synanon's model of communal living was relevant to the union, but everyone acknowledged that a common purpose and a shared community had drawn them to the movement in the first place. As Chavez ran down the list of board members in attendance for their vote, each hesitated to give his final answer and each expressed trepidation about paying wages. Mack Lyons warned, "If we start paying, we can't come back [to a volunteer system]," a sentiment with which everyone in the room agreed.

Just as Chavez took the straw poll on whether to pay members, Jerry Cohen stepped into the room, cracking wise about the bizarre behavior of the Synanites and requesting a rundown of the board's business up to that point. Medina, who seemed to harbor resentment toward the legal department for its proposal, delivered an early shot across Cohen's bow. "Why do we pay lawyers $600 bucks, as opposed to other people?" he asked. "That seems to me a radical departure from what we're doing." When Chavez responded that they had made an exception for lawyers and doctors in the beginning because the board did not think they could attract them without wages, Medina smugly joked, "I thought lawyers were coming because of Jerry's magnetic personality." Chavez returned the humor, confirming, "Well, that and $600." Medina feigned ignorance about the policy, pointing out, "You have people who are getting a salary that is considerably above and beyond what other people are getting."

As the straw poll came around to Cohen, he delivered the strongest position on the matter. Rather than shrink from Medina's challenge, Cohen addressed what was on everyone's mind: "I want to take a clear position, and my position is that we're going to have to pay people." A cagey tactician, Cohen coyly admitted, "I'm having trouble understanding some of the things that are being said," but still he offered an unambiguous answer to every issue raised to that point. Cohen worried aloud about the danger of experiencing turnover in staff at a moment when the union needed stability. In addition to the recruitment work of the field offices, he warned that the upcoming certification of contracts in their third and renewable year required members with experience in such negotiations or the union stood to lose hard-fought ground. He explained what would happen if they decided not to pay wages: "I don't think we'd have the continuity and . . . the competence and I think it is a question of survival, at least when it comes to some jobs." Turning his attention to Medina, he confirmed that the lawyers "*do* like the union" and "there is an element of the love for the fight but, without salaries there's going to be turnover." Citing a recent example in which several resignations in the legal department made for difficulties during an antitrust case, Cohen opined, "I think we wasted a lot of time by not paying people." For these reasons, Cohen told the board, he supported the paralegals' proposal, which he regarded as "well-thought out" and "reasonable." Ultimately, Cohen landed squarely on the side of paying people across the board for the simple reason that it ensured "competence and continuity." When Chris Hartmire suggested that the "continuity of [Cohen's] leadership" would produce the same security in the legal department that his had created in the Migrant Ministry, Cohen strongly disagreed. Echoing the earlier points made by Ganz and Medina, Cohen retorted, "I think it comes to feeling people's problems out there in the fields. It comes to servicing contracts. It comes to administering contracts. There's a problem there."

Although Medina disagreed with Cohen's position on wages, he appreciated his acknowledgment of the problem of attrition among the staff and used the opening to make his point. "In my opinion," he told the board, "we're overextended. We're doing too many goddamned things without enough people." He recited a list of departments that he believed needed to be cut, including the health clinics, the campesino centers, and the retirement village. Taken together with the requirements of operating the boycott, field offices, the legal department, and administering contracts, these tasks prevented the union from doing anything well. "Goddamnit, we should close the goddamned clinics," he angrily advised, adding that they should force the workers to go "to whatever doctor they want to go to in town." Sharpening his position, Medina argued that the union needed to concentrate on organizing workers. To do this, the union should "close everything that is not related to organizing and administering contracts."

Chavez agreed with the call to reduce staff costs but grew frustrated with the board's refusal to embrace his solutions. He seized on Medina's idea for cutting staff, announcing that less than 20 percent of the union's money came from dues and warning of massive layoffs if the board did not make a decision about paying wages. When dire predictions failed to spur the board into agreeing with his plan to concentrate on La Paz, he lashed out, "I can't manage the union unless I get some direction from you." "For many years," he insisted, "I didn't ask the board, I just did it." Although clear proposals had emerged during the meeting—Cohen's idea of paying people; Medina's plan to cut departments; Ganz's proposal to shift resources toward organizing and increasing dues-paying members; and Velasco and Vera Cruz's plan to improve living conditions for volunteers—Chavez refused to work out scenarios whereby any of these ideas could give the union some relief from its staffing woes and financial burdens. Instead, he pushed harder for his solution of community building at La Paz. "I think there is another way of getting people into the union," he announced, "but we need to have real discipline. We need to have a community."

Unconvinced, board members continued to discuss alternatives to Chavez's plan. Milne sought a middle ground between Cohen's position on paying salaries and Medina's preference for remaining an all-volunteer organization by suggesting that they determine which jobs constituted "missionary work" and pay some according to their value in the union. "You're not going to pay them and not pay others," Chavez sternly answered. When Milne asked why, Chavez upped the stakes. "Why not? Because I won't be here and be a part of that," he threatened. Asserting a veto power that most on the board never knew he had, Chavez added, "No way in the world I would let that happen."

Chavez's brinksmanship did not sit well with members, least of all Jerry Cohen, who challenged Chavez to seriously consider Milne's idea. When Chavez refused, Cohen scolded him, "Why do you prejudge it and say 'not gonna?' . . . That's a big weapon to trot out, you know." He paraphrased Chavez mockingly: "'If you do it that way, you're not going to have me around.'" Cohen warned that such an approach had a dampening effect on board members' willingness to try new ideas. When Chavez tried to redirect Cohen's challenges to "philosophy," the way he had with Ganz a day earlier, Cohen stood up to him. "Well . . . philosophy," Cohen groaned in disgust. "I always hated philosophy in college because it was never relevant to the facts." The confrontation invited other challenges, including one from Richard Chavez, who worried aloud about his own value to the union and accused his brother of not caring about the well-being of his or other volunteer's families.

The charges irritated Cesar Chavez, precipitating another sibling squabble. "I'm gonna tell you something," he asserted. "It's not threatening; it's just plain fucking facts. If this union doesn't turn around and become a movement, I don't want no part of it!" Moments later he accused everyone of ignoring his "special needs." "My needs are not being met," he claimed, "so when you don't meet my needs, then what do I do to defend myself? I say, 'fuck you!'" The tirade was a thinly veiled threat to withhold union resources when members in the field requested them. He placed the onus of the union's failures on the board, complaining, "We need to really stop all the crap and make some goddamned, hard-ass decisions." According to Chavez, their "farting around" and obsessions with negotiations—ironically, the work of a union—had made him an ineffective leader. "Pretty soon I become a goddamned fucking little clown. I don't do anything. I just bounce from one to the other." "Nah," he half-heartedly concluded, "I can't do it."[71]

The contentious nature of the conversation worried Chris Hartmire, who, unbeknown to most board members, had been drafted into service by Chavez to research communes and promote similar development at La Paz. Seeking to get his friend back on track, Hartmire invited Chavez to spell out what he meant by a community. When Chavez emphasized that it began with restricting access to the kitchen at La Paz and forcing people to eat communally as they do at Home Place, Ganz expressed skepticism, arguing that Synanon did not fit the UFW model. "Most of these communities spend a hell of a lot of time on each other," he argued. Chavez tried to defend Synanon by asserting that they spent time "on people," but Ganz corrected him forcefully, *"On each other."* The two went back and forth like this before Chavez finally erupted, "If we don't shape up we're going to have a goddamned union on our hands!"[72]

Sensing opposition from a majority of the board, Chavez finally just asked for their permission to try the Game at La Paz. Cohen, a skeptic, advised Chavez to first focus on delegating more duties, but Chavez would not have it. "No, Jerry," he responded, "I can't do that until we find something else to do . . . and that is The Game." Chavez informed the board that none of them would be expected to participate; rather, he had identified a group at La Paz willing to play. Ganz still objected, arguing, "I have a hard time believing that's the best use of your time. What about all those farm workers out there, who need you to go out there and talk to them?" In response, Chavez offered to leave La Paz four nights each month to minister to the grassroots. His plan revealed the depths of his withdrawal from the farm worker communities and the degree to which he had committed to turning La Paz into his own version of Home Place.

Chavez launched into a defense of the Game, arguing that the practice would help people "develop muscle" in confronting their wasteful behavior and anti-authority tendencies. He promised to take eight to ten people to Synanon every week to start and eventually expand to include everyone living at La Paz within two years. To help convince the board, Chavez called in Game master Matt Rand to describe how the practice had begun at Synanon and to answer any questions the board might have. Cohen worried aloud about the intensity of the insults exchanged within the Game, and suggested that some members would "carry their wounds" into daily life. Both Rand and Chavez tried to reassure him that the boundaries between what happened inside and outside of the Game would be strictly monitored, but Cohen refused to accept it, based on his experience in the legal department. He noted that although some of his staff could "fight and work" at some level, there were members, "if I jump them, it would really fuck things up." When Chavez suggested that this problem would be avoided because he would invite people to "game" him, Cohen retorted, "The problem is, they wouldn't say 'screw you.'" Both Hartmire and Milne warned Chavez that staff members regarded him differently than their fellow volunteers. Not recognizing the weight of their concerns, Chavez promised to "deal with my ego first" and "ritualize" the Game to mitigate any potential conflicts.

Milne asked Chavez to describe how the community at La Paz had received the news. Chavez noted that the vast majority "were afraid but in an inquisitive sort of way," although a small, vocal contingent worried that the Game would destroy relationships. Labeling these people "politicals," he attributed their reactions to their having a problem with his authority rather than legitimate concerns. One resident who had been recalled from the boycott to live at La Paz chose to quit in reaction to the announcement, but Chavez stated, "He was just looking for an excuse to leave." Unwittingly going back on his promise to separate what happened within the Game from what happened outside of it, Chavez added, "[If] I [got] the son of a bitch in The Game I might find out why he really is leaving."[73]

Many board members acknowledged that there would be few among them who could be as forthcoming in the Game as Chavez hoped, and many doubted it would be the "equalizer" Chavez and Rand promised. Cohen predicted that the Game would not be particularly helpful in making decisions that had political ramifications for board members. He argued that some matters were better handled through a subtle process of indirect communication rather than confrontation. "The Game may allow you to be honest," he admitted, "but there's a price that might be paid because I am not sure some of the people in this room would be honest back."[74] Tellingly, no one questioned Cohen's assertion.

That night, the union attended another demonstration of the Game, this time with an invitation from Dederich to participate. Cohen showed his willingness to mix it up with "the old man" when Dederich charged him with disloyalty to Chavez for his insistence on maintaining the legal department in Salinas rather than moving it to La Paz. Cohen laughed it off, dismissing

Dederich as "Chuck the Shmuck"; however, the accusation signaled that Chavez had confided private concerns to Dederich.

At the start of the morning meeting the next day, many joked about the incident, and most people seemed energized by the evening. Medina enthused about the communal meal experience, while Dolores Huerta, who had arrived just in time to partake in the evening's events, marveled at Synanon for taking "people [who] are broken and [making] them whole." Even Cohen, who had been skeptical, softened his opposition, seeing some value in the Game.

Ganz, however, persisted in challenging Chavez, pleading with him to acknowledge the differences between Synanon's mission and the work of the union. "There's a point where the [UFW] staff become so important to itself," he argued, "that that becomes more important than the work out there with the people." Chavez ignored his concerns, allowing the meeting to drift into personal grievances among members until Chuck Dederich arrived for a question-and-answer session. Only Chavez and Hartmire showed real interest in engaging Dederich, while Ganz wriggled in his seat, anxious to salvage some results from the weekend.

As the meeting wound to a close, Medina and Ganz tried to push their agenda even though the time for making critical decisions had long since passed. In the closing ten minutes Medina appealed for more support in Coachella for the upcoming harvest. When Chavez instructed Ganz to transfer his staff from the Imperial Valley to Coachella to help Medina at the conclusion of the elections, Ganz protested, arguing that organizers working with him needed at least a two-week break, and the board needed time to think through the strategy more carefully. Irritated, Chavez permitted the Imperial Valley staff a one-week break, but Ganz responded that he had already promised them two. "Why'd you give them my commitment without me knowing it?" Chavez angrily asked. Ganz offered an apology, but Chavez cut him off. "No, no, don't be sorry," he told Ganz. "Just follow the rules so I know what the hell you're doing." Ganz tried to respond, but Chavez would not be consoled. "Remind me to screw you next time, okay? All I want is a little respect."

The situation remained tense as Medina tried again to work in a request for more support, but neither Ganz nor Chavez would let it go. Finally, when Chavez quipped sarcastically that Ganz's "guilt" would eventually free up "troops" for the ensuing fight in Coachella, Ganz erupted. "What troops?!" he demanded. "You're imagining troops, too? See that's what I thought we were going to talk about at this meeting, you know, instead of, well ....," Ganz caught himself. Chavez, however, continued the fight, now asserting that he would "decide where the fucking staff goes." Ganz responded mockingly, "Be sure you have all the facts too." Chavez retorted that he did not need facts, and promised to do things according to his "own little whims . . . from now on." He added, "I get fucked every time I start trying to please everybody and we wind up doing shit."

Chavez quickly ordered Ganz, Richard Chavez, and Jim Drake to ride back to Delano together and work out strategy on the way. Worried about the magnitude of the undertaking, Richard complained that the task would take more than a car ride to plan. Ganz, still angry, added, "That's what we shoulda done for two days." "No," Chavez replied angrily, "this is *my* meeting." Ending the conflict on a note of personal bitterness, he added, "You guys just think about your needs. I also have needs. This is my meeting, so I can take care of what *I* need to do."[75]

In the end, the meeting failed to live up to anyone's expectations. In the past, Chavez had recognized the challenges facing the union at critical moments and leaned on his staff of advisors to achieve solutions to their problems. This time, however, Chavez repeatedly resisted the counsel of those in the field who could give him a different perspective. Ganz, who had earlier circulated a white paper arguing for the redeployment of personnel to vegetable farms, walked away from the meeting frustrated and confused by Chavez's behavior. "It was really bizarre," he commented in retrospect. "He always was a little weird. . . . I mean, weird in good ways." Ganz and the board had become accustomed to Chavez's eccentricity and had even come to accept his profane, often combative style in board meetings. Prior to the Home Place meeting, Ganz had seen these qualities as evidence of what he called Chavez's "strategic creativity," in which he argued with board members to come to some policy decisions. This had been "the joy of the whole movement" for Chavez, Ganz believed, in which he fed off the give-and-take with his comrades. At the Home Place meeting, however, he seemed to take on everyone, accusing them of holding him back, resisting his authority, and ultimately sabotaging the future of the union. Ganz recalled, "It was like all of a sudden, we were like a negative. The sense of humor went out of things."[76]

What motivated this shift is open to conjecture, although many acknowledge the defeat of Proposition 14 as a moment when Chavez experienced feelings of vulnerability for the first time. The purge of Nick and Virginia Jones was his attempt to place blame for the loss at someone's feet other than his own. The refusal of volunteers to accept that storyline accentuated his sense of responsibility for the debacle. Their rebellion also highlighted his fallibility as a leader and suggested to many that something was awry within the leadership. That most of these rebels had been white gave the conflict racial overtones that threatened the multicultural underpinnings of the movement. Unwittingly, Medina's insistence that more farm workers—by which he meant Mexicans and Filipinos—move into staff positions had fueled a growing resentment toward white volunteers who increasingly questioned the direction of the union. Oddly, these worries also facilitated bitterness toward the very people whose lives they aimed to improve: farm workers. The union's success in raising wages made volunteering less appealing to a population whom many on the board now saw as too dependent on them. Board members' indignation stemmed from feelings of insecurity and deprivation associated with the struggle to make ends meet under an outdated volunteer system. The board's unwillingness to grapple with the compensation question delayed reckoning with the institutional responsibilities of a union that now, for better or worse, functioned as the primary spokesperson for workers in California fields.

These observations, of course, assume that the National Executive Board was a democratic organization. It was not. In spite of his appeals to the board to make "hard-ass decisions," Chavez encumbered the process of collective decision making by narrowing the options to fit his own desired outcomes. When he did not get his way, he asked board members to step aside while he conducted his "experiment" at the union's headquarters.

Chavez increasingly relied on a smaller and smaller circle of advisors who supported his beliefs and facilitated his dream of achieving the control he perceived Dederich had at Synanon. His obsessions with "philosophy" and "community" only partially revealed his true intent to consolidate power at La Paz and weed out disloyal members whose resistance he attributed to an attachment to communism or their unwillingness to acquiesce to his authority. Up until the Home Place meeting, most board members had ignored Chavez's abuse of power. Some, such as Dolores Huerta and Chris Hartmire, even justified his actions. Their support notwithstanding, it was Chavez who demanded the power to hire, fire, and redeploy staff members as he saw fit. He also insisted on having all executive decisions regarding resources and contract negotiations pass by his desk for approval. Such requirements made him primarily responsible for the direction of the union at this critical time.

Historians usually avoid analyzing the psychological state of their subjects, largely because such an analysis assumes we can achieve a conclusion tantamount to a medical diagnosis when one is impossible. Certainly, in my encounters with veterans of the movement, the word *crazy* has been uttered by more than one person, but I believe such an interpretation of Chavez's thoughts and actions betray the complexities of the moment and the man. For example, no one on the board thought Chavez's concerns about the effects of mechanization unfounded, and even Ganz admitted during the meeting that the coming of machines threatened the future of vegetable workers in the Imperial Valley and Salinas (a development, incidentally, that has yet to occur).

Chavez's interest in purchasing land and moving toward what he misguidedly called "cooperativism"—to avoid the label of communism—offered a solution that, in retrospect, appears peculiar. His obsession with Synanon seems particularly troubling; however, it is worth remembering that the demise of urban living had become a topic for discussion by 1977. His back-to-the-land ideas cohered with a growing rejection of the city and a willingness to explore alternative solutions to participating in white flight to the suburbs. One can even interpret his yearning for community at La Paz as perhaps an unconscious desire to retrieve the lost paradise of his family's farm that had been taken from him during the Great Depression.

Chavez's turning away from a legislative solution is harder to explain. For him, the passage of the Agricultural Labor Relations Act in 1975 had imposed a process of professionalization that he neither anticipated nor ultimately favored, largely because it involved a shift from the act of maintaining a movement to building a union. He was not alone in his concern. Medina at one point quipped, "We ought to go to the Legislature and get 'em to repeal the ALRA and go back to the boycott!"[77] Indeed, the demands elections placed on the union, even and perhaps especially when it won, made the work of the union much more officious and less "missionary" than Chavez remembered it in the beginning. Rather than embrace that reality, as Cohen, Ganz, and even Medina had, Chavez conjured new objectives in private consultation with Dederich and Hartmire that he thought would lead the organization back to the glory days of the first strikes and the boycott. Dederich's advice to focus on the youth of the union encouraged Chavez to place less stock in the counsel of old friends and advisors such as Gilbert Padilla and Jerry Cohen. By the time everyone had arrived at Home Place, Chavez had clearly fashioned himself a reality that he anticipated would be embraced as another product of his "strategic creativity." When this did not happen, he saw their opposition as a consequence of their failure to see reality from his unique and singular viewpoint. Worse, he began to see the opposition of board members in the same light as he had seen the criticism from volunteers whom he had labeled "communists," "politicals," or simply "assholes" over the past several months.

SEVEN

Rotting from the Inside Out

THE UNITED FARM WORKERS' DEFEAT in Proposition 14 came largely by way of urban voters who understood the question of access to private property in much different terms than those who earned their living harvesting crops. While the campaign produced the regretful tactic of withdrawing the boycott from cities, it also enabled organizers like Eliseo Medina and Marshall Ganz to invest more time and resources into building strong ranch committees that formed the foundation of what the union referred to as "Ranch Nation." Ganz described the concept: "The Ranch Nation was like a little metaphor for describing the situation where the grower and the foreman, through their control over employment, exercise power over everybody in the ranch, namely the workers. So now, how do the workers get justice? Well, they have to develop their own power. Well, so how do they do that? Well, they have to develop their own leaders [as a] ranch committee in the union, and take the power away from the foreman. So it's . . . a power struggle. . . . In order to free the Ranch Nation, we have to create this parallel power structure."[1] By 1977 Ganz had built a very secure "nation" among vegetable workers in the Imperial Valley and Salinas, while Medina had developed a sturdy one of his own among the citrus workers in Oxnard and Ventura.

Ganz believed that the future of the union lay in organizing local workers involved in the ranch committees. "That was going to be the source of strength for the union," he reflected years later. On the face of it, such a strategy seemed to address the growing concern articulated by Medina that young, white volunteers were now running the union. The composition of the UFW's staff, however, indicated an opposite trend: about 50 percent of the union's directory contained Spanish surnames in 1977, compared to just 30 percent in 1974.[2] Still, most people on the board appeared to have agreed with Medina's call for more farm worker volunteers. In response to this concern, he and Ganz devoted much of their time to developing the leadership capacity of the workers and avoiding the madness that was percolating at La Paz.

The loose governance structure of the union permitted such retreats from the nerve center of the union, but the lack of connection had its consequences. Chavez's harsh reaction at the Home Place meeting in February 1977 to Ganz's granting a two-week vacation to volunteers was just one example. According to Ganz, the executive board had talked about a more coherent structure leading up to the 1973 convention, but the confrontation with the Teamsters and the loss of virtually all the contracts that season created a "meeting of the government in exile" that put off such a discussion. In its absence, Chavez ruled by fiat over a vast, unwieldy political terrain that produced more autonomy than obedience to the union leader. Rather than embrace the diversity of opinions and conditions extant among organizers, workers, and volunteers, Chavez tried to suppress expression. "Cesar was very, very suspicious," Ganz recalled. "[He] didn't want to have locals [because] locals develop their own politics."[3]

As a consequence, the distance between the ranch committees and the National Executive Board was greater than it should have been. "There was the national board and there were ranch committees," Ganz remembered, "but there were no elected bodies [and] no elected officers in between." At most, workers relied primarily on field organizers such as Ganz and Medina to carry their concerns to the board. The lack of a democratic process placed enormous pressure on the field organizers to achieve results on behalf of the workers. The pent-up demand for democracy led to the election of local leaders in the field, but such actions only delayed demands for more democracy. "The structure that emerged," Ganz remembered, "was one in which there was no political accountability."[4]

The arrangement suited Chavez, given his new obsession with creating a commune-like setting at La Paz. At the February meeting of the executive board, he expressed contempt for the rank and file and facilitated a "they'll take whatever we give them" attitude among some of the leaders. Ganz, who thought this position was both politically and morally reprehensible, found it nearly impossible to reach Chavez because of an inner circle of followers who now surrounded him. "Cesar was sort of floating up [at La Paz], being apotheosized in this domain, having some real personal challenges with no one able to really help him with it."[5] During the February meeting, Chavez disclosed to the board that his wife, Helen, had separated from him and was now living in Delano. His family also split on the idea of playing the Game;

his son, Paul "Babo" Chavez, was the only enthusiast for the experiment. Chavez's closest friend and confidant outside of La Paz, Chris Hartmire, took on the responsibility of answering questions from skeptics. According to Ganz, Hartmire's training as a minister should have given him the ability to help Chavez; instead, he ended up "amplifying" the problems by facilitating the Game and covering up his friend's eccentric behavior.

Without anyone to check him, Chavez embarked on a mission that deviated dramatically from the efforts of those most engaged with the workers in the field and from the legal battles waged by Jerry Cohen and his team of young lawyers in Salinas. At the time, Cohen worried little about the separate track on which his legal team moved. He had acquitted himself quite well in the Game at Badger, putting Chuck Dederich in his place and averting a showdown on the question of raising the pay of the lawyers or moving the legal department to La Paz. These questions, however, were secondary; as Cohen later admitted, "I [was] not a political threat [to Chavez]. I [was] talking in English to judges and growers and [Governor] Brown," whereas Ganz and Medina "were talking in Spanish to workers," organizing and empowering them to think of the union as their own.

Cohen believed that Chavez recommitted to winning the battle in the grape fields not because he believed strongly in the mission, but because it prevented Ganz and Medina from building up a base in areas outside of his influence. "I think he lost a sense of control," Cohen reflected. "I think that that's part of why he felt more comfortable in the grapes, because when it comes to grapes, he knew the game was boycott."[6] Although Chavez had significantly diminished the power of the boycott, the nerve center remained at La Paz. The move maintained his position of authority and, for the time being, kept the locus of power with him.[7]

What emerged in this crucial year of 1977 was an unnecessary showdown between "two different cultures": one in the fields among the organizers and the legal team, and another one festering in the home place of the United Farm Workers, La Paz.[8] Given Chavez's overwhelming influence, the fight would not be a fair one. Such struggles, of course, came about not because Ganz or Medina hoped to wrest control of the union away from the man they both respected. Rather, in the absence of a democratic structure, Chavez had to employ skills of self-restraint, diplomacy, and power sharing that by this time were beyond him.

On the trip back from Badger in February 1977, Richard Chavez, Jim Drake, Eliseo Medina, and Marshall Ganz tried to make up for lost time by planning their campaign in the grape fields of Coachella. Ganz questioned the strategy, given that Coachella had been a graveyard for the union in 1973. "We had this whole history in Coachella," he recalled, "especially with the migrants." The union's seniority system in the hiring halls favored workers who lived in close proximity to the fields and could sign up for job placements much earlier than workers who migrated. Such a system appealed to workers in Delano whose residency in the Central Valley permitted them to build stable, permanent communities.

In Coachella, where the growing season was much shorter and worker residency was much lower, the seniority system grated on workers. Coachella's location near the border also meant that Mexican immigrants constituted a much higher percentage of the workforce, adding to the union's challenge. Although Chavez had reversed himself on the question of support for restrictive immigration policy, the UFW's track record of cooperation with the Immigration and Naturalization Service in reporting undocumented immigrants made many migrants suspicious of the union. As Ganz recalled, "The migrants were sort of the least secure and the most hostile [to the union]."[9]

Ganz questioned why the union had begun its first campaign for ALRB electoral victories among a workforce as transient and undependable as the one in Coachella. Seeing things through the more familiar point of view of the vegetable industry, he analogized, "You wouldn't try to organize the vegetable industry by going to Huron [West Central Valley], where the season lasts for like three weeks, and everybody's passing through. You'd go to Salinas or you'd go to Imperial Valley, the home base; that's where you organize." Previously, although the union had secured the first contracts in grapes with Steinberg and Larson in Coachella, the pressure for those victories had begun by organizing workers in Delano. "The logic," Ganz explained, "is that you would start and end in Delano, because Delano is the heart of the grape industry, and if you could organize Delano, you could easily organize Coachella and Arvin [South Central Valley]."[10]

Ganz had already lost the battle over strategy when everyone on the executive board except Jerry Cohen ignored his admonition about organizing in Coachella first. Against his advice, his peers committed the union to winning back what had been lost in grapes. The decision proved to be fateful not only for the strategic points raised by Ganz, but because Chavez had wasted valuable planning time at the meeting with his failed attempt to convince the board of the value of the Game. As a consequence, the union was not prepared to take on the challenges in Coachella. Although the UFW retained control of Steinberg's David Freedman Ranch, they lost most of the others, including K. K. Larson, with whom they had held contracts since 1969. As Ganz later saw it, "We [went] to Coachella and [got] our asses kicked."[11]

As these challenges unfolded in the field, Chavez remained obsessed with La Paz. Throughout the spring, he focused on instituting reforms that drew the union into line with his vision of building a community. He began with the implementation of "high holy days" that celebrated the union's accomplishments in the tradition of "feast days" common in the Catholic Church. Among the first of these was "Martyr Days," in which he hosted elaborate dinners at La Paz in honor of Juan de la Cruz and Nagi Daifallah, two farm workers killed in the tumultuous summer of 1973. Chavez assumed that the union would evolve into a religion as Synanon had and that one day the community would "canonize them." In creating the days, he explained to the executive board, "The first step is [to] beatify our martyrs . . . and then about 150 years from now, 200 years from now, we make them saints."[12]

The most peculiar high holy day was Founding Day, a celebration to be held each year on March 31. The date supposedly marked the day Chavez officially resigned from the CSO to start the Farm Workers Association, although coincidentally, it also fell on his birthday.[13] Chavez created a new community life department run by Chris Hartmire, who took responsibility for organizing the events. On Founding Day, staff were encouraged to reflect on the achievements of everyone in the movement, but the actual execution of the celebration involved La Paz children drawing pictures of the leader and residents repainting Chavez's house in preparation for his birthday party. On the day of the event, mariachis and residents serenaded Chavez with the Mexican birthday song "Las Mananitas" outside his window at 6 a.m., followed by a *menudo* breakfast, mass, and a day-long celebration involving live music, a barbeque, and dancing into the evening.[14]

The merriment of these events belied a growing distrust that simmered just below the surface between Chavez and some in the movement. Chavez continued to purge volunteers from the boycott whom he believed were organizing against the union. In Denver, he targeted Mike Wilzoch, a popular but radical young director who had been under surveillance since the Proposition 14 vote for his decision to reassign "unauthorized non-staff" members from his team to Los Angeles to work on the campaign. Many of these volunteers were later sacked in the housecleaning after the election. Labeled "the Mike Wilzoch affair" within the inner circle of the union, Chavez asked Ganz and Chavez's future son-in-law, Arturo Rodríguez, to interview Wilzoch on charges that he had attended a meeting of Maoists. Wilzoch confirmed that he had been recruited by the group and unfairly implicated a fellow organizer, Jerry Ryan, in the meeting. His actions and misstatements earned him the ire of the executive board and expulsion from the union.[15]

Closer to home, suspicion swirled as morale deteriorated among residents at La Paz. Chavez had long blamed the executive board for "running down" the community and creating the perception that the union headquarters was a difficult place to live and work. In March 1977, he ordered mailroom staff to open all mail prior to its distribution, an ill-advised policy that had been in place since the founding of La Paz but had rarely been enforced. When a number of checks from contributors turned up lost in the mail, Chavez became enraged, declaring that the privacy of residents had superseded the economic viability of the union and demanded that the practice be restored. Although Kent Winterrowd instructed volunteers to have their mail marked "personal" and promised not to open packages or envelopes that appeared to belong to someone, the order upset many volunteers. Privately, some members began to question the surveillance now being practiced in their community.[16]

The deteriorating physical conditions at La Paz also made the union's headquarters nearly intolerable. During the February 1977 meeting, a number of executive board members, especially Pete Velasco and Philip Vera Cruz, pointed out that many volunteers slept on broken-down mattresses or the floor, and unsanitary conditions prevailed in most of the headquarters' eight kitchens.[17] Rather than address their concerns, Chavez blamed the residents for a lack of discipline, especially in the main kitchen in a building everyone called "the Hospital." He complained that the situation had become chaotic: cooking duties rotated among fifty-four individuals, and residents were permitted to eat at any time of the day. The open-kitchen policy existed as a consequence of the various diets at La Paz, including vegetarian, and the desire to give people access to food as they wished. Rather than discuss the situation with the community, Chavez ordered the kitchens closed except to a handful of cooks who would prepare communal meals served three times a day. "We're going to force the community," he told the board and predicted that half of the residents would resign as a consequence of his decision. "Let 'em leave," he added, hoping that the move would rid La Paz of troublemakers and "save a little money." Chavez also believed that the ritual of eating together would have the added benefit of creating a "church community" that mirrored the meals at Home Place.[18]

The proposal to reduce access to the kitchen especially troubled a group of volunteers who used the Hospital for what they called the "Veggie Kitchen" to prepare vegetarian meals. At gatherings, participants occasionally discussed their frustrations and compared experiences in their respective jobs. Two members of the group, Deirdre Godfrey and Judy Kahn, had worked in the union for four years, the past eighteen months of which had been shared in the accounting department. The monotony of their work, located far from the rest of the financial management department, had produced feelings of alienation. For Godfrey, the job was a dramatic departure from how she began in the union, working on the boycott in Toronto under Ganz. In Canada, Godfrey had learned valuable lessons about how to transcend what she described as her "privileged middle-class Anglo" background and connect with farm workers and people from all walks of life. In La Paz, she had lost that sense of camaraderie and eventually her passion for *la causa*. When she tried to take the matter up with Gilbert Padilla and Chavez, both lacked the sensitivity shown by Ganz. By the spring of 1977, she had decided to take a break from the union at the end of June, although she continued to participate in the Veggie Kitchen until her departure.

Chavez's irritation with the state of the kitchen raised his suspicions about the group. Since the February meeting he had played on the sympathies of allies and family members, encouraging them to become informants on anyone suspected of oppositional behavior. The group of loyalists included his son Babo, as well as Dolores Huerta's son and daughter, Emilio and Lori Huerta, Gilbert and Esther Padilla, Kent Winterrowd, Larry Tramutt, and Chavez's bodyguard and son-in-law, David Villareno.[19] Godfrey's failed attempt to resolve her concerns in a private meeting with Chavez made her a target for surveillance, and someone within this group began reporting on her every move and the actions of those with whom she kept company. When Chavez believed he had enough evidence to indict members of the Veggie Kitchen on charges of conspiracy, he met with his loyal group of followers to plan a community meeting designed to purge them from the union.

Known as "the Monday Night Massacre," the community meeting on April 4, 1977, quickly devolved into a Game-like atmosphere, with the Veggie Kitchen occupying center stage. During the meeting, Chavez allowed his team of loyalists to accuse members of holding "chicken shit little meetings" in private to plot the overthrow of the union. Before a packed hall in the North Unit, Larry Tramutt reported that he had heard members of the Veggie Kitchen call Chavez a "fascist" and charged them with the crime of counterorganizing. One of the newest volunteers, David McClure, had recently relocated from the South to work on the failing heating system at La Paz. When Tramutt accused him of being "an agent for the growers," McClure rose to defend himself but was quickly surrounded by Chavez loyalists.

Chavez interrupted the attack to wage an accusation of his own against McClure. According to one of his informants, McClure had been reporting on union activities to Senator S. I. Hayakawa, an ultraconservative California Republican opposed to the United Farm Workers. The charge turned out to be false. McClure confirmed that he had indeed made calls to a "Mr. Hayakawa," although not the senator. In his attempt to fix the furnace at La Paz, he had called a local company, Ayers & Hayakawa Energy Management.[20]

Undeterred by the error, Chavez and the loyalists continued their expletive-laden assault, forcing McClure to leave the building. Next they turned their attention to other alleged conspirators, including Kahn and Godfrey. Godfrey was shocked by the viciousness of the attack. Although she admitted to being worn down by her job, she believed that she had confined her "grumbling to those people who were similarly disillusioned." She admitted to complaining about the union's failure to rotate volunteers from job to job after a reasonable amount of time, but nothing approaching counterorganizing had ever taken place in their casual conversations during their preparation of meals. Kahn and McClure offered similar testimony, but Chavez and his supporters rejected such defenses. Anyone who dared to defend the alleged conspirators also came under suspicion. Godfrey later recalled, "I shall never forget the frenzied, hate-filled faces and voices of people who had been warm and friendly with me right through to the hour of the meeting."[21] In the end, Chavez ordered seven of the eight members of the Veggie Kitchen out of the union and off the premises.

That night the terror continued as expelled members packed their belongings and made arrangements with family and friends outside of La Paz. Organizers of the forum assumed McClure would not go quietly, given his resistance at the meeting, and called local law enforcement officials to have him arrested on trespassing charges. In a letter to the executive board later, McClure once again defended himself and reminded them that the union had abrogated his rights as a legal tenant by evicting him without due process. Others experienced harassment from Chavez's bodyguards. In a letter following her departure, Godfrey told Chavez and members of the executive board, "I have never spent such a fearful night as the one following that meeting." The security team restricted access to pay telephones and forced the expelled members to walk to the nearby town of Keene to make their calls. When Godfrey could not arrange for a pickup immediately, she returned to her room at La Paz, where guards "march[ed] through the halls every two minutes" in an attempt to flush her out prematurely.[22]

The events of April 4 did not produce the harmony Chavez sought. Because of his singular authority within the union to hire and fire anyone he wished, his decision to hold a public witch-hunt instead of private meetings seemed curious. Why hadn't he just called the accused into his office to fire them? He had used this more direct method in March, when members of the day care center in Delano had questioned his reduction in staff. Although farm workers regarded the child care service as essential, Chavez and Dolores Huerta suspected counterorganizing among some employees and decided to eliminate them from the union. David Train and Edy Scripps, two purged members of the center, wrote letters of protest but were ignored.[23] In another case, Chavez fired a volunteer, Roger Brooks, for questioning the mail policy and reportedly comparing him to Richard Nixon.

In all of these meetings, Chavez exhibited his infamous flashes of anger, shouting obscenities at the volunteers and berating them for having a poor work ethic and a bad attitude. Such private encounters, however, allowed residents to offer unsolicited criticism that further infuriated Chavez and reminded him that not everyone agreed with his vision for La Paz. In this context, the Monday Night Massacre served an additional purpose: it scared residents into obedience and extracted the kind of loyalty enjoyed by Dederich at Home Place. The "community meeting," as it was known at La Paz, polarized the community, forcing residents to take sides. As David Train later wrote, the public pursuit of conspirators "put [volunteers] in a position of either complete loyalists or complete traitors."[24] In the wake of the Monday Night Massacre, an estimated fifteen to twenty people either were fired or left the union voluntarily, many of whom had committed their lives to the farm workers' struggle.

Loyalty to the movement compelled critics of the Monday Night Massacre to restrict their complaints to Chavez and the members of the executive board rather than go public. McClure, for example, reminded the board of his restraint in writing a private letter, given that the extreme nature of the meeting would "damage liberal support and build the morale of the Union's *real* enemies" if word got out. In spite of his troubles, he held on to the belief that "the union [would] remain an example to unorganized working people everywhere." Godfrey also avoided circulating her concerns widely by carefully numbering each of her response letters so as to keep track of to whom she wrote. Most volunteers whose experience with the union had recently become negative avoided bringing disfavor on the UFW at all cost.

Within these circumscribed boundaries, purged members and critics expressed their earnest desire to save the union by offering constructive criticism. McClure and Godfrey expressed disappointment more than anger, and each addressed the "tremendous chasm" that had opened between "long-time core members of the Union and the recruited volunteers."[25] McClure opined, "An air of contempt towards volunteers" prevailed among the leadership and served as "the largest single cause of low morale" at La Paz.[26] Acknowledging the significant number of departures since the Proposition 14 loss, both encouraged the union to get to the source of the problem. Godfrey echoed what had become Chavez's common berating of volunteers, asking, "Isn't the answer likely to be more complex than that these people were not quite selfless, dedicated, and hard-working enough?" Citing the absence of the same rights for UFW employees that the union supported for farm workers, she pointed out the glaring "contradiction between the Union's expressed goals for farm workers and the ways in which it often treats its own staff." She concluded, "The divergence of principles and practice regarding the respect and dignity of all people is bound to weaken and sicken the Union at its very heart."[27] Both offered a vigorous defense of the role of the volunteer and strongly denounced the accusations of counterorganizing as "the very greatest violence" that could be done to the members who had served the union faithfully.

Chavez and his allies responded by dismissing their critics' claims as the opinions of people hell-bent on destroying the union. An internal document that circulated among the leadership at La Paz after the Monday Night Massacre reveals a hardening of their position, arguing that the expulsion of these members cohered with the "desire [of] Cesar Chavez and [the] National Executive Board that more farm workers be moved up into leadership positions." Although during the spring meetings the board had complained of a dwindling workforce and the need for more rank-and-file members to participate in the execution of policy, Chavez chose to deal with only the latter concern. "In [the] past [the] UFW tried to recruit people for specific needs," the document reads. "Now [we] want to recruit and train farm workers for some of those jobs." The position implicitly conveyed that their initial approach had led to the unfortunate consequence of bringing representatives into the union who did not reflect the interests of the farm workers. Repeatedly, the document labels the conspirators as "non-farm workers" in an attempt to undermine their legitimacy and insists that the "small group" had pushed the "overwhelming majority of [the] La Paz community" to the actions taken on April 4. The document defends the mail policy and reiterates the goal of "building a community at La Paz," adding without irony, "We want it to be the showcase of discipline, cooperation, friendliness, and production for [the] entire movement."[28]

As former members of the union shared their experiences with friends who had had similar encounters with Chavez, many began to formulate a critical response. Roger Brooks, for example, became increasingly troubled by the circumstances surrounding his firing. Afterward he moved to San Francisco, where many veterans of the movement remained in contact with volunteers at La Paz and received early word of the events surrounding April 4. He recognized the "vengeance and hatred" reportedly displayed in the meeting, having suffered similar threats of violence from Chavez's security guards, David Villareno and Carlos Rodriguez, during his last night at La Paz. In a series of letters from May 1977 to October 1978, Brooks recounted the offenses committed against him and tried to set the record straight. Of particular concern was the charge of "racism" leveled by Chavez for speaking out on the mail policy. "It was both shocking and a grievous disappointment to me," Brooks wrote, "to see you, an espoused leader of the nonviolent movement shouting obscenities . . . and calling me 'a goddamn racist.'"[29] He found the charge particularly preposterous given the nature of the recent purges: not only had the members been committed, hardworking volunteers, but they were white. If anything, it was Chavez who seemed to use race as a reason for purging volunteers. "You must resist the temptation," Brooks scolded Chavez, "to categorize us whites as liberal do-gooders, students and the like. There are many people who will support and work for the union regardless of skin color."[30] In a later correspondence, Brooks, having time to research the matter for an article he titled "Sour Grapes," found that of the thirty people who left the union in March and April 1977, only one person was Mexican American.[31]

Whether Chavez and the executive board had intended it or not, the call for more farm workers in the administration combined with the purges of mostly white individuals produced the appearance that the UFW had begun to spurn the help of some due to their background. Unquestionably, cliques had formed at La Paz, with many whites forming friendships and affinity groups that invited a narrowing of their perspectives. Indeed, in her prescriptions of remedies, Godfrey offered the somewhat condescending recommendation that Chavez spend more time getting to know who the volunteers were and why they had come to the union. That her solutions began with Chavez acquiring a deeper understanding of the whites and their sacrifices might have struck UFW leaders and Mexican American staff as self-centered, signaling a drift away from the integrated workforce that had always been the hallmark of the union. In some ways, Godfrey's opinions manifested a real need for community building that had become Chavez's agenda, but not in the ways he framed it. Rather than break down cultural barriers, Chavez used schisms within La Paz and the anxiety over the lack of farm workers in the leadership as a pretext to reach for more control. By framing the issue as a problem of authenticity and representation in the union, Chavez and the board fed the perception that the UFW now depended on the labor of Mexican and Filipino volunteers first and everyone else second. The struggle to staff all of the departments of the union suggested that Chavez could hardly afford to be so particular, yet he and some leaders pursued the policy anyway, regardless of the consequences to the union's multicultural image.

Chavez anticipated these charges by surrounding himself with white members who either spoke for him or carried out his orders. He relied on two white volunteers, Kent Winterrowd and Terry Carruthers, to enforce many of his demands at La Paz, and Larry Tramutt often handled the most difficult tasks of removing people whom Chavez deemed "troublemakers." Marc Grossman also served as the official spokesperson for the union, often handling questions from the media about the purges. To be sure, non-Anglos played a role in the crackdown, such as Esther Padilla, who functioned as the unofficial "mayor" of La Paz, although Gilbert's doubts about Chavez's sanity began to creep into her consciousness.[32] Family members such as Babo Chavez and David Villareno offered filial loyalty to their father and father-in-law, respectively, and Lori and Joaquin Huerta obeyed Chavez like a father. Helen Chavez's absence from the headquarters, however, made it evident that not all in the family condoned the world Chavez had created.[33]

Among those who spoke for Chavez, Chris Hartmire figured prominently. Amid the controversies surrounding the purges and the implementation of the Game, Hartmire's endorsement of Chavez's vision for a new community provided legitimacy that seemed to be slipping away from the leader. As a Presbyterian minister Hartmire brought a moral force to his work. He also had credibility with volunteers, rank-and-file members, and the leadership because

FIGURE 16. Cesar and Helen Chavez with their six children, California, 1969. ALUA, UFW Collection, 215.

of his involvement with the movement from the beginning. As the head of the new department of community life, Hartmire had accepted the responsibility of harmonizing relationships across the wider union community, including those outside the headquarters who heard rumors about strange behavior and mass firings. Although Chavez wanted him to live at the headquarters, Hartmire's living arrangement outside of La Paz enabled him to move much more easily among the various constituencies that made up the union. An articulate and passionate defender of Chavez, he took his position seriously and did much research on "best practices" in communal living settings. In fact, Hartmire and his wife, Pudge, had been out of the country during the Monday Night Massacre, spending time on a kibbutz in Israel and in a Hutterite settlement in France.

When Hartmire returned, he encountered a task far greater than any he had previously taken on: cleaning up the mess created by the new round of purges. In addition to the letters that came to him from former volunteers, he received inquiries from fellow workers, friends, contributors, and concerned members who had learned of the firings and forced resignations. Hartmire tried to strike a sympathetic tone in his responses, but his role as a self-professed "true believer" biased his opinion. He shared his delicate letters with Chavez before putting them in the mail to ensure that his message stayed within boundaries acceptable to his friend.

Hartmire's response to Sister Mary Catherine Rabbit, a volunteer in the Denver boycott house and a member of Hartmire's National Farm Worker Ministry board, served as a model for the many letters he was forced to answer throughout 1977. Rabbit knew Mike Wilzoch well and wanted Hartmire to explain his firing and the alarming rumors of a "witch-hunt" for conspirators in the union. Although he had not been around during Wilzoch's sacking and promised to get to the bottom of the case, Hartmire defended the general cuts in staff as part of a plan designed to make the boycott a more effective tool for the union. "That process," he told her, "will be slow and deliberate," especially because the union had to place an emphasis on organizing in the fields in the coming months. As with most of the policy decisions in the union in 1977, there was little logic to his argument since the union needed more volunteers to cover the wide array of tasks it could not handle with the workforce it currently had.

Only concerns about former members' political beliefs and intentions could explain their firings and forced resignations, but Hartmire worked hard to convince Rabbit that such worries had not been behind the union's recent actions. "It is unfair to conclude that the union was terminating people only or primarily because of political affiliations or ideas," he told her, although he knew better. Aware of the thinness of his argument, Hartmire admitted, "Not everything that happens within the movement is wise, right or just." The statement was a shocking admission of the leadership's fallibility, and still he asked her to accept their decisions. His and Rabbit's own experiences within the church, he explained, should have reminded her of the difficulty of running a large organization and given her reason to pause before criticizing the UFW. He added, "I don't know about and/or understand everything that happens within the union and I am a lot closer than most supporters. I can't imagine myself making judgments about the heart and soul of the movement based on what happens to some volunteers, even to some of the best and most dedicated volunteers. The UFW is a farm workers' movement!"[34]

Hartmire's message of volunteer expendability confirmed the feelings of many purge victims, who sensed that union leaders did not value their service. Moreover, his allusion to the farm workers being "the heart and soul of the movement" conflated the inspiration for the union with what some were now projecting as the ideal organization: a union by and for the farm workers. This position, of course, ignored that the union had always depended on the labor and contributions of people from various backgrounds.

Hartmire's duties also extended to the promotion and defense of the Game. His willingness to embrace Chavez's plan to forge more formal relations with Synanon endeared him to the leader and made him a valuable asset in managing the transference of ideas from Home Place to La Paz. Following Dederich's lead, Chavez wanted to move more aggressively toward buying property, but Hartmire channeled his energy instead toward the Game. He had visited Synanon's headquarters in Santa Monica during the early 1960s and respected some of Dederich's methods. He especially enjoyed the Game, although he admitted that it was not for everyone. "The Game is sensitivity training for the street," he explained. "I mean it's rough." Hartmire learned this firsthand when Chavez called him up to Home Place for an introduction. In his initial Game with Synanon participants, they verbally assaulted him for choosing to live in Los Angeles, far from La Paz where Chavez needed him. "It was a ferocious Game" and an "unpleasant experience," but he grew to appreciate how it taught him self-defense.

The ranks of those willing to ask questions about the direction of the union grew as word of the purges and the Game spread. Fred Ross Jr. and Richard Chavez, two of Cesar's most trusted confidantes, struggled to extinguish rumors about a "cultural revolution" at La Paz and contacted Hartmire for help. Hartmire defended Chavez's "strong, determined, persistent leadership" and rebuffed claims that he was cultivating a "cult of personality." "These same people," he wrote, "are *very* respectful of Castro, Ho Chi Minh, John L. Lewis, Mao Tse Tung, Mahatma Gandhi, etc." He advised the two to answer critics by pointing out "the blatant contradiction" in their positions. Hartmire compared Chavez to Chairman Mao, confirming that he had initiated "a mini-cultural revolution within the UFW" worthy of their support. "He is determined to carry it through and he is certain that it will help the movement." He also tried to allay their fears about the Game, citing his own experiences at Synanon as a testament to its value. Whether he was covering for its failings or had been blinded by his loyalty to Chavez, Hartmire asserted that the Game conjured "genuine tenderness, love and affirmation" among early participants and that such feelings had already become "the most powerful part of the Game."[35]

The growing questions about the Game and the endless stream of letters from former and current volunteers to the leadership compelled Chavez to take a stand against his critics. He targeted a set of meetings scheduled for late June and July 1977 to make his strongest pitch yet to the board. In preparation, he told the first Game group that they would play during a session for members of the executive board to observe and comment on. He explained that he would participate too, but also reminded them that this Game had a purpose: to convince the board that the union and La Paz would be better off with the Game than without it. These instructions, of course, violated the "say anything" rule, although the stakes were much too high to allow a free flow of indictments and risk creating a negative impression.

Executive board members came to the meeting prepared to discuss strategies for organizing workers and winning elections. The failures in the grape fields had caused a crisis of confidence among some organizers, while the persistent problems with the general counsel for the ALRB, Henry Delizonna, and the antitrust lawsuit against the growers occupied a majority of the legal department's attention. Few on the board had thought deeply about the problems at La Paz since the meeting in Badger in February, preferring to avoid discussions about the rumors of purges, hostility among La Paz residents, and surveillance of members. Ganz later admitted, "I just tried to kind of ignore it, you know, look the other way."[36] Instead, he saw the growing debacle in grapes as evidence that he had been right about the need to shift resources to vegetables and spent the weeks leading up to the meeting preparing a sixty-page treatise on the potential for gains in the Imperial Valley and Salinas.

Jerry Cohen also saw the failure in grapes as a painful yet positive indication that the union needed to shift its base of power from the external pressure of the boycott to an energized group of new members willing to seize control of the vegetable fields. "When you look at the grape boycott," Cohen observed, "you don't have the same kind of organizational punch in the fields." The boycott, he argued, functioned like "an economic gun to [the grower's] head," bringing about contracts that required relatively little negotiation. With the implementation of the ALRB and the increased savvy of growers regarding marketing, the union could not rely as much on these tactics. Under these new conditions, Cohen, like Ganz, placed stock in the fervent support growing among Salinas vegetable workers who were developing a "separate source of power" that the union should have been cultivating. "These guys in Salinas wanted to be in the fields," Cohen remembered. "There was real power generated there." Both Cohen and Ganz believed in this power, in part, because they had witnessed its development while living among the workers and watching the culture of the fields take on a life of its own.[37]

Both arrived at the executive board meeting hopeful that Chavez shared their interpretation of events, but neither really had any expectations, given their distance from La Paz. According to Ganz, "[La Paz] was a problem to the extent that it facilitated Cesar's withdrawal." The constant presence of people feeding Chavez's ego in a remote community fostered what Ganz called "the worst kind of loneliness and isolation."[38] These conditions, Ganz believed, caused Chavez to lose his connection to the rank and file, but most on the executive board did not detect the extent of his alienation. The meeting, however, would prove just how withdrawn Chavez had become by the summer of 1977.

INSIDE IS REVULSION

The June-July board meeting in 1977 began as usual, with the requisite departmental reports on the union's business. At the start, Chavez tried to impose the unusual practice of referring to fellow board members as "prophets" to cast a religious tone over the proceedings, but most took it as a joke and reverted back to the common union referents of "brother" and "sister."

During the first two days, the question of how to increase the number of dues-paying members dominated discussion. The cuts in boycott staff and the streamlining of departments through firings had brought down expenditures, noted Sister Florence Zweber, the head of the finance department, but the union drew only 2 percent of its operating budget from membership dues. The situation, Chavez noted, was untenable, not only because the dependence on donations placed the union in a precarious position, but also because he was getting tired of fundraising. Ganz recommended that the union take organizing more seriously, but Chavez chose to table the discussion.

Although Chavez waffled on a number of important matters of financial importance, he once again exhibited a determination to gain the board's approval of the Game. He closed the first day of the meeting for a session of the Game for the board to observe. He tapped a loyal group of staff and family members to participate, including Babo Chavez, David Villareno, Lori Huerta, Marc Grossman, and Kent and Esther Winterrowd. Chavez inserted himself into the session in an attempt to convey the message that he was open to being indicted for his behavior too and that anyone, regardless of office, could be gamed.

Some moments of tension surfaced, but on this day the Game came across as staged and heavily orchestrated by Chavez. Showing signs of having been coached, Villareno used the opportunity to game Chavez for his inadequacies as a boss. "You get on my ass about not being tough on the guys," he complained; however, when he attempted to arrange security for an upcoming trip to the Philippines, Chavez declined in order to save money. Villareno yelled, "You're inconsistent [and] chicken shit!" Lori Huerta accused Chavez of "trying to prove how macho he is" by traveling without union protection. When Chavez assured them that President Ferdinand Marcos of the Philippines would provide two presidential guards as security, Kent Winterrowd responded, "That's what Kennedy thought. . . . Money should never be a consideration when it comes to your safety."[39]

The contrivance fooled few on the board. When it ended, Chavez attempted to defend the authenticity of the session by observing, "I was gamed; not hard, but I was gamed." Skeptical board members groaned at the claim. When Chavez solicited feedback from the board members, most were critical of the practice. Richard Chavez, Eliseo Medina, Pete Velasco, Philip Vera Cruz, Jessica Govea, and Marshall Ganz all voiced their disapproval when asked their opinion. Vera Cruz offered the first critical comments, calling the Game "indefensible" and "aggressive." Chavez assured him that the indictments were not true and that the Game encouraged people to "say what you fear," but Vera Cruz saw no value in such an exercise. Govea offered her own indictment of the Game as inauthentic to the culture of farm worker families. "This is not the way I grew up," she commented, adding that her parents would strongly disapprove of the practice. "The other thing I didn't like," she told Chavez, "was that you didn't get gamed. They deferred to you a lot."[40]

Govea's comment struck a nerve with both Chavez and the participants who had hoped to sell this particular Game as an honest exchange among equals. When Chavez and Lori Huerta tried to defend the session as authentic, an incredulous Cohen expanded on Govea's point. "We've always had fights with Cesar about security," he told the group, recounting how Manuel Chavez nearly came to fisticuffs with his cousin over the issue when he managed the bodyguards for the union. Cohen continued, "Cesar knows they're fighting about it because they care about him. That's not a real game on Cesar." Cohen had not been a strong opponent of the Game, having played it effectively himself, but he hated that the group had tried to fake some of the exchanges to win the approval of the board. Although Chris Hartmire, Mack Lyons, and Dolores Huerta tried to defend the practice, it was evident by the end of the night that Chavez had failed to convince most board members of the Game's usefulness to the union.[41]

Chavez's inclination to table discussions came to a halt as the meeting entered the weekend and tensions came to a head. Many had grown frustrated with Chavez's failure to assume a leadership role in guiding the board on anything other than changes at La Paz. He had also permitted tensions to simmer among board members, and in some cases pitted one against the other to maintain his authority over the union. Ganz and Dolores Huerta, for example, had not seriously spoken to each other since negotiations during the Giumarra agreement in 1970 had strained relations between them. Huerta resented the close relationship between Chavez and Ganz and regarded Ganz as a "spoiled brat" and "Cesar's little boy."[42] Chavez also facilitated conflict between Ganz and Medina, two of the most vociferous advocates for rank-and-file empowerment, by tacitly favoring Medina's work with citrus and grape workers while ignoring Ganz's constant appeals to step up organizing efforts in vegetable fields.

Virtually everyone had conflicts with Dolores Huerta, whose esteem in the union had diminished since the early 1970s. Her tendency to pick fights with younger staff had earned her the ire of many volunteers, especially those in the Huelga School, an educational program for the children of farm workers in Delano funded by the Migrant Ministry, whom she suspected of counterorganizing. "None of them can fuck me up with the members," she told the board in a fit of insecurity, "because my roots go back many years."[43] Indeed, some veteran farm workers chose to remember her in her better days, but her circulation of rumors that conspirators were trying "to fuck her, fuck Cesar, and fuck the union" generated an unhealthy air of suspicion in the community and, in the case of the Huelga School, contributed to the purging of the entire staff. Her inclination to question Richard Chavez, with whom she lived in a common-law relationship and whom Cesar had placed as director of operations in Delano, led the brothers to secretly discuss moving her to La Paz without her consultation. At board meetings, however, Chavez openly used (and abused) Huerta as either his one-woman cheering section or a punching bag, depending on the circumstances. His dependence on her sycophancy and his tendency to make her the butt of his jokes did little to improve her confidence at a time when she most needed it.

At the weekend Chavez promised to tackle the big issue of how to deploy dwindling staff in the service of expanding membership. He saw two options: either finish negotiating contracts at ranches where the union had won elections, or organize workers for election victories at ranches that had not yet been tapped by the union. Gilbert Padilla, the head of the contract administration department and the person most responsible for training negotiators, shared his dismal report on the status of contract negotiations. Since the beginning of the year only fourteen new contracts had been signed, bringing the total number to seventy-one contracts covering 13,475 workers. Although the union had rights to negotiate with 109 certified companies, they engaged only forty-six because the union maintained just six full-time negotiators. "It's not a very pretty picture," Padilla sadly reported.[44]

The dearth of resources forced the union to concentrate on one function or the other, Chavez argued, but Ganz objected to such a Manichaean framing of the issue. "Concentration does not have to mean organizing or negotiations," Ganz challenged. "Concentration can mean [concentrating resources] on certain areas." He offered Delano as an example of a place where both organizing and negotiating contracts would be beneficial to the union, but Chavez dismissed his suggestion, insisting without evidence, "We know what would happen." He encouraged the board to "make a ballsy decision," repeatedly steering the discussion toward a narrow consideration of one option or the other. Ganz saw Chavez's set of hypothetical questions as contrived, given his unwillingness to engage Salinas workers. When Ganz pushed for a wider discussion of options, Chavez lost his cool. "Your mind is so fucking closed this morning," he told Ganz without irony. "I can't penetrate it."

Only Fred Ross Jr. demonstrated any sympathy for Ganz's position. He attempted to bring honesty to the brainstorming session. "We're having this discussion because of the grapes," he told the board. Ross cautioned his colleagues not to interpret the failed struggle against grape growers as a sign that they could not be successful recruiting new workers. He acknowledged that the board might feel some trepidation about organizing after the beating the union had taken in Coachella; however, he warned against seeing that experience as representative of their capacity to win elections. "We couldn't control the conditions," he told the board, referring to the high number of migratory workers in the area and the short amount of time the union had to prepare for the campaign. "We shouldn't have gone in," he argued. "We did it because we felt we had to do it to save what we had invested." Ross contended that the lettuce and fruit industries would be different, a position that supported Ganz's contention that the union could deploy its resources to individual crops rather than limit them to one function or another.

Ultimately, however, Ross agreed with the rest of the board's support for concentrating union resources in negotiations. The union had the greatest control over the boycott, he argued, because "it is our ballgame," yet the boycott department was in no condition to lead a campaign of any consequence now or in the near future. Ross diagrammed the options and ranked the strategy that best served the union. "The most control is enforcing the contracts," he admitted, but that would merely retain what the union had already negotiated. To add more members, the union had to decide between negotiations or organizing. In Coachella, Ross had witnessed the condition of organizers who had recently suffered crushing defeats. "The board has to face that staff in these campaigns are being chewed up," he reported. He acknowledged the heroic efforts by Ganz and Medina to rally the troops, but the curve had been too steep. Ross found the organizers ill-prepared, lacking "solid judgment about human relations," and not having the basic understanding or respect for the concept of "the ranch nation" and the people within it.[45] Mistakes had been made that could be overcome with training, but that would take time that the union did not have. Ross argued, "We owe it to those workers [to concentrate on negotiations]. No one should be defensive."[46]

The board's preference came as an incredible disappointment to Ganz, who rejected calls to "consolidate" resources to survive. "How can we talk about consolidating?" he asked. "There's nothing to consolidate there. It still has to be organized. It has to be negotiated. We've got to win more elections. There needs to be an overall strategy of attack which involves elections, negotiating, bargaining, where you wind up with signed contracts." He worried, "If there isn't a big election campaign, it's going to simply give credibility to the company propaganda that the union got its ass kicked in Coachella and therefore is not going to have these elections up here [referring to Delano]." Tapping into his belief that an organization must continue to grow or die, he added, "Either you go forward or you wind up going back."[47]

Chavez showed no interest in engaging Ganz's ideas, nor did Ganz's position evoke support from his peers. Although the final resolution would not come until the last day of the meeting, the board had decided to go all out on negotiations. Predictably, Ganz was silent for most of the remainder of the day, lamenting the missed opportunity to convince his fellow board members of the opportunity the Teamsters' evacuation of the fields had afforded the union.

Cohen's relative silence on the matter was the most curious, given his belief that the union should move more aggressively toward organizing vegetable workers in Salinas. Like many, however, he had grown tired of Ganz's self-righteous behavior and his tendency to blame anyone but himself for the failures of the union. When Ganz accused one negotiator on loan from the

UAW, Ernie Moran, of failing to secure contracts, Cohen erupted. "You can sit in this room and shit on Ernie," he told Ganz, "but Ernie didn't have a lot to work with." He reminded Ganz that the board had given Moran his instructions and that Ganz shared in the responsibility as a board member for what happened.[48]

Cohen's reaction to Ganz revealed his general dissatisfaction with his peers, which had been growing for some time. He especially resented Chavez's recent tampering with the legal team, including his attempted firing of Bob Thompson, an effective but opinionated attorney whom Cohen had refused to dismiss just because Chavez did not like him. Cohen had never been one to wallow in self-pity, nor did he appreciate passive-aggressive leadership, two traits that Chavez had increasingly incorporated into his style and encouraged in others by example. The long, tedious meetings that had become the standard practice of the National Executive Board also bothered Cohen, especially the episodic fights between Huerta and Chavez that prevented the board from making progress. Although Chavez believed the conflicts produced useful, frank discussions, Cohen saw them as annoying, counterproductive, and unnecessary.

When Huerta took exception to Chavez's questioning whether she had done enough in Delano to get contracts, Cohen decided he had had enough. He interrupted and announced that he would be "going to the mountains for six weeks" to think about whether he wanted to continue in the union. "You know, what makes me tired isn't fighting with the [ALRB] or growers," he told the board. "This is what makes me tired, really tired. The most dishonesty is right here at the board level." He accused Ganz of being a "fucking perfectionist" when it came to contract negotiations, whereas Vera Cruz was guilty of the opposite sin of not contributing anything at all. "Philip, you don't say a goddamn word at board meetings," he told him, "and it makes me sick!" Turning to Huerta, he yelled, "Dolores, don't be so fucking defensive!" "We better get our act together," he warned. "It's disgusting to sit back here and watch it."[49]

Cohen's outburst triggered strong reactions from the members and set in motion a landslide of accusations and confrontations. Richard Chavez shared, "I agree with every goddamn word Jerry said. We are not fucking honest in this circle here. People are not free to say what they want to say because they'll get in trouble." He revealed that, in the past, when he said something controversial at board meetings, his brother appeared at his house soon after to draw him back in line. Vera Cruz accused his peers of discriminating against Filipino members. Jim Drake claimed that they had lost a sense of trust among themselves. When Padilla disputed Drake's assertion, Huerta confronted Padilla for conspiring against Chavez. "We haven't gotten along since you were badmouthing what was [going on] up here at La Paz," she said, "making fun of Cesar, making fun of the Game, making fun of everyone here, and I don't think that's a way for a goddamn leader to act. You've been going around behind Cesar's back, and you've been undermining what he's doing and you haven't got the goddamn guts to face him and tell him face to face." When Padilla asked her, "How do you know we haven't had a face to face?," Huerta stumbled and stammered, prompting Padilla's angry order "Shut up." Huerta shot back that she should have been named secretary of the union, not Padilla, revealing yet another layer of insecurity now consuming her.

Rather than intervene, Chavez let the malevolence consume the board. His failure to channel the ugly exchanges into a productive dialogue had become part of his management style. He had learned how to use confrontations among volunteers and union officials as a mechanism for dealing with people whom he deemed troublemakers, allowing him to impose discipline and order without sacrificing his own image as a benevolent leader. He told the board, "I use my aura to run [the union]," but his contention rang hollow in light of the expletive-laden firings of some individuals over the past year. Still, Chavez had grown fond of the pressure he witnessed in the Game, achieving conformity through a combination of peer pressure and intimidation that came from multiple directions but rarely came directly from him. The tactic put anyone who had the slightest doubts about the direction of the union on edge, yet few felt empowered to challenge the leader for fear of being labeled a traitor to the union. If Chavez cared whether expressions of loyalty came by way of fear or respect, he did not show it, but many loyalists began to question why they were following a path that many in the field saw as unproductive and self-indulgent.

Members of the board began to penetrate Chavez's self-proclaimed aura of piety and questioned the illusion of democracy. Mack Lyons accused Chavez of being dishonest when he challenged board members to be more responsible. According to Lyons, Chavez possessed the ultimate responsibility to lead the board. "You're trying to give people the opportunity to pop up and do something," he told Chavez, but added, "That's bullshit." He informed Chavez that he had an obligation as president to lead, but he had abdicated that responsibility for some time now. Jim Drake agreed, going so far as to call the board "a charade." Drake challenged Chavez, "You got the power. Now either you're going to use it or let it go, but you can't be halfway in between." When Chavez used Huerta's temper tantrums as an excuse for not being more assertive, Lyons objected. "We can't think of [losing somebody] as a fucking disaster. You're talking about the survival of the movement!"

Chavez tried to evoke sympathy by telling the board he knew assassins were lurking in the shadows ready to kill him at any moment. No one took the bait. Finding the courage to confront Chavez, Drake replied, "That's . . . the ultimate argument because we can't argue with you. . . . I don't think you can pull that. That's a fucking cop-out." Lyons added, "You're worried about the future. You should worry if you don't do your job."

Surprised by their challenges, Chavez attempted to command loyalty by arguing that he had come under extreme pressure from subversive forces. "It has become fashionable to criticize me," he told them. He claimed that an "Anglo volunteer syndrome" permeated the union staff, conditioning them to judge any strong actions on his part as evidence that he had become a dictator. Chavez complained that the attitude encumbered his ability to act decisively and prevented him from enacting a vision that would lead the union out of its current morass. "I know there are smarter people than I am," he demurred, but added, "not fucking cagier . . . I'm the cagiest." Such a trait, he argued, had come in handy in dealing with most board members who had been too quick to side with his critics. "It's there," he told them. "I need to feel comfortable that I can get in a fight and nothing is going to stay there." Except for Ganz, Huerta, and Cohen, Chavez explained, he worried that most on the board would "bring out the skeletons in [his] closet" or label him a "fucking dictator" if he pushed too hard. "It hurts," he complained. "It really does."

Chavez's depiction of himself as an embattled but patient leader belied the reality of his exercise of power during the past year. The move sought to circumvent personal accountability and avoid confronting his shortcomings. In spite of his complaints, Chavez had found the means to do the things he wanted to do: pursuing Proposition 14, contracting the boycott network, implementing the Game, and purging "assholes" from La Paz. When the union failed—the loss of Proposition 14, the failure to capitalize on the pact with the Teamsters, and the recent losses in Coachella—he sought to deflect the blame onto the board. Even the rumors of dissension among staff at La Paz he attributed to the actions of board members. Their failure to be good role models by not accepting the Game and their habit of "running down" La Paz while talking about the union with workers in the field offices set a bad example for members throughout the union. Regardless of the problem, Chavez seemed to always place blame at the feet of the board.

Chavez's complaints quickly coalesced into his familiar appeal for building community. "I am convinced if we don't form a community . . . we'll never get to a point where we will act as one." He recognized the need to consider alternative viewpoints, yet accommodation had its limits. "Unless we release some of those individual rights for the good of one," he warned, "we're never going to make it." He asked the members for the freedom to follow his instincts, no matter the consequences. He acknowledged the presence of skeptics within the wider orbit of the union and again offered the self-serving prediction that his vision could be interrupted by assassination. His greatest fear, however, was not being "bumped off." "What I am really afraid of," he told the board, "is having a schism in this movement." He expanded: "Because, once it starts, then you're in trouble. See, then you have no choice. . . . I don't have to tell you. I don't like to fight inside. There's something inside of me. I'll fight the outside forces day and night. Inside is *revulsion*. I'm afraid. I don't like it. The only thing that would make me walk out is . . . a split on the board. . . . I wouldn't be able to deal with it. I'm not built that way."

Chavez's airing of concerns served to articulate a fear of disunity shared by most, if not everyone, in the room. Since Proposition 14, most board members had privately expressed anxiety about the direction of the union, and some openly questioned the implementation of the Game. Few, however, plotted against Chavez. Only Padilla had seriously questioned Chavez's fitness as a leader, although his conversations with other board members had come during field visits rather than in any well-orchestrated plan to overthrow his friend. Indeed, Padilla's primary concern was to get Chavez into psychological counseling rather than remove him from power. Most felt burned out by a string of losses dating back to Proposition 14, and some even wondered whether the union had lost its way when it had agreed to the Agricultural Labor Relations Act. Others, such as Medina, felt the burden of not becoming a self-sustaining farm workers union. Medina imagined hearing donors say, "We've been supporting you for 13 years, why don't you get your act together?" Whatever the source or the starting point of each member's individual doubts, the group now felt a strong urge to flee rather than to fight.

The first board member to actually broach the subject of leaving was perhaps the one with the least amount invested in the union. Philip Vera Cruz had come to the board as one of a handful of Filipino leaders who had participated in the 1965 grape strike. Since then, however, he had gently eased into inactivity, marrying a former legal volunteer and spending most of his time maintaining their home in Delano rather than tending to his duties as a board member. Seventy-two at the time of the board meeting in 1977, Vera Cruz was well past his prime, but he always found the time to speak to Filipino college students and radical labor organizations eager to hear stories of the union's founding. His most captivated audiences had been in the San Francisco Bay Area, a location of first retreat for many of the union's recent exiles. Chavez and Huerta had heard rumors that Vera Cruz criticized the union leadership in his speeches. More recently, during the spring of 1977, Vera Cruz had shared his plans with Kent Winterrowd to write a tell-all book about the union with the help of his wife, Debbie Vollmer, that promised to put Chavez and some members of the board in a negative light.

Now in strong disagreement with Chavez's position taken during the meeting, Vera Cruz saw an opening to announce his resignation. "I think there is a great problem with the union today," he announced. He objected to the prevailing assumption that anyone who dared to criticize the leadership was "speaking against the union," and accused Chavez of extracting conformity through intimidation and fear. "I hate authority when I am not given the freedom to express myself," he told him. "I found out that the power struggle here in the union is a kind of dirty politics and I hate that." He knew his speeches had rankled Chavez, admitting, "When I find myself very controversial I think I should keep my mouth shut because I wouldn't want to disrupt the operations of the union." Knowing he could no longer abide by such silence, Vera Cruz concluded, "And so I have decided that my stay in the union will no longer be useful. I am leaving."

The reaction from board members was swift and ferocious. "I am sick and tired of that guy," Lyons responded. "He's full of shit." Medina complained that Vera Cruz had not said anything for four years but now had the temerity to complain about how he had been treated. Cohen agreed, informing Vera Cruz that he had an obligation as a board member to tell them what he was feeling. Huerta recounted an incident in Delano when Vera Cruz missed an important strike meeting to stay home and cook supper for his wife. "You can make a speech in San Francisco," she observed, "but you can't go to the Friday night meeting?" Padilla and Drake accused him of shirking his responsibilities in the field, while Richard Chavez chastised him for giving a lackluster eulogy at Larry Itliong's funeral. "The Filipino brothers have a hard

FIGURE 17. Philip Vera Cruz (center), vice president of the United Farm Workers, and unidentified men at a boycott meeting, ca. 1970s. ALUA, UFW Collection, 3361.

time holding on to their dignity," Huerta shouted, adding, "They want you to do more." Richard Chavez noted that the tension over Vera Cruz's reputation as a leader had recently provoked a nasty fight in Delano between two Filipino farm workers that nearly ended in a gun battle.

Vera Cruz evoked near universal condemnation from his peers with his announcement. Some may have resented his ability to find the courage to say what they had not dared to utter. Judging by the level of vitriol in the room, however, most had legitimate gripes, because everyone at one point or another had carried Vera Cruz's load of work for him. Some may have been thinking of their own shortcomings as board members and worried about how their service might look between the covers of his forthcoming book. Whatever the motivation, virtually everyone in the room took a turn lambasting Vera Cruz.

Eventually Chavez weighed in. "We fucked up," he told the board. He reported that he knew of Vera Cruz's plans for a book. Chavez had received a detailed report from Kent Winterrowd about it and suspected that the copious notes Vera Cruz wrote in silence during every meeting would be part of his source material. Still, Chavez told the board, he had not taken it seriously enough to do something about it. He then launched into an insult of his own followed by a threat: "Philip is the most revolutionary guy here . . . in his mind. He couldn't get a revolution because he won't do the work. He thinks about it and he talks about it. I know his speeches. He's very international. It's a syndrome that we've had in the union for some time. He doesn't like authority. That's number one. He said it and I know it. He resents it. It's the kind of people who wouldn't mind praising Mao, who was out and out the greatest dictator the world has ever known, but shits on Cesar Chavez because I'm a little dictator." He chastised himself for accommodating Vera Cruz instead of ordering him to "shape up, asshole." He admitted that Vera Cruz had the right to criticize the union but also noted that his actions gave the board the right to "fuck him up if we can." "You want to struggle inside the union?" Chavez asked him menacingly. "Okay, but I also have a right to struggle back."

Several members followed Chavez's threat by insisting that Vera Cruz air his differences then and there rather than save them for the book. Vera Cruz responded with evasion, which stoked Cohen's anger. "I'll do my best to fuck it up," he told Vera Cruz, promising to use whatever legal means at his disposal to block the book. "I've been here ten fucking years and no one is going to fuck me without getting fucked back. Especially a friend." Feeling the pressure, Vera Cruz finally admitted that he had serious differences with Chavez over the recent firings. "I didn't think too many of them were conspiring against the union," he told Chavez. "I think there were some mistakes."

Vera Cruz's questioning of the firings upset Chavez, who launched into a long explanation of why each person had been let go. He claimed that he had fired only two people and that the majority had been forced out by the collective will of the community. As always, Chavez tried to have it both ways, depicting himself as strong and decisive while at the same time benevolent and democratic. In one case, he bragged about how he had confronted one volunteer for pushing marijuana on the children of La Paz. "There's three things that can fuck up a movement," he told the board, "money, pussy, and dope." He confronted the "dirty asshole," he explained, to protect the children of La Paz from being corrupted.

Chavez then introduced a laundry list of other firings, including many in Delano that he had not necessarily initiated but condoned in the interest of purging conspirators from the union. In a brief moment of introspection, he admitted, "There were some good people that got fucked in the process . . .

[mainly because] they got emotional." He saw these mistakes as necessary, however, since the acts proved the existence of a loyal group of staff at La Paz who would protect the community at all costs. "When I give you an order in La Paz," he said with pride, "you're going to carry it out." Backing away from his direct culpability in the affairs, he concluded, "I gave them permission to stand up and do what they thought needed to be done and I'm really proud of that."

Among the board members, no one had been more loyal to Chavez than Dolores Huerta, who used the discussion of conspirators to make unsubstantiated charges of her own. Addressing the board with an urgent, even manic cadence in her speech, she described how she had moved from doubt to certainty that "the assholes are trying to sabotage us." She recounted a number of incidents that hinted at a conspiracy but offered no concrete evidence. In one case, she latched onto Chavez's crude assertion that "money, pussy, and dope" could be used to corrupt the union by suggesting that one young volunteer and friend of Nick Jones, Mark Silverman, had pledged his undying love to her in an attempt to infiltrate the union and disrupt its affairs in the service of a socialist organization. "They're going to marry people just to get us," she cautioned board members. For her, the repeated fights among the leadership had little to do with substantive differences about the direction of the union; rather, they were the result of a divide-and-conquer strategy by alleged saboteurs. She warned, "If anyone tells me anything about Cesar right now, man, I got my antenna up! Before I'd just listen to it.... From now on, I've got a whole goddamn different attitude. If somebody starts giving me a bad time, man, I'm going to start noticing. Before I thought it was because I wasn't popular, that people didn't like me. But now I know that's not it at all. It's that people are trying to fuck me and they *are* fucking me!" Huerta's emotional tirade revealed more about her deteriorating state of mind than it did the existence of a well-planned conspiracy against the union during the summer of 1977. When Drake and Govea challenged the facts of her stories, she shot back angrily, "If someone fucks me, they assume it is my fault." She complained, "I can't go to one person on this board to defend me."

Chavez showed his appreciation for Huerta's loyalty by indulging her fantasies of a conspiracy and adding some of his own. "Dolores is getting a lot of attacks," he pointed out, but admitted, "It is very hard to prove [her accusation of a conspiracy]." According to Chavez, this was exactly the plan of the communist conspirators, who had a history of infiltrating the labor movement and were now breeding "like flies" within the organization. "We know they're doing this with the steel workers and the auto workers. We know for sure. We know this is the plan. We know that with agriculture they've been salivating at the mouth for us."

Chavez shared a number of suspicions he had about counterorganizers in the movement based on hearsay rather than solid evidence, and his opposition to volunteers' values and lifestyle. One included a member of Cohen's legal team, Steve Hopcraft, whom he wanted to fire because Huerta reported that he might be gay. In another case Chavez alleged that a UFW volunteer, Kathy McCarthy, used a combination of sex and lies to entangle key members of the union in controversy. Chavez had fired a long-time UFW boycott organizer in Chicago, Marcos Muñoz, for an attempted rape of McCarthy. Now he questioned his decision, telling the board, "I'll be a son of a bitch if I didn't blame him." When Padilla tried to defend the decision, Chavez admitted that Muñoz "wasn't the most perfect guy," but still clung to McCarthy's culpability in the affair and suggested that other women were out to get the leaders of the union.

Chavez counted himself as the number one target for these alleged femmes fatales. Extending the discussion to his personal life, he announced, "They fucked up my marriage. Well, maybe." During the late spring of 1977, Helen Chavez had received several anonymous letters "in perfect Spanish" revealing the details of a love affair between her husband and a young Mexican American woman. Before leaving on a trip Chavez had sought to blunt the impact of his accuser's testimonials by telling Helen that he had been set up by conspirators angry about the recent purges. The details in the letter convinced her otherwise. "She picked [the letter] up, and when I came back, she [was] just going out of her mind." In spite of his best efforts to explain, Helen moved out of La Paz to Delano. Still, the letters kept coming. "Two weeks later, another fucking letter," Chavez groused to the board. She also received several phone calls from women while her husband was traveling. Although some among them knew of Chavez's infidelities, no one challenged his assertions for fear of their own indiscretions being revealed. Indeed, Chavez tried to draw sympathy by alluding to skeletons in the closets of Larry Tramutt, Jerry Cohen, and Fred Ross. Few took the bait, except Huerta, who returned to her lament about nearly giving in to Silverman's romantic overtures.

Most in the room remained silent throughout Chavez's and Huerta's dizzying rants about vague plots to overthrow the union and moments of personal weakness. Although Cohen, Govea, and Drake tried to interject some sanity by suggesting that not all the mistakes by staff had been part of a pattern of conspiracy, their challenges only produced more unsubstantiated charges from Chavez and Huerta. Finally, Chris Hartmire, whose conscience had grown weary from trying to defend the purges of innocent staff, had had enough. "How far do you want to go into this today?" he asked Chavez. "Because Dolores and I are coming apart at the seams over Shelley [Speigel]." Speigel had been an effective director of the Huelga School. Although members of the community deeply appreciated the services and trusted Speigel, Huerta disliked her and told Chavez that she had been fomenting revolution among her staff during the first half of 1977. Hartmire knew this to be untrue, but Chavez had moved ahead anyway with the firings of the staff and the dismantling of the program. As always, he had left the fallout to be handled by Hartmire, who, in this case, refused to excuse the behavior of his boss or Huerta.

Now, in front of the board on July 3, 1977, Hartmire found the courage to confront Huerta. "You're so emotionally involved with the attack on you at Delano," he told her, "[that] you are out to get certain people, even if you have to exaggerate and lie." The accusation stung Huerta, who angrily threatened Hartmire, "Where I come from, we kill people for calling someone a liar." Not cowed by her, Hartmire pressed on: "The first time I talked to you about it, you accused me of defending the whole goddamn conspiracy. The second time I talked to you about it, you said 'I guess you're calling me a liar.'" The two fell into an argument about the details, in which Hartmire challenged Huerta to back up her claims that Speigel had been holding meetings at her home to conspire against the union. Her suspicions of Speigel amounted to holding a birthday party on the same day as a march in Coachella, and another social gathering to which Huerta had not been invited. "I saw the party and went by," Huerta complained, adding, "I wasn't invited." In the end, Huerta failed to substantiate anything more than her exclusion from the parties, an act that had earned Speigel her ire. "I think that she's a fantastic teacher," Huerta finally admitted, but added, "At this point, if I can't stand to be in the same fucking room with [the Huelga School staff], I'll be goddamned if I'm going to send my kids to be taught by them. . . . It's nothing about her ability, man. But I just think she's fucked up politically." Rather than acknowledge the shaky foundation of her conspiracy theory, Chavez defended Huerta, and called on Tramutt, who offered the unsubstantiated allegation that Speigel had encouraged her roommate to seduce him while they worked in Los Angeles on the boycott.

Hartmire's challenge invited an incredulous board to pounce on the absurdity of the moment. The mutiny began with Chavez's brother, Richard, who had grown tired of the whole affair and offered to tender his resignation. As the director of operations in Delano, it was his responsibility to follow up on any charges of misconduct, but he found nothing on which to indict Speigel. Huerta and his brother, however, had gone over his head to purge Speigel and the Huelga School. "For God's sake," Cesar desperately pleaded with his brother, "open your fucking eyes and see what's happening." He suggested that their fighting had been caused by the same "assholes" who had disrupted his marriage, had strained his relations with his daughter, and were trying to break up the union. Unmoved, Richard sarcastically retorted, "So, okay, look at everybody."

Padilla also doubted the conspiracy, including the involvement of those purged during the Monday Night Massacre. Since 1965 he had tolerated the various "goofies" and castoffs who had come to the union, some of whom he had profound disdain for because of their lack of decorum or seriousness about their work. He had participated in the purge on April 4, 1977, only to get rid of some of these people, but in its aftermath he recognized that the firings had gone too far and had fed Chavez's paranoia.[50] "You and Dolores are the only ones who follow the patterns," he told Chavez, and added that he could no longer go along with what he did not see. Rather than fight him, Chavez tried to guilt Padilla into submitting to his will by reminding him that he had trusted Padilla's request in earlier days to sack members in Fresno because Padilla asked him to. He now expected Padilla to give him the same benefit of the doubt, but Padilla's conscience would not allow it.

Hartmire also objected to Chavez's position and increased the urgency of his original message. "All I am pleading for," he told Chavez, "is that we listen to other interpretations so we don't screw good people." It had taken all of the courage he could muster to make his request. "Cesar, let me tell you, we're afraid. All of us are afraid, from time to time, to raise those other interpretations from within. . . . I think a lot of other people are afraid to fight with you on this issue . . . [but] we've got to do that because you also are capable of making a goddamn bad mistake about a person."

When Chavez insisted that he had consulted the board on the firings but got "dead silence," Jim Drake found the courage to weigh in. "The reason there is dead silence sometimes," he told Chavez, "is because it's a type of frightening thing to take you on." Drake admitted being ashamed of his role in allowing the madness to continue over the first half of 1977; however, now, he believed, it was time to speak the truth about Chavez's unchecked power. He shared that Hartmire had come to him recently to talk about his disagreement with the purges. During those conversations, Hartmire had told Drake of his reluctance to challenge Chavez out of fear of being accused of conspiracy too. "My God, what are we, then?" Drake asked. "What have we become? Chris Hartmire is afraid to express things openly because he is afraid to be accused of being part of a conspiracy. What more is there to say? If he's afraid, I'm going to be a little afraid." "I'm afraid too," Richard Chavez immediately added. "Everybody's afraid, but we're too goddamn chicken shit to say anything."

The admission of fear should have been sobering for Chavez, but he failed to grasp the gravity of the moment. Instead, he denied their right to their feelings by arguing that they encumbered his ability to lead. He chastised the board, "If every time I fire someone you're going to be fearful, then I can't do my job. I got to have the right to fire people and I got to have the right to make mistakes in doing that. . . . If you say you're afraid, then you're really fucking me up!" He argued that their unreasonable fears also prevented him from tackling the major issues confronting the union in 1977, foremost in his mind the expulsion of subversives. He told the board, "We are fucked today in the union. Because, you know why? We haven't got the balls to face reality."

Hartmire refused to back down. "I get a lot of shit from the outside world over all that's happened in the last five months," he said angrily. "I defend the union and I think I interpret it better than anybody else probably does." This period of the union's history had "not been exactly normal," he opined, and he now found it too difficult to offer the explanation "Cesar simply wants to come down and fuck people who we know." He believed others sitting in the room agreed with him, though they were too "chicken shit" to join in his condemnation of Chavez's actions. Now confronting his friend and boss as he'd never done before, Hartmire offered a different interpretation of "asshole" than the one Chavez had so often promoted: "There are also other kinds of assholes in the union besides agents who are trying to fuck us. They are mechanistic assholes who do every goddamn thing you say just because you say it, whether or not they believe in it, just because they are kissing ass. And they're going to kiss ass, and kiss ass, and kiss ass, and kiss ass and they're going to screw some real good people that you don't intend to screw. Because their way of living life is just to kiss your ass."

A shocked Chavez rejected Hartmire's message and moved to quash what he saw as insubordination. "Chris, let me tell you, I think it's a total bunch of fucking horseshit," he replied angrily. When Hartmire tried to stand up to him, Chavez grew more insistent and moved into lecture mode. "Let me tell you what happens. Fucking people do things for me because I do fucking things for them! Don't you ever fucking forget that! If you keep that fucking perspective then you shouldn't be afraid of anything!" Not seeing how this changed what he had just said, Hartmire restated his position. "There are some people whose existence in life is made meaningful by kissing your ass," he clarified. His point clearly alluded to Huerta, with whom he had recently sparred, but he also took aim at many other staff members in the room, including the Winterrowds and Tramutt, who had tried futilely to support Chavez's conspiracy theories throughout the day. Hartmire added, "They're dangerous people also. And they're going to go around hurting good people in the union just because they're kissing your ass. I think we have to watch for them too. Now, does no one agree with me? Am I the only one who thinks that?"

Initially no one spoke up, likely out of fear of Chavez's menacing anger. Chavez continued to defend the few firings for which he personally took credit, most notably that of Joe Smith, which he knew several people on the board questioned. "What's so fucking strange that I fire one fucking son of a bitch that didn't agree with me?" he asked. "Now, just assuming that it's true that I made mistakes, why should it be so fucking disastrous and you get affected because I fire Joe [Smith]?" Regaining his courage, Drake once again chimed in. "That's the question you have to answer," he told Chavez. "It's not the question to ask, it is the question to *answer*." Drake's question, however, required Chavez to engage in a level of reflection that his anger and self-righteousness could not permit. He refused to accept that his actions, ill temper, and false accusations had created an air of suspicion in the union that turned officials against one another and paralyzed some with fear.

Chavez insisted that his position as president gave him a unique, bird's-eye view of the union that permitted him to see things hidden from plain sight. The argument constituted another desperate attempt to mark out an exclusive perspective and a special set of powers that no one could challenge. He told the board, "If I say you have to have a fucking clean-up and I've got to make it my union and fuck it, I've got to be a fucking king or I leave."

The suggestion that he might resign was a threat that he hoped would draw people back into line. Sounding defeated and exhausted, he launched into a self-pitying speech. "I've been used," he said dejectedly. "I've been used by the people. I've been used by my own ideas. And I've been used by everyone in this room to get to a goal. We made a deal. And so you wear out. You wear out your friendship. You wear out your Blue Chip stamps." Chavez now strove to make the point in a way that he hoped would create shame. "I see certain things in the union that I think have to be dealt with. But most people don't agree with me. They don't. Let's face it. The Game, they don't agree with me. This idea that we're being had, they don't." Things had changed in twelve years, he admitted. He waxed nostalgic for a time when he "had total and absolute power," but those days were gone. Rather than stay around to be dragged "out like a fucking dog," it was time to prepare for a smooth transition in which he would become a "president emeritus" at La Paz, left to pursue his vision of a community separate from the union. "There's the whole naked truth," Chavez told the board. "Now it's come out. I think I should leave."

Although most knew he would never give up power, predictably Dolores Huerta took the bait and begged him to stay. Huerta recounted her own moments of grandeur, telling the group how she stood next to Bobby Kennedy at the Ambassador Hotel in Los Angeles just minutes before his assassination. The experience, she argued, made her contemplate life without Chavez either by his voluntary departure or, worse, by murder. "I couldn't take over the union," she admitted. "Who could?" The question was meant to be rhetorical and served to launch an appeal to the board. "We don't really care that much about the union to make it survive. Basically, we all care about him. I care about him because of his great genius, and what we have in his talent as an organizer and as a leader. But none of us really care that much to really follow and try to keep the organization together. We're all just fighting each other. We're all just cutting each other's throats." Among the board members, only Richard Chavez agreed with Huerta. "We're so fucking dumb," he told the board. "He's way out there, way out there in front, and we can't follow." Perhaps regretting his earlier challenges to his brother, he lamented, "I feel ashamed sitting right here today."

Few shared his embarrassment, including Gilbert Padilla, who added his name to the list of people who had lost confidence in Chavez. "I don't know where we are going," he admitted, adding that he had become profoundly unhappy in his job and unsure of what the mission of the union had become. He disagreed with Chavez and believed he had exhausted his options in saving the union from self-destruction. "The day I disagree with you," he told Chavez, "I think I better leave." Several people tried to convince him to reconsider, but Padilla identified Chavez's plans to create a community in the likeness of Home Place as the main reason why he could not stay. Rather than create controversy before the upcoming convention, he would choose not to run for office, take a leave of absence, and quietly move on.[51]

Although silent for much of the meeting on July 3, 1977, Marshall Ganz was now roused to life, criticizing Chavez for his lack of leadership since the spring of 1975. "It's sort of surprising that more people haven't left the union given the degree of frustration that obviously exists among the leadership," he told everyone. Like many on this day, he reflected on his own life and the impact of the union on it. The lack of direction, the isolation from fellow board members, and, most important, the failure of Chavez's leadership had produced a feeling of "drift" that he argued was almost universal. "I don't think we have the time to drift [and] I don't want to drift with my life. I want to use it to do something." He complained that they had been "back-doored" into doing Proposition 14 and had wasted valuable time with the "Twinky Land" of Synanon. Reflecting on the board meeting in Badger, Ganz admitted, "I was pissed off by the whole thing." No longer holding back his opinion of Dederich, the Game, and Home Place, he told Chavez that he thought "it was phony" and "a bunch of bullshit." Ganz expanded: "It was a big diversion from what we ought to be doing, which is dealing with where we're going to organize. How are we going to recruit more people? How are we going to train organizers? What are we going to do about negotiations? When are we going to get to the citrus industry? How are we going to get to Florida? All of these things that, in my thinking, was like where the union had to go." Like Padilla, he objected to concentrating energy and resources into forming Game groups and reconstructing La Paz as a new Home Place for the union. "I didn't find that idea [and] I still don't find that idea particularly appealing." He admitted to thoughts of leaving at least three times during the past year and was not convinced now that he should stay. "Are we really building a workers' union?" Ganz asked, not certain of the answer Chavez would give him.

Chavez circumvented the question and indeed avoided engaging virtually every serious challenge to his leadership at the meeting. Perhaps he had grown weary, having entered the fifteenth day of one of his routine fasts. More likely, however, he had begun to approach board meetings as he approached the Game, exercising his "caginess," thinking of how to "get the Game off him[self] and onto some else," and initiating indictments and "carom" attacks on individuals about whom he had suspicions. The meeting had revealed signs of all these elements, yet Chavez had done his best to uphold the distinctions between inside and outside of the Game. For example, when Lyons and others identified the indictment of Vera Cruz earlier in the meeting as a Game-like maneuver and suggested that they had, in fact, entered a de facto Game, Chavez insisted otherwise. The distinction between the two had become blurry to many on the board and perhaps to Chavez too, though he failed to acknowledge it. The meeting provided more evidence of his failure to facilitate true democracy; rather, he encouraged confrontations to prove his point that conspirators had infiltrated the union and caused the conflicts among them. He now managed meetings as he did the Game, letting attacks among board members become nasty and personal. Although some valued the honesty expressed in the meeting, the indictments, challenges, and testimonies failed to produce confidence in the direction of the union, in Chavez, or in one another.

Chavez saved the last and most vicious attack for the end of the day. Prior to the meeting, he had discussed Vera Cruz's book with a small cadre of board members, including Cohen and Padilla. Together they hatched a plan to circulate a confidentiality agreement among the board in which each member would promise not to disclose the contents of meetings after the fact. Chavez believed the move would reveal Vera Cruz and Debbie Vollmer as "spies." He especially distrusted Vollmer, although Padilla had discounted both of them as threats to the union. "She was a little dingy," Padilla admitted of Vollmer, but she was no conspirator. Of Vera Cruz, Padilla opined, "Philip was a very honest human being, I mean really honest, up straight [and] very democratic." He recognized that Vera Cruz had Marxist ideas, but he failed to see this as evidence of treason. Padilla went along with the scheme if only to see Chavez's far-fetched claims of a conspiracy blow up in his face.[52]

The results turned out far worse than Padilla or Cohen expected. Before adjourning the meeting on July 3, 1977, for the evening, Chavez announced that Cohen had drawn up the agreement to which, he asserted, they had already agreed verbally earlier in the day. He asked everyone to sign it, though predictably Vera Cruz refused. Still shaken from the earlier attack on him, Vera Cruz admitted to having ambitions of publishing but denied ever calling the union corrupt. "I don't want to waive my rights," he told his peers, "because you people have been very mad at me today." He worried that if he signed away his rights, he would not be able to defend himself in an uncertain future that could produce more hatred and personal attacks.

True to the plan, board members weighed in against Vera Cruz. "Legally, it doesn't make a goddamn bit of difference whether you sign it or not," Cohen told Vera Cruz. "I can get your ass under federal law. I can get your ass with the oral agreement. One way or another," he promised, "I'll get your ass." Cohen saw Vera Cruz's refusal to sign as both a personal affront to their friendship and a betrayal of his responsibility to the workers who had elected him. "It makes me sick to my stomach," he added in disgust. "I am going to crank up the propaganda machine and get your ass," Hartmire too threatened Vera Cruz. Medina reminded Vera Cruz that he had committed his life to work for the farm workers and poor people. Now Medina doubted the truth of his statements. "You're going to give a weapon to the imperialists [by writing a book]," Medina alleged. "Everyone in this state will know that this Philip Vera Cruz was a pile of shit," he predicted, and accused him of selling out. Drake went further, announcing, "I don't think the meeting should continue in the presence of this filth." When Chavez reminded Drake that Vera Cruz had been elected by the membership, he told him, "[Then] why don't you [Vera Cruz] die right now so we can have our decent meeting without you listening with your big fat ears?" Chavez also invited staff members—most them more than half Vera Cruz's age—to berate the elder board member, accusing him of lying and deceiving the membership.

Chavez hung back as the indictments flew at Vera Cruz from all angles, diminishing a man who had served the union since its founding twelve years earlier. Padilla later recalled with regret, "What we did to Philip was ugly, ugly. . . . That's all I can say . . . just plain ugly." Padilla remembered Vera Cruz trying to stand his ground, but by this point the long day had turned into a seemingly interminable night, and he had now begun to feel his age. He admitted to being "confused" and pleaded with the group to let him leave, telling them, "I cannot think straight now. All of you are trying to scare me!" But the insults and accusations kept coming.

When Hartmire paused the attack to ask Chavez what he was thinking, Chavez broke his silence. "They worked on Philip a long time ago," Chavez contemplated aloud. "Philip wasn't like this when we started. I know exactly when it started." He claimed that he and Vera Cruz had been the targets of "commie" conspirators years ago, though only Vera Cruz had given in. "They fucked him up," he alleged. Chavez bragged, "I used them as much as I could," but admitted that he paid for his subterfuge by making the union a target. He knew that Vera Cruz traveled to San Francisco to "pal around" with the union's enemies, who lavished praise on him to get him to do their dirty work. "Philip made friends outside of the union," he told the board, "[and] the day of reckoning has come."

Chavez gave Vera Cruz the coup de grace, but the damage had already been done. When Vera Cruz reiterated his innocence and his desire to leave in peace, Chavez called for a break to allow him to collect his things and leave the board meeting for good. When the meeting resumed, a confident Chavez smirked that he did not feel as bad as they apparently felt about the attack because, in his mind, it proved the existence of a conspiracy he had been telling them about all along. "It should be fucking clear to you," he chastised the group. He spent the next three hours deep into the night reviewing a number of possible suspects throughout the union, from Delano to Salinas to Coachella. He returned to his problems with Helen as evidence that a conspiracy was afoot, lamenting, "I have to have a meeting with my family tonight to see if I am still married. . . . It's really fucking ridiculous." The marital problems of others also passed as evidence that white women conspirators were out to sabotage the union. Every conflict, from a fight he had with Ganz in 1968, to opposition in the medical clinics and questions about the upcoming convention was proof that conspirators had infiltrated the union. "There's others that are going to come up," Chavez predicted without evidence. "I can't tell you now because if I did tell you now, I can't prove it."

Too exhausted to challenge his circular arguments, the board mostly relented. Chavez told them he would continue to purge suspicious characters from the union, concentrating on white volunteers because he knew "they got some more members," and because "getting a Chicano and a farm worker out is a different story." "We'll make some mistakes," he predicted, but assured the group that he would do it "with class" and avoid taking them "by storm" as they had done in April 1977. He would use special powers to run patterns in his mind to detect suspicious behavior and "find a nice way" to expel them. Either way, he told the board, "we gotta clean them" or else they would destroy the union.

In the end, the executive board meeting of June 30 through July 4, 1977, did little to lift the union out of its current malaise. The decision to concentrate on negotiations over organizing constituted a major retreat from ALRA elections and a forfeiture of the advantage they had gained by reaching a truce with the Teamsters. In retrospect, Cohen suggested that the decision to concentrate on one or the other had been a false choice created by Chavez to counter the growing power of vegetable workers in Salinas. He later explained, "It's a false choice in that these guys in the vegetables were willing not only to organize their own companies; they wanted to go organize the competition."[53] One Salinas worker close to Ganz, Mario Bustamante, had begun to talk about moving ahead with or without Chavez's approval. The move fed Chavez's already well-developed paranoia about conspirators in Salinas, prompting him to doubt Ganz's intentions in 1977. Although Cohen agreed with Ganz, he found it impossible to support him, given his stubbornness and his tendency to rebel by refusing to respond to phone calls. Cohen later remembered that Ganz's behavior "sort of poisoned the atmosphere," making it hard for anyone to support him.

In general, the deep feelings of distrust stopped the board from making decisions in June and July 1977. Such conditions could be interpreted as a collective failure, but the lack of democracy either in the union or on the board meant that much of the responsibility for the union's dithering fell on Cesar Chavez. He maintained the ultimate authority to hire and fire. In addition, the board functioned only as effectively as he managed it. Consumed by fears of a conspiracy, and with no one in his inner circle to check his anxieties, Chavez let his imagination run wild. His embrace of the Game colored his dealings with the board, as his behavior, especially on July 3, 1977, revealed. His attack on Vera Cruz bared the telltale signs of the Game: a contrived, mean-spirited indictment, in which Chavez relied on others in the room to lead the attack. The verbal assault came at a moment when board members had launched their most critical challenge to his leadership, with many expressing an interest in quitting. The attack on Vera Cruz effectively "got the Game off of him" and served to temporarily unify members, but the deep divisions remained. The indictment of Vera Cruz also placed board members on notice that anyone who dared to question Chavez's fitness as a leader—even veterans of the movement—would be subject to community scrutiny and condemnation.

Chavez, who now ruled through a mysterious combination of fear, intimidation, and self-pity in an imaginary world of conspirators and double agents, considered the meeting a tremendous success. Just three days later he convened a Game session at La Paz in which he began the day by reflecting on the past weekend. He proudly recounted the details of Vera Cruz's purge and announced that it had produced "probably the best debate we ever had in the history of the board." He saw a transformation in the board members, who, he asserted, now understood the threat the union faced. "I've known for a while and the board didn't believe me," he explained. "Now, I think they all believe. They all believe now. . . . So, we're going to be also trying to get more assholes out of the union."[54] In this way, Chavez offered a self-serving interpretation of the UFW's health in 1977, one that denied his slow strangulation of the union he had once led so skillfully.

EIGHT

Some Were More Equal Than Others

AMONG THE MANY TOPICS that divide former members of the United Farm Workers, the Game and the influence of Synanon remain the most controversial. Although it is difficult to pinpoint the moment at which Chavez became convinced of its value to the union, by mid-1977 he had committed to the Game's integration into La Paz and made plans to extend it to the legal department in Salinas and the field offices throughout California. At the executive board meeting in June–July 1977, he revealed that the Game constituted the cornerstone of his "little cultural revolution" and speculated, "It may lead us to heaven."[1] Within the span of four months, from March to July 1977, Chavez had moved aggressively from inaugurating the first Game groups at Home Place to playing the Game three times a week at the union's headquarters with two separate groups, composed mostly of young residents. By July 1978, union records indicate, more than a hundred people had played the Game as frequently as nine times a month. As someone partly responsible for monitoring its growth, Chris Hartmire watched the Game unfold before his eyes. Like many who came to regret the union's experimentation with the Game, he reached a new understanding of its purpose over time. Although Hartmire initially believed Chavez when he said that he wanted to implement the practice to inspire greater honesty among staff, he later realized Chavez's true intent. "In retrospect," Hartmire reflected, "I think Cesar was looking for disloyal staff." He added, "The Game came to La Paz for control."[2]

How much the Game contributed to conflict among UFW leaders and hastened the retreat of the union from the fields is a matter of debate. Some, such as Jerry Cohen, saw the odd behavior at La Paz as an unfortunate distraction that took Chavez away at a time when they most needed him. Others remain committed to Chavez and his legacy, refusing to admit that the Game had any influence in the decline of election victories or contributed to the differences that emerged between Chavez and field representatives in the late 1970s.[3] Indeed, when I spoke to Marc Grossman in 2006, he declined to be interviewed for this book but assured me that Chavez had maintained only a fleeting interest in the Game and that the experiment ended without having any influence on the union.[4] The discussion among movement veterans on a listserv created by LeRoy Chatfield in 2004 belies such an interpretation. For example, Glenn Rothner, a former member of the UFW legal department, wrote, "I'm not sure why [Synanon and the Game] warrants so many postings (including my own), but surely we can agree that the alliance with Synanon, particularly at a time when that organization had proven internally toxic (and externally venomous) was not one of Cesar's finer moments."[5] That not everyone could agree to his interpretation is a testament to the gulf between most histories of the movement and the memory of those who participated in it.[6]

The relationship with Synanon and the integration of the Game introduced a way of doing business that dramatically deviated from what had been the norm. The union began as a multiethnic and multigenerational movement in which volunteers applied their passion and skills according to their strength; most were welcome to participate regardless of their background. Although at times this made for some awkward exchanges and a clash of cultures, the principles of nonviolence—most dramatically modeled by Chavez in his fasts, marches, and speeches—smoothed over these differences and facilitated a feeling of beneficence among staff. The decision to privilege the recruitment of those perceived as being closer to farm work began a slide away from these principles, establishing a hierarchy that fed Chavez's suspicion of non-Mexicans in the union. Dederich's recommendation that the youth constituted the future also set in motion a growing irreverence toward senior members, most viciously demonstrated in the purging of Philip Vera Cruz. The Game became the vehicle for this transition, introducing to members aggressiveness heretofore unknown to the movement. In the numerous letters of protest that came into La Paz during this time, many former members and allies outside of La Paz tried to point out the violence inherent in the words and threats that flowed from the Game. Chavez dismissed the concerns as further evidence of agents conspiring to bring down the union, creating greater distance between the two cultures that had emerged: a permissiveness and obedience to Chavez at La Paz and resistance and nonconformity away from it.

This clash of cultures created a poisonous environment that had already afflicted most board members and caused many inside and outside of the headquarters to contemplate a life without the movement. Throughout the end of the decade, those who opposed Chavez's direction struggled over priorities and goals in an attempt to pull the union out of the tailspin it had begun during the fateful campaign for Proposition 14. The result would not remedy what ailed the union; however, it would prevent La Paz from becoming another failed intentional community and remind many that there was still important work to be done.

NO ONE IS REALLY A LEADER

According to Chris Hartmire, Cesar Chavez claimed to have brought the Game to La Paz to "manage the union better."[7] Most UFW volunteers, however, came to loathe the Game and likened it to the kind of democracy practiced in George Orwell's *Animal Farm,* in which the governance of the farm by the animals provided only the illusion of democracy and actually accentuated inequality. Marc Coleman, who lived at La Paz from 1975 to 1977, recalled, "I think everyone at La Paz who played The Game (and we were all required to do so) understood . . . 'some were more equal than others.'" He, like others who played a Game with Chavez, "never heard anyone attempt to 'game' him."[8]

At La Paz, Game participants went after each other with a vengeance, an approach that thrilled Chavez. He had grown tired of the legal maneuverings and political dealings he had to engage in with the state and appreciated the rawness of the conflicts in the Game. "We deal with [old questions] intellectually but not from the gut," he complained. The Game, he told the board, allowed the group "to go to the innards."[9] Chavez believed that the confrontations among Game participants would encourage them to reflect more deeply on the quality of their service to the union and renew their commitments to him.

But the Game often had the opposite effect, producing distrust and enmity among people who had formerly trusted one another. Players routinely criticized their peers for their sexual practices, their age, their relationship to their parents, their limited intellect, or their poor hygiene. Issues spoken in private between members would frequently make their way into sessions, creating suspicion about who could be trusted with personal information.

Similarly, indictments voiced within sessions infected relations in the day-to-day lives of members, violating one of the key rules of the Game: the maintenance of a firewall between the inside and outside of the Game. The violation also broke one of Chavez's promises to police such transgressions, although ultimately they helped instill fear among members and contributed to his desire to control the behavior of La Paz residents.

Chavez officially began his experiment on March 15, 1977, when he asked Chris Hartmire and Kent Winterrowd to take a small group of twelve volunteers to Badger once a week to learn. "I selected the ones who I thought had more possibility not to fail on [the] first try," he told the executive board.[10] Esther Padilla, who had been slated to be in the group but postponed her participation due to pregnancy, thought that there was more to Chavez's choice of participants. "When [Chavez] came back [from Home Place in February]," she recalled, "he decided he was going to get all the young minds, the young virgin minds, and start with them." The group included Cesar's son, Babo, as well as Dolores Huerta's daughter, Lori, and a number of other young people whose parents participated in the union.[11]

According to Gilbert and Esther Padilla, Chavez selected young people whom he planned to move into leadership roles as the new community matured. The Padillas saw the emphasis on youth as a peculiar and cynical approach to addressing a lack of farm workers in the union since few of them possessed experience either as field laborers or as organizers. In the case of Chavez's children, Helen Chavez had been very protective of her children while they were growing up, avoiding the limelight and restricting them from participating in strikes or serving on boycott picket lines.[12] Nevertheless, Chavez invested hope in them as the future of the union.

Chavez occasionally accompanied the youth to Badger but entrusted much of the early responsibility of teaching the Game and monitoring the group to Hartmire and Winterrowd, whereas Matt Rand imparted lessons on how to play at Synanon. Among this first group, Hartmire remembered, "most people got a kick out of it," but Gilbert and Esther received a very different report from Babo Chavez. Esther remembered, "Babo came to our house in tears to talk to Gilbert. Those kids were scared shitless." Babo confided in Gilbert that the Game was difficult for him, but he apparently felt he could not challenge his father.[13]

The Games in Badger took a physical toll on the participants since sessions went until 1 a.m., and the group often did not arrive home until 4 a.m. prior to a busy day of work. Some participants also began to avoid the trips altogether due to the unpleasant nature of the encounters. Chavez's son-in-law and head of security, David Villareno, received harsh treatment throughout March and April 1977, prompting him to skip out on the Game when Chavez did not accompany the group. Consequently, Chavez moved the Game to La Paz and invited members of Synanon to facilitate sessions there.

The first Game at La Paz took place on May 3, 1977, and involved members of the first two Game groups, though only a handful participated in the gaming. Rand brought four experienced gamers from the Synanon community who had participated in the training at Home Place. If the shift to La Paz was meant to produce more constructive exchanges, the planners mostly failed in their attempts.

Villareno was the first to be chastised by the group. Rand initiated the attack, taking note of his absences from the Game at Home Place and scolding him for missing an assignment to provide security at a rally in Santa Barbara. After Chavez accused him of dereliction of duties, Villareno had skipped the event and headed to San Diego, where his car broke down. "You make a lot about laying down your life and taking several bullets in your keister," Rand told him, "[but] the fact [is] that you got your feelings hurt and so you went away to San Diego and you got stuck there." Rand derided Villareno for being a "fucking kid," a charge that invited others to call him a "liar" and "a damn sissy." Few relented when Villareno finally admitted his mistakes. "David," Gerri from Synanon told him, "I don't know you very well, but I think you're a liar. . . . I don't think you're very honest at all. I think most of the people feel that way about you." Following a cascade of insults, Chavez finally weighed in, stating that he didn't think talking to Villareno would make the situation better, and concluded, "I'll get him the hell out and find some goddamn organized company or something [for him to work at]."[14]

Lori Huerta also received harsh treatment. Marc Grossman began the indictment, sharing that Huerta had refused to read stories critical of the union in the newspapers because it made her depressed. Instead, he told the group, she spent her time reading advice columns, the comics, and the horoscope. "We mentioned the name of *the Wall Street Journal*," Grossman told his fellow gamers, "and [she] didn't even know what it was!" When Huerta confirmed that the news did depress her, Grossman shouted her down, asking her, "Does that mean you have license to be an ignoramus all your life?" Rand asked, "Why do you crack your gum like some kind of fucking broad?" From there, the indictment descended rapidly into an attack on her hygiene, dress, and general lack of decorum before members of the

Synanon team redirected the discussion toward strategies for her self-improvement. Although Huerta claimed that she had made efforts since the first Game sessions to clean up, Gerri from Synanon offered, "You kinda got a big mouth. You're kinda feisty, like me. But you're kinda dumb. And I don't think you're doing anything at twenty-five to improve.... If you were eighteen, you would be cute. But, you're not cute at this age."[15]

The Game spared no one; even those thought to be making positive contributions came in for petty, often personal criticism. Whereas in one moment, the Synanon group used Grossman's attack on Huerta to question her behavior, in another they turned the focus on Grossman, pointing out that he had failed by not correcting Huerta when she misspoke or acted inappropriately. Gerri of Synanon mocked Grossman's "skills with the free press" and ultimately determined that he lacked "any value to this group." Babo took his turn at Grossman, making the attack personal. "What was the most exciting thing that he ever did in his life?" the young Chavez asked the group. Answering his own question, he said, "[Marc] told us the other day [he] lost his virginity at nineteen or something like that." As people in the room giggled, Rand added the insult, "It took about four hours to get him to come to the fact that the first time he got laid . . . he was twenty-four and he did it through the hole in his pajamas!"

Although some of the discussion dealt with on-the-job issues, more often the Game invited people to exploit character flaws of individuals for laughs or self-promotion. Rand and his Synanon team stoked the fires of conflict in an attempt to initiate indictments, a goal he believed he achieved. "From our standpoint," Rand wrote Chavez in May 1977, "no one has approached the proposition [of incorporating the Game] with as much enthusiasm and initial success as our friends from UFW."[16] Unquestionably, the Game had begun to transform people formerly uncomfortable with the exercise into expert gamers who exhibited a willingness to confront other members. Babo Chavez, for example, seemed to become more aggressive the more he played, and he developed a knack for striking at people's greatest vulnerabilities.

Equally telling, however, were the number of people who sat quietly in the room, refusing to participate for fear of becoming the target of an attack or because they disapproved of the exercise. Their silence betrayed "the theory" that everyone felt the freedom to indict anyone in the Game, including those higher up on the organizational food chain. As their ultimate supervisor and the person who had sole power to hire and fire individuals, Chavez produced anxiety by his presence and encouraged competitiveness at the expense of peers. Although he invited everyone to indict him and promised that "no one is really a leader" inside the Game, in practice most people respected his power and left him alone. Rand revealed more than he intended when he told the group, "One of the things that we were afraid of . . . in getting together a group of younger people and having them play the Game is that somehow they would think that they're anything other than what they are . . . dumb fuckin' kid[s]." Such a position not only denigrated the "future of the union" but also demanded obedience to Chavez. Moreover, neither Chavez nor anyone charged with implementing the Game saw the contradiction in achieving more honesty and respect through telling lies and ridiculing one another.

Several people living beyond La Paz began to challenge the practice as absurd and inconsistent with the principles of the union. Hartmire, who received many letters during 1977 and 1978, remembered, "The people out there in the field offices and the legal department, they just thought, 'What's going on?!'" At a time when the union should have been organizing for the first elections since the Proposition 14 debacle, the Game produced distractions and sapped the energy of volunteers. In his travels throughout California during the 1977 spring harvest, Hartmire heard mutterings among incredulous members: "We have a war out here in the fields, [and] they're playing the Game three times a week?! Cesar's calling us back to La Paz to learn and play the Game?! What in the world is going on?!"[17]

Hartmire began to see the ill effects of the Game in July 1977, after a particularly brutal session that forced one member to confide her distaste for the practice.[18] Ann McGregor, a shy, middle-aged white woman, had been a reluctant participant in the first Game group. Chavez had selected her, in part, because of her role as the head of the department that managed retirement benefits for members. During Games, her tendency to remain quiet only invited participants to attack her more. The Game on July 7, 1977, had been particularly difficult for her because she had allowed unauthorized members working beneath her to sit in on the recent June–July executive board meeting. Once inside the Game, her peers attacked her mercilessly for not showing more assertiveness with her staff. Babo Chavez, now quite comfortable in the Game, angrily criticized her for allowing the unauthorized members to remain until his father finally had to play the heavy and remove them from the meeting. "This man's got an image," he shouted at McGregor, "and he's not gonna have a very good image if he keeps on telling people they cannot come to board meetings. That's your fucking job!" McGregor refused to engage the indictment, which only fueled their anger. Lori Huerta

FIGURE 18. Chris Hartmire, director of California Migrant Ministry and head of the UFW department of community life, and Cesar Chavez prepare to tape an advertisement in favor of Proposition 14, 1976. Courtesy of Chris Hartmire.

objected to her silence, telling her that her "glassy-eyed" look reminded her of her mentally ill sister. "That's just how my sister acts when she's getting sick . . . the same fucking way." "She's not getting sick," Cesar Chavez added, "she's been sick for a long time."

The personal attack only forced McGregor more deeply into a shell, precipitating nastier observations about her from her peers. Kent Winterrowd faulted her for taking more of her share of food during communal meals. "[The cooks] have to count heads so they can know how much [to serve] . . . and here comes that great big cow," he told the group. As he accused her of eating for two, Lori Huerta screamed, "Fat bitch," but the insult did little to prompt a response from McGregor. When the group criticized her management of her department, McGregor admitted to having difficulty with some employees, especially men who did not respect her authority. The revelation did not garner sympathy. Grossman accused her of destroying her own credibility, while others suggested that she needed to give her staff more "haircuts," a euphemism for discipline. McGregor's claims that she had disciplined them only invited more derision. Another gamer responded sarcastically, "Yeah, you combed and styled their hair [too]."[19] Afterward McGregor asked Hartmire to excuse her from any further participation.[20]

The exchanges between Lori Huerta and Babo Chavez were especially malicious given the contentious relationship of their parents, in which Cesar frequently insulted Dolores, and Dolores often cried and stormed out of meetings. In the July 7, 1977, Game, Babo charged Lori with sharing details of what happened within the Game to union staff members. He recalled how someone had reported her complaining about him picking on her and replicating his father's treatment of her mother during Game sessions. "You're spreading fucking rumors and playing the Game outside of the Game," he angrily asserted. When Lori protested, Babo peppered her with insults, calling her "a fucking hypocrite," "a fucking bitch," and "a goddamn cunt," while others joined in the verbal assault. Ann McGregor and Kent Winterrowd accused Huerta of gaming McGregor in front of McGregor's mother. Someone else opined that she spoke and looked like "a fucking chimp," and Villareno compared her to a dog that must be punished repeatedly before she learns to behave. "Fuck you all!" Lori shouted, but the barrage continued. Finally, Cesar Chavez intervened. "Lori," he told her, "you're too fucking defensive for your own fucking good. This is a fucking big problem. If you don't start doing something about that defensiveness, you're gonna end up in a fucking mental institution or something." "Like her fucking crazy sister," Babo added. "Fucking bitch. She's like a goddamn parrot, just like her crazy mother."

Lori tried to defend herself, but the indictment by Cesar and Babo became more intense and invited a more aggressive game against her, pushing her to her limits. When Cesar accused her of being "fucking neurotic," Lori confessed that she did not understand his insult. "If you're gonna call me something, call me something I understand." "Cunt!" Babo yelled. Cesar asked for substantive criticism of her, precipitating a deluge of complaints: she had been aggressive with staff; she spread lies about others; she made impetuous decisions in her job; and she was defensive whenever someone gave her feedback on her performance. Babo admitted his resentment that Lori had been assigned to an advisory position in the president's office. "The only reason you're there," he complained, "is because [my father is] playing favorites." Lori offered her resignation so that he could take the job, but it did little to salve Babo's or anyone else's anger. Some reminded her of what happened when she had previously left the union. "You fucking went and got laid," several people yelled. Babo observed that Lori and her mother had made a mistake by having children, given how poorly they performed their maternal duties. Dolores, he opined, at least showed more responsibility by having her fallopian tubes tied rather than break union policy as Lori had done by taking the pill.[21] Cesar threw fuel on the fire by reciting Lori's long track record of failure: "She fucking left Stockton. She fucking left Delano. She left *teatro campesino*. She fucking left Oakland. She fucking left school." In the end, Cesar saw her as a "fucking sorry mess" that evoked more pity than anger from him. "I feel very sorry for her," he concluded.[22]

Ultimately, Lori decided against leaving the union, but her decision to quit the Game encouraged a growing number of individuals to refuse to play. Several veterans of the union, such as Pete Velasco and his wife and David Burciaga, understood the destructive nature of the Game and resisted playing. Those less secure about their place in the union or with shorter tenure felt compelled to try it, even though Chavez initially indicated that participation would be voluntary. In these situations, Chavez used peer pressure, relying on loyal members in the pilot group to cajole, harass, and even threaten those who were not playing to change their minds. Cynthia Bell, for example, recalled how loyalists forced her to participate by telling her she would be fired if she did not play. She joined, but the experience did not go well. "I was accused of being a bad mother and pimping my daughters with the Filipino brothers," she remembered. She walked out. Within fifteen minutes of her departure, angry members of the group descended upon her trailer, shouting at her to return. Although she feared she would be expelled from La Paz for her decision, she turned up her stereo to drown out the protest that continued outside her door for about an hour. To her surprise, she was not asked to leave the union, but she never played the Game again.[23]

During the summer of 1977, members of the La Paz Game group exported the practice to staff offices in Delano, with more tragic consequences. Several veterans of the union believe the Game played a role in purging a union paralegal, Steve Hopcraft, on the basis of his alleged homosexuality. Jerry Cohen had assigned Hopcraft to duties in Delano, where he had butted heads with Dolores Huerta. Although according to Cohen, "[Steve] was doing a lot of really good work," Huerta objected to him purely for personal reasons. She began spreading the rumor that he was a *jota* (faggot) among farm workers and convinced Chavez that he was a threat to the union. When Cohen caught wind of the attack, he defended Hopcraft and his staff in no uncertain terms. "I said [to Chavez], 'I don't want you fucking around with the legal department.'"[24] In their rant against suspected conspirators during the June–July 1977 board meeting, both Chavez and Huerta expressed their "strong doubts" about Hopcraft, although they waited until Cohen had left for the Rockies to formally accuse him of being a homosexual and a conspirator. Mark Sharwood, a veteran of the movement from 1976 to 1982, remembered that they used the Game to force Hopcraft out. Sharwood recalled, "He was [accused of] causing problems (which were never specified) for the union just because of who he was."[25] Hopcraft denied all charges; however, Chavez used Huerta's testimony and evidence supposedly unearthed during the Game to fire him. The incident angered Cohen, who saw Chavez's actions as a betrayal of their trust and a sign that Cohen needed to begin his departure from the union.[26]

In another case, Lorraine Agtang (Mascarinas) Greer, a Mexican Filipina volunteer and the daughter of farm workers, experienced the wrath of Dolores Huerta inside and outside of the Game. Born and raised in Delano, Agtang joined the union during the 1973 Delano grape strike. During the mid-1970s, she worked closely with Chavez's long-time assistant, Ben Maddock, and served as the first manager of the Agbayani Retirement Village for aging Filipino workers. She left for a short break in 1975, but returned to find the union community in Delano besieged by Huerta's fits of insecurity and explosive anger.

In 1977, the union struggled to maintain its influence over Filipino workers, many of whom had trouble gaining a foothold in the new hiring halls after 1970. Several Filipinos had also recently become irritated with Chavez over his acceptance of Ferdinand Marcos's invitation to visit the Philippines, an act that defied the wishes expressed by the membership at the 1973 convention in Fresno.[27] Huerta asked Agtang to move to Santa Maria for an undetermined amount time to shore up support among these workers, but Agtang declined because of her responsibilities as a single mother of three. Although a mother herself, Huerta took exception to Agtang's decision. Agtang remembered, "She proceeded to tell me that maybe I should leave the union since I had so many personal problems." After that, Huerta reported her as a troublemaker to Chavez and vowed not to speak to her again.[28]

Huerta reversed her vow of silence when the Game came to Delano. Agtang remembered the day vividly: "Several months later while in a staff meeting at Forty Acres, all of a sudden the doors opened, and in came a number of La Paz staff. Everyone got quiet because we all recognized the prized 'game' team." In the Game, Huerta angrily indicted Agtang for her lack of respect and questioned her dating choices. "It was real ugly," Agtang remembered. "Then systematically others joined in." Like Bell, Agtang stood up and left the room, but she eventually succumbed to peer pressure based on the promise that she would not be fired if she returned. Once she rejoined the group she quickly agreed to reform her behavior to get the Game away from her and on to the next victim. She later said, "I should have known that this was not the end."

Displeased by her inability to force Agtang from the union, Huerta proceeded to intimidate her by staking out her house at night for hours on end. Although Agtang tried to ignore her, Huerta became more insistent, eventually confronting her at home in the middle of the night. She remembered, "A week or so later it was 1:30 a.m. when I heard my roommate calling my name. I was asleep in bed with my three children. The next I knew my roommate opened the door and Dolores barged in behind her. Before I could wipe the sleep from my eyes she started telling me how I had not followed through with the agreements from The Game. . . . She again began to tell me how I had too many problems and so maybe now was not a good time for me to work with the union and so I should not go to work the next day." Shaken by the confrontation, Agtang asked for advice from trusted members in the union, but no one dared to cross Huerta. "That was my last day with the UFW," Agtang sadly recalled.[29]

The purges of Hopcraft and Agtang were just two examples among many in which Chavez and Huerta used the Game to make good on their threats to remove alleged troublemakers from the union. Although some might see this as an abuse of the Game, for those familiar with it such outcomes were consistent with Chavez's intent.[30] Tom Dalzell, a member of the legal team, opposed the Game from the start. "When Cesar turned to Synanon as a role model for the Union and embraced The Game," Dalzell commented years later, "it was pretty clear what his thinking was on free speech zones."[31] Like many in the legal department, Dalzell saw the Game as a mechanism for creating conformity through fear. Another member of the legal team, Charlie Atilano, recalled how effective the Game had become at La Paz: "We (the legal department) were individuals that protested being subjected to draconian treatment, and when we spoke against having to participate [in the Game] all the La Pazians were like insulted. It was like they were in some hypnotic trance; like zombies. I remember going back to visit La Paz and, man, it was like going to Stepford and seeing everyone acting like the wives."[32]

Few volunteers at La Paz found the courage to leave given the influence Chavez wielded over residents' lives. In some instances, people played the Game out of a sense of obligation to the movement, especially those who did not come from a farm worker background. The claims that the Game made everyone equal appealed to some who harbored guilt about their privilege.

One legal volunteer, Mary Mocine, admitted, "In some odd way, The Game was liberating. I found I had survived it and felt that some of my 'liberal, legal dept' guilt was washed away."[33] Like others, however, she came to regret her participation. More often, people subjected themselves to the Game out of misplaced loyalty to the farm workers, disbelief that Chavez could welcome such a cancer into the union, or a real fear of being put out on the street at a time when they had become dependent on the union for food, shelter, and a job.

Many veterans of the union still debate the significance and the consequences of the Game to the UFW in 1977 and 1978. Kathy Murguia, for example, began playing the Game after the Monday Night Massacre in 1977 with the hope that it would quiet the conflict and *chisme* (gossip) floating within the community. "I had rationalized it as a method of managing interpersonal conflict," she remembered, but added, "I was wrong as I came to see that at times it intensified conflict." In her experience, she saw participants struggle with the indictments outside of the Game and believed that "it had the potential to become psychologically damaging."[34] Abby Flores Rivera, however, dismissed the Game as "a speck in time": "[It] did not teach me anything I did not already know." She believed that the community compelled Chavez to experiment with the Game by "creat[ing] such a negative atmosphere that we became more of a burden than an asset to the union."[35] Yet she predicted, "When they read our history [some] will find [the Game] acceptable and will wonder what all the fuss is about."[36]

RESISTING CHAVEZ

Beyond La Paz, staff members and former volunteers saw the Game, the purges, and the trip to the Philippines as a reason to confront Chavez in order to save the union from self-destruction. Chavez succeeded in extending the Game to the offices in Delano but met with resistance elsewhere. Staff farther out, in Coachella, the Imperial Valley, Salinas, and Santa Maria, heard rumors about its practice and received some encouragement to participate; however, the difficulties with sustaining interest at La Paz and in Delano meant that Chavez had no ability to enforce the practice in these offices. For volunteers in the boycott network who now had been mostly inactive since the Proposition 14 debacle, questions arose as to the direction and purpose of the union. The purges sent several disgruntled members into the stream of progressive networks, where they began to speak about red-baiting, abusive treatment, and cultish behavior within the inner sanctum of the union's headquarters. These revelations produced a strong reaction from boycotters, who wrote protest letters to Chavez and members of the executive board, and challenged some of the new priorities and policies now being implemented.

The first signs of resistance appeared at the United Farm Workers Convention in Fresno at the end of August 1977. Chavez anticipated his critics by announcing that the union had made the important decision over the past several months to fire staff who he alleged were disrupting operations at La Paz. Before a giant mural of himself holding a child aloft on his shoulders, Chavez spoke of the expelled members: "Instead of helping the farm workers to build their own union, some volunteers have come with the notion that they would do the work for the farm workers. Some come with the idea of saving the farm worker from the union. Some have come with their own political and social values and have attempted to convince the workers to adopt them." Chavez articulated, for the first time publicly, a growing animosity toward non–farm workers, by which most understood him to mean white, educated, middle-class volunteers. The position cast aside concerns about the shrinking number of volunteers and privileged a movement built on the elusive service of people with field experience. Speaking to journalist, Sam Kuschner, Larry Tramutt emphasized that the union would now look for "quality rather than quantity" in staffing positions. Marc Grossman offered a cruder explanation, stating, "Many people [in the past] joined in support of the UFW for their own purposes." Sharing the paranoia of Chavez and others within his inner circle, Grossman told Kuschner, "We now say if any S.O.B. comes in with his own political or social agenda and tries to impose that agenda on the union, we will kick him out."[37]

Chavez also sought to head off debate about his unpopular trip to the Philippines as a guest of dictator, Ferdinand Marcos, just prior to the convention. He had ignored the counsel of Gilbert Padilla, who had privately withdrawn from the trip in protest and advised Chavez not to go. Chavez stubbornly went anyway, based on advice from Andy Imutan, a former member and Filipino activist who, according to many within the Filipino and farm worker communities, was an apologist for Marcos.[38] Imutan led Chavez to believe that the trip would shore up flagging support among Pinoy field workers and stem the flow of Filipino members from the union. When the trip did the opposite, Chavez refused to admit his mistake and instead pushed his position harder by inviting Blas Ople, secretary of labor for Marcos, and Roman Arguelles, consul general of the Philippines, to address the farm workers at the convention. The action upset many Filipinos within the union, including Rudy Reyes, a volunteer and former boycott worker in Philadelphia, who seized the floor immediately after their speeches to denounce martial law in the Philippines.[39] Following the convention, Reyes organized with the interfaith community to demand an apology from Chavez for his blunder.[40]

The protest grew so intense that Chavez finally agreed to a public meeting with an anti–martial law collective in the Bay Area that had its own newspaper, *Ang Katipunan*, and the backing of many religious leaders. Rather than use the event as an opportunity to heal wounds and draw attention to the plight of farm workers in the Philippines, Chavez unilaterally invited representatives from the Philippines Consulate in Los Angeles to provide a pro-Marcos position just three days before the meeting. Pinoys reacted angrily, picketing the Consulate office in protest and denouncing the UFW as antidemocratic and Chavez as a friend to dictators. Philip Vera Cruz, who now talked openly about his differences with Chavez, joined the fray by granting an interview to *El Cuhamil*, a newspaper associated with Tony Orendain, a former UFW member who had broken with Chavez to create the Texas Farm Workers Union. "By accepting the invitation [from Marcos]," Vera Cruz told his interviewer, "Cesar showed that he does not believe in [a] democratic process." He pointed out that Chavez's embrace of Marcos stood in stark contrast to the union's resolution to condemn the Nicaraguan dictator Anastacio Somoza and offended many Pinoys who had committed their lives to the union. He also called his former colleagues on the board "figureheads" who acquiesced to Chavez's "dominating power." The situation, Vera Cruz opined, had facilitated the creation of an idol in the form of Cesar Chavez whose word now was accepted as gospel by many. "The danger," he concluded, "is that Cesar is misleading the people."[41]

Protests from Filipino leaders and opponents of Marcos in the United States began to sway public opinion against Chavez. His high-handed attempt to counter the Filipino protest backfired terribly, especially among religious leaders who had their own issues with Marcos and now questioned whether the union had abandoned its principles of nonviolence. A bevy of religious organizations, including the National Council of Churches and the U.S. Conference of Catholic Bishops, wrote to Hartmire and Chavez expressing their deep concern and regret for Chavez's decision to visit the Philippines. In response, Chavez held a community meeting, which many concerned religious leaders and community groups attended. One observer noted that Chavez told the group "how fucking pissed off" he was at the media for obsessing about Marcos's political prisoners and ignoring the Philippine leader's great strides in land reform.[42] Over the course of the next several months, the controversy persisted, grabbing the attention of mainstream newspapers and television and radio outlets. As a consequence, protest letters continued to flow to Hartmire, who heard from several clergyman, religious leaders, and nuns regarding their objections to the union's position.[43]

Although several radical organizations counted themselves critics of Chavez, it was the resistance from former friends of the union and those within the Catholic Church that stung the most. Chavez had drawn on the symbols of the Virgin Mary and Christ to show his affinity with the principles of sacrifice and nonviolence present in the most progressive wing of the Church. During the heyday of the boycott, he had depended on many Catholic organizations to man the picket lines. He relied heavily on Catholic clergy and lay leaders to persuade congregants across the nation and in Canada to participate in the movement and counted among his own staff former nuns and priests who served him faithfully throughout the most difficult years of struggle. Hartmire maintained a cadre of Catholic allies and contacts on his National Farm Worker Ministry board who, in times of solidarity, helped convey a message of peace and brotherhood that lent credibility to the United Farm Workers.

Chavez's support for Marcos, his experimentations with Synanon, and news of aggressive behavior and threats of violence against volunteers in 1977 compelled some Catholics to speak out, most notably members of the Pax Center in Erie, Pennsylvania, a leading Catholic peace organization. Juli Loesch belonged to the Center and served as a writer and editor for the *Erie Christian Witness*, a local newsletter that covered the activities of members and other allied organizations. Loesch had volunteered on the UFW boycotts in Delano, Detroit, Cleveland, and elsewhere dating back to 1969 and knew many of the volunteers recently purged from the union. The stories she had heard from at least a dozen ex-volunteers compelled her to ask Hartmire to explain Synanon's role in the union and to justify the reduction of the boycott network and the firing of people whom she knew to be trustworthy and committed staff members.

Still enthralled by Synanon and the potential of the Game, Hartmire offered his usual labored defense of Chavez and his practices. "The union *is* doing something about the status of volunteers," he assured Loesch. "The end product will be good for the staff and for the farm workers' cause." He confessed that "getting there is rocky" and predicted that "plenty of rough times internally and externally" lay ahead for the union, but he felt confident that all the new developments, including the Game, were helping the union mature. He acknowledged that "people who are down on the union and the leadership" had been asked to leave, but this decision had contributed to the improvement of staff morale. Hartmire reminded Loesch of her obligation to defend the union against critics and asked her to take an active role in fighting back against "those people who attack Cesar or the UFW." "Tell them that an attack on Cesar is an attack on the movement," he instructed. "If you can't do that, Juli, then I don't know what to tell you."[44]

Hartmire's words of advice rang hollow to Loesch, given the news of the purges and Chavez's increasingly authoritarian behavior. Loesch accused Hartmire of being "defensive" in his reply to her and dismissive of her concerns. Feeling the stress of the situation and overwhelmed by the number of critical letters, Hartmire lashed out at Loesch, explaining, "I do not have time to carry on a continuing correspondence with you or others who have written me. The union's future shape will be determined by those who have made it their life, with no consideration of alternative ways of living and struggling." Unwittingly, his response to Loesch confirmed the insular, "us against them" mentality that had taken root within the union and articulated the kind of blind loyalty Chavez expected of his staff. Ending his letter with a bitter postscript, Hartmire lectured Loesch on the true meaning of being an ally. "You are a 'supporter,' Juli. That does not mean your ideas have no merit. But it does mean you end up *supporting* what others have given their lives *to do*." Amid Hartmire's condescension, he missed the irony of the moment, neglecting to see how the union's recent behavior had forced out the people who had, in fact, committed their lives to the UFW only to be betrayed by its leader.[45]

Loesch responded by taking her challenge directly to Chavez. In a letter to him on June 22, 1977, she professed her love for the UFW, but worried that three general problems had "grown from bad taste into something considerably worse." Citing the purges since the Proposition 14 campaign and the stifling of internal criticism at La Paz, she claimed that an "intolerance of dissent" had produced an unhealthy paranoia in the union that turned staff members against one another. "I *do* mean that even the mildest private criticism of the Union's affairs is treated as objective treason," she told Chavez. She accused him of cultivating an unhealthy "cult of personality" that had been "fostered as a matter of policy." Such a condition, she argued, had made the union an extension of his will rather than an organization committed to farm workers' self-determination. Finally, she criticized Chavez for his exploitation of volunteers, or what she called the "burn 'em up and throw 'em out" approach. "People come to the UFW willing to work long hours, to accept strict union discipline, and to live in poverty," she contended, "but nobody wants to be a sheer instrument, to be drained to the max and then discarded with the comment, 'Well, there's more where YOU came from!'"[46] She explained that she had learned of these problems through former volunteers who began to appear at churches and colleges in the Midwest where she had intended to rally support for the union. "I could hardly... talk about the Farmworkers," she told Chavez, "without somebody popping up and saying, 'Well, I'm an ex-UFW volunteer (or my wife or my older brother is) and... I was manipulated, I was intimidated, I was used to the max and then kicked in the head!'" The shear number of encounters compelled her to talk to these people, who convinced her that something was amiss. "That's why I wanted you to know," she concluded, "that many of us out here can see a large and growing problem in the UFW in relation to its treatment of volunteers."[47]

Chavez took what had become the union's accepted approach to critics, ignoring Loesch's letter and her concerns. His silence, however, only propelled Loesch to move forward with her investigation, reaching out to former members through a network of religious leaders and former boycott volunteers to obtain greater familiarity with the problems. Her inquiries turned up a number of old and new complaints from people who had firsthand experience or knowledge of the new culture now dominating at La Paz, as well as outside observers who had heard similar stories of dysfunction. Monsignor George Higgins, who had been counted as an early ally of the union, wrote Loesch, expressing hope "for a greater degree of internal self-criticism" in the union. Jim Forest wrote Loesch from Holland, where he had encountered rumors of purges and cultish behavior from two former members of the Philadelphia boycott house.

Closer to home, Mike Yates, an economics professor at the University of Pittsburgh at Johnstown, had recently taken a six-month sabbatical to work at La Paz but ended his service prematurely in response to Chavez's revolution. "I was shocked [and] shaken by the turn taken at La Paz," he confessed to Loesch. Yates had been present for the Monday Night Massacre and the implementation of the Game, developments that disturbed him profoundly. According to Yates, when staff resisted the Game, Chavez used his raw power to thwart dissent. "There's now outright repression going on at La Paz, to which I am an eyewitness," he told Loesch. In one case, he watched as Chavez verbally accosted a volunteer who questioned the mail policy. "Cesar, in a rage, summoned the volunteer into his office, screamed at him in the most vulgar and abusive way, [telling] him to 'shove his civil liberties up his ass' and fired him."[48]

Several others responded to Loesch, recounting the firings and the growing paranoia of Dolores Huerta and Chavez. Bruno Hicks, a priest and anti–martial law community activist in San Francisco, reported that Huerta routinely espoused the belief that "infiltrators with revolutionary, radical ideology [were] urging armed struggle" to overthrow the current leadership in the union. Others complained about the severe reduction in the boycott network without an adequate explanation, and a few expressed disapproval of Larry Tramutt's "rigid and fairly ruthless" approach to creating a "new, lean, loyal" boycott. The recent experiences of one volunteer associated with the newspaper *Catholic Worker* made her question whether it was time to expose the union for its own good. Rather than write about the festering problems, however, she chose to move on to the women's movement.[49] Jeff Ames, a legal volunteer who left California and the union, objected to the "heavy collectivist La Paz Synanon Monastic trip" Chavez had imposed on residents living at the headquarters. As a member of the legal department, he opposed playing the Game, a position that earned him Chavez's ire. "Cesar called the Legal Department 'a cancer on the union,'" he reported to Loesch, an insult that compelled him to leave the union for good.[50]

Ultimately, Loesch decided to write about the problems for the *Erie Christian Witness*.[51] In anticipation of her article, she wrote her informants expressing her gratitude for their "strong, honest, corrective criticism." "If we're loyal UFW supporters and we believe in justice," she told them, "the most loyal support we can give is to *look into* the allegations of injustice, ask probing questions, and criticize directly the people who are most responsible." Responding to Hartmire's private admonishment, she added, "Uncritical, unquestioning, unprincipled 'support' is not support at all; it's a kind of patronizing sentimentality." The article, entitled "Trouble in the UFW," appeared in the Christmas edition and contained the contents of her letter to Chavez and a number of testimonials from people within her network. To this, she added the judgment "What the Teamsters and the growers and poverty and repression could not do, the UFW could do to itself; suicide by moral suffocation." She encouraged sympathetic readers to criticize the union leadership and to join her in praying for the union. Many allies in Loesch's network associated with newspapers heeded her advice, publishing critical articles in religious, leftist, and community newspapers.[52] In addition, several individuals and groups sent letters to Hartmire and Chavez well into 1978, expressing disapproval of the union's direction.[53] Chavez, Hartmire, and those vested in the changes at La Paz dismissed the charges as the product of disgruntled idealists and radicals who had little idea of how the union worked.

Chavez had a much more difficult time ignoring criticism coming from the UFW legal department. The lawyers, who had already become the target of suspicion given their request for pay, resisted the Game. One of Loesch's informants, Jeff Ames, privately testified that Cohen "[couldn't] stand the Synanon shit," although the verdict on whether the lawyers would play remained unsettled at the beginning of 1978.[54] The Hopcraft affair proved that some lawyers working in places like Delano had already become ensnarled in the practice, and Chavez had made overtures to Cohen about drawing the legal staff from Salinas to La Paz to participate. The attorneys anticipated these plans and began to organize against it, calling it a "waste of time" and a diversion from the "real work" "out there." Many in the legal department saw the La Paz staff as "brown-nosing moonies" (a reference to Reverend Moon and the Unification Church) and took issue with Cohen over his belief that they should play the Game to appease Chavez. Cohen believed their training to defend themselves in a court of law would give them the ability to hold their own in the Game. For a brief moment, he also saw the value of using the Game to check some of the strong personalities on his staff. In anticipation of the legal department's arrival, Hartmire and Cohen had some hard words about what had transpired with the Game to date, but they also worked out some combinations for a session that would check "legal staff who clearly jump over the net" when it came to respecting Cohen's authority. Cohen encouraged Hartmire "to take off the gloves" with these individuals.[55]

The matter came to a head on April 15, 1978, when the attorneys boarded four rented white vans bound for La Paz. Cohen had called a meeting earlier in the week to announce that Chavez was making their participation in the Game for six consecutive weeks a condition of their continued employment. Charlie Atilano noted the irony of "being fired as a volunteer" if they did not agree to play.[56] According to Tom Dalzell, Cohen also saw the absurdity of the situation but pleaded with the group to participate since he was not ready to quit the union. "Nobody-nobody-nobody wanted to play The Game," Dalzell remembered, but the attorneys had too much respect for Cohen to let him down.[57] Rather than resist the visit, the group devised a plan to mock the Game and expose Synanon's beliefs as inconsistent with the stated philosophy of Chavez and the United Farm Workers. Dalzell remembered, "We decided to go [to La Paz] but to do so in a way that nobody would miss our resistance."[58]

A minority among the twenty-five to thirty members of the legal team initially suggested that they take direct aim at Synanon, given the increasingly negative press the organization had recently received. In October 1977, Synanon had come under investigation by the state health department and a Marin County grand jury for the abuse of children at the Tomales Bay facility. Dederich had responded with self-righteous incredulity, threatening to surround the investigators with "10 guys twice their size within 1 foot of them." He did little to hide his belief in corporal punishment and revealed a degree of megalomania when he boasted, "I have done exactly like the rest of the guys that run the world. I could run a state, a country, a city; it doesn't make any difference. I'm one of those guys. I know that magic."[59] In its investigation, the county discovered a stockpile of recently purchased weapons that prompted supervisors to threaten Synanon with expulsion from Marin County.[60]

In December 1977, *Time* magazine responded to a growing chorus of former Home Place residents who had broken ranks with Dederich over his "changing partners" policy, which required couples to dissolve their marriages and take another partner. Dederich responded in his typical bombastic fashion, denouncing the magazine and instructing his followers and allies to harass *Time* shareholders. Taking a page out of the union playbook, Dederich ordered a boycott of the magazine and other media outlets that dared to paint Synanon in a negative light. Unlike the UFW boycott, however, Synanon's campaigns bordered on violence. In one instance, Synanites picketed a stockholders meeting of the American Broadcasting Corporation in New York City for airing negative stories about Synanon on the San Francisco Bay Area affiliate, KGO-TV. In the course of the protest, Matt Rand threatened ABC executives and their families with violence on their way home from work and at their residences. Another Synanite spoke of the "irrational" rage among members and warned that the organization could not promise to control it. Meanwhile, news leaked that Dederich had assembled a small paramilitary force at Home Place known as the "Imperial Marines" to do anything he asked to protect the organization.[61]

UFW attorneys recognized similarities between the blind allegiance of Synanites to Dederich and the culture of obedience Chavez was trying to impose on the volunteers. Some attorneys wanted to draw out the contradictions between Chavez's espoused belief in nonviolence and Dederich's turn toward armed struggle. "There was a small but vocal faction that advocated showing up at La Paz dressed and acting like Synanon's Imperial Marines," recalled Dalzell. Some wanted to do a full-scale protest by arriving with "shaved heads, coveralls, shotguns, and chants of Dederich's to-the-point [message]: 'Don't Fuck with Synanon!'" Although the attorneys had a laugh—including the men on staff who joked that they would all have to get vasectomies to carry out the ruse faithfully—the majority settled on a milder demonstration. The group arrived wearing short-sleeved white shirts and skinny dark ties, a look that Dalzell described as an "approximation of Mormon missionaries or LaRouche droids at the airport."[62] The appearance captured the uniformity of behavior that derived from Synanon but had come to dominate the actions and thoughts of people living within La Paz as well.

Upon their arrival, Charlie Atilano, a former U.S. Marine, started a boot camp–style march around the grounds of the headquarters, leading the group in a call-and-response chant ("I don't know but I've been told / I don't know but I've been told"). The display drew incredulous residents to the windows as the group broke into a loud rendition of "When the Saints Go Marching In." Perhaps a bit tamer than their initial plans, the protest still conveyed the point the attorneys were hoping to make. Dalzell remembered, "We were suggesting a certain cultishness in the embrace of Synanon while at the same time mocking ourselves as self-anointed saints." The latter reference acknowledged the resentment of some organizers within the union, such as Eliseo Medina, who groused that members of the legal department pulled in larger stipends than the average volunteer, or that they had the benefit of jobs that many still considered "missionary" work. Larry Tramutt, who had prepared to receive the group in the North Unit, embraced the challenge by attempting to take the edge off the protest with a demonstration of his own. Calling his response a "stroke of genius," Dalzell remembered what came next: "[Tramutt] stood up, joined us in singing, and formed a conga line behind us with La Paz volunteers, weaving through the room, singing along with us."[63]

Tramutt's actions notwithstanding, the attorneys' performance shattered any expectations that the legal department would go along with the new culture that was dominating at La Paz. No one could remember if Chavez witnessed their display of insolence, but the news traveled quickly throughout the union, prompting him to take action against the lawyers. "We had two meetings between the legal department and Cesar that summer in which [Cesar] fired all of us," Dalzell lamented.[64] Marshall Ganz and Jessica Govea tried to stand up for the lawyers, refusing to go along with the decision. In the end, however, Chavez cobbled together enough votes on the executive board to support his proposal.[65] Although Dalzell joked that the purge earned the department the distinction of being "the biggest group fired at once," he remembered the meetings with Chavez as "civil, respectful, and sad." Not all shed a tear for the attorneys. "You guys danced yourselves right out of good standing and out of a job," Abby Flores Rivera told Dalzell years later.[66] Her feeling captured the opinions of some within La Paz who refused to see the attorneys' work as essential to the continued success of the union or resistance to the Game as a worthwhile fight.

In the wake of the firings, Chavez transferred the legal operations to La Paz, as he had always wanted to do. He instituted a program to train young, mostly Mexican American lawyers to serve as the new, all-volunteer legal department, a move that severely diminished the legal-organizing collaboration that had been so successful up until that point. Over the next three years, the union dramatically withdrew from pursuing ALRB elections and concentrated almost exclusively on negotiating the contracts they had won in 1975 and 1976.[67] Without an experienced legal team, however, moving union election victories to bona fide contracts became more difficult and left many frustrated workers wondering when, if ever, they would have representation.[68] During that time, growers had begun a new strategy of bringing civil suits against the union for damages related to strikes, thereby circumventing the ALRB and limiting the state's influence over labor-employer relations. The absence of an effective legal team only hastened the union's decline and permanently imperiled the goal of reaching 100,000 members by 1978.[69]

In 1979 a sense of urgency compelled vegetable workers in the Imperial Valley and Salinas to make a final push for ALRB electoral victories through the use of strikes, but the effort happened without the approval of Chavez. "I worked with those workers," Ganz recalled. "There was tremendous potential there. We thought we could accomplish a lot, and eventually we did. We got great contracts out of that thing. But there was no commitment from Cesar to turning that base into a success."[70] As workers celebrated their achievements, Chavez sat out the festivities, wondering how he might rein in the autonomous vegetable workers. Ganz, who had encouraged the workers, now came under suspicion, as did Jessica Govea, who joined him in advocating for their right to strike. Through the end of the decade, Chavez sought to curb the influence of the two, targeting them for internal investigations regarding their alleged treason against the union. Under the weight of this pressure, Ganz and Govea resigned in 1981. That same year, Chavez unilaterally reinterpreted union rules to block the candidacy of three vegetable workers for a spot on the executive board at the UFW convention, all but ending a chance for anything resembling representative democracy in the union.[71]

The dismantling of the base of power in Salinas also corrupted what had been a tense but respectful relationship between Cesar Chavez and Jerry Cohen. After firing his staff, Chavez invited Cohen to join the new team at La Paz, but Cohen declined. "I told him 'no,' and . . . resigned as general counsel, but I wanted to stay and negotiate [contracts] and he wanted to keep me around on any terms," Cohen remembered. Cohen continued to work for the union from Salinas, where his wife inherited land and they built a home. He enjoyed the break from being surrounded by other lawyers, but the honeymoon did not last long. "Finally, it was sometime in '80 [when Chavez] began to sort of switch up the signals." Cohen had worked out a deal with a big grower, Sam Andrews, to adjust the controversial hiring hall process to involve only new workers. They also mutually agreed on a seniority list for those workers already in the system. Although Chavez had agreed to the terms, he changed his mind at the last minute, embarrassing Cohen and thwarting the will of many Salinas workers who had fought hard to win union representation. Rather than fight with Chavez, Cohen resigned, bringing to an end his long distinguished career with the UFW.[72]

Chavez's attempts to maintain the Game through the end of the decade did not fare any better than his attempts to fend off criticism from those outside of La Paz. Chavez must have noticed that the Game had become controversial and instructed the union spokesperson, Marc Grossman, not to talk about it to the press. According to Tom Dalzell, throughout the summer and fall of 1977, Chavez went so far as to deny the existence of the Game to the outside world, even as he added a Spanish-language game group and extended it to Delano.[73]

The decision of some members to quit the Game and others to outright refuse participation signaled that not all was well. Hartmire, who evaluated the emotional state of participants, grew increasingly pessimistic about the prospects of continuing the practice. Throughout 1977 and 1978, numerous volunteers expressed significant reservations about playing, including Grossman, who now told Hartmire he was "having serious problems."[74] Chavez worked to assuage Grossman's concerns, but he could not do the same for others, who stated unequivocally that they wanted out. Hartmire reported that the Spanish-language version of the Game, known as La Broma (the Joke), was in "wobbly shape." Given the dire situation, Hartmire advised Chavez to "forget the Spanish game" or perhaps salvage some of the Spanish-dominant members' participation through the inclusion of "some bilingual action" in other sessions.[75]

The news from English-dominant Game groups did not look much better. Hartmire reported at the beginning of 1978, "Lots of absenteeism recently. Sickness, kids sick and 'maybe sickness.' I have sent for people the last two games." When he confronted individuals, many either refused to play or offered excuses why they were not ready. "Judy Scheckel played one (1) game and then exercised her option to stop," Hartmire reported. Another volunteer, Toni Barela, also expressed her desire to withdraw from the Game, but Hartmire attempted to discourage her from doing so. He reported to Chavez, "I told her she did not have that option. She did *not* show up Wed nite." Another resident of La Paz, Bobby Reyes, asked for an exemption. "[He] says 'he doesn't feel like playing until he is clearer on his commitment to the union.'" In spite of his trepidations, Hartmire convinced Reyes to remain in the Game for a little while longer.

Hartmire's powers of persuasion did not work with everyone. Betty Wolcott objected to the Game on the grounds that she felt hesitation in waging indictments and harbored unresolved anger against those who maligned her. Hartmire hoped that he had persuaded her to continue, although he could not be sure she had changed her mind. "She knows [missing] is serious and will talk to you *if* she comes to a final decision on not playing," he told Chavez.[76] A former priest, Ken Doyle, refused to play and challenged the Game as inconsistent with the nonviolent tenets of the union. "He came on with a lot of intellectual questioning of The Game," Hartmire reported to Chavez. "I told him that was a cheap cop-out. If he wants to make the game better, join us and help." In spite of Hartmire's accusation that "it was screwing other people up to have him absent," Doyle continued to stay away. "He said he would leave La Paz if his *not* playing was such a huge problem," Hartmire told Chavez.[77] When Hartmire and Kent Winterrowd conducted a survey to assess the popularity of the Game in June 1978, they found that Doyle was not alone in his negative opinions. "The pioneering, enthusiastic spirit that prevailed with groups 1 & 2 is faltering or weakening," they wrote Chavez. When people did play, they found "a preference for discussions [rather than the] rough and tumble gaming" that Chavez believed was more productive.[78]

The avoidance of the Game and complaints from allies outside eventually compelled Chavez to admit, "[The] Game is good for us personally but not so good for the Union."[79] Rather than dispense with it, however, he chose to re-form the practice during the summer of 1978 by bringing in Synanon advisors and discussing alterations to the practice with the first Game group. The ugliness of indictments, including false accusations and comments about people's sexual behavior, led Chavez to change the rules regarding personal attacks and lying.[80] In the "new, new Game," as they called it, those doing the gaming were expected to draw on a "kernel of truth" in their indictments, while those being indicted were encouraged to remember "it's not you personally, it's the fuck-up" that was at issue. Kathy Murguia, who played through these transitions, remembered, "The Game was only supposed to relate to work issues and NOT personal issues."[81] Participants could now remain silent in sessions. Game groups were instructed "to take the time needed to put a person back together after a hard game." Couples were now off limits for indictments because, leaders recognized, "it is hard for the mate to sit there and watch while the other is taken apart."[82]

These changes, however, did little to assuage the concerns of skeptics who had already made up their mind that the Game did not belong in the union. For Hartmire, who tried to navigate between Chavez's wishes to maintain and expand the practice and his own need to manage the outcry from former and current members to end it, the protests from outside the union pushed the matter to a breaking point. "We were saved from becoming a cult because of the boycott," Hartmire later admitted. Although Chavez and the board had done much to disable the network in the intervening months since the Proposition 14 campaign, enough people affiliated with the boycott had stayed in touch with the union, waiting and hoping for direction. The firing of Nick Jones followed by the consolidation of houses and changes in leadership piqued awareness among critics who questioned what Chavez and the union were doing with the momentum they felt they had created through their collective actions. "We had to constantly be communicating with the people out there in the world," Hartmire remembered. "If we hadn't had to, god knows where we would have gone."[83]

No one can quite recall when the Game officially ended. According to Hartmire, "At some point, the outside world was raising so many questions, and some of them were people who had given us money and support, Cesar just called it off." Records show July 1978 as the last month in which Chavez attempted to salvage the Game on a communitywide level, although some recall that he held smaller Game sessions well into 1979.[84] In the end, the experiment with the Game had lasted a solid fourteen months at La Paz, from May 1977 to July 1978, long enough to sow distrust among the leaders and divert attention from the work of building a union.[85]

On January 31, 1978, Chavez and the executive board called off the boycott of grapes, lettuce, and Gallo wine, bringing to an end an era in which the United Farm Workers had made its presence felt throughout the United States and beyond.[86] Chavez's promise to downsize the department at the union convention the previous summer anticipated this move, and the announcement confirmed what numerous former volunteers had felt since the demobilization of the boycott for the Proposition 14 campaign in 1976. Throughout the turmoil of 1977, Larry Tramutt had presented a positive outlook in his monthly reports while quietly carrying out Chavez's wishes to purge boycott staff and consolidate houses. At Chavez's request, Tramutt had compiled a month-by-month tally of volunteers in the boycott who had been fired or forced to resign and a brief explanation of how the individual had arrived at his or her fate. Submitted to Chavez on August 31, 1977, the five-page list contained a total of 109 individuals sacked between January and July that year, most identified as victims of the Proposition 14 campaign or the "Nick Jones Fallout." The list stands as a record of the remarkable efficiency of a union motivated by fear and paranoia. It also marked the end for many young, dedicated people, most of whom had little personal connection to the farm workers but had fought tenaciously on their behalf nonetheless. By the time the official announcement came, Tramutt had moved on to other business in the union. He was replaced by former New York volunteer, Mike Lacinak, who functioned primarily as a caretaker for the transfer of resources from the boycott to other departments in the union.[87]

The list did not account for one of the boycott's most beloved figures, Elaine Elinson, although it easily could have. Elinson had continued to work for the union on a volunteer basis, functioning as the boycott coordinator for all of Britain, oblivious to the changes going on at La Paz. In 1977, she traveled to Ireland, where she showed transport workers the film *Fighting for Our Lives* and raised approximately 500 British pounds. When Elinson sent the money with her report to Nick Jones, however, she heard nothing in return. After several attempts to make contact with La Paz, she finally received an angry letter from Tramutt, who demanded that she explain her actions. She recalled its contents: "The letter [said], 'who the heck are you? Who do you think you are representing the United Farm Workers? Who told you you could go show this movie? What did you tell these unions so that you could raise this money?'" A shocked Elinson wrote directly to Chavez, who promptly replied with a letter of gratitude for her service, but the experience led her to ask questions. Eventually, during a visit to the United States the following year, she met Nick and Virginia Jones, who told her what had happened to them and many others in the union. As a consequence, Elinson pulled back on her fundraising for the UFW and focused on her job in London.

In 1980, Elinson had one final encounter with Tramutt. She had returned to the United States to begin what turned out to be a long career working for the American Civil Liberties Union. She remained sympathetic to *la causa,* and, although the Jones affair troubled her, she still wanted to help the union now that she was living in the Bay Area. When she called the Oakland office to volunteer, a familiar voice answered the phone. "Oh, well, this is Larry Tramutola," the person identified himself. Elinson had heard that Tramutt had changed his name, and she took the opportunity to communicate her displeasure with him after all these years. She recalled her response: "I'm like, 'You know what? Screw you! You sent me the worst letter that I've ever received in my life. . . . You made me feel worse than I've ever felt. And I will never work in any boycott office with you. Good bye.'" In the years that followed, Elinson, like many other former volunteers, found other ways to help farm workers, but she never again gave her time to the union that had been such an important part of her life.[88]

A QUESTION OF STRATEGY

The decision to dismantle the boycott was not well received by the radical left, who had trouble understanding why the union would forfeit what had been a successful strategy. Most believed that the boycott still held sway over the public in the battle for the hearts and minds of consumers, made evident by a poll in 1975 showing that 12 percent of the American people were boycotting grapes, 11 percent were boycotting lettuce, and 8 percent refused to purchase Gallo wines.[89] Indeed, an evaluation from the *Los Angeles Times* proclaimed that the UFW had constructed "the most effective union boy-cott of any product in the history of the nation."[90] Why then, asked one writer, would the union give up this tool for social change so easily?

Most outside of the United Farm Workers believed that Chavez and members of his inner circle had turned their backs on the movement in favor of a more ordinary union concerned with the nonmissionary work of win-ning ALRB elections and litigating labor disputes. Promises at the union convention in 1977 to professionalize the staff and involve more rank-and-file workers in the day-to-day operations signaled this turn toward a model that resembled the UAW more than it did CORE or SNCC. The antiradi-cal purges were consistent with the politics of organized labor during the cold war, a position that discouraged many social justice activists from seeking solutions by way of unions. Moreover, Chavez's apparent faith in the government seemed inconsistent with either the character of the movement during its heyday in the late 1960s and the early 1970s or the record of suc-cess under the new law. Although the union won more elections than it lost, critics were quick to point out that many of the victories failed to translate into real gains for workers because the process of appeals and ratification of votes often delayed the achievement of a contract. "The UFW now has 100 contracts in California," one observer wrote, "but there are 100 other ranches where the union has won representation elections but still hasn't obtained a contract."[91] In the final analysis, Chavez's decision to dismantle the boycott was "a question of strategy," one that neither the radical left nor volunteers in the boycott agreed with.[92]

As the audiotapes of the executive board meetings show, Chavez and the union struggled more than anyone in the public knew with the question of how to merge a social movement with the requirements of becoming a state-recognized union. The boycott, for all its value in drawing growers to the bar-gaining table and gaining public sympathy, had taken a backseat to the elec-tions after the passage of the ALRA in 1975. "[The law] changed everything," Chavez often lamented, an acknowledgment that he too missed the mission-ary work of building a movement that counted among its goals more than just earning collective bargaining rights for farm workers. Hartmire, who had a front-row seat to the changes in his friend, later reflected, "I think the Agricul-tural Labor Relations Act threw Cesar off course." He saw Chavez as a master tactician in what he called "a guerilla movement," of which the secondary boycott served as the ultimate weapon. "But now," Hartmire remembered,

"the law and lawyers, and the government, which he never much trusted ...
threw him off his natural course."[93]

What that "natural course" may have been is up for interpretation, although Chavez tried to indicate, in both word and deed, what he intended during the tumultuous years immediately after the ALRA was signed into law. In an interview in October 1977 with the Catholic publication *Sojourner*, Chavez laid out the challenges before the union, the first of which was to consolidate the gains made by negotiating contracts where they had won elections. Such a task, he contended, depended on the stabilization of a long-term staff that he believed had eluded the union due to a lack of common understanding and commitment among volunteers. "I am convinced," he told his interviewer, "that we have to do something to replace what we lost. We had a kind of community."[94] Chavez wanted to turn back the clock to a time before the ALRA, when volunteers flocked to the movement out of a willingness "to give up some of those individual rights ... for the good of the group." "We're at a crossroads now as to whether we're a 9-to-5 group or a more disciplined, more religious community," he explained. Only those on the inside and those who had been alerted to the transformation in the union understood that Chavez's community had more of an affinity with Dederich's Synanon than with the Catholic Church. "If we choose this community style," he said, "we will have some kind of religion—either we invent one or we keep what we have, but we cannot be without one."[95] For those who opposed Chavez and his plans, such a public admission must have been demoralizing.

Ultimately, Chavez's vision for a new community died under the combined weight of volunteer opposition and the discrediting of the commune model. As current and former volunteers resisted the influence of Synanon on the union, Dederich and Synanon itself imploded. Dederich became increasingly combative as the state investigated claims of child abuse and Synanon dissidents and relatives tried to extract loved ones from the community. The success of one attorney, Paul Morantz, to win a $300,000 lawsuit against Synanon precipitated an act of bizarre retribution from Dederich. Angered by the settlement, Dederich allegedly ordered two members of his Imperial Marines to kill Morantz by planting a rattlesnake in his mailbox. Morantz survived the bite; however, the failed plot all but ended Synanon when authorities arrested the two suspects. Dederich fled into the Arizona desert, where he began drinking and taking drugs again. Throughout the spectacle, Chavez defended his friend, at one point asking Governor

Jerry Brown not to extradite Dederich to California to stand trial for attempted murder. Chavez's actions endeared him to Dederich's family and Synanon loyalists, but the defense of his friend confirmed critics' belief that Chavez had lost his way.[96]

In truth, Chavez had not abandoned his principles as much as his critics believed. Although his experiments with the Game and his relationship with Dederich certainly raised eyebrows, his "one man, one vision" approach had been the hallmark of his leadership since before the founding of the union. As an organizer in the Community Service Organization, he resented the growing influence of professionals and their refusal to take up advocacy work on behalf of farm workers. Rather than compromise and work within the strictures of an organization that resisted becoming a union, Chavez issued an ultimatum that resulted in his resignation. The action demonstrated his sincere commitment to help a people and an occupation to which he felt intimately attached; it also revealed stubbornness and autocratic tendencies that would flourish within a farm worker movement closely identified with his charismatic leadership. The years of struggle to build the movement—not yet a union—had been incredibly challenging, yet his ability to draw people in with marches, rallies, and fasts validated his approach. Through this process, he alienated allies—most notably Filipino leaders and some rank-and-file members—but the continued appeal of the boycott and the initial success in winning ALRB elections justified his choices, helping him to overcome any moments of self-doubt.

These successes, however, had much more to do with the work of volunteers and organizers than Chavez cared to admit. The boycott had materialized as a strategy for social change due largely to experimentation by diverse groups of people who interpreted the conditions on the ground and mobilized citizens and allied unionists. The embrace of the boycott—and not the strike—as the critical tool that put the union over the top in the struggle to get growers to the bargaining table demonstrated a flexibility in Chavez that seemed to disappear as the movement evolved into a union. The UFW initially experienced more victories than defeats in this new role, thanks in large part to Jerry Cohen and his team of attorneys, who outsmarted expensive Teamster and grower lawyers and maneuvered their way into the political process to craft a law that favored the UFW.

In the aftermath of the ALRA, the UFW legal team and union organizers, such as Eliseo Medina and Marshall Ganz, adapted to the new realities of state-sponsored farm worker justice and its limits under the ALRB, but the process frustrated Chavez. Interaction with the state changed the rules of the game from winning hearts and minds in the fields, on the docks, and in front of supermarkets to winning votes in union elections and unfair labor practice suits in Sacramento. As a consequence, the union's tactics shifted from the missionary work of marches, fasts, and boycotts to the bureaucratic work of lawyers and contract negotiators. These requirements also empowered volunteers within the union to demand a greater say over the future of the organization. Such challenges threatened the tight control to which Chavez had grown accustomed, leading to a contest of wills that served no one.

In the end, Chavez's greatest failure may not have been his flirtations with communal living, creating a new religion, or attempting to control the minds of his followers through a bevy of devices borrowed from self-made prophets. Rather, his failures were quite familiar to social movements that have harbored a dream of institutionalizing social justice: Chavez failed to adapt his strategy to fit the demands of a dynamic situation.[97] The ability to move the locus of power from the strike to the boycott in the earlier days was not matched in the late 1970s by an equal ability to move from the boycott to a fight for victories in ALRB elections and arbitration and, if necessary, California courtrooms. That Chavez and his lieutenants failed to handle with grace the transition from the boycott to more state-sponsored solutions was only part of the problem. He and the executive board recognized the need for greater skill and specialization among their team of organizers and lawyers but resisted a process of professionalization out of fear of becoming like the unions, state bureaucracies, and political parties they distrusted. Social theorists who have studied the relationship between social movements and the state would suggest that they had much to be fearful of, given the ability of state institutions, especially political parties, to absorb and diffuse much of the enthusiasm and agenda for reform present in social movements. In the most pessimistic readings of this relationship, movements that concede to pursuing justice on the state's terms usually end up perpetuating the "injuries" inflicted upon them by extending the coercive influence of the state and replicating its oppressive features in their own governance. Ultimately, some theorists argue, it should be the objective of the poor and the dispossessed to avoid being governed altogether.[98]

With the United Farm Workers, the answer to whether the state would have helped or hindered their pursuit of social justice is incomplete. Chavez and the executive board chose to go halfway in working within the new reality of the ALRA. In spite of their great frustration with the Agricultural Labor Relations Board, the exhaustion of state funds in 1976, and the failure of Proposition 14, the record still shows that the union was winning more elections than it was losing, and growers disliked the ALRB for its tendency to favor the UFW.[99] In essence, Chavez had chosen to work with the state by acceding to the ALRA yet failed to follow through with this strategy by withdrawing from organizing in 1977 and dismantling the legal team in 1978. The lack of democracy and the reliance on Chavez's charismatic leadership permitted him to pursue a path that doomed the union to failure.

Meanwhile the growers adapted their strategies to meet the challenges confronting them. Prior to 1970, the failure of industry leaders to anticipate the power of the boycott and to acknowledge differences among them led to Coachella growers' split from San Joaquin Valley growers and a breakdown in industry solidarity. Through this experience, grape growers like Martin Zaninovich never became reconciled to the reality of a unionized workforce; however, like most of them, he learned that they could not run a business and a publicity campaign at the same time. "Although I still managed to handle sales and make contracts and arrange for brokers and dealers to handle our product," Zaninovich recalled, "I did not spend as much time in the office or on the ranch as I had previously." He and others longed to return to managing farm operations and leave the work of public relations to those with more skill and knowledge. As a consequence, the growers embraced a degree of collectivity that, unbeknown to them, made the industry stronger and more cohesive. Zaninovich said, "The Table Grape Commission was approved during this time, and has been tremendously important to us as a marketing tool for our products." He added, "Table grape growers approved it and financially supported it probably because we were, as an industry, in trouble. It is highly questionable whether we would have approved the commission otherwise."[100]

As the president of the California Table Grape Commission and the main force behind the growers' opposition to the boycott, Bruce Obbink witnessed the United Farm Workers at their most potent as well as their most vulnerable. Obbink began at a time when other grape grower organizations, such as the Grape & Tree Fruit League and the South Central Growers Association, failed to stem the tide of losses associated with the grape boycott that culminated in the 1970 contracts. "One thing led to another," Obbink recalled, "so in 1967, [the growers] went to Sacramento and said, 'We need to organize ourselves.'" The California state legislator sanctioned the creation of the commission, which functioned as a quasi-public agency similar to a chamber of commerce charged with bolstering the image of the industry. Once the majority of growers voted for it, everyone had to contribute dues. According to Obbink, growers preferred the noninvasive structure of the commission that allowed them to market their own products while getting support from the state for the promotion of the entire industry.[101]

By the late 1970s, as growers became more savvy about articulating an identity that appealed to consumers, the Table Grape Commission was thriving. Like Harry Kubo and the Citizens for a Fair Labor Law, Obbink and the commission avoided taking a reactionary position vis-à-vis the UFW and Chavez, and instead engaged in media campaigns designed to advance an image sure to resonate with the public. The commission functioned primarily as an advertising and public relations organ for the industry, focused exclusively on raising the esteem of table grapes regardless of where they were grown. Under Obbink, the commission cultivated new sales pitches. Although some resisted, the majority of growers voted to fund the enterprise by deducting .0005 percent per box of grapes sold. The organizational structure gave Obbink and his employees the incentive to succeed in their media campaigns to maintain growers' faith in the commission. The boycott also helped define and cultivate their mission and gave purpose to the commission. In essence, the longer the boycott ran and the wider it spread, the stronger and more defined the commission's work became.

The collapse of the boycott and the internal strife in 1977 and 1978 made the union vulnerable at a time when it needed to be strong. Obbink remembered the year as a watershed moment, not for what the commission did, but for the failures of the union to capitalize on its momentum after the pact with the Teamsters. Like Kubo, Obbink respected Chavez and anticipated a vigorous offensive in the fields following a year of struggle to improve the ALRB. "There's just no doubt in [my] mind," Obbink asserted, "that Cesar Chavez was an incredibly charismatic guy ... whether he was marching or fasting or whatever the hell he was doing." Yet for reasons that are still inexplicable to Obbink, Chavez lost his focus and withdrew from the fight. In that moment, Chavez managed to snatch defeat from the jaws of victory, laying the conditions for the expansion of the grape market and the ascendancy of the commission. Obbink opined, "Had [Chavez] not got off sideways here, somehow, with that Synanon bunch and then started firing all these competent people . . . you never know."

The formation of a state-sanctioned, quasi-public commission paid dividends as time wore on. According to Obbink, the commission began with a modest budget of $600,000 during the 1967–68 harvest. Once growers had settled the conflict and returned to profit in 1970, the commission's budget rose due to the per box deductions. "When I left [in 1996]," Obbink explained, "[my budget] was 12 million dollars." With that money, he and his team expanded their operations beyond fighting the United Farm Workers to developing slogans like "The natural snack" and "One bite at a time," which dramatically increased the popularity of table grapes despite intermittent boycotts throughout the 1980s and 1990s. Obbink explained, "[We went] from 20 million boxes [sold in 1967–68] to 90 million [in 2008]." During that same period, Obbink observed a dramatic change in both the number of growers and the per capita consumption: "When I started with the Table Grape Commission, there were 1,500 farmers producing 20 million boxes of grapes. Per capita consumption was 1.2 pounds in 1967–68. Today, there are 500 farmers producing 90 million boxes of grapes, and the per capita consumption is over eight pounds." These changes signaled that the boycott had eliminated smaller, less profitable growers from the business, while growers with more capital and land survived and ultimately thrived.

The increase in profits also tells another important story. Such changes came as a consequence of the expanded sales of table grapes in markets in which growers had a negligible presence prior to the UFW boycott. The boycott forced growers to develop marketing campaigns in nontraditional domestic markets such as the South and the Mountain West, and in international markets such as Canada, England, Scandinavia, and Asia to try to beat the boycott. When the boycott ended, the traditional urban markets returned to the growers, but so did these new markets that had been cultivated in the heat of the battle. In the years following the grape boycott, the commission succeeded in incorporating Mexican and Chilean grapes into their promotions, enabling the industry to coordinate seasons north and south of the border and expand to a twelve-month, or year-round, consumer market for grapes in the United States. Obbink attributed these successes to expansion and organization required to fight the boycott.

Until his death on April 23, 1993, Chavez occasionally appealed to consumers not to buy grapes, but the boycott never was the same. Without the extensive network of volunteers, organizers, and lawyers to back it up, the UFW relied on mailing lists to generate financial support for a union that had little contact with workers in the field. Regrettably for farm workers, such "hi-tech boycotts" transformed the UFW into a farm worker advocacy group more concerned with maintaining the legacy of Chavez than addressing the persistent problem of rural poverty that inspired the movement in the first place.[102] Despite the efforts of this once mighty union, the search for farm worker justice continues.

Epilogue

BEYOND THE LEGEND

We must ask of our historians and of those who write about us to be more thorough, more dedicated to seek the full truth and to be more disciplined and rigorous about their evaluating and characterizing of our peoples' struggles, of the roles played by our organizations and by our significant leaders. We demand that our history be analyzed from the perspective of the fundamental contradictions present in the society as a whole during its making. We demand that the most important consideration be given to the role of our workers in determining our history and that this last be the measuring stick for giving significance to this or that event, this or that organization or leader.

BERT CORONA
"Analyzing the Writing of Our History and Its Importance,"
unpublished manuscript, Stanford University Library

Plaster saints are not real. We don't learn anything from plaster saints; we don't write plays about them over and over. We write plays about tragic heroes, because we can identify with them.

MARSHALL GANZ
interviewed by the author, March 26, 2008

This is the West, sir. When the legend becomes fact, print the legend.

MR. SCOTT
in John Ford's *The Man Who Shot Liberty Valance,* 1962

IN JOHN FORD'S CLASSIC WESTERN FILM, *The Man Who Shot Liberty Valance,* audiences are challenged to reconsider the meaning and importance of heroes in the development of the American West. Although Jimmy Stewart's character, Ransom Stoddard, did not kill the fearsome Liberty Valance, a man who had terrorized the townspeople of Shinbone, Arizona, in the name of protecting the land and interest of cattle barons, he received credit for it, rising to the level of U.S. senator for his supposed act of courage. Years later, when Valance's real murderer, John Wayne's Tom Doniphon, dies, Stoddard tries to set the record straight with the local newspaper. The editor, however, will not have it. Beleaguered from carrying the burden of this lie for so long, an incredulous Stoddard asks, "You're not going to use the story, Mr. Scott?" For Scott and his readers, however, the lie had become a convenient myth that provided Shinbone and the state of Arizona with a useful creation story that no one wanted to abandon in the name of truth. "This is the West, sir," Scott replied. "When the legend becomes fact, print the legend."

Released the same year as the National Farm Workers Association began, Ford's cautionary film about the superficiality of heroes has surprising resonance with the history of the farm worker movement and the way historians and the public have remembered its Arizona-born leader, Cesar Chavez. Although Chavez has always had his critics, most historians, both popular and professional, have celebrated him as a visionary, pious, and virtuous leader who would have achieved a national farm workers union if not for the forces mounted against him.[1] This literary approbation has precipitated a surfeit of public memorials in Chavez's honor, ranging from the renaming of public streets and schools, to statues and a postal stamp. Most recently, U.S. Secretary of the Interior Ken Salazar designated the birthplace of the movement, Forty Acres, a National Historic Landmark for the purpose of remembering the "national significance of the life and work of Cesar E. Chavez."[2] The students and professors of Chicano and Latino academic programs have been among the most vested in the Chavez legend, celebrating his birthday and offering scholarships in his name to those whose humble background or commitment to social justice mirrors those of the late labor and civil rights leader. Although these are all laudatory actions, they draw a picture of Chavez's leadership that is far removed from the complex history that I have told in this book.

From the Jaws of Victory contributes to a critical reassessment of Chavez and the United Farm Workers union. In the process of sharing my findings, I have encountered concerned true believers of the Chavez legend who have questioned the value and intent of this project. My purpose has been to hold the UFW leadership accountable to the thousands of farm workers who were let down by the union's retreat from the fields and to produce a usable past for those who wish to advance the cause of farm worker justice today.

This has been the common sentiment among many veterans of the movement whom I have consulted for this book, especially the desire to reconsider the decisions Chavez made from the mid-1970s to the end of that decade. To be sure, a consensus does not exist on the significance and meaning of Chavez's leadership among all who dedicated their lives to the struggle. Yet, the debate that raged among 275 former UFW volunteers on LeRoy Chatfield's online listserv in 2004 and 2005 suggests that neither the public nor those close to the UFW have been well served by more than forty years of hagiography. Oral histories, the listserv, and an evaluation of many hours of recorded executive board meetings have led me to a new interpretation that accounts for the mix of pride and disappointment experienced by the men and women who invested deeply in the project of farm worker justice. Such an accounting is necessary if we hope to learn from Chavez's mistakes as well as his successes.

Although I began this project with the zeal of a labor historian intent on telling the story of the United Farm Workers from the point of view of the volunteers, I became convinced that no accurate picture of the union during its heyday is possible without confronting the legacy of Cesar Chavez. The control Chavez exercised over the union meant that most decisions passed across his desk. There were exceptions to this rule, which I have explored in vivid and sometimes harrowing detail. In the field, volunteers and staff members adapted their strategy to the particular conditions of the fight, whether it was Jerry Cohen negotiating a settlement with the Teamsters, Gilbert Padilla and Marshall Ganz organizing field workers, or Jessica Govea and Elaine Elinson appealing to consumers, storeowners, or dock workers not to buy, sell, or unload grapes. Yet the lack of democracy in the union meant that Chavez more than anyone determined the net impact of these people's efforts. In the end, I found it impossible to downplay or explain away his role in favor of privileging the story of the rank and file and the staff.

Nor should I have. In telling this story, I have tried to avoid presenting Chavez as the fake that Stoddard turns out to be. As Ganz has admitted, Chavez was no "plaster saint"—colorful and noble on the outside, hollow and devoid of substance on the inside. Chavez possessed many valuable qualities that inspired hundreds of volunteers to dedicate their lives to the union and millions of people around the world to rally behind *la causa*. His "single-minded doggedness," as Fred Ross put it, may have been his most important quality, encouraging people not to give up when prospects for success looked grim.[3] Chavez's leadership proved to be especially important in the early years, when someone needed to show the courage necessary to walk away from a secure paycheck and trusted organization in order to build a movement that addressed the specific needs of farm workers. That this same impulse led him to ignore warning signs and reject the counsel of close friends in favor of pursuing what he believed to be the right course of action makes his failures and the deterioration of the union all the more painful. Rather than continue to see Chavez in the narrow light of celebration, I have widened the lens to show him as the tragic hero he was. Such a perspective allows us to honor his tremendous virtues as a leader while not forgetting the perils that come with autocratic leadership.

My measure of the man has been the health and security of the farm workers he purported to serve. Such a perspective conforms to the prescription for responsible history offered by Mexican American leader, Bert Corona. As Corona suggests, fundamental contradictions between employees' rights to fair and humane treatment in the workplace and the desire of wealthy and more powerful entities to flourish in our society were at play in this tragic drama. The failure of farm workers' collective bargaining rights to keep pace with the expansion of growers' profits reveals the degree to which this system privileges owners over workers. The continued suffering of farm laborers, even as California grapes are sold worldwide and grape sales flout the old conventions of seasonal markets, offers an important reminder of the need for more advocacy on their behalf. The dilemma of H2-A guest workers and undocumented food producers today sadly resembles the experience of braceros and farm workers in the 1950s and early 1960s that precipitated the farm worker movement in the first place. If their lives constitute the measuring stick by which we determine the success or failure of Cesar Chavez and the United Farm Workers, then the story would be a depressing one indeed.

The value of history, however, is not simply to determine winners and losers. I have focused equally on issues of strategy, particularly how the poor, the young, and the disfranchised overcame tremendous odds to win more battles than they lost. The story of the boycott in particular offers a vision of hope for humanity by demonstrating the capacity for consumers and volunteers to take action in the interest of people far removed from them and their station in life. Although the current orientation of food consumer activism signals a disturbing drift away from the welfare of farm workers, the grape boycott lives in the memory of many people who either volunteered on the picket lines or refused to buy grapes. Recent campaigns by the Coalition of Immokalee Workers to add a penny-per-pound to fast-food meals in order to increase farm worker pay in Florida echo the activism of UFW boycott volunteers begun more than four decades ago.[4] The language and strategy of the boycott is also ubiquitous in the pursuit of justice for immigrants, from the threat of Latino residents boycotting the U.S. census in response to federal neglect of immigration reform to a national boycott of the state of Arizona to protest harassment of ethnic Mexicans under the 2010 law SB1070. The grape boycott, whether acknowledged or not, informs these new conflicts and shapes the strategy of current labor and civil rights organizations. For those who wish to employ boycotts today, it behooves them to study the grape boycott and see that it succeeded due to constant organizing and adapting of strategies that propelled the movement forward.

The history of the boycott also reminds us of the capacity of people to overcome differences to work together. At the height of the boycott, volunteers from diverse backgrounds lived and worked in boycott houses far from their homes and comfort zones to build effective networks that shut down the grape markets and forced growers to seek a strategy of moving sales beyond their traditional strongholds. These movements precipitated new coalitions among farm worker advocates, including cooperation with labor unions abroad. It is worth noting that many of the key volunteers in the grape boycott network came from Jewish families, including Elaine Elinson, Marshall Ganz, and Jerry Brown, to name just a few. Their identities occasionally had meaning in the struggle. Elinson, for example, cited her grandmother's radical political beliefs as a motivating force behind her activism, while Ganz and Brown cited their affinities with Jewish storeowners as levers for change in the Toronto markets. When viewed in the wider context of the union's history, we see the presence of Jews in important staff positions, such as Jerry Cohen and Sandy Nathan, who were essential to the advancement of the union. Their ability to see affinities with nonwhite and poor workers demonstrates the elasticity of a "family of resemblance" among people who stood outside the WASP majority in the 1960s and 1970s.[5] Viewed from the perspective of Mexican and Filipino farm workers, the embrace of young college students and white religious volunteers demonstrates a similar inclusivity and willingness to adapt to difference in pursuit of a shared goal.

The United Farm Workers survived the end of the boycott, but the political upheavals of the late 1970s still reverberate through the union and the lives of veterans today. In the years immediately following 1978, Chavez's refusal to decentralize power and welcome contributions from organized workers in Salinas led to an unfortunate standoff between him and the rank and file. By 1981 he was working with a small cadre of loyalists to expel rebellious members at the national convention, forever closing the possibility of democratic reform in the union. By then, however, most of the critics from within the union leadership had either resigned or become suspected of treason themselves. Sadly, the vitriol and distrust that pervaded the union in the final years of the 1970s continue to shape exchanges among veterans of the movement.[6] Such anger and suspicion seem an unfitting way to remember anyone who participated in the union's heyday.

The United Farm Workers continues to pursue farm worker justice, but its strategies have not produced the kind of results that the boycott achieved in 1970. In 2005, the United Farm Workers broke from the AFL-CIO to join the labor coalition Change to Win, which included, among other unions, their old rival, the International Brotherhood of Teamsters. The change, however, did them little good, as they failed to gain the support from workers at Giumarra Vineyards to represent them in contract negotiations with the son of the grower who signed the first historic grape contracts in the San Joaquin Valley.[7] More recently, in 2010, UFW president and Chavez's son-in-law, Arturo Rodríguez, joined with comedian, Stephen Colbert, in the "Take Our Jobs" campaign that invites average Americans to do field work and eliminate the need for foreign nationals to do this labor. The strategy has attracted much publicity, although the union's objectives remain somewhat murky. Colbert and Rodríguez have drawn attention to the hypocrisy of politicians who harangue against undocumented immigrants, but their joke rests in part on the premise that farm work is an undesirable job. This uneasy interpretation has not escaped everyone, least of all Doug Adair, a veteran of the grape boycott and the grape fields of Coachella Valley. "The truth is," Adair writes, "if the very thought of doing farm work didn't make so many Americans laugh, we'd all be better off."[8] For him, the union would be truer to its mission if it honored the occupation that feeds the nation by working for contracts rather than chuckles.

Today not one field worker laboring on grape farms in California is covered by a labor contract. Gone are the days of "double minimum wage," paid vacations, unemployment insurance, and the modest pension plan that the United Farm Workers fought for and won in the 1970s. Today most farm workers in California are indigenous migrants from Mexico or Guatemala making $5 an hour, far below the state's minimum wage of $8.[9] Few have the courage to challenge inhumane treatment because of their undocumented status and the lack of faith in the United Farm Workers. In fact, the name of

Cesar Chavez has slipped so far from the consciousness of those in the field that workers are more inclined to associate his name with the retired Mexican boxer Julio Cesar Chavez than the labor leader who led the campaign for their rights.[10] Meanwhile, the California Table Grape Commission campaigns to sell table grapes worldwide, producing record profits for growers who now worry more about escalating land values than the cost of labor.[11] This is not the result anyone could have imagined at the height of the grape boycott.

If the story of the United Farm Workers teaches us anything, it is that the gains made on behalf of workers cannot be taken for granted as permanent and immutable. Contrary to Martin Luther King Jr.'s famous statement, the arc of history does *not* bend toward justice for farm workers. The rights won for farm workers in the 1960s and 1970s were not a moveable feast—sustainable gains that could be extended across time and place. Rather, this history proves that it takes constant and accountable engagement with workers and consumers to defend the interests of food producers whose rights have been and remain the most tenuous among us.

NOTES

INTRODUCTION

1. The United Farm Workers is the most popular name of the organization. The union became the United Farm Workers Organizing Committee in August 1966, after a merging of the National Farm Workers Association (NFWA) and the Agricultural Workers Organizing Committee (AWOC). The AFL-CIO granted UFWOC an independent charter as the United Farm Workers in February 1972, and the name was formally adopted at the constitutional convention in Fresno, California, in September 1973. To simplify the narrative, I refer to the union as the United Farm Workers (UFW) unless it is necessary to distinguish it from its other iterations.

2. Marshall Ganz, interviewed by the author, March 26, 2008.

3. García, *The Gospel of César Chávez*, 1. In addition to the books produced during Chavez's life, all of which are mostly celebratory, see recent books such as Stavans, *Cesar Chavez, an Organizer's Tale;* Ferriss and Sandoval, *The Fight in the Fields;* Griswold del Castillo and García, *César Chávez.*

4. The term *boycott* was not coined until the 1880s, in Ireland, but the act of preferential purchasing extends back to the antislavery movement. See Glickman, *Buying Power,* 2.

5. For a discussion of contemporary uses of the boycott, see Frank, *Buy American.*

6. Glickman contends, "Consumer activism lacks the signature victory that we associate with such social movements as abolitionism, organizer labor, women's suffrage, temperance, and Civil Rights" (*Buying Power,* 2). The labor contracts signed by the UFW in 1970, however, are one such "signature victory" achieved by means of a boycott.

7. For a discussion of early consumer boycotts, see Sklar, *Florence Kelley and the Nation's Work.*

8. An exception to this rule is the UFW's predecessor, the National Farm Labor Union (NFLU). In 1948, they pursued a secondary boycott of DiGiorgio products to accompany a strike in the fields. I discuss the NFLU boycott briefly in

chapter 1, but for a thorough history of the union and its boycott, see Street, "Poverty in the Valley of Plenty."

9. Friedland and Thomas, "Paradoxes of Agricultural Unionism in California," 57; Fletcher and Gapasin, *Solidarity Divided,* 32–33. For a definition of social movement unionism in another context, see Johnston, *Success While Others Fail,* 28–30.

10. Newton-Matza, "Boycott," 171–74.

11. Consumers considered lettuce much more important to their diets and chose not to conform to boycotts of that product as much. Wine was also boycotted; however, wine producers tended to be less resistant to negotiations with the UFW.

12. Growers saw their profits the same way Christians regard holy days set by the ever-shifting Easter Sunday: no matter when or where it occurs, a feast would not be denied. Ernest Hemingway also called his glorious time as a young man in Paris in the 1920s "a moveable feast," by which he meant that the experience would always stay with him regardless of his age. Ernest Hemingway, *A Moveable Feast* (New York: Scribner's, 1964).

13. Michael Pollan, for example, has raised awareness about the ills of an industrialized and globalized food system, yet, oddly, farm workers figure as minor characters in his crisis. His book titles alone—*Food Rules: An Eater's Manual; In Defense of Food: An Eater's Manifesto;* and, of course, *The Omnivore's Dilemma: A Natural History of Four Meals* (and the "Young Readers Edition" with the subtitle *The Secrets behind What You Eat*)—signal his primary interest in appealing to *consumers* for the benefit of *consumers.* Fortunately, scholars have begun to deepen the study of food politics to include farm workers. Similarly, some students have connected with farm labor organizations to build support for labor and immigration reform. For new studies on the United Farm Workers, see Bardacke, *Trampling Out the Vintage;* Pawel, *The Union of Their Dreams;* Ganz, *Why David Sometimes Wins;* Shaw, *Beyond the Fields.* On the turn toward a greater consciousness of worker rights in food politics, see DuPuis and Goodman, "Should We Go 'Home' to Eat?" Students have embraced the Coalition of Immokalee Workers' "Campaign for Fair Food" to bring justice to tomato pickers in Florida, see www.ciw-online.org. Similar student-worker coalitions have been created since the heyday of the UFW with Pineros y Campesinos Unidos Noroeste (Treeplanters and Farm Workers Northwest United, or PCUN) in the Pacific Northwest and the Farm Labor Organizing Committee (FLOC) throughout the Midwest and the Southeast. See Garcia and Sifuentez, "Social Movement Unionism and the 'Sin Fronteras' Philosophy in PCUN." Finally, the Southern Poverty Law Center has released two studies that have contributed to a focus on farm worker justice: *Injustice on Our Plates* and *Close to Slavery.*

14. In subsequent years, Chavez and UFW advocates expanded the appeal to include the harmful effects of pesticides on consumers, but the overall goal remained focused on achieving justice for farm workers. Here, I use the term *producer* as a reference to the farm workers who literally produced the food we eat.

15. Jeremy Varon, *Bringing Home the War: The Weather Underground, the Red Army Faction, and Revolutionary Violence in the Sixties and Seventies* (Berkeley: University of California Press, 2004).

16. Clayborne Carson, *In the Struggle: SNCC and the Black Awakening of the 1960s*, 2nd edition (Cambridge, MA: Harvard University Press, 1995); Manning Marable, *Race, Reform and Rebellion: The Second Reconstruction and Beyond in Black America, 1945–2006*, 3rd edition (Jackson: University of Mississippi, 2007).

17. Laura Pulido, *Black, Brown, Yellow and Left: Radical Activism in Los Angeles* (Berkeley: University of California Press, 2006); Ian Haney López, *Racism on Trial: The Chicano Fight for Justice* (Cambridge, MA: Belknap Press of Harvard University Press, 2004).

18. Special Organizing Meeting, November 24, 1976, Miscellaneous UFW Audiovisual Boxes, Tape 8, ALUA.

19. Here, I am thinking of the model created by the Bracero Archive History Project. See www.braceroarchive.org. This book also touches on Chavez's relationship with the Chicano movement, although David Gutiérrez's *Walls and Mirrors: Mexican Americans, Mexican Immigrants, and the Politics of Ethnicity* remains the authoritative treatment of that subject. My focus is on the relationship between Chavez and the volunteers on the grape boycott.

CHAPTER ONE

1. *International Directory of Company Histories*, vol. 12.

2. Street, "Poverty in the Valley of Plenty."

3. Ibid., 30–31.

4. Ibid., 36–37.

5. Andres, "Power and Control in Imperial Valley, California," 202.

6. Smith, "A Study of Social Stratification in the Agricultural Sections of the U.S.," 498, 508–9.

7. Garcia, *A World of Its Own*, 174–77; García y Griego, "The Importation of Mexican Contract Laborers to the United States," 45–85. See also braceroarchive.org.

8. Garcia, *A World of Its Own*, 174–88; Vargas, *Labor Rights Are Civil Rights*, 278; Ngai, *Impossible Subjects*, 127–66.

9. "Contract Mexican Nationals in California Agriculture, 1964," San Joaquin Valley Farm Labor Collection, Fresno State University, Special Collections.

10. Ibid., 17–20.

11. Ibid., 23–24. One employer, Gillian's, maintained a camp for braceros but abandoned this option due to the cost of housing (29). Jack Wolff, owner of Giffen Ranch, operated ten labor camps housing 10,000 people four to five years prior to the study, though he divested from it in favor of mechanization (49). The authors of the report concluded, "Growers prefer contracts to large scale labor camps" (54).

12. Ibid., 30.

13. Ibid., 44.

14. Ibid., 12.

15. Ibid., 62.

16. Ibid., 13.

17. Garcia, "Cain contra Abel."

18. Miguel Figueroa, interviewed by the author, Riverside, California, March 25, 2008.

19. Ibid.; U.S. Commission on Civil Rights, *Mexican Americans and the Administration of Justice in the Southwest*, 3.

20. Miguel Figueroa interviewed by the author.

21. Galarza, *Strangers in Our Fields*. For reaction to *Strangers in Our Fields*, see García y Griego, "The Importation of Mexican Contract Laborers to the United States," 69.

22. Galarza, *Strangers in Our Fields*, and *Merchants of Labor*. For perspective on Galarza's career as an activist, see Pitti, *The Devil in Silicon Valley*, 136–47; Loza, "Braceros on the Boundaries." For the best discussion on the termination of the program and its legacy, see García y Griego, "The Importation of Mexican Contract Laborers to the United States," 69–75; Gutiérrez, *Walls and Mirrors*, 152–60.

23. "Western Water," *MacNeil/Lehrer Report*, January 3, 1978; "The Imperial Gadfly," *Upland Courier*, February 2, 1978; "Dogged Doctor Refuses to Give Up Case against Big Farmers," *Los Angeles Times*, June 22, 1980; *60 Minutes*, CBS, January 14, 1973, transcript, Ben Yellen Papers (MSS 193), Mandeville Special Collections, UCSD. For information on how Paul Taylor supported Yellen, see Taylor, "Mexican Migration and the 160-Acre Water Limitation," 734–35.

24. Gilbert Padilla, interviewed by the author, January 11, 2010.

25. Garza, *Organizing the Chicano Movement*, 149–50.

26. Padilla interview.

27. Ibid.

28. Garza, *Organizing the Chicano Movement*, 146–48. "Gilbert Padilla, 1962–1980," Farm Worker Movement Documentation Project (FMDP).

29. Dolores Huerta, interviewed by Margaret Rose, 41.

30. Ibid., 44.

31. Ibid., 8, 23.

32. Ibid., 24–26, 29.

33. Ibid., 21.

34. Padilla interview.

35. Ibid.

36. Ibid.

37. Ibid.

38. Ibid.

39. Garza, *Organizing the Chicano Movement*, 153; Padilla interview.

40. Garza, *Organizing the Chicano Movement*, 154–55.

41. Letter from Fred Ross [to "Carl"] about hiring Gilbert Padilla, July 16, 1963, FMDP.

42. "Gilbert Padilla 1962–1980," FMDP; Padilla interview.

43. "Wayne 'Chris' Hartmire, 1962–1989," FMDP.

44. "Gilbert Padilla, 1962–1980," FMDP; Gilbert Padilla to Artie Rodriguez, president, UFW, AFL-CIO, July 23, 2008, Padilla's private collection (also reprinted in Garza, *Organizing the Chicano Movement*, 174).

45. "Wayne 'Chris' Hartmire, 1962–1989," FMDP.

46. "Jim Drake, 1962–1978," FMDP.

47. Garza, *Organizing the Chicano Movement*, 170. As a member of the CSO staff in Stockton, Padilla had witnessed two Irish Catholic priests, Father Thomas McCullough and Father John Duggan, organize farm workers under the Agricultural Workers Association, but backed away from the enterprise when their efforts ran afoul of the archdiocese in San Francisco.

48. Padilla interview.

49. Letter from Fred Ross [to "Carl"] about hiring Gilbert Padilla, January 16, 1963, FMDP.

50. Padilla interview.

51. Ibid.

52. "Jim Drake, 1962–1978," FMDP; Garza, *Organizing the Chicano Movement*, 188.

53. Padilla interview.

54. "LeRoy Chatfield 1963–1973"; "Rent Strike," FMDP.

55. Louis Krainock to Larry Itliong, February 13, 1961, UFW Larry Itliong Collection, Box 2-4, ALUA; "Ceiling on the Employment of Foreign Workers," A. J. Norton to U.S. Department of Labor, June 1, 1962, Larry Itliong Collection, Box 2-4, ALUA.

56. Gilbert Padilla, interviewed by the author, August 19, 2009.

57. Cesar Chavez, "Eulogy for Fred Ross," October 17, 1992, in Stavans, *Cesar Chavez, an Organizer's Tale*, xiv.

58. Ferriss and Sandoval, *The Fight in the Fields*, 82.

59. Alex A. Esclamado, obituary of Larry Dulay Itliong, *Philippine News*, February 12–18, 1977, UFW Larry Itliong Collection, Box 1, Folder 12, ALUA.

60. Ferriss and Sandoval, *The Fight in the Fields*, 86.

61. Padilla interview, January 11, 2010.

62. Ibid.

63. Ferriss and Sandoval, *The Fight in the Fields*, 86; Padilla interview, January 11, 2010.

64. Padilla interview, January 11, 2010; Ferriss and Sandoval, *Fight in the Fields*, 88.

65. Padilla interview, January 11, 2010.

66. Ibid.

67. Pawel, *The Union of Their Dreams*, 27.

CHAPTER TWO

1. Jerry Brown, interviewed by the author, January 16, 2009.

2. Ibid.

3. Jim Drake, "Two Unpublished Manuscripts," FMDP, 6.

4. Rudy Reyes to Leroy Chatfield, June 4, 2003, in FMDP.

5. Gilbert Padilla, interviewed by author, August 19, 2008, Fresno, California.

6. Hijinio Rangel, untitled essay, FMDP, 1–2.

7. Payne, *I've Got the Light of Freedom.*

8. Marshall Ganz, interviewed by the author, March 26, 2008.

9. Ibid.; Mike Miller, "The Farmworkers and Their Allies in the Early to Mid-1960s," FMDP, 3.

10. "Some Facts on the New Grape Boycott, September, 1973," UFW Office of the President, Part 2, Box 33-10, ALUA.

11. Letter to Boycott Committees from Mike Miller and Jim Drake, December 17, 1965, National Farm Workers Ministry Collection, Part I, Box 25-9, ALUA.

12. Meister and Loftis, *A Long Time Coming,* 143–44.

13. James Woolsey, "Statement of Schenley Industries, Inc.," California Senate Fact Finding Committee on Agriculture, Delano, July 20, 1966, 7 in Ganz, *Why David Sometimes Wins,* 303n166.

14. Ganz, *Why David Sometimes Wins,* 158.

15. Ibid., 159.

16. Taylor, *Chavez and the Farm Workers,* 190–95.

17. The United Farm Workers Organizing Committee was shortened to the United Farm Workers when the AFL-CIO granted it an independent charter in 1972 and the union ratified it in February 1973. For the sake of continuity, I use the acronym UFW before and after the change in title.

18. Taylor, *Chavez and the Farm Workers,* 197.

19. Ibid.; Chris Hartmire, interviewed by the author, September 2, 2008.

20. Taylor, *Chavez and the Farm Workers,* 208. Dunne, *The Story of the California Grape Strike,* 171–73; Ganz, *Why David Sometimes Wins,* 226.

21. Quoted in Ganz, *Why David Sometimes Wins,* 159–60.

22. Zaninovich and Thomas, *Turmoil in the Vineyards,* 4–7.

23. Ibid., 8.

24. Ibid.; Bruce Obbink, interviewed by the author, August 21, 2008.

25. Quoted in Zaninovich and Thomas, *Turmoil in the Vineyards,* 9.

26. Street, *Photographing Farmworkers in California,* 196–237. For more on SCFC and Zaninovich, see Ganz, *Why David Sometimes Wins,* 151; Taylor, *Chavez and the Farm Workers,* 159.

27. Marshall Ganz interview.

28. Brown, "The United Farm Workers Grape Strike and Boycott," 136. Marshall Ganz explains that the union, now under the AFL-CIO, spent hours deliberating on the direction of the movement after the defeat of Perelli-Minetti. Bill Kircher favored

further organizing among winery workers to consolidate their victory over all California vintners, but the majority of UFW leaders favored a campaign against table grape growers, because many workers had come from those plantations and had seen little in the way of progress since the beginning of the struggle. Ganz, *Why David Sometimes Wins*, 227–28.

29. Of their 12,170 acres, Giumarra owned 6,430 in the Delano district, dedicated to table grape cultivation (Brown, "The United Farm Workers Grape Strike and Boycott," 136).

30. Ibid., 143.

31. Ibid., 34.

32. Ibid., 128–29.

33. Drake, FMDP, 14.

34. Brown, "The United Farm Workers Grape Strike and Boycott," 183.

35. Jessica Govea, interviewed by William Taylor, July 21, 1976, William Taylor Collection, Oral History Tape 211 (Audio Visual), ALUA.

36. Jerry Brown interview.

37. Ibid.

38. Brown, "The United Farm Workers Grape Strike and Boycott," 204–5.

39. Dolores Huerta, quoted in ibid., 205.

40. Brown, "The United Farm Workers Grape Strike and Boycott," 207.

41. Noé G. Garcia, who worked for Safeway as a butcher for more than thirty-five years, said that the reference to "Slave-way" was common within his family and used frequently among fellow workers. Interviewed by author, May 24, 2008.

42. Brown, "The United Farm Workers Grape Strike and Boycott," 206. Brown found that six of Safeway's directors sat on executive boards for twelve major agricultural producers, including three who served as board members for J. G. Boswell Company and Kern County Land Company, both of which were targets of UFW strikes.

43. Nick Jones, interviewed by William Taylor, July 24, 1976, 22, William Taylor Collection, Box 1, Folder 1, ALUA.

44. Jerry Brown interview.

45. Brown, "The United Farm Workers Grape Strike and Boycott," 210.

46. Nick Jones interview, 19, 21, William Taylor, Box 1, Folder 1, ALUA.

47. Chris Hartmire, interviewed by the author, September 2, 2008.

48. "California Table Grape Industry, Study of Boycott Effect—1968 & 1969 Seasons," March 1970, Chapter 6, UFW Office of the President, Part 2, Box 34, Folder 32, ALUA.

49. Jerry Brown interview.

50. Brown, "The United Farm Workers Grape Strike and Boycott," 218–19. Because a poor crop in 1967 had reduced total shipments well below the norm for the table grape industry, 1966 became the benchmark. Therefore, 1966 shipment totals represented a much truer condition of the market.

51. Jerry Brown interview.

52. Brown, "The United Farm Workers Grape Strike and Boycott," 198.

53. Ibid., 201.

54. Jerry Brown interview.

CHAPTER THREE

1. Elaine Elinson, "UFW Memoir: The UFW Grape Boycott in Europe," FMDP, n.d., 10.

2. Brown, "The United Farm Workers Grape Strike and Boycott," 214–15. Brown reported that table grape growers sent 65 percent of their harvest, or 10 percent more table grapes from 1966 to 1968, to be crushed for wine and juice production.

3. "Sales at Record High, Grape Growers Claim," *Los Angeles Times*, June 25, 1969

4. Taylor, *Chavez and the Farm Workers,* 235. Growers paid the public relations firm $1 million per year.

5. Ibid., 236–38.

6. Chavez to Ganz, March 9, 1969, UFW Administration Files Collection, Box 26-25, ALUA.

7. Brown, "The United Farm Workers Grape Strike and Boycott," 202.

8. Ibid.

9. Ibid., 211.

10. Jerry Cohen, interviewed by the author, August 18, 2008, 30; Cohen, "Gringo Justice."

11. Hijinio Rangel testimonial, FMDP, 2.

12. Ibid., 3.

13. "Grower Quits Grape Group, Hits Reports," *Los Angeles Times*, June 27, 1969.

14. Marshall Ganz, interviewed by the author, March 26, 2008; Jerry Brown, interviewed by the author, January 16, 2009.

15. Brown, "The United Farm Workers Grape Strike and Boycott," 217.

16. Jessica Govea to Chavez, February 4, 1969, UFW Administration Files Collection, Box 26-28, ALUA.

17. Shaw, *Beyond the Fields,* 30; Mark Day essay, FMDP, 5.

18. Juanita Brown to Marshall Ganz, December 31, 1969, UFW Marshall Ganz Collection, Box 6, Folder 8, ALUA.

19. Jessica Govea to Cesar Chavez, February 4, 1969, UFW Administration Files Collection, Box 26-28, ALUA; Marshall Ganz to Juanita Brown, January 7, 1970, UFW Administration Files Collection, Box 26-28, ALUA; Marshall Ganz to Larry Itliong, January 27, 1970, UFW Administration Files Collection, Box 26-28, ALUA.

20. Marshall Ganz to Juanita Brown, January 7, 1970, UFW Administration Files Collection, Box 26-28, ALUA, 3.

21. Ibid., 4.

22. Jerry Brown interview.

23. Ibid.

24. Ibid.

25. Mark Silverman essay, FWDP, 2.

26. Jessica Govea to Larry Itliong, February 10 and February 13, 1970, UFW Administration Files Collection, Box 26-28, ALUA; Marshall Ganz to Juanita Brown, January 7, 1970, UFW Administration Files Collection, Box 26-28, ALUA.

27. Ganz to Itliong, February 10, 1970; Govea to Itliong, February 13, 1970, UFW Montreal Boycott Office, Box 3, File "Delano Correspondence #5," ALUA.

28. Jessica Govea to Cesar Chavez, June 4, 1970, UFW Administration Files Collection, Box 26-25, ALUA.

29. Peter Standish to Cesar Chavez, June 4, 1970, UFW Administration Files Collection, Box 26-25, ALUA.

30. Ibid.

31. Govea to Chavez, June 4, 1970, UFW Administration Files Collection, Box 26-25, ALUA.

32. Standish to Chavez, June 4, 1970, UFW Administration Files Collection, Box 26-25, ALUA.

33. Elaine Elinson, interviewed by the author, December 8, 2009.

34. Ibid.

35. Brown to Elinson, October 8, 1968, UFW Administration Files Collection, Box 26-33, ALUA.

36. Ibid.

37. *The Port*, December 19, 1968; "Grape Boycott Reaches Europe with Girl's Aid," *Los Angeles Times*, January 20, 1969; "Hon vädjar i Sverige: Bojkotta USA—druvor!," *Aftonbladet (Sweden),* 1969, UFW Administration Files Collection, Box 26-33, ALUA.

38. Elaine Elinson interview.

39. Govea to Chavez, December 3, 1969, UFW Marshall Ganz Collection, Box 6-17, ALUA; Govea to Chavez, March 4, 1970, UFW Administration Files Collection, Box 26-25, ALUA.

40. Elaine Elinson interview.

41. Brown to Elinson, January 21, 1969, UFW Administration Files Collection, Box 26-33, ALUA.

42. Elaine Elinson interview.

43. Brown to Elinson, October 8, 1968, UFW Administration Files Collection, Box 26-33, ALUA.

44. Ibid.

45. Elinson essay, FMDP, 2.

46. Brown to Elinson, December 7, 1968, UFW Administration Files Collection, Box 26-33, ALUA.

47. Elinson essay, FMDP, 4.

48. Brown to Elinson, December 24, 1968, UFW Administration Files Collection, Box 26-33, ALUA.

49. Brown to Elinson, October 19, 1968, UFW Administration Files Collection, Box 26-33, ALUA; Brown to Elinson, October 31, 1968, UFW Administration Files Collection, Box 26-33, ALUA.

50. Brown to Elinson, October 31, 1968, UFW Administration Files Collection, Box 26-33, ALUA.

51. Ibid.; Elinson essay, FMDP, 3.

52. Brown to Elinson, October 31, 1968, UFW Administration Files Collection, Box 26-33, ALUA. Historically, Britain had imported table grapes from Spain and South Africa, but after World War II, U.S. imports of fresh produce dramatically cut into this business.

53. Elinson essay, FMDP, 3.

54. Ibid., 5.

55. Ibid., 2.

56. Brown to Elinson, November 18, 1968, UFW Administration Files Collection, Box 26-33, ALUA.

57. Elinson essay, FMDP, 6–7.

58. Chavez to Victor Reuther, January 5, 1969, UFW Administration Files Collection, Box 26-33, ALUA.

59. Brown to Elinson, December 7, 1968, UFW Administration Files Collection, Box 26-33, ALUA.

60. TGWU, "Resolution, Support of Grape Workers Strike," UFW Office of the President, Part I, Box 75-9, ALUA.

61. Brown to Elinson, December 17, 1968, UFW Administration Files Collection, Box 26-33, ALUA; Don Watson, interviewed by the author, June 15, 2009.

62. Brown to Elinson, December 17, 1968, UFW Administration Files Collection, Box 26-33, ALUA.

63. Elinson essay, FMDP, 5.

64. Don Watson interview; Elaine Elinson interview.

65. Chavez to Victor Reuther, January 5, 1969, UFW Administration Files Collection, Box 26-33, ALUA.

66. Elaine Elinson essay, FMDP, 7.

67. Elaine Elinson interview.

68. Brown to Elinson, November 20, 1968, UFW Administration Files Collection, Box 26-33, ALUA.

69. Elinson essay, FMDP, 7.

70. Brown to Elinson, January 10, 1969, UFW Administration Files Collection, Box 26-33, ALUA.

71. Brown to Elinson, January 14, 1969, UFW Administration Files Collection, Box 26-33, ALUA.

72. *Aftonbladet*, January 12, 1969, UFW Administration Files Collection, Box 26-33, ALUA.

73. Elinson essay, FMDP, 9. Svenska Lantarbetareforbundet is the farmers union in Sweden.

74. Brown to Elinson, January 21, 1969, UFW Administration Files Collection, Box 26-33, ALUA.

75. Brown to Elinson, December 17, 1968, UFW Administration Files Collection, Box 26-33, ALUA.

76. Elinson essay, FMDP, 9.

77. Haber to Chavez, June 9, 1970, UFW Administration Files Collection, Box 26-28, ALUA.

78. Elaine Elinson interview.

79. Brown to Elinson, December 7, 1968, UFW Administration Files Collection, Box 26-33, ALUA.

80. Senator Walter Mondale, U.S. Senate Hearings (pesticides), August 1, 1969, "Statement of Jerome Cohen," Cohen Papers, Amherst College; Cohen, "Gringo Justice," 19.

81. Taylor, *Chavez and the Farm Workers,* 243–44.

82. Marshall Ganz interview.

83. Ibid.

84. Ibid.

85. Taylor, *Chavez and the Farm Workers,* 246.

86. Marshall Ganz interview.

87. Ibid.; Taylor, *Chavez and the Farm Workers,* 246–48.

CHAPTER FOUR

1. Nixon White House Tapes, March 1972, audiotape 698-2, National Archives, Washington, DC. Transcribed by the author.

2. "Teamsters President Proposes Alliance with Growers Group," *Los Angeles Times,* December 13, 1972.

3. Friedland and Thomas, "Paradoxes of Agricultural Unionism in California," 57. Friedland and Thomas call it a "paradox" when, in fact, it is an irony.

4. Marshall Ganz, interviewed by the author, March 26, 2008. Ganz explained, "Our moments of greatest vulnerability were our moments of greatest success."

5. David Harris, "The Battle of Coachella Valley," *Rolling Stone,* September 13, 1973.

6. "Chavez' Union Scores Major Farm Victory," *Los Angeles Times,* June 7, 1970 and "Battle between Teamsters and Chavez Looms," *Los Angeles Times,* August 5, 1970.

7. "Battle between Teamsters and Chavez Looms," *Los Angeles Times,* August 5, 1970; Taylor, *Chavez and the Farm Workers,* 257–59.

8. Taylor, *Chavez and the Farm Workers,* 259–60.

9. Ibid., 261.

10. Ibid., 262.

11. Harris, "The Battle of Coachella Valley," 6.

12. Fujita-Rony, *American Workers, Colonial Power.*

13. Scharlin and Villanueva, *Philip Vera Cruz,* 31.

14. Ibid., 49.

15. Ron Taylor, "Chavez Aide Quits, Raps 'Brain Trust,'" *Fresno Bee*, October 15, 1971; Larry Itliong Papers, Box 1-12; Letter to Larry Itliong from Bill Kircher, November 15, 1971, Larry Itliong Papers, Box 1-12, ALUA.

16. Letter to Bill Kircher from Larry Itliong, March 30, 1972, Itliong Papers, Box 1-12, ALUA.

17. Letter to Sid Valledor from Larry Itliong, December 20, 1971, Itliong Papers, Box 1-2, ALUA. Itliong wrote, "Brother Philip and I have never hit it right although God knows I try my best to adjust myself to gain his trust and confidence.... When I said I will quit UFWOC, because I felt that our cababayans [Filipino country men] were not being given a fair shake in the Union, do you know that brother Philip, said in that meeting 'good riddance.'" Itliong's defection did not sit well with Vera Cruz, nor did Itliong's support of the Teamsters during the mid-1970s nor his support for the Marcos regime in the Philippines.

18. Vera Cruz commented, "The union wanted the Filipinos there—their membership, their presence, looked good for the union.... But Cesar and the others weren't willing to put the same time and money into organizing the Filipinos as they did with the Mexicans." Scharlin and Villanueva, *Philip Vera Cruz,* 91–92.

19. Doug Adair, interviewed by the author, January 10, 2006.

20. Rey Huerta, interviewed by the author, January 6, 2006.

21. Ibid.

22. Doug Adair interview.

23. Ibid.

24. Ibid.

25. Ibid.

26. Ibid.

27. Ibid.

28. "The Anglo Army behind Cesar Chavez," *Los Angeles Times*, April 6, 1972; Fujita-Rony, "Coalitions, Race, and Labor." For growers' perspective on Filipino defections, see Zaninovich and Thomas, *Turmoil in the Vineyards,* 71–73.

29. Many Filipinos who expressed discontent with the UFW also voiced their opposition to the Teamsters. In 1974 Lemuel F. Ignacio, a Filipino farm worker organizer, wrote to Reverend Phil Park, who had reiterated the popular perception that the Filipinos preferred the Teamsters over the UFW. Copying the letter to his friend Larry Itliong, Ignacio wrote, "Your statement [that] 'most of the Pilipino farm workers are now a part of [the] teamsters' is gravely wrong. Pilipino farm workers believe in the union but are presently lukewarm to both the UFWA and the teamsters. The concept of organizing is very real and rich in their history in this country. In the 1930s there was an independent union of Pilipino agricultural workers." Letter to Reverend Phil Park from Lemuel F. Ignacio (Larry Itliong cc'd), October 31, 1974, Larry Itliong Papers, Box 1-4, ALUA.

30. "Comparison of Health and Welfare Plans of Teamsters and United Farm Workers of America," n.d., UFW Information and Research, Part I, Box 31-1, ALUA.

31. Taylor, *Chavez and the Farm Workers,* 26–28.

32. "The Anglo Army behind Cesar Chavez," *Los Angeles Times*, April 6, 1972.

33. "Cesar Chavez—Out of Sight but Still in Fight," *Los Angeles Times*, February 14, 1972; "The Anglo Army behind Cesar Chavez," *Los Angeles Times*, April 6, 1972.

34. "Chavez Union Starts New Boycott," *Los Angeles Times*, July 3, 1971; "Heublein Offer to Acquire 80% of United Vinters Approved," *Los Angeles Times*, August 2, 1968; "Chavez Union Opens Worldwide Boycott against Wine Firm," *Los Angeles Times*, August 10, 1971; "Chavez, Wine Firm Set Up Company Hiring Hall in Pact," *Los Angeles Times*, August 19, 1971.

35. "Growers Will OK Farm Unions in Policy Change, Official Says," *Los Angeles Times*, January 20, 1971.

36. Ibid.

37. "Two Salinas Valley Growers Prepared to Sign with Chavez," *Los Angeles Times*, August 30, 1970; "Chavez Signs 3rd Big Salinas Grower: Pic N' Pac Contract Ends National Boycott Activities," *Los Angeles Times*, October 10, 1970.

38. Marshall Ganz interview.

39. "Teamster Boycott Hits Lettuce Picked by Chavez' Union," *Los Angeles Times*, February 9, 1971; "Chavez Signs Nation's Largest Independent Lettuce Producer," *Los Angeles Times*, April 24, 1971.

40. "The New Rules of Play," *Time*, March 8, 1968.

41. "Reagan Acts in N.Y. Grape Boycott Threat," *Los Angeles Times*, June 8, 1968; "Boycott of Grapes Has Failed, Reagan Says," *Los Angeles Times*, October 5, 1968.

42. Alistair Cooke, "Harvesting the Grapes of Wrath," *The Guardian*, December 28, 1967.

43. "Voters Hand Stern Rebuttal to Costly Proposition Drives," *Los Angeles Times*, November 9, 1972.

44. Jerry Cohen, interviewed by the author, August 18, 2008. Cohen explained, "I'm right out of law school. I don't know a goddamn thing, right, and I told [Cesar] that when he said, quit. You know, I was griping about CRLA not being able to do a damn thing and he said, 'Well, just come and work for us.' And I said, 'I don't know anything.' . . . And he said, 'I don't know anything either. We'll learn it together.'"

45. Jeffrey Kahn, "Ronald Reagan Launched Political Career Using Berkeley Campus as a Target," *UC Berkeley News*, June 8, 2004.

46. Harris, "The Battle of Coachella Valley," 35.

47. Peter M. Flanigan organized New Yorkers for Nixon and directed Volunteers for Nixon-Lodge during Nixon's unsuccessful 1960 presidential campaign. In 1968, Flanigan served as Nixon's deputy campaign manager and initially served as an assistant to the president in 1969. In January 1972, he became the assistant to the president for international economic affairs. The following month, Nixon named him executive director of the Council on International Economic Policy. NARA, White House Special Files, Staff Member Office Files, "Peter M. Flanigan."

48. "Agriculture: Biggest Growth Industry in the U.S.," *Business Week*, April 28, 1973, 71.

49. Announced on August 15, 1971, NEP leaned heavily toward an activist, interventionist government that appropriated many of the policy recommendations

of the Democrats and made possible Nixon's victory in 1972. Matusow, *Nixon's Economy*, 14–16.

50. Samuel Rosenberg, *American Economic Development since 1945*, 198–99

51. "Nixon Proposal Slows Action on Farm Legislation," *Los Angeles Times*, May 8, 1969. Chavez charged that Nixon had "entered into an unholy alliance with Reagan and Senator Murphy to destroy our movement." During his election campaign, Nixon opposed the grape boycott and the UFWOC. He mistakenly called it "illegal," claiming, "We have laws on the books to protect workers who wish to organize. We have a National Labor Relations Board to impartially supervise the election of collective bargaining agents and to safeguard the rights of organizers. . . . The law must be applied equally to all." The UFWOC pointed out that farm workers were, in fact, excluded from the NLRA. "Nixon's Stance on Grape Boycott," *Los Angeles Times*, September 20, 1968; "Nixon's Opposition to Grape Boycott May Help Chavez," *Los Angeles Times*, September 25, 1968.

52. "Farm Union Discloses Soaring Grape Purchases for Vietnam," *Los Angeles Times*, June 6, 1969.

53. Memorandum from Charles Colson to President Nixon regarding meeting with Frank (Fitz) Fitzsimmons, March 30, 1972. Nixon Files, Charles W. Colson, Box 24, Conversation No. 698-2, NARA.

54. Unidentified "Teamster leader," quoted in Brill, *The Teamsters*, 82.

55. "Teamsters' Ties to Mafia—and to White House," *Los Angeles Times*, May 31, 1973; Brill, *The Teamsters*, 101.

56. "Teamsters' Ties to Mafia—and to White House," *Los Angeles Times*, May 31, 1973. According to one anonymous FBI agent, "This whole thing of the Teamsters and the mob and the White House is one of the scariest things I've ever seen. It has demoralized the bureau. We don't know what to expect out of the Justice Department."

57. "Possible Mafia-Teamsters Link Got Lost in Watergate Shuffle," *Sacramento Bee*, June 22, 1975; "U.S. Said to Bar Bugging on Teamsters-Mafia Link," *New York Times*, April 29, 1973; Brill, *The Teamsters*, 104.

58. Brill, *The Teamsters*, 105. Another version of this scheme is recounted in Summers and Swan, *The Arrogance of Power*, 398–99. Quoting a 1981 *Time* magazine article, Summers and Swan write, "[In a purported 1972] meeting between Nixon and Fitzsimmons in one of the private rooms of the White House, [Attorney General] Kleindienst had been summoned to the session and ordered to review all investigations pending against the Teamsters and to make sure that Fitzsimmons and his allies were not hurt. The meeting supposedly occurred after Nixon's 1972 re-election campaign, to which the Teamsters contributed an estimated $1 million." Summers interviewed Harry Hall, an IRS agent tracking Fitzsimmons's nefarious investments, in 1997. According to Hall, Fitzsimmons arranged for $500,000 to go to Nixon through his former campaign advisor, Murray Chotiner.

59. Summers and Swan, *The Arrogance of Power*, 399; "Teamsters' Ties to Mafia—and to White House," *Los Angeles Times*, May 31, 1973; Harris, "The Battle of Coachella Valley," 33.

60. Brill, 101. *Fresno Bee*, December 8, 1972, A1, A4.

61. *Westgate*, June 18, 1973.

62. Jerry Cohen, interviewed by the author, August 18, 2008.

63. Taylor, *Chavez and the Farm Workers*, 294.

64. "Labor Votes Fund for Chavez Union," *New York Times*, May 10, 1973; Jerry Cohen, interviewed by the author, September 14, 2009.

65. Jerry Cohen interview, September 14, 2009. He mentioned that the lettuce boycott "was never really successful."

66. "Some Facts on the New Grape Boycott, September, 1973," UFW Office of the President, Part 2, Box 33-10, ALUA.

67. Taylor, *Chavez and the Farm Workers*, 275.

68. Jerry Cohen interview, August 18, 2008.

69. Ibid.

70. Ibid.

71. Friedland and Thomas, "Paradoxes of Agricultural Unionism in California," 59.

72. Ibid.

73. Zaninovich and Thomas, *Turmoil in the Vineyards*, 76–78.

74. Ibid., 61. Friedland and Thomas, "Paradoxes of Agricultural Unionism in California," argue that this organizational strategy was the legacy of a Trotskyite faction among Minnesota Teamsters that took over the union during the 1930s and was carried through to the era of the farm worker movement by Jimmy Hoffa.

75. Harry Bernstein, "Duel in the Sun: Union Busting, Teamster Style," *Progressive*, July 1973, 20. Also quoted in Taylor, *Chavez and the Farm Workers*, 326.

76. "Farm Union Halts Picketing; Rites Held for Striker," *Los Angeles Times*, August 18, 1973; *Fight for Our Lives* (documentary film, The United Farm Workers, 1974).

77. "Teamsters Open Massive Drive to Eliminate Chavez Farm Union," *Los Angeles Times*, March 29, 1974.

78. Taylor, *Chavez and the Farm Workers*, 327.

79. Congressional Budget Office, "Agricultural Export Markets and the Potential Effects of Export Subsidies," June 1983, www.cbo.gov/ftpdocs/50xx/doc5024/doc03-Entire.pdf (accessed September 26, 2011).

CHAPTER FIVE

1. Sarat and Scheingold, *Cause Lawyers and Social Movements*, 2. For history related to cause lawyers in the UFW, see specifically Gordon, "A Movement in the Wake of a New Law."

2. Sandy Nathan, quoted in an interview with Jacques Levy, September 25, 1975, Levy Papers, Box 29, Folder 577.

3. Ibid.

4. Inaugural Address, Edmund G. "Jerry" Brown, January 6, 1975, http://gov ernors.library.ca.gov/addresses/34-Jbrown01.html.

5. Cesar Chavez, "Why the Farm Labor Act Isn't Working," *Los Angeles Times*, November 17, 1975. Chavez declared the ALRA a "good law," but explained that collusion between growers and Teamsters was undermining it.

6. Sec. 1140, ALRA, Levy Papers, Box 28, Folder 538.

7. Ibid. For more on the creation and impact of ALRA, see Wells and Villarejo, "State Structures and Social Movement Strategies."

8. "Assembly Sends Farm Bill to Brown for Signing: Brown's Farm Labor Bill Wins Final Approval," *Los Angeles Times*, May 30, 1975; Brown, quoted in Wells and Villarejo, "State Structures and Social Movement Strategies," 296.

9. Jerry Goldman, quoted in an interview with Jacques Levy, September 25, 1975, Levy Papers, Box 29, Folder 577, 35.

10. Ibid.

11. "Dawn of a New Era for Farm Workers," *Los Angeles Times*, May 30, 1975.

12. Ibid.; Wells and Villarejo, "State Structures and Social Movement Strategies," 297.

13. Levy Papers, ALRA, Box 28, Folder 538.

14. Cohen, June 13, 1975, Levy Papers, Box 28, Folder 553.

15. Notes on ALRA, Burton-Alatorre Bill, Levy Papers, Box 28, Folder 536; ALRA, Levy Papers, Box 28, Folder 538.

16. Wells and Villarejo, "State Structures and Social Movement Strategies," 298.

17. Chavez, June 13, 1975, Levy transcription, Levy Papers, Box 28, Folder 553.

18. Ibid., 5–6.

19. Ibid., 6–7.

20. Ibid., 6.

21. Ibid., 5–7.

22. Ibid., 16.

23. Interview transcript with Sandy Nathan, Levy Papers, Box 28, Folder 577.

24. Ibid.

25. Ibid.

26. Ibid., 57.

27. Jerry Goldman, Levy Papers, Box 28, Folder 577, 29–30.

28. Ibid., 46.

29. Ibid., 49.

30. Ibid.

31. Levy Papers, Box 29, Folder 577, 55.

32. Ellen Greenstone to Levy, Levy Papers, Box 29, Folder 577, 17–18.

33. Esther Padilla, interviewed by author, January 11, 2010, in Fresno, California, 75.

34. "Terror amid the Tomatoes," *Los Angeles Times*, September 4, 1975.

35. Ibid.

36. Jerry Goldman to Levy, Levy Papers, Box 29, Folder 577, 29.

37. Ellen Greenstone to Levy, Levy Papers, Box 29, Folder 577, 17.

38. Ibid., 19. Greenstone reported, "For example, on one team of three was a woman who has worked for the UFW. She worked in '73 and was a farm worker at one time and grew up in the valley and her team labeled her as totally biased. . . . I heard the two other [agents] talking one night and one woman saying, 'Well, I just can't believe that everyone in Salinas goes down to Mexicali every weekend. That's just impossible for me to believe. No one could do that.'"

39. Ibid., 13.

40. Ibid., 19.

41. Rick Rodriguez, "ALRB to Bear Duke's Stamp," *Sacramento Bee*, December 25, 1985. Also see Wells and Villarejo, "State Structures and Social Movement Strategies," 312.

42. Wells and Villarejo refer to the law as "social reform policy," which I believe aptly describes both the nature and the intent of the ALRA ("State Structures and Social Movement Strategies," 300). If we acknowledge that the legislation is an attempt at social reform, then it requires that we recognize the disorder that the legislation is addressing. I contend that the intent of the law was to rectify years of injustice toward farm workers in California.

43. Ellen Greenstone to Levy, Levy Papers, Box 29, Folder 577, 19; UFW Documentation Project, online discussion, Glen Rothner, May 24, 2004, FWDP, 66; Case No. 77-CL-7-C, 4 ALRB No. 42, United Farm Workers of America, AFL-CIO and Kelvin Keene Larson, aka K. K. Larson, July 7, 1978, www.alrb.ca.gov/legal _searches/decisions/4_42(1978)ocr.pdf (accessed April 9, 2012).

44. Jerry Goldman to Levy, Levy Papers, Box 29, Folder 577, 31.

45. Sandy Nathan to Levy, Levy Papers, Box 29, Folder 577, 45.

46. Greenstone to Levy, Levy Papers, Box 29, Folder 577, 20.

47. "Union Access to Fields Curbed," *Los Angeles Times*, September 4, 1975.

48. Ibid.; "Teamsters Win Major Victory," *Los Angeles Times*, September 13, 1975; "UFWA Wins State High Court Ruling," *Los Angeles Times*, September 19, 1975; "Enforcement of Farm Law to Be Tightened," *Los Angeles Times*, September 30, 1975; "Brown, High Officials Meet on Farm Labor Complaints," *Los Angeles Times*, October 2, 1975.

49. June 17, 1975, meeting, Levy Papers, Box 28, Folder 553, California ALRA, 1975 Notes, 29–33.

50. Elaine Elinson interviewed by the author, December 8, 2009.

51. Levy Transcript, Levy Papers, Box 28, Folder 553, California ALRA , 1975 Notes, 15.

52. "UFWA Leads in Voting on Unions Despite Setbacks," *Los Angeles Times*, September 17, 1975.

53. "Brown, Officials Meet on Farm Labor Complaints," *Los Angeles Times*, October 2, 1975; "Farm Labor Picture: Will Democracy Blossom?," *Los Angeles Times,* December 26, 1975.

54. "Farm Labor Picture: Will Democracy Blossom?," *Los Angeles Times*, December 26, 1975.

55. Election Analysis, January 1976, Levy Papers, Box 29, Folder 561. In the final analysis, according its *Annual Report* for 1975, the board received 604 election petitions and held 423 elections involving 47,812 voting farm workers.

56. Election Analysis, January 1976, Levy Papers, Box 29, Folder 561.

57. The board began canceling hearings "due to budgetary considerations" as early as January 23, 1976. California Agricultural Labor Relations Board Press Release, 1975–76, Levy Papers.

58. "Farm Labor Picture: Will Democracy Blossom?," *Los Angeles Times*, December 26, 1975.

59. "Emergency Aid for Farm Board Denied," *Los Angeles Times*, January 28, 1976.

60. "Farm Board Closes Up as Funding Ends," *Los Angeles Times*, February 7, 1976.

61. "Farm Violence Erupts Again in Imperial County," *Los Angeles Times*, February 14, 1976.

62. "Chavez Plans Boycott against Big Growers," *Los Angeles Times*, February 12, 1976.

63. Daniel Martinez HoSang, *Racial Propositions: Ballot Initiatives and the Making of Postwar California* (Berkeley: University of California Press, 2010), 2–3, 91–93.

64. Ibid.; NEB, June 13, 1976, UFW Office of the President, Part II, Box 1-19, 5.

65. "General Counsel of State Farm Labor Board Quits," *Los Angeles Times*, April 17, 20, 1976; "Third Member of Farm Board Quits," *Los Angeles Times,* April 20, 1976; "Farm Initiative Qualifies for Nov. 2 Ballot," Los *Angeles Times,* May 29, 1976. The union acquired 729,965 signatures—more than the 312,000 required under state law. "Report to the U.F.W. Executive Board on the Farm Worker Initiative," uncatalogued materials, Wayne State University.

66. "UFW Initiative Drive Past Halfway Mark," *Los Angeles Times*, April 15, 1976.

67. Esther Padilla interview.

68. "Chavez: Farm Worker Initiative Is Needed to Guard against Abuses," *Los Angeles Times*, April 8, 1976.

69. "UFW Initiative Drive Past Halfway Mark," *Los Angeles Times*, April 15, 1976.

70. "Who Is Harry Kubo?," *Fresno Bee*, February 22, 1976.

71. Susan Sward, "California Agriculture: Campaigns Gear Up on Farm Initiative," *Associated Press*, September 15, 1976; "Yes on 14" poster, n.d., UCLA Political Literature Collection.

72. "Who Is Harry Kubo?" *Fresno* Bee, February 22, 1976.

73. Citizens for a Fair Farm Labor Law press release, August 6, 1976, Scrapbook April 16, 1975–August 20, 1976, Table Grape Negotiating Committee Papers, Fresno State University; Harry Kubo, interviewed by Sam Suhler, Fresno County Library, October 13, 1978.

74. Kubo interviewed by Sam Suhler, 29. Gilbert Padilla now jokingly says he "organized Kubo" by sending picketers to his property and forcing Kubo to become organized. Gilbert Padilla, interviewed by the author, January 11, 2010.

75. Larry Kubo, interviewed by the author, January 6, 2010; "Who Is Harry Kubo?" *Fresno Bee.*

76. "Who Is Harry Kubo?," *Fresno Bee.*

77. Ibid.; Kubo interviewed by Sam Suhler, 32–33. With additional satellite groups in Stockton, Los Angeles, and San Diego County, the total membership topped out at 2,200 in 1976.

78. "Debate Grows over Farm Labor Proposition: NO," *Los Angeles Times,* October 24, 1976.

79. Ibid.

80. Ibid.

81. Cesar Chavez letter to supporters, September 1976, UCLA Political Literature Collection.

82. Kubo interviewed by Sam Suhler, 33, 36.

83. Ibid., 16.

84. Ibid., 10.

85. For a history of farming and Japanese Americans in the Central Valley, see Matsumoto, *Farming the Home Place.*

86. Kubo interviewed by Sam Suhler, 36.

87. Council of California Growers Newsletter, September 20, 1976 and October 4, 1976, Scrapbook April 16, 1975–August 20, 1976, Table Grape Negotiating Committee Papers, Fresno State University.

88. Council of California Growers Newsletter, September 13, 1976 and November 1, 1976, Scrapbook April 16, 1975–August 20, 1976, Table Grape Negotiating Committee Papers, Fresno State University.

89. Coalition for Economic Survival letter to Coalition for Economic Survival Members and Friends, November 2, 1976, UCLA Political Literature Collection.

90. *National City Star-News,* September 19, 1976, UCLA Political Literature Collection.

91. Flyers, n.d., UCLA Political Literature Collection.

92. "Carter's Forces Move to Smooth Convention Path: Carter Forces Move to Smooth Convention," *Washington Post,* July 14, 1976; "Brown, Tunney Endorse Farm Labor Initiative," *Los Angeles Times,* September 4, 1976.

93. "Chavez Vows Farm Workers Will Continue Their Fight," *Fresno Bee,* November 3, 1976, Office of the President, Box 55, Folder 20, ALUA; Council of California Growers Newsletter, November 8, 1976, Fresno State University.

94. Council of California Growers Newsletter, November 8, 1976, Fresno State University.

95. "Proposition 14 Foes End with a Deficit," *Fresno Bee,* January 19, 1977.

96. Lipsitz, *The Possessive Investment in Whiteness,* 114; Elinson and Yogi, *Wherever There's a Fight,* 148–49. HoSang, *Racial Propositions,* 70–71.

97. In 1983, a congressional committee issued the report *Personal Justice Denied,* recommending compensation to the victims, and in 1988, President Ronald Reagan signed the Civil Liberties Act, offering $20,000 in redress to surviving detainees.

98. Poster, n.d., UCLA Political Literature Collection.

99. Ferriss and Sandoval, *The Fight in the Fields,* 208–9; President's Report, December 1976, ALUA.

100. Marshall Ganz, interview with the author, March 28, 2008.

101. Gilbert and Esther Padilla, interviewed by the author, January 11, 2010.

102. Sharon Delugach, May 10, 2004, Listserv entry, "RE: PROPOSITION 14," FWDP, 11–12.

103. Tom Dalzell, May 9, 2004, Listerv entry, "RE: PROPOSITION 14," FWDP, 6.

CHAPTER SIX

1. Nick Jones interviewed by William Taylor, July 24, 1976, La Paz, California, William Taylor Collection, ALUA.

2. Tramutt's Report, December 15, 1976, Office of the President, Part II, Box 18-9, ALUA; "Farm Labor Erupts Again in Imperial Valley," *Los Angeles Times,* February 14, 1976; *El Malcriado,* September 17, 1976, ALUA.

3. Nick Jones interviewed by William Taylor, 30, 35–36.

4. "Nick Jones 1966–1976," FWDP, 1.

5. Boycott minutes, August 24, 1976, Jones folder, ALUA; Nick Jones to NEB of United Farm Workers of America, September 14, 1976, UFW Office of the President, Part II, Box 18-9.

6. Resignation Letter, Nick and Virginia Jones to National Executive Board, November 14, 1976, UFW Office of the President, Box 3-22, ALUA.

7. "Nick Jones 1966–1976," FWDP, 1.

8. Pawel, *The Union of Their Dreams;* Shaw, *Beyond the Fields;* Bardacke, *Trampling Out the Vintage;* Wells and Villarejo, "State Structures and Social Movement Strategies"; Gordon, "A Movement in the Wake of a New Law."

9. "Teamsters to Withdraw, Leave Field to Chavez," *Los Angeles Times,* March 11, 1977; National Executive Board Meeting audiotapes (henceforth referred to as "NEB Meeting"), June 30, 1977, UFW Collections, ALUA.

10. Special Organizing Meeting, November 24, 1976, Miscellaneous UFW Audiovisual Boxes, Tape 8, ALUA.

11. Ibid.; MLK. report, March 14, 1977, on Calexico, audio recording, ALUA; MLK Report to UFW Board of Directors, March 15, 1977, Office of the President, Part II, Box 18-10; Special Organizing Meeting, November 24, 1976, UFW Information and Research, Box 11-10, ALUA.

12. Marshall Ganz, interviewed by the author, March 26, 2008.

13. Ibid.; Special Organizing Meeting, November 24, 1976, UFW Information and Research, Box 11-10, ALUA.

14. Marshall Ganz interview.

15. Ibid.

16. Miami Boycott Staff to Cesar Chavez, December 13, 1976, and Claudia Shacter, December 14, 1976, UFW Office of the President, Part 2, Box 3-22, ALUA.

17. Nick Jones to Cesar Chavez, October 28, 1975, UFW Office of the President, Part 2, Box 3-22, ALUA.

18. Jon Heller to Cesar Chavez, December 11, 1976, and Larry Tramutt to John Heller [sic], Southeast Division Director, December 11, 1976, UFW Office of the President, Part 2, Box 3-22, ALUA.

19. "Larry Tramutola 1971–1981," FWDP.

20. Nick and Virginia Jones to National Executive Board, United Farm Workers of America, November 14, 1976, UFW Office of the President, Box 3-22, ALUA.

21. Atlanta Branch Staff to Cesar Chavez, December 10, 1976, UFW Office of the President, Part 2, Box 3-22, ALUA. For transformations in the southern economy and landscape toward urban development, see Shulman, *From Cotton Belt to Sunbelt;* Lassiter, *The Silent Majority.*

22. Jon Heller to Cesar Chavez, December 11, 1976, ALUA.

23. Ibid.

24. Larry Tramutola quoting Fred Ross Sr. in "Larry Tramutola 1971–1981," FWDP.

25. Larry Tramutt to John [sic] Heller, December 11, 1976, ALUA.

26. Claudia Shacter to Larry Tramutt, ca. December 14, 1976, UFW Office of the President, Part 2, Box 3-22, ALUA.

27. Susan Sachen to Cesar Chavez, January 10, 1977, UFW Office of the President, Part 2, Box 3-22, ALUA.

28. Susan Sachen to Cesar Chavez and Members of the National Executive Board, January 8, 1977, and Susan Sachen to Cesar Chavez, January 10, 1977, UFW Office of the President, Part 2, Box 3-22, ALUA.

29. Seattle UFW Staff to Cesar Chavez and Executive Board Members, December 13, 1976, UFW Office of the President, Part 2, Box 3-22, ALUA.

30. Staff Members, New York City Boycott, to Cesar Chavez, "Re: Demoralization Resulted from De-organization of Boycott," December 12, 1976, UFW Office of the President, Part 2, Box 3-22, ALUA. The Boston and New Jersey houses also sent letters in support of New York; however, later New Jersey members sent a separate letter apologizing for signing the New York letter. New Jersey staff never explained their apology. Irv Hershenbaum, Diane Cohen, and March Johnson (Boston) to Cesar Chavez, December 14, 1976, and Norbert Herold, Robin Brownfield, Eugene Dougherty (New Jersey) to Cesar E. Chavez, January 12, 1977, UFW Office of the President, Part 2, Box 3-22, ALUA.

31. Charlie March to Larry Tramutt, December 19, 1976, UFW Office of the President, Part 2, Box 3-22, ALUA.

32. Dale Van Pelt to Cesar Chavez, December 8, 1976, and Mary Dynes and Dave Shapiro to Cesar Chavez, November 29, 1976, and Bill Ferguson to Cesar Chavez, January 5, 1977, and Susan Sachen to Cesar, January 10, 1977, UFW Office of the President, Part 2, Box 3-22, ALUA.

33. "UFW Aide Quits, Alleges Chavez Antileftist Bias," *Los Angeles Times*, December 22, 1976.

34. Janzen, *The Rise and Fall of Synanon*, 11.

35. Kent (Winterowd) to Cesar Chavez, n.d., UFW Office of the President Collection, Part 2, Box 3-24, ALUA.

36. Synanon's residential population was 1,301 in 1977, although not all of these people lived in Badger. At Home Place, Dederich maintained a select group of adults minus "17 and 18 and 25 year old kids," whom he described as "dumb, ignorant, poor manners, ass-kissing." Janzen, *The Rise and Fall of Synanon*, 162, 172.

37. Synanon most resembled a utopic or "intentional" community. The Fellowship for Intentional Communities defines an intentional community as "ecovillages, cohousing communities, residential land trusts, communes, student co-ops, urban housing cooperatives, intentional living, alternative communities, cooperative living, and other projects where people strive together with a common vision" (www.ic.org/, accessed December 11, 2011). For an early study of these communities and how they functioned in the late 1960s and early 1970s, see Kanter, *Commitment and Community*.

38. Janzen, *The Rise and Fall of Synanon*, 47.

39. "Notes of Meeting with Charles Dederich at Synanon Home Place," February 27, 1977, UFW Office of the President Collection, Part 2, Box 9-18; Janzen, *The Rise and Fall of Synanon*, 64.

40. Judge James H. Lincoln, Probate Court, Juvenile Division, Wayne County, Michigan, UFW Office of the President Collection, Part 2, Box 3-24, ALUA.

41. Janzen, *The Rise and Fall of Synanon*, 13; Ralph Waldo Emerson, "Self-Reliance," www.emersoncentral.com/selfreliance.htm; NEB meeting, February 27, 1977, Badger, California, UFW 7 of 8 side 1, audio recording, UFW Collections, ALUA.

42. NEB audiotape, UFW Collections, ALUA.

43. Janzen, *The Rise and Fall of Synanon*, 14.

44. Matt Rand, NEB Meeting, February, 1977, UFW 4 of 8 side 1, audio recording, UFW Collections, ALUA.

45. In 1966, Synanon began its first "game clubs" for use among non-Synanites and by the mid-1970s had facilitated its practice among a number of groups, including a joint session with Oakland police officers, the Black Panthers, and players on the Oakland Raiders. Janzen, *The Rise and Fall of Synanon*, 47–48. When Chavez began planning for the use of the Game at UFW is unclear, but formal conversations began in the spring of 1977. Matt Rand to Cesar Chavez, May 6, 1977, UFW Office of the President, Part 2, Box 3-24, ALUA.

46. Janzen, *The Rise and Fall of Synanon*, 14–16.

47. Judge James H. Lincoln, Probate Court, Juvenile Division, Wayne County, Michigan, UFW Office of the President Collection, Part 2, Box 3-24, ALUA.

48. NEB meeting, February 26, 1977, UFW 5 of 8 side 2, audio recording, UFW Collections, ALUA. On Helen's opinion, NEB meeting, February 26, 1977, UFW 4 of 8 side 1, audio recording, UFW Collections, ALUA.

49. As quoted in Janzen, *The Rise and Fall of Synanon*, 174.

50. Ibid., 141.

51. Gilbert and Esther Padilla, interviewed by the author, January 11, 2010.

52. Mary Mocine, June 14, 2004, Listserv, (2) "RE: EVEN-HANDED SCHMEVEN-HANDED," FWDP.

53. Rod Janzen, a Synanon historian, holds that members, especially women, began shaving their heads on their own accord as a joke in order to fit under a beam in the Tomales Bay facility. The practice, however, eventually became "a policy" imposed on the members by Dederich. Janzen, *The Rise and Fall of Synanon,* 125–28.

54. Cynthia Bell, June 10, 2004, "Re: Synanon," FWDP.

55. Kent to Cesar, n.d.; handwritten notes, "2-27-77 Synanon," author not identified; Matt Rand to Cesar Chavez, May 6, 1977, all at UFW Office of the President Collection, Part 2, Box 3-24, ALUA.

56. Boycott Dept, April 1, 1977, ALUA; NEB 3.14.77, audiotape 1, UFW Collections, ALUA; *Los Angeles Times* March 2, 1977; "Independent Union Wins in Lettuce Worker Vote," *Los Angeles Times,* March 4, 1977.

57. NEB audiotape, UFW Box 04, Tape 12-3/3.14.77, UFW Collections, ALUA.

58. "Teamsters to Withdaw, Leave Field to Chavez," *Los Angeles Times*, March 11, 1977.

59. "Patience . . . Patience . . ." *Los Angeles Times*, March 4, 1977; "UFW Names Farm Board Counsel in $2 Million Suit," *Los Angeles Times,* March 8, 1977.

60. Marshall Ganz interview.

61. NEB audiotape, 3.14.77, UFW Collections, ALUA.

62. For this reason, Ganz also disagreed with Medina's desire to direct more resources into organizing among grape workers in Coachella, but he supported his work in Oxnard. The union had suffered from poor management of grape contracts in the Central Valley, where workers had resided the longest but had the least amount of confidence in UFW management of contracts. Ganz explained, "The logic of grapes is that you would start and end in Delano, because Delano is the heart of the grape industry, and if you could organize Delano, you could easily organize Coachella" (Marshall Ganz interview).

63. Ibid.

64. Jerry Cohen, interviewed by the author, August 18, 2008.

65. Ibid.

66. NEB meeting, February 25, 1977, UFW 1 of 8 side 1, audio recording, UFW Collections, ALUA. All quotes, henceforth, come from this source unless otherwise indicated.

67. NEB meeting, February 25, 1977, audio recording, UFW 1 of 8 side 2, UFW Collections, ALUA. All quotes, henceforth, come from this source unless otherwise indicated.

68. UFW 2 of 8 side 1, audio recording, UFW Collections, ALUA.

69. Ibid. For the Hutterites and Hartmire, NEB audiotape, 3.14.77, UFW Collections, ALUA.

70. UFW 2 of 8 side 1, audio recording, UFW Collections, ALUA. All quotes, henceforth, come from this source unless otherwise indicated.

71. Ibid.; UFW 3 of 8 side 2, audio recording, UFW Collections, ALUA.
72. Ibid.
73. Ibid.
74. Ibid.
75. UFW 8 of 8 side 1, audio recording, UFW Collections, ALUA.
76. Marshall Ganz interview.
77. UFW 6 of 8 side 1, audio recording, UFW Collections, ALUA.

CHAPTER SEVEN

1. Marshall Ganz, interviewed by the author, March 26, 2008.
2. Ron Taylor, *Chavez and the Farm Workers,* 26–27.
3. Marshall Ganz interview.
4. Ibid.
5. Ibid.
6. Jerry Cohen, interviewed by the author, August 18, 2008.
7. Ibid.
8. Ibid.
9. Marshall Ganz interview.
10. Ibid.
11. Ibid.
12. NEB audiotape, November 24, 1976, cassettes 5 and 6, UFW Collection, ALUA.
13. His official resignation was April 12, 1962. Garza, *Organizing the Chicano Movement,* 153; Gilbert Padilla, interviewed by the author, August 15, 2010.
14. President's newsletter, April 15, 1977, UFW Collections, ALUA; NEB 3.21.77, audiotape 3, UFW Collections, ALUA.
15. "Wilzoch" Document, n.d., "Victim of a Purge?," UFW Office of the President, Box 3-22, ALUA; Juli Loesch, Box 1-8 , ALUA.
16. Kent Winterrowd to the La Paz Community, "Personal Mail," March 22, 1977, UFW Office of the President, Part 2, Box 3-23, ALUA.
17. NEB, February 25–27, 1977, UFW 3 of 8 side 1, audio recording, UFW Collection, ALUA.
18. NEB, February 25–27, 1977, UFW 3 of 8 side 2, audio recording, UFW Collection, ALUA.
19. Ibid.
20. David McClure to Members of the Executive Board, May 5, 1977, UFW Office of the President, Part 2, Box 3-22, ALUA.
21. Godfrey to Chavez, UFW Office of the President, Part 2, Box 3-22, ALUA.
22. Ibid.
23. David Train to Cesar Chavez, March 29, 1977; Edy Scripps to Cesar Chavez, March 30, 1977. Their firing also provoked a friend and fellow volunteer, Deni

Howley, to tender his resignation. Deni Howley to Cesar E. Chavez, March 30, 1977. All documents in UFW Office of the President, Part 2, Box 3-22, ALUA.

24. Train to Chavez, March 29, 1977, 2, UFW Office of the President, Part 2, Box 3-22, ALUA.

25. Godfrey to Chavez, ALUA.

26. McClure to NEB, Office of the President, Part 2, Box 3-22, ALUA.

27. Godfrey to Chavez, ALUA.

28. Untitled, undated document, UFW Office of the President, Part 2, Box 3-22, ALUA.

29. Roger Brooks to Cesar Chavez, May 10, 1977, UFW Office of the President, Part 2, Box 3-22, ALUA.

30. Brooks to Chavez, May 10, 1977, UFW Office of the President, Part 2, Box 3-22, ALUA.

31. Roger Brooks to Cesar Chavez, October 31, 1978, 3; Roger Brooks, "Sour Grapes: The Revolution Is Revolting. Inside Cesar Chavez and the UFW," unpublished manuscript, ca. October 20, 1978, UFW Office of the President, Part 2, Box 3-22, ALUA.

32. Esther and Gilbert Padilla, interviewed by the author, January 11, 2010.

33. Ibid.

34. Chris Hartmire to Sister Mary Catherine Rabbit, May 16, 1977, UFW Office of the President, Part 2, Box 3-22, ALUA.

35. Chris Hartmire to Fred [Ross] and Richard [Chavez], "Subject: Cultural Revolution," May 31, 1977, UFW Office of the President, Part 2, Box 3-24, ALUA.

36. Marshall Ganz interview.

37. Jerry Cohen interview.

38. Marshall Ganz interview.

39. UFW Tape 6 A, UFW Collection, ALUA.

40. UFW Tape 6 B, UFW Collection, ALUA.

41. Jerry Cohen, UFW Tape 6 B, UFW Collection, ALUA.

42. UFW Tape 10 A, UFW Collection, ALUA.

43. Ibid.; Pawel, *Union of Their Dreams*, 220.

44. UFW Tape 8 B, UFW Collection, ALUA.

45. Fred Ross Jr., UFW Tape 9 A, UFW Collection, ALUA.

46. Ibid.; Meeting log, July 4, 1977, for page 24, reel 8, side 1, UFW Collections, ALUA.

47. Marshall Ganz, UFW Tape 9 A, audio recordings, UFW Collections, ALUA.

48. UFW Tape 9 A, audio recordings, UFW Collections, ALUA; Jerry Cohen, interviewed by the author, August 12, 2010.

49. UFW Tape 9 A, audio recordings, UFW Collections, ALUA. All quotes, henceforth, come from this source unless otherwise indicated.

50. Padilla later recalled, "There was no conspiracy . . . none of them. Nobody was a conspirator." Gilbert Padilla interview.

51. UFW Tape 10 A, audio recordings, UFW Collections, ALUA. All quotes, henceforth, come from this source unless otherwise indicated.

52. Gilbert Padilla interview.

53. Jerry Cohen interview, August 12, 2010.

54. The Game, July 7, 1977, La Paz, tape 1, audio recording, UFW Collections, ALUA; Gilbert Padilla interview.

CHAPTER EIGHT

1. "NEB June.July 1977," audio recording, UFW Collections, ALUA.

2. Chris Hartmire, interviewed by the author, September 2, 2008.

3. Wells and Villarejo, "State Structures and Social Movement Strategies." Wells and Villarejo write, "In sum, what is most striking about the ALRA election data is the sharp drop in election activity and union wins after 1977–1978 (with the exception of the 1980 upswing), coupled with a rise in the proportion of decertification and 'no union'-won elections" (302).

4. When I approached Marc Grossman to arrange for a meeting with union officials for oral histories, he refused access and would not go on the record. In 1977, Grossman also reported to the press that residents were not playing the Game when, in fact, they were playing frequently and, internally, Chavez was celebrating its success in his newsletters. See Tom Dazell, July 12, 2004, FWDP, 88–89.

5. Glenn Rothner, June 10, 2004, "RE: 1966 Santa Monica Synanon," FWDP.

6. For example, Abby Flores Rivera disagreed with those who criticized the Game on the listserv. Her comments are part of a longer dialogue that had numerous entries, criticizing and defending Cesar Chavez and the Game. Abby Flores Rivera, June 1, 2004 (3), 5, FWDP.

7. Chris Hartmire interview.

8. Marc Coleman, May 13, 2004, FWDP. Orwell's full quote: "All animals are equal, but some animals are more equal than others." *Animal Farm* (New York: Harcourt, Brace, 1946), chapter 10.

9. "NEB June.July 1977," audio recording, UFW Collections, ALUA; Janzen, *The Rise and Fall of Synanon*, 14.

10. UFW, Box 4, Tape 12-3/3.14.77, audio recording, UFW Collections; NEB Meeting, March 14–16, 21, 1977, 23–28, UFW Vice President Pete Velasco, Box 4-43, ALUA.

11. Esther and Gilbert Padilla, interviewed by the author, January 11, 2010. According to the Padillas, this group also included Joaquin Murguia, Terry Vasquez, and Kent and Esther Winterrowd, to name a few.

12. Ibid.

13. Ibid.; Chris Hartmire interview.

14. Game Tape, 5.3.77, Synanon Game at La Paz, audio recording, UFW Collections, ALUA.

15. Ibid., 250.

16. Rand to Chavez, May 6, 1977, Office of the President, Part 2, Box 3-24, ALUA.

17. Chris Hartmire interview.

18. Ibid.

19. The Game, July 7, 1977, La Paz 1, audio recording, UFW Collections, ALUA.

20. Chris Hartmire interview.

21. Chavez eliminated abortion and restricted access to birth control as a service in UFW health clinics at the end of 1976. "Ethical Directives for Health Facilities for the United Farm Workers of America," UFW, Information and Research Department Collection, Box 21-9, ALUA.

22. The Game, July 7, 1977, audiotape 2, UFW Collections, ALUA.

23. Cynthia Bell, June 10, 2004, 75, FWDP.

24. Jerry Cohen, interviewed by the author, August 12, 2010.

25. Mark Sharwood essay, FWDP.

26. Marc Coleman, May 13, 2004, 31, FWDP; Steve Hopcraft, May 10, 2004, 14, FWDP; Jerry Cohen interview.

27. At the 1973 UFW convention, the membership passed a resolution condemning the dictatorships of Anastasio Somoza in Nicaragua and Ferdinand Marcos in the Philippines. Tom Dalzell, June 8, 2004, "Re: Ferdinand Marcos," 65, FWDP.

28. Lorraine Agtang (Mascarinas) Greer, June 2, 2004, 13, FWDP.

29. Ibid.

30. Chris Hartmire interview.

31. Tom Dalzell, May, 2004, 61, FWDP.

32. Charlie Atilano, June 23, 2004, 187, FWDP. Atilano is making reference to the 1975 film *The Stepford Wives*, based on the novel by Ira Levin published in 1972. *The Stepford Wives* is a satirical thriller in which a new wife in the idyllic setting of Stepford, Connecticut, discovers that husbands in the community have turned their wives into submissive robots who cater to their every whim.

33. Mary Mocine, May 11, 2005, 23, FWDP.

34. Kathy Murguia, June 10, 2004 (2), 81, FWDP. Murguia's son, Joaquin, was forced to leave the union when he became critical of the Game and stopped playing. See Joaquin Murguia, listerv, June 14, 2004 (2), 103, FWDP.

35. Abby Flores Rivera, June 22, 2004 (1), 173, FWDP.

36. Abby Flores Rivera, June 25, 2004 (3), 200–201, FWDP.

37. "Farmworker Convention Marked by Controversy," *In These Times*, September 7–13, 1977, UFW Office of the President, Part 2, Box 3-22, ALUA.

38. Philip Vera Cruz did not refer to Imutan by name in the press, but referred to him as "a Filipino ex-member who is pro–martial law." Padilla went further in his interview with me, naming Imutan as the advisor and calling him a "whore." Philip Vera Cruz quoted in *El Cuhamil*, November 20, 1977, UFW Office of the President, Part 2, Box 3-22, ALUA; Gilbert Padilla, interviewed by the author, August 15, 2010.

39. "Farmworker Convention Marked by Controversy," 5.

40. Bernier to Loesch, telephone conversation, September 14, 1977, 4; Ed Kinane to Cesar E. Chavez, August 19, 1977; Doug Barnhisel to "Friends," February 23, 1978, all in UFW Office of the President, Part 2, Box 3-23, ALUA; Gilbert Padilla interview.

41. *El Cuhamil,* November 5, 1977, 4, UFW Office of the President, Part 2, Box 3-22, ALUA.

42. Ed Kinane to Cesar E. Chavez, August 19, 1977, UFW Office of the President, Part 2, Box 3-23, ALUA; "Chavez Trip Upsets Key Church Backers," *Los Angeles Times,* October 22, 1977.

43. Brenier to Loesch, November 1977; Ed Kinane to Cesar E. Chavez, August 19, 1977; Sister Carol Dougherty to Cesar, July 11, 1977; Father Robert Murray, Erie, Pennsylvania, January 6, 1978, all in UFW Office of the President, Part 2, Box 3-23, ALUA.

44. Hartmire to Juli Loesch, May 24, 1977, UFW Office of the President, Part 2, Box 3-24, ALUA.

45. Hartmire to Juli Loesch, June 13, 1977, Juli Loesch Collections, Box 1-1, ALUA.

46. Juli Loesch to Cesar Chavez, June 22, 1977, UFW Office of the President, Part 2, Box 3-23, ALUA.

47. Ibid.

48. Loesch's notes on Mike Yates to Juli Loesch, telephone conversation transcript, April 20, 1977, Juli Loesch Collections, Box 1-4, ALUA. On the Game, Yates wrote, "I think the Game (a kind of mutual-criticism encounter team) is a ploy to contain and de-politicize dissent by making it 'private'—what's discussed by the group in the Game is *not* to be discussed on the 'outside'—kind of a seal of confessional."

49. Loesch's notes, Adams to Loesch, August 24, 1977, San Francisco; Robert Ellsberg to Loesch, August 30, 1977, New York, both in UFW Office of the President, Part 2, Box 3-23, ALUA.

50. Loesch's notes on phone conversation with Jeff Ames, Roanoke, Virginia, June 1977, UFW Office of the President, Part 2, Box 3-23, ALUA.

51. The *Ernie Christian Witness* was a publication associated with the Catholic peace movement and the Pax Center.

52. Newspapers that published stories include the *Denver Post,* the *National Catholic Reporter, In These Times,* the *Catholic Agitator, Crisis, The Militant, The Nation,* and *Ang Katipunan.*

53. Juli Loesch, "Trouble in the UFW," *Erie Christian Witness* 5, no. 7, November-December 1977, 4, 8; Farmworker Support Committee, Iowa City, Iowa, to the United Farmworkers Union, January 23, 1978, UFW Office of the President, Part 2, Box 3-23, ALUA. Yates was also quoted in *The Nation* on November 19, 1977, and was cited again in *The Militant.* Yates told *The Nation,* "In the past year there have been at least two mass firings.... Dedicated, hard-working men and women ... were accused, on little or no evidence, of being radicals, spies for the employers, troublemakers, complainers.... The union's central staff had been reduced by more than a third." *The Militant,* n.d., UFW Office of the President, Part 2, 3-22, ALUA.

54. Jeff Ames to Juli Loesch, June 1977, Loesch's notes, UFW Office of the President, Part 2, Box 3-23, ALUA.

55. Chris Hartmire to Esther Winterrowd, May 8, 1978, UFW Office of the President, Part 2, 9-18, ALUA.

56. Charlie Atilano, June 23, 2004, 187, FWDP.

57. Tom Dalzell, June 23, 2004, 184–85, FWDP.

58. Ibid.

59. *Los Angeles Times*, October 6, 1977, UFW Office of the President, Part 2, Box 3-24, ALUA.

60. *Fresno Bee*, April 13, 1978, UFW Office of the President, Part 2, Box 3-24, ALUA.

61. Mailgram, March 16, 1978; *Washington Post*, May 18, 1978, both in UFW Office of the President, Box 3-24, ALUA.

62. Dalzell, June 23, 2004, 184–85, FWDP. Lyndon LaRouche was an American political cult leader.

63. Ibid.

64. Ibid.

65. Wells and Villarejo found that the decision to dismantle the legal department came by way of an executive board vote heavily manipulated by Chavez. Like the decision to abandon organizing for contract negotiations, Chavez wore down opposition on the nine-member board by holding a lengthy debate on a decision he had already made. Based on consultation with historian, Paul Henggeler, Wells and Villarejo write, "Four of the nine board members voiced their strong opposition to the proposal, including Eliseo Medina, Jessica Govea, Mack Lyons, and Marshall Ganz. Once it was clear that Chavez's proposal was going to get a majority, Lyons and Medina switched their votes, so that the final formal vote was seven to two" ("State Structures and Social Movement Strategies," 307, 323n36).

66. Abby Flores Rivera, June 22, 2004 (1), 173–74, FWDP.

67. Wells and Villarejo, "State Structures and Social Movement Strategies," 302.

68. "Where Is UFW Headed? End of the Boycott Reflects Shift in Strategy," *The Militant*, 1978, UFW Office of the President, Part 2, Box 3-22, ALUA. See also Wells and Villarejo, "State Structures and Social Movement Strategies," 307.

69. Wells and Villarejo, "State Structures and Social Movement Strategies," 308–9.

70. Marshall Ganz, interviewed by the author, March 26, 2008.

71. Wells and Villarejo, "State Structures and Social Movement Strategies," 307.

72. Jerry Cohen, interviewed by the author, August 18, 2008.

73. Tom Dalzell, June 12, 2004, 88–89, FWDP. Abby Flores Rivera believed there was nothing out of the ordinary in denying the press access: "They are extremely good at taking things out of context. It is not a question of hiding anything." She defended Grossman, calling him a "professional" and "an expert at dealing with the media." Abby Flores Rivera, June 13, 2004 (2), 92, FWDP. In the fall of 1977, Chavez proposed to play an especially intense version of the Game called Dissipation. Participants were thought to lose, or "dissipate," their individuality within a

Game lasting between thirty-six and seventy-two hours. Dederich claimed that his followers experienced quasi-hallucinations during Dissipation and saw him as the Savior. Chavez chose not to follow through with his plans after privately consulting with possible participants. For Dissipation, see Ofshe, "The Social Development of the Synanon Cult," 118; Kathy Lynch Murguia, June 10, 2004 (2), 81–82, FWDP.

74. Chris Hartmire to Cesar Chavez, December 22, 1977, UFW Office of the President, Part 2, Box 9-18, ALUA. In a survey regarding the Game, Grossman wrote, "99% of [the] time, I DO *NOT* enjoy the Game." "Marc Grossman," Memorandum, 6-78-9, UFW unprocessed material, 11-30, ALUA.

75. Chris Hartmire to Cesar Chavez, n.d., UFW Office of the President, Part 2, Box 9-18, ALUA.

76. Chris Hartmire to Cesar Chavez, February 13, 1978, UFW Office of the President, Part 2, 9-18, ALUA.

77. Ibid.

78. Chris Hartmire and Kent Winterrowd to Cesar Chavez, n.d., UFW Office of the President, Part 2, 9-18, ALUA.

79. "Problems—Cesar," n.d., UFW Office of the President, Part 2, 9-18, ALUA.

80. "Emphases for the New, New Game, July 1978"; Chris Hartmire to Ester Winterrowd, handwritten note, "Subject: Rules for New, New Game," July 28, 1978, both in UFW Office of the President, Part 2, 9-18, ALUA.

81. Kathy Lynch Murguia, June 10, 2004 (2), 81–82, FWDP.

82. Notes of Sylvester's Talk to Game 1, July 5, 1978, UFW Office of the President, Part 2, 9-18, ALUA.

83. Chris Hartmire interview.

84. "Cesar's Notes from Saturday, 7/5/78"; Chris Hartmire to Ester Winterrowd, July 28, 1978, both in UFW Office of the President, Part 2, 9-18, ALUA.

85. "The Game 4/29/78," UFW Office of the President, Part 2, 9-18, ALUA.

86. "UFW Announces End of Grape, Lettuce Boycott," *The Militant*, February 17, 1978, 7, UFW Office of the President, Box 3-23, ALUA; *Los Angeles Times*, February 1, 1978, UFW Office of the President, Part 2, 15-9, ALUA.

87. Larry Tramutt to Cesar Chavez, "Boycott Staff List of Terminations (January–September 1977)," August 31, 1977, UFW Information and Research Department, Box 3-36, ALUA; Mike Lacinak to Cesar Chavez, January 9, 1978, UFW Information and Research Department, Box 3-37, ALUA.

88. Elaine Elinson interviewed by the author, December 8, 2009.

89. "Chavez Favored 6 to 1 by Public in Farm Dispute," *Long Beach Press Telegram*, October 20, 1975; Wendy Batson to Cesar Chavez, October 30, 1975, UFW Office of the President, Part 2, 15-9; Harry Ring, "Where Is UFW Headed?," *The Militant*, ca. February 1978, UFW Office of the President, Part 2, Box 3-23, ALUA.

90. As cited in *The Militant*, Office of the President, Part 2, Box 3-23, ALUA.

91. *The Militant*, UFW Office of the President, Part 2, 3-23, ALUA.

92. Ibid.

93. Chris Hartmire interview; Pat Hoffman, "An Interview with Cesar Chavez," *Sojourner*, October 1977, UFW Office of the President, Part 2, 36-26, ALUA.

94. Hoffman, "An Interview with Cesar Chavez," 22.

95. Ibid., 23. This interpretation is somewhat at odds with Mario T. García's belief that Chavez was an "organic theologian" whose spirituality derived mostly from a distinctly Mexican American brand of Catholicism influenced heavily by women (*The Gospel of César Chávez*, 12, 18–23). García's perspective does not consider the influence of Dederich and the counterculture of the 1970s in the creation of his "religious" beliefs. See García, *The Gospel of César Chávez*.

96. *Los Angeles Times*, October 31, 1978, UFW Office of the President, Part 2, Box 3-24, ALUA; "Friends of Charles E. Dederich, Human Rights and Justice Hold a Press Conference," January 13, 1979, UFW Office of the President, Part 2, Box 3-25, ALUA.

97. Piven and Cloward, "Movements and Dissensus Politics." Wells and Villarejo argue that the state and the farm worker movement achieved "symbiosis" between 1975 and 1977–78. They attribute the UFW's withdrawal of "pressure necessary to preserve and capitalize on existing gains and consolidate new ones" as the primary reason for a change in this condition ("State Structures and Social Movement Strategies," 318, 319).

98. Fox Piven and Cloward write, "The record of these efforts in the past argues that the hope for a synthesis of party and movement is likely to be disappointed" (ibid., 248). On the question of extending the power of the state and replicating its oppressive features in the movement, see Brown, *States of Injury*. On resistance to governance altogether, see Scott, *The Art of Not Being Governed*.

99. Wells and Villarejo, "State Structures and Social Movement Strategies," 316–18.

100. Zaninovich and Thomas, *Turmoil in the Vineyards*, 112–14.

101. Obbink explained the formation of the commission this way: "The grape farmers didn't want it to be quite that structured. So they convinced the legislature to give them this Commission, which took them about one-half of a step away from where the marketing [cooperatives] were. It gave a little bit more autonomy, though the state still maintained control of it. They appointed the board members; you had to do all that through the state structure. But not quite as tight as the marketing order structure." Bruce Obbink, interviewed by the author, August 21, 2008. All quotes, henceforth, come from this source unless otherwise indicated.

102. Bardacke, *Trampling Out the Vintage*, 732.

EPILOGUE

1. García, *The Gospel of César Chávez*; Stavans, *Cesar Chavez, an Organizer's Tale*; Ferriss and Sandoval, *The Fight in the Fields*; and Griswold del Castillo and García, *César Chávez*.

2. U.S. Department of the Interior, "Dedication Ceremony for the Forty Acres National Historic Landmark," February 21, 2011, Delano, California.

3. Ross, *Conquering Goliath,* 144.

4. "The Campaign for Fair Food," Coalition of Immokalee Workers, www.ciw -online.org/101.html.

5. For more on the concept of "families of resemblance," see Lipsitz, *Time Passages,* 136.

6. This has been especially true in the listserv exchanges among veterans on Leroy Chatfield's website, the Farm Worker Documentation Project. See the Listserv archive, May 2004–January 2005, www.farmworkermovement.us/.

7. Miriam Pawel and Mark Arax, "Vineyard's Workers Appear to Reject Joining UFW," *Los Angeles Times,* September 2, 2005.

8. Douglass Adair, "What the Fields Taught Me," *Los Angeles Times,* July 10, 2010.

9. Ibid.; Southern Poverty Law Center, *Injustice on Our Plates,* 13.

10. Fletcher and Gapasin, *Solidarity Divided,* 74.

11. The Southern Poverty Law Center writes, "Today, the U.S. grape industry generates $3 billion in sales each year." This, while "harvesters earn 1 to 5 cents per pound for grape clusters that sell in grocery stores for $1.40" (*Injustice on Our Plates,* 13).

SELECTED BIBLIOGRAPHY

ARCHIVES

Amherst College, Special Collections, Amherst, Massachusetts (AC)

Archive of Urban and Labor Affairs, Wayne State University, Detroit, Michigan (ALUA)

Beinecke Library, Yale University, New Haven, Connecticut (BL)

Bracero History Archive, www.braceroarchive.org (BHA)

David Harris Papers, San Francisco, California

Farm Worker Movement Documentation Project, www.farmworkermovement.org (FMDP)

Fresno County Public Library, Fresno, California (FCPL)

Fresno State University, Madden Library, Special Collections, Fresno, California (FSU)

Huntington Library, San Marino, California (HL)

Mandeville Library, Special Collections, University of California, San Diego (UCSD)

National Archives and Records Administration, Washington, DC (NARA)

Stanford University Library, Department of Special Collections, Palo Alto, California (SUL)

University of California, Los Angeles (UCLA)

U.S. Department of Agriculture Library, College Park, Maryland (USDA)

ORAL HISTORIES

Debbie Adair, interviewed by the author, January 6, 2006, Coachella, California.

Doug Adair, interviewed by the author, January 6, 2006, Coachella, California.

Jerald "Jerry" Brown, interviewed by the author, January 16, 2009, telephone.

Jerry Cohen, interviewed by the author, August 18, 2008, Carmel, California.

Elaine Elinson, interviewed by the author, December 8, 2009, and June 15, 2009, San Francisco, California.

Miguel Figueroa, interviewed by the author, March 25, 2008, Riverside, California.

Marshall Ganz, interviewed by the author, March 26, 2008, Cambridge, Massachusetts.

Noé G. García, interviewed by the author, 2009, South Hadley, Massachusetts.

Jessica Govea, interviewed by William Taylor, July 21, 1976. William Taylor Collection, ALUA.

Wayne "Chris" Hartmire, interviewed by the author, September 2, 2008, Claremont, California.

Dolores Huerta interviewed by Margaret Rose, March 16, 1984, Transcribed by Paula Owen, California Agricultural Oral History Project, California State College, Bakersfield, "Women Unionists of the United Farm Workers of America," Oral History Collection, ALUA.

Rey Huerta, interviewed by the author, January 6, 2006, Coachella, California.

Nick Jones, interviewed by William Taylor, July 24, 1976. William Taylor Collection, ALUA.

Harry Kubo, interviewed by Sam Suhler, Fresno County Library, October 13, 1978.

Larry Kubo, interviewed by the author, January 6, 2010, Fresno, California.

Sandy Nathan, interviewed by Jacques Levy, September 25, 1975, Levy Papers, BL.

Bruce Obbink, interviewed by the author, August 21, 2008, Pacific Grove, California.

Esther Padilla, interviewed by the author, March 28, 2008, January 11, 2010, and August 15, 2010, Fresno, California.

Gilbert Padilla, interviewed by the author, March 28, 2008, August 19, 2008, January 11, 2010, and August 15, 2010, Fresno, California.

Don Watson, interviewed by the author, June 15, 2009, Oakland, California.

NEWSPAPERS/NEWSLETTERS

Aftonbladet
Ang Katipunan
Catholic Agitator
Council of California Growers Newsletter
El Cuhamil
Crisis
Denver Post
Ernie Christian Witness
Fresno Bee
Guardian
In These Times
Long Beach Press Telegram
Los Angeles Times

El Malcriado
The Militant
The Nation
National Catholic Reporter
National City Star-News
New York Times
The Packer
Philippine News
The Progressive
Rolling Stone
Sacramento Bee
San Francisco Chronicle
Sojourner
UC Berkeley News
Washington Post
Westgate

OTHER SOURCES

Andres, Benny, Jr. "Power and Control in Imperial Valley, California: Nature, Agribusiness, Labor and Race Relations, 1900–1940." Ph.D. dissertation, University of New Mexico, 2003.

Bardacke, Frank. *Trampling Out the Vintage: César Chávez and the Two Souls of the United Farm Workers.* New York: Verso, 2011.

Brill, Steven. *The Teamsters.* New York: Simon and Schuster, 1978.

Brown, Jerald Barry. "The United Farm Workers Grape Strike and Boycott, 1965–1970: An Evaluation of the Culture of Poverty Theory." Ph.D. dissertation, Cornell University, 1972.

Brown, Wendy. *States of Injury: Power and Freedom in Late Modernity.* Princeton, NJ: Princeton University Press, 1995.

Coalition of Immokalee Workers. "Campaign for Fair Food." www.ciw-online.org (accessed September 10, 2011).

Cohen, Jerry. "Gringo Justice: The United Farm Workers Union, 1967–1981." Unpublished paper, 2008, Cohen Papers, Amherst College.

Dunne, John Gregory. *The Story of the California Grape Strike.* New York: Farrar, Straus & Giroux, 1967.

DuPuis, E. Melanie, and David Goodman. "Should We Go 'Home' to Eat? Toward a Reflexive Politics of Localism." *Journal of Rural Studies* 21 (2005): 359–71.

Elinson, Elaine, and Stan Yogi. *Wherever There's a Fight: How Runaway Slaves, Suffragists, Immigrants, Strikers, and Poets Shaped Civil Liberties in California.* Berkeley, CA: Heyday Books, 2009.

Ferriss, Susan, and Ricardo Sandoval. *The Fight in the Fields: Cesar Chavez and the Farmworkers Movement.* New York: Harcourt Brace, 1997.

Fletcher, Bill, Jr., and Fernando Gapasin. *Solidarity Divided: The Crisis in Organized Labor and a New Path toward Social Justice.* Berkeley: University of California Press, 2008.

Frank, Dana. *Buy American: The Untold Story of Economic Nationalism.* Boston: Beacon Press, 1999.

Friedland, William H., and Robert J. Thomas. "Paradoxes of Agricultural Unionism in California." *Society,* May/June 1974.

Fujita-Rony, Dorothy. *American Workers, Colonial Power: Philippine Seattle and the Transpacific West, 1919–1941.* Berkeley: University of California Press, 2003.

———. "Coalitions, Race, and Labor: Rereading Philip Vera Cruz." *Journal of Asian American Studies* 3.2 (June 2000): 139–62.

Galarza, Ernesto. *Merchants of Labor: The Mexican Bracero Story.* Charlotte, CA: McNally and Loftin, 1964.

———. *Strangers in Our Fields.* Washington, DC: Fund for the Republic, 1956.

Ganz, Marshall. *Why David Sometimes Wins: Leadership, Organization and Strategy in the California Farm Workers Movement.* New York: Oxford University Press, 2009.

García, Mario T., ed. *The Gospel of César Chávez: My Faith in Action.* Lanham, MD: Sheed & Ward, 2007.

Garcia, Matt. "Cain contra Abel: Courtship, Masculinities, and Citizenship in Southern California, 1942–1964." In *Race, Nation, and Empire in American History,* edited by James Campbell, Matthew Guterl, and Robert Lee. Chapel Hill: University of North Carolina Press, 2007.

———. *A World of Its Own: Race, Labor and Citrus in the Making of Greater Los Angeles, 1900–1970.* Chapel Hill: University of North Carolina Press, 2001.

Garcia, Matt, and Mario Sifuentez. "Social Movement Unionism and the 'Sin Fronteras' Philosophy in PCUN: A New Paradigm for American Labor." In *Labor's New World: Essays on the Future of Working-Class America,* edited by Daniel Katz and Richard Greenwald. New York: New Press, forthcoming.

García y Griego, Manuel. "The Importation of Mexican Contract Laborers to the United States, 1942–1964." In *Between Two Worlds: Mexican Immigrants in the United States,* edited by David G. Gutiérrez. Wilmington, DE: Jaguar/SR Books, 1996.

Garza, Humberto. *Organizing the Chicano Movement: The Story of CSO.* San José, CA: Sun House Publishing, 2009.

Glickman, Lawrence. *Buying Power: A History of Consumer Activism in America.* Chicago: University of Chicago Press, 2009.

Gordon, Jennifer. "A Movement in the Wake of a New Law: The United Farm Workers and the California Agricultural Labor Relations Act." In *Cause Lawyers and Social Movements,* edited by Austin Sarat and Stuart A. Scheingold. Stanford, CA: Stanford University Press, 2006.

Griswold del Castillo, Richard, and Richard García. *César Chávez: A Triumph of Spirit.* Norman: University of Oklahoma Press, 1995.

Gutiérrez, David G. *Walls and Mirrors: Mexican Americans, Mexican Immigrants, and the Politics of Ethnicity*. Berkeley: University of California Press, 1995.

Hahamovitch, Cindy. *The Fruits of Their Labor: Making of Migrant Poverty, 1870–1945*. Chapel Hill: University of North Carolina Press, 1997.

International Directory of Company Histories. Vol. 12. Jefferson, MO: St. James Press, 1996.

Janzen, Rod. *The Rise and Fall of Synanon: A California Utopia*. Baltimore: Johns Hopkins University Press, 2001.

Johnston, Paul. *Success While Others Fail: Social Movement Unionism and the Public Workplace*. Ithaca, NY: ILR Press / Cornell University Press, 1994.

Kanter, Rosa Moss. *Commitment and Community: Communes and Utopias in Sociological Perspective*. Cambridge, MA: Harvard University Press, 1972.

Lassiter, Matthew. *The Silent Majority: Suburban Politics in the Sunbelt South*. Princeton, NJ: Princeton University Press, 2007.

Lipsitz, George. *The Possessive Investment in Whiteness: How White People Profit from Identity Politics*. Philadelphia: Temple University Press, 2006.

———. *Time Passages: Collective Memory and American Popular Culture*. Minneapolis: University of Minnesota Press, 1990.

Loza, Mireya. "Braceros on the Boundaries: Activism, Race, Masculinity, and the Legacies of the Bracero Program." Ph.D. dissertation, Brown University, 2010.

Majka, Linda C., and Theo J. Majka. *Farm Workers, Agribusiness, and the State*. Philadelphia: Temple University Press, 1982.

Majka, Theo J., and Linda C. Majka. "Decline of the Farm Labor Movement in California: Organizational Crisis and Political Change." *Critical Sociology* 19.3 (1992): 3–36.

Matsumoto, Valerie. *Farming the Home Place: A Japanese American Community in California, 1918–1982*. Ithaca, NY: Cornell University Press, 1994.

Matusow, Allen J. *Nixon's Economy: Booms, Busts, Dollars and Votes*. Lawrence: University Press of Kansas, 1998.

Meister, Dick, and Anne Loftis. *A Long Time Coming: The Struggle to Unionize America's Farm Workers*. New York: Macmillan, 1977.

Mooney, Patrick, and Theo J. Majka. *Farmers' and Farmworkers' Movements: Social Protest in American Agriculture*. New York: Twayne, 1995.

Newton-Matza, Mitchell. "Boycott." In *Encyclopedia of U.S. Labor and Working-Class History*, vol. 1, edited by Eric Arnesen. New York: Routledge, 2007.

Ngai, Mae. *Impossible Subjects: Illegal Aliens and the Making of Modern America*. Princeton, NJ: Princeton University Press, 2004.

Ofshe, Richard. "The Social Development of the Synanon Cult: The Managerial Strategy of Organizational Transformation." *Sociological Analysis* 41.2 (1980): 109–27.

Orwell, George. *Animal Farm*. New York: Harcourt, Brace, 1946.

Pawel, Mariam. *The Union of Their Dreams: Power, Hope and Struggle in César Chávez's Farm Workers Movement*. New York: Bloomsbury Press, 2009.

Payne, Charles. *I've Got the Light of Freedom: The Organizing Tradition and the Mississippi Freedom Struggle.* Berkeley: University of California Press, 1995.

Pitti, Stephen J. *The Devil in Silicon Valley: Northern California, Race, and Mexican Americans.* Princeton, NJ: Princeton University Press, 2003.

Piven, Frances Fox, and Richard A. Cloward. "Movements and Dissensus Politics." In *Cultural Politics and Social Movements,* edited by Marcy Darnovsky, Barbara Epstein, and Richard Flacks. Philadelphia: Temple University Press, 1995.

Pollan, Michael. "Farmer in Chief." *New York Times Magazine,* October 12, 2008.

———. *The Omnivore's Dilemma: A Natural History of Four Meals.* New York: Penguin, 2007.

Rosenberg, Samuel. *American Economic Development since 1945: Growth, Decline and Rejuvenation.* New York: Palgrave Macmillian, 2003.

Ross, Fred. *Conquering Goliath: Cesar Chavez at the Beginning.* Keene, CA: El Taller Grafico Press, 1989.

Sarat, Austin, and Stuart A. Scheingold, eds. *Cause Lawyers and Social Movements.* Stanford, CA: Stanford University Press, 2006.

Scharlin, Craig, and Lilia V. Villanueva. *Philip Vera Cruz: A Personal History of Filipino Immigrants and the Farm Workers Movement.* Los Angeles: UCLA Labor Center, Institute of Industrial Relations, and UCLA Asian American Studies Center, 1994.

Schlosser, Eric. *Fast Food Nation: The Dark Side of the All-American Meal.* New York: Harper Perennial, 2005.

Scott, James C. *The Art of Not Being Governed: An Anarchist History of Upland Southeast Asia.* New Haven, CT: Yale University Press, 2009.

Shaw, Randy. *Beyond the Fields: Cesar Chavez, the UFW, and the Struggle for Justice in the 21st Century.* Berkeley: University of California Press, 2008.

Shulman, Bruce. *From Cotton Belt to Sunbelt: Federal Policy, Economic Development, and the Transformation of the South, 1938–1980.* Durham, NC: Duke University Press, 1994.

Sinclair, Upton. *The Jungle.* New York: Doubleday, Jabber, 1906.

Sklar, Kathryn Kish. *Florence Kelley and the Nation's Work: The Rise of Women's Political Culture, 1830–1900.* New Haven, CT: Yale University Press, 1995.

Smith, T. L. "A Study of Social Stratification in the Agricultural Sections of the U.S.: Nature, Data, Procedures, and Preliminary Results." *Rural Sociology* 34.4 (1969): 498–509.

Southern Poverty Law Center. *Close to Slavery: Guest Worker Programs in the United States.* Montgomery, Alabama, 2007.

———. *Injustice on Our Plates: Immigrant Women in the U.S. Food Industry.* Montgomery, Alabama, 2010.

Stavans, Ilan, ed. *Cesar Chavez, an Organizer's Tale: Speeches.* New York: Penguin, 2008.

Street, Richard Steven. *Photographing Farmworkers in California.* Stanford, CA: Stanford University Press, 2004.

———. "Poverty in the Valley of Plenty: The National Farm Labor Union, DiGiorgio Farms, and Suppression of Documentary Photography in California, 1947–1966." *Labor History* 48.1 (2007): 25–48.

Summers, Anthony, with Robyn Swan. *The Arrogance of Power: The Secret World of Richard Nixon*. New York: Penguin Putnam, 2000.

Taylor, Paul. "Mexican Migration and the 160-Acre Water Limitation." *California Law Review* 63.3 (1975): 732–50.

Taylor, Ronald B. *Chavez and the Farm Workers*. Boston: Beacon Press, 1975.

U.S. Commission on Civil Rights. *Mexican Americans and the Administration of Justice in the Southwest*. Report. March 1970.

Vargas, Zaragosa. *Labor Rights Are Civil Rights: Mexican American Workers in Twentieth-Century America*. Princeton, NJ: Princeton University Press, 2007.

Wells, Miriam J., and Don Villarejo. "State Structures and Social Movement Strategies: The Shaping of Farm Labor Protections in California." *Politics & Society* 32 (2004): 291–326.

Zaninovich, Martin John, with Edward H. Thomas. *Turmoil in the Vineyards*. Self-published, n.d.

INDEX

Chatfield, LeRoy, 257; Agricultural Labor Relations Act and, 156, 164; in boycott, 54–55, 76–78; Brown and, 45, 71; Ganz and, 54; grocery store picketing and, 72–73; in Los Angeles, 63, 65, 90; in Tulare rent strike, 35–36; in United Farm Workers formation, 57

Chavez, Alicia Margaret St. John, 28

Chavez, Cesar, 26*fig.*, 42*fig.*, 48*fig.*, 53*fig.*, 165*fig.*, 172*fig.*, 194*fig.*, 227*fig.*, 263*fig.*; AFL-CIO and, 137–38; Agricultural Labor Relations Act and, 147–51, 213–14, 284–86; AWOC-NFWA merger and, 57; background of, 25; Brown, Jerry and, 44–46; *caminata* of, 183; Catholic Church and, 70–71; in Community Service Organization, 26–29; Community Service Organization and, 25–26; decline of, 176–77; Dederich and, 190–93; Drake and, 237–38; early success of, 3; erratic behavior of, 180–81; on Europe, 103; "the Game" and, 190–92, 208–9, 232; Ganz challenges, 201, 210–11, 234; García, Mario T. on, 4; García, Pete and, 25; Govea and, 90–91, 232; on grape boycott, 73; Harper, Valerie and, 176; Hartmire and, 227–28; Hartmire confronts, 247–48; Heller and, 185–86; Huerta and, 243–44; imprisonment of, 117; isolation of, 4; Jones, Nick and, 178–80, 184–85, 188–89; King and, 69–70; Kubo on, 170; leadership of, 3; Loesch and, 272–73; Lyons and, 237; marriage of, 244; McClure and, 222–23; "Monday Night Massacre" and, 221–22; in National Farm Workers Association inception, 31–32; on organizing philosophy, 36–37; overview of, 2; Padilla and, 25–26, 249; Padilla's concerns about, 239; in Philippines, 269–70; Proposition 14 and, 174–77; racial accusations against, 225–26; recruitment of, by Ross, 25; Smith, Joe and, 179–80; on Teamsters, 116; Vera Cruz and, 240–42

Chavez, Helen Favela, 25, 26*fig.*, 226, 227*fig.*, 244

Chavez, Manuel, 137, 150

Chavez, Paul "Babo," 217, 221, 226, 227*fig.*, 259, 262–64

Chavez, Richard, 194*fig.*; Cohen and, 236; conspiracy ideas and, 246; "the Game" and, 232; in grape boycott, 193, 218; hiring halls and, 139; Huerta and, 233; La Paz and, 201–2, 229; Teamsters and, 158–59; Vera Cruz and, 240–41; on volunteer system, 199, 204, 207

Chicago, 78, 83*t*, 157

Chicago Women's Liberation Union, 52

child care, at La Paz, 223

Citizens for a Fair Farm Labor Law, 168, 171, 289

Civil Liberties Act, 317n97

class system: in Imperial Valley, 15

Cleveland, 78, 83*t*

Coachella Valley, 17*map*; "Battle of Coachella," 136–37; braceros in, 16; grapes and AWOC in, 38; San Joaquin Valley and, 81; strategy in, 218

Coalition for Economic Survival, 171

Coalition for Immokalee Workers, 295–96

Coca-Cola Company, 133

Cohen, Jerry, 126*fig.*, 207; AFL-CIO and, 146; Agricultural Labor Relations Act and, 156–57; Agricultural Labor Relations Board and, 147; in "Anglo Brain Trust," 125; in California Rural Legal Association, 130; on Chavez, 217; Chavez, Richard and, 236; confidentiality agreements and, 251; "the Game" and, 208–9, 232, 275–76; Ganz and, 235–36, 254; on Giumarra, 139; grape boycott failure and, 230; hiring of, 311n44; Huerta and, 236; in legal team, 64; in pay debate, 205–7; pesticide use and, 79, 108; in philosophy of movement, 196–98; resignation of, 279; on Teamster feud, 137; in Teamster legal battle, 117–18; in Teamster negotiations, 181; Teamster violence against, 117; on undocumented workers, 149; in union negotiations, 110; Vera Cruz and, 252

Cohen, Sam, 160

Colbert, Stephen, 297

Colemna, Marc, 258

Filipino American Political Association, 120–21

Filipino Hall, 40–41, 44, 55, 75

Filipinos: AWOC and, 37–38; opposition of, 122–23; Rancho Blanco and, 39–41; Teamsters and, 43, 310n29; UFW and, 119–20

Finast, 65

Finland, 106

Fisher, Dixie Lee, 91

Fitzsimmons, Frank E., 113–14, 124, 132–36, 140–42, 181, 312n58

Flanigan, Peter, 311n47

Flanigan Report, 131–32

Flores, Gil, 27

Flowers, Dickie, 54

food justice, 9

Ford, John, 292–93

Founding Day, 219

Freedom Summer, 52–53

Fresno: braceros in, 16–17

Fresno State College, 16

Fresno State University, 16

Galarza, Ernesto, 14, 23, 30

Gallin, Dan, 107

Gallo Wines, 58, 149, 157, 159, 283

Gallyen, LeRoy, 55

"Game, the": Agtang and, 266–67; background of, 190; in Badger, 259–60; board and, 229–32, 254; Chavez defends, 208–9; Chavez's family and, 216–17, 259; Cohen on, 209; comes to La Paz, 193, 208–9; as contributor to conflict, 256–57; Dederich and, 190–91; Dissipation version of, 328n73; first, 259–60; Ganz and, 250; Grossman and, 260–61, 324n4; growth of, 256; Hartmire and, 229, 256, 262, 279–80; at Home Place, 191–92; Huerta, Lori and, 260–61, 264–65; inspiration for, 190; McGregor, Ann and, 262–63; meetings as, 251, 254; negative effects of, 258–59, 262; resistance to, 275–76, 280–81; spread of, 265–66; Vera Cruz on, 232; withdrawal from, 279–81

Ganz, Marshall, 53fig., 109, 194fig.; Agricultural Labor Relations Act and, 197–98; in "Anglo Brain Trust," 125; background of, 52; Black, Eli and, 129; challenges Chavez, 201, 210–11, 234; Chavez and, 183; on Coachella strategy, 218; Cohen and, 235–36, 254; Delizonna and, 194–95; "the Game" and, 232, 250; in grape boycott, 60–62, 66–67, 84–89; on grape boycott, 230; Greer and, 146; Huerta and, 233; Jewish growers and, 81; on La Paz, 231; in Mississippi Freedom Summer, 52–53; in Montreal, 88–89; on organization, 195–96; ranch committees and, 215–16; Ross and, 234; in San Joaquin Valley, 110; on Standish, 91; on Steinberg, 109; in Student Nonviolent Coordinating Committee, 53–54; Teamster assault of, 136; Teamster boycott and, 128; in Toronto, 63, 66–67, 84–85, 87; on UFW hierarchy, 216

García, Mario T., 4

García, Noé G., 305n41

García, Pete, 25

Geijer, Arne, 106

Gentle, Janice, 169

Gerard, Linda, 84

Giffen Ranch, 301n11

Gilbert, Brother. *See* Chatfield, LeRoy

Gillian's, 301n11

Gines, Ben, 37, 119

Giumarra, John, Jr., 138

Giumarra Vineyards Corporation, 60–61, 110–11

Godfrey, Deirdre, 221, 223

Goldman, Jerry, 148, 155–56

González, Alfredo, 136

Goodman, Andrew, 54

Govea, Jessica, 78–79, 84–86, 85fig., 88–91, 157–58, 232

Grami, Bill, 137

grape boycott, 5–6; AFL-CIO and, 55, 127; in Boston, 73, 82; Brown, Jerry and, 44–46, 63–64; building support for, 62–63; Catholic Church and, 81–82; Chavez on, 73; in Chicago, 78; circumvention of, 82; civil rights movement and, 52; in Cleveland, 78; Cohen on, 230; college students and, 52–53; in Detroit, 79–80, 82; DiGiorgio

United Farm Workers (UFW): Agricultural Labor Relations Act and, 151–67; composition of, 215–16; Filipino opposition to, 122–23; funding crisis of, 181–82; grape boycott and, 47–49; Heublein and, 127; immigrants and, 119; Immigration and Naturalization Service and, 218; Loesch criticizes, 274–75; name of, 299n1; Nixon and, 133–34; as peaceful, 9; Proposition 14 and, 164–73; restructuring of, 182–83; start of, 3–4, 57; Teamsters and, 115–44; Teamsters *vs.*, 115; TGWU and, 101

United Fruit Company, 128

United Kingdom, 97–102, 159, 308n52

United Mine Workers, 22, 27

United Vintners, 127

Unity Leagues, 25

Uribe, Alicia, 115, 136

Valdez, Luis, 51

Vancouver, 86

Van Pelt, Dale, 188

Vasquez, Mark, 108

"Veggie Kitchen," 221–22

Velasco, Peter, 37, 157–58, 194*fig.*, 198–99, 220, 232, 265

Venezuela, 108

Vera Cruz, Philip, 18, 28, 37, 57, 119–21, 194*fig.*, 198, 204, 232, 236, 239–42, 241*fig.*, 251–55, 310n17

Vietnam, 133

Viklund, Victor, 104

Villareno, David, 221, 225, 232, 260, 264

Villegas, Jesus "Chui," 145–46

"Viva Kennedy!" campaigns, 22–23

Vollmer, Debbie, 240

Volpey, Steve, 109

wages: of day-haul laborers, 18; at ranches, 18–19; at Weeth Ranch, 18–19

Wagner Act. *See* National Labor Relations Act (NLRA)

Walbaum's, 65

Waldie, Jerome, 156

Walsh, Denny, 135

Walther Reuther Library of Labor and Urban Affairs, 5

Watergate, 135–36, 140

Watson, Don, 101

Wayne State University, 5

Weather Underground, 9

Weeth Ranch, 18–19

Weinstein, Leon, 85, 88

Western Growers Association, 128, 167

West Food, 178

Westgate, Murray, 137

Weyerhaeuser Paper Company, 167

Wilzoch, Mike, 219–20, 228

Windsor, Ontario, 84–86

Winterrowd, Kent, 220–21, 226, 240, 259, 263–64

Wolcott, Betty, 280

Wolff, Jack, 301n11

Woodcock, Leonard, 133

Woolsey, James, 55–56

World Peace Council, 159

Yates, Mike, 273–74, 326n48

Yellen, Ben, 24

"yellow sheet," 24

Yippies, 7, 67

Young Lords, 9

Youth International Party, 7, 67

Zaninovich, Martin, 59–60, 288

Matt Garcia is Professor of History and Transborder Studies at Arizona State University, where he also directs the School of Historical, Philosophical and Religious Studies, and the Program in Comparative Border Studies. He is the author of *A World of Its Own: Race, Labor, and Citrus in the Making of Greater Los Angeles, 1900–1970*.

Mattgarcia.org

TEXT
11/14 Adobe Garamond Premier Pro

DISPLAY
Adobe Garamond Premier Pro

COMPOSITOR
Westchester Publishing Services

PRINTER AND BINDER
Maple-Vail Book Manufacturing Group